Praise for *Family Business*

'An absorbing and often moving record of an intense relationship . . . We have here an important part of the record of a major figure's development, and a rare example of the power of certain family pieties.'

The New York Times Book Review

'Surprisingly poignant . . . Schumacher's thorough, amiable introduction sets the stage for the remarkable father-son performance that follows . . . what overwhelms throughout is the adamantine bond of affection that connected the two . . . An eloquent, affecting collection that offers lessons in poetry, in love, and in family.' *Kirkus Reviews* (starred review)

'This volume . . . presents some of the most astonishing correspondence in American literature . . . Anyone interested in either Ginsberg, the beats, American poetry or the '60s should not miss this ferociously tender and comical collection.' *Publishers Weekly* (starred review)

'Tracing their journey toward a shared conviction that poetry has the power to change history makes *Family Business* important reading for us all.'

San Francisco Chronicle

'Inspiring . . . behind the anger and anguish, what shines through these letters is love.' *The Forward*

'*Family Business* charts in surprisingly affecting eloquence the gradual, wonderful radicalization of the king of the Beats.' *Orlando Sentinel*

'Allen and Louis' correspondence demonstrates a mutual respect, a strong desire for reconciliation, and pride in each other's poetic accomplishments . . . Highly recommended.' *Library Journal*

'A look at 30 years of love and words between the Beat poet and his father.'

The Record (Hackensack, NJ)

'Rich . . . the three decades of exchanges between Allen Ginsberg and his father offer a backstage pass to the post-World War II cultural drama in which Ginsberg and associates such as Jack Kerouac, William Burroughs, and Lawrence Ferlinghetti played starring roles.' *The Indianapolis Star*

'As much an intellectual exchange of ideas as a personal family dialogue, these letters provide material for studies of differences between two generations of writers who had much to say regarding US culture.'

Choice (Middletown, CT)

ALSO BY MICHAEL SCHUMACHER

FAMILY BUSINESS

SELECTED LETTERS BETWEEN
A FATHER AND SON

ALLEN AND
LOUIS GINSBERG

Edited by Michael Schumacher

BLOOMSBURY

PICTURE CREDITS: Courtesy of Elsa Dorfman (Elsa@photo.net): page 1;
Courtesy of the Allen Ginsberg Trust: page 2, page 3 *top* and *bottom*, page 4 *top
left* and by Allen Ginsberg *top right*, page 5 *top* and *bottom*, page 6, page 7 *top*
and by Allen Ginsberg *bottom*; Courtesy of John Cohen: page 4 *bottom*; Courtesy
of Layle Silbert: page 8.
Jacket photograph © Richard Avedon, 1970
Every reasonable effort has been made to ascertain and acknowledge the
ownership of copyrighted photographs included in this volume. Any errors that
have inadvertently occurred will be corrected in subsequent editions provided
notification is sent to the Publisher.

Published by Bloomsbury, New York and London
Distributed to the trade by Holtzbrinck Publishers

Library of Congress Cataloging-in-Publication Data

Ginsberg, Allen, 1926-1997
Family business : selected letters between a father and son / by Allen Ginsberg and
Louis Ginsberg ; edited by Michael Schumacher.
p. cm.
Includes bibliographical references.
ISBN 1-58234-107-9
1. Ginsberg, Allen, 1926-1997--Correspondence. 2. Ginsberg, Louis, 1895-1976---
Correspondence. 3. Poets, American--20th century--Correspondence. 4. Fathers and
sons--United States. I. Ginsberg, Louis, 1895-1976. II. Schumacher, Michael.
III. Title.

PS3513.I174 Z485 2001
811'.54--dc21
[B]
2001035431
Paperback ISBN: 1-58234-216-4

First published in hardcover in the United States by Bloomsbury in 2001
This paperback edition published in 2002

10 9 8 7 6 5 4 3 2 1

Typeset by Hewer Text Ltd, Edinburgh, Scotland.
Printed in Great Britain by Clays Limited, St Ives plc

In Memoriam
Eugene Brooks
1921–2001

CONTENTS

BOOKS BY ALLEN AND LOUIS GINSBERG

BY ALLEN GINSBERG

Howl and Other Poems (1956)
Kaddish and Other Poems (1961)
Empty Mirror, Early Poems (1961)
Reality Sandwiches (1963)
The Yage Letters (with William Burroughs) (1963)
Planet News (1968)
Indian Journals (1970)
The Fall of America, Poems of These States (1972)
The Gates of Wrath, Rhymed Poems 1948–52 (1973)
Iron Horse (1973)
Gay Sunshine Interview (1974)
Allen Verbatim: Lectures on Poetry, Politics, Consciousness (1974)
First Blues (1975)
Chicago Trial Testimony (1975)
To Eberhart from Ginsberg (1976)
As Ever: Collected Correspondence Allen Ginsberg & Neal Cassady (1977)
Journals Early Fifties Early Sixties (1977)
Mind Breaths, Poems 1971–76 (1978)
Composed on the Tongue: Literary Conversations 1967–1977 (1980)
Straight Hearts Delight, Love Poems and Selected Letters 1947–1980 (with
    Peter Orlovsky) (1980)
Plutonian Ode, Poems 1977–1980 (1982)
Collected Poems 1947–1980 (1984)
White Shroud, Poems 1980–1985 (1986)
Howl, Original Draft Facsimile, Fully Annotated (1986)
Cosmopolitan Greetings, Poems 1986–1992 (1994)
Journals Mid-Fifties: 1954–1958 (1994)
Selected Poems 1947–1995 (1996)

Luminous Dreams (1997)
Death and Fame, Last Poems 1993–1997 (1999)
Deliberate Prose: Selected Essays 1952–1995 (2000)
Spontaneous Mind: Selected Interviews 1958–1996 (2001)

BY LOUIS GINSBERG

The Attic of the Past and Other Lyrics (1920)
The Everlasting Minute (1937)
Morning in Spring (1970)
Collected Poems (1992)

ACKNOWLEDGMENTS

I originally approached Allen Ginsberg about editing this book in 1992, shortly after the publication of *Dharma Lion*. I told Allen that, during the course of writing his biography, I had reached the conclusion that his relationship with his father had never been properly explored, and I felt that their correspondence would be valuable to readers and scholars interested in a longer, more detailed look at his development in poetics and politics. As I mention elsewhere in this volume, Allen used his father as a sounding board for both his poetry and politics, and their correspondence found him honing his position in literary and world affairs. Allen liked the idea of the project, though he complained that he couldn't consider working under another deadline. I worked on it on my own, with neither deadline nor publisher, but, unfortunately, Allen passed away before he had the opportunity to see this book in its final form. So it's too late, although still very necessary, to thank Allen for his faith in this project.

Edith Ginsberg, Allen's stepmother and Louis's wife, was a wonderful, witty, and intelligent woman, and she was very excited about the prospects of this book's publication. I spent a lovely afternoon with her, going over photo albums and talking about Allen and Louis. Sadly, she, too, passed away before she could see this volume in print.

Eugene Brooks also spent an afternoon talking to me about his father and brother. Gene, a fine poet himself, also provided me with missing letters and generously agreed to allow me to publish one of his own.

Anyone who has ever worked with the "Ginsberg people" knows how valuable they are, as friends and as associates devoted to overseeing Allen's continuing literary legacy. I owe them a huge debt of gratitude. Bob Rosenthal, Allen's secretary, has been incredibly helpful over the years, dating back to my early work on *Dharma Lion* and continuing through the editing of this book; running the office has always been a prodigious chore, but Bob manages to accomplish it with grace and efficiency. Bill Morgan, Allen's archivist and bibliographer, has provided great assistance, never failing to answer one of my (countless) questions, as well as providing me with photocopies of many of Louis Ginsberg's letters. Peter Hale was always very obliging when I called for a telephone number or needed information, and he, along with Bill Morgan, assisted me greatly in the selection of the photographs for this book.

Thanks to Polly Armstrong and the staff of the Department of Special Collections and University Archives, Green Library, at Stanford University, and to Bernard Crystal and the staff of the Butler Library at Columbia University, where most of the enclosed letters are housed.

Ann Charters, the Kerouac biographer and scholar, and Gordon Ball, who managed Allen Ginsberg's farm and edited three volumes of his work, offered valuable advice on the editing of this book. David Carter, editor of *Spontaneous Mind*, also chipped in with needed advice.

Thanks for assistance and friendship to: Peter Spielmann, Judy Hansen, Paula Litzky, Judy Matz, Rochelle Kraut, Simma Holt, and Amelie Littell.

A book is always a collaborative adventure, and in this case, it seemed especially so. Thanks to Jeff Posternak and the staff at the Andrew Wylie Agency; to Kim Witherspoon, Maria Massie, and David Forrer at Witherspoon Associates; to Karen Rinaldi, Panio Gianopoulos, Andrea Lynch, Colin Dickerman, Jason Baskin, Susan Burns, and the staff at Bloomsbury USA. Carol Edwards did her usual incredible job copyediting and fact-checking the manuscript.

As always, I owe an enormous debt of gratitude to my wife, Susan, and to my children, Adam, Emily Joy, and Jack Henry, who support me in every way imaginable.

Finally, I'd like to acknowledge a long overdue debt to my father, Alvin J. Schumacher, author of three books (including a wonderful young adult biography of Roger Taney) and, to a great extent, the inspiration for my own career. In reading through the Allen Ginsberg–Louis Ginsberg correspondence, I found myself reflecting on my relationship with my father – often in ways that were rather uncomfortable. Like Allen and Louis Ginsberg, my father and I have differed in our politics and outlooks on life and society, and we have been known to engage in more heated exchanges than either of us cares to remember. And, like Allen Ginsberg, I grew up in a household in which I was accustomed to seeing my father working on his writing, struggling to get the word on the page while holding a teaching job and raising a family. Finally, like Allen and Louis Ginsberg, my father and I know something about the ties that bind, and how those ties are stronger than all the forces that separate. I love you, Dad, and I owe you more than these few words could ever state or repay.

INTRODUCTION

Allen Ginsberg often remarked that writing poetry was the "family busi-ness." His father, Louis, earned a modest reputation as a lyric poet, and his older brother, Eugene Brooks, published poetry in a number of newspapers and magazines. Neither, of course, would ever come close to achieving Allen's lofty status in the literary community, but that never stopped Allen from promoting the merits of their work. He often appeared at joint poetry readings with his father and, on a rare occasion, with his brother. He wrote introductions for poetry collections by Louis and Eugene. He was proud of his father's and his brother's work, even though it was vastly different in style and content from his own.

Like Allen, Louis looked at his family's interest in writing poetry as being almost inevitable. "Asking why we write is like asking why fire burns," he said. "It's our nature. . . . How can we perpetuate ourselves? One way is by children, another is by art."

When I was researching *Dharma Lion*, my biography of Allen Ginsberg, it occurred to me that Allen's relationship with his father, as well as the lineage of poetry and political interest passed on from father to son, had always been overshadowed by the interest in Allen's relationship with his mother. To a certain degree, this made sense: Allen's masterwork, "Kad-dish," was a heartwrenching homage to – and biography-in-poetry of – his mother, and Naomi Ginsberg's story, in terms of sheer drama and emo-tional impact, seemed to have so much more to offer.

Still, Allen's debt to his father is undeniable, and the debt extends far beyond Allen's following in his father's footsteps as a poet and, later, teacher. Allen had many literary influences, but Louis was his first, and even after Allen met such important friends and literary contemporaries as Jack Kerouac and William S. Burroughs, who strongly influenced the direction of his writing, he continued to discuss his work with his father. Perhaps even more important was the ongoing debate on political issues. Since neither Burroughs or Kerouac cared much for politics, Allen used his father as a sounding board, which becomes very clear in this volume of letters. You can just feel Allen working his material, running statements past his father, and developing his position for later writings and political proclamations.

I remember mentioning all this to Allen when I proposed this book project to him many years ago. He was overwhelmed with work, as he always was, but he was intrigued by the idea. He remembered his letters to his father in only the most general of terms, but when he reread a small sampling of them, he agreed that they might be useful to scholars and biographers in the future, as well as to general readers fascinated by twentieth-century American history and politics.

Louis Ginsberg, the first of Pinkus and Rebecca Schectman Ginsberg's five children, was born on October 1, 1895, in Newark, New Jersey. Both of his parents were of Russian Jewish ancestry. Pinkus, a socialist, was active in politics, and both Pinkus and Rebecca belonged to the Yiddish Arbeiter Ring, also known as the Workman's Circle. Louis would recall his father's taking him to socialist meetings, where he had occasion to hear Eugene Debs speak. Pinkus ran a small laundry business, which barely earned enough to pay the family's bills. Louis occasionally accompanied his father on the horse-drawn cart, picking up laundry and making deliveries, but he had very little interest in the business.

Louis attended Barringer High School, one of the first high schools in the country, where he excelled in his studies and began writing poetry. In a 1990 interview, Hannah Litzky, Louis's youngest sister, accredited Margaret Coult, one of Louis's high school English teachers, as the one responsible for Louis's initial interest in writing poetry.

"She had given the class an assignment to write a poem in imitation of Milton's 'L'Allegro,'" Litzky remembered, "and Lou went home and did it. She was absolutely amazed, and that was a very meaningful experience for him, that he should have been so successful at it. That's what started him on his career in poetry."

While at Barringer, Louis met Naomi Levy, a short, slender, attractive girl his age. Naomi had emigrated from Russia to the United States in 1905, when she was ten years old, at the time a pogrom forced the Russian Jews to flee the country for their safety. Naomi was Louis's intellectual equal, and her strongly stated opinions, especially on political affairs, led to many discussions and arguments. Like many of the Russian Jews living in the western part of the country, near the Polish border, Naomi was a Communist.

Neither of Louis's parents had much use for Naomi, largely because of her politics: She made very little secret of her disdain for socialism, and she wasn't afraid to confront the elder Ginsbergs, especially Rebecca, with her views. For a while, Louis and Naomi's relationship was put on hold, while Louis attended Rutgers University and Naomi attended a two-year college to earn her teacher's certification, but in 1919, against the wishes of Louis's parents, they married.

Naomi's politics weren't the only reason Louis's parents objected to the marriage. Just months before the wedding, Naomi suffered a nervous breakdown, beginning what turned out to be a tormented adult life of gradual mental deterioration. She quit teaching and, in 1921, bore her first son, Eugene Brooks Ginsberg, named after Eugene Debs. Almost exactly five years later, Irwin Allen Ginsberg was born.

Life was never easy for the Ginsbergs. As Louis's teaching jobs took him from Woodbine to Newark and then to Paterson, the family moved frequently. With Naomi unable to work, Louis had to scramble to find ways to support a family of four, as well as pay for Naomi's mounting medical bills, on a teacher's salary. The lack of money, along with Naomi's increasingly irrational behavior, led to great tension. When they grew a little older, Eugene and Allen were occasionally kept out of school so that they could keep an eye on their mother.

Although teaching took up most of his time, Louis continued to write poetry. He joined the Poetry Society of America and associated with the likes of Marianne Moore, Maxwell Bodenheim, John Dos Passos, and Edwin Arlington Robinson. He published poems in numerous literary magazines and newspapers, and he privately published two books of poetry, *The Attic of the Past and Other Lyrics* (1920) and *The Everlasting Minute* (1937). His poem "Fog" was included in Louis Untermeyer's important anthology *Modern American and Modern British Poetry*. Although he would never reach the stature of some of his contemporaries, he was well known on the East Coast, and he liked to call himself "Paterson's principal poet."

Allen Ginsberg was always "high-maintenance," to use a current expression. He demanded more attention than his older brother, and his need for physical affection was so great that his father jokingly referred to him as "my little kissing bug." Allen would often crawl into bed with Louis, which, in all likelihood, was precipitated by his anxiety over his mother's manifestations of insanity and subsequent institutionalization, but which, nevertheless, contributed to confusing semierotic thoughts in a child already mixed up by his sexual identity. (Throughout his life, Allen would have erotic dreams involving himself and his father, much the way he was plagued by disturbing nightmares about his mother's insanity and the guilt he felt in authorizing her eventual lobotomy.)

Allen would never characterize his childhood as being a joyous one, but he never wrote it off as unhappy, either. Hannah Litzky remembered him as being "happy, playful," while her husband depicted his nephew's childhood as strongly family-oriented.

"I remember him as a happy, frolicking kid, who would be with the family down at the shore," Leo Litzky said in 1990. "He loved to frolic in the water and play with his cousins and ride bikes in the street. He'd just have a wonderful time. And race with the adults: Louie and he would race for a hundred yards. Louie was very agile, and frequently Louie would win. That camaraderie in the family was very strong and prevalent."

There's no doubting Louis's early influence on Allen. For as long as Allen could remember, his father recited poetry from memory, often while he was doing domestic chores – "the way people sing or hum while they work," as Allen pointed out. Every night after dinner, Louis would retreat to his desk in the corner of the living room, where he'd sit and grade his students' papers and, if he had the time, write poetry. For Allen, the desk became an important memory and symbol: After his father's death, he claimed it, moved it to his apartment, and used it himself.

Allen said nothing about his desire to write poetry, mainly because, as he noted later, he wanted Louis to think he was "normal." Allen had once overheard his father joking that Allen, as the only nonpoet in the family, was the only normal member of the household, and he took his father's words seriously. Although his early journals indicate that from a very early age he felt that he would be a writer someday, he kept these ambitions a secret. When he began attending Columbia University in 1943, he intended to study labor law.

The mid- to late 1940s was a tumultuous period for both Allen and Louis Ginsberg. Louis and Naomi, separated since 1943, were finally divorced in 1948. A short time later, Louis married Edith Cohen, a divorcée with two teenaged children, Harold and Sheila, and the family moved into a new house in Paterson. The marriage provided Louis with the kind of companionship and stable home life that he had lacking for most of his adulthood. Vivacious and intelligent, Edith had an enormous influence on Louis, particularly in matters involving his youngest son.

During this period, Allen confronted one crisis after another. In 1944, three of his closest friends – Lucien Carr, Jack Kerouac, and William Burroughs –

ran afoul of the law in the now-legendary David Kammerer murder; Carr was imprisoned for manslaughter, while Kerouac and Burroughs faced minor charges, stemming from their neglecting to report the crime, and because Kerouac had assisted Carr in hiding evidence. The following year, Allen was expelled from Columbia for housing an unauthorized guest (Kerouac) in his dorm, and for scribbling obscene slogans and drawings on his gritty dorm windows. That same year, Allen met Neal Cassady (a Denver native and hero of Kerouac's *On the Road*), and though Cassady was essentially heterosexual, the two began an on-again, off-again affair, which lasted for nearly a decade. When Cassady initially tried to break off the relationship in 1947, Allen traveled to Denver to rekindle the affair, and when that trip ended in failure, Allen found a job on board a ship bound for Dakar.

Up until this point, Louis had no inkling of his son's sexual preferences, but he was understandably quite concerned about the direction Allen's life was taking. Louis never had much use for Allen's friends – particularly Burroughs and Cassady – and he exploded when Allen finally told him that he was homosexual. Fortunately, Edith, who loved Allen deeply, acted as a buffer between father and son.

But the turmoil was far from over. In 1948, Allen confessed to Louis that he'd had a series of "visions" involving William Blake and the mystic poet's work, and a year later – the same year that Naomi Ginsberg was permanently committed to Pilgrim State Hospital – Allen was arrested for allowing Herbert Huncke, a friend, and Huncke's small burglary gang to store stolen goods in his apartment. In lieu of a jail sentence, Allen was sent to Columbia Presbyterian Psychiatric Institute for treatment.

The stress on Louis Ginsberg during all of this was immense.

"When I think of Louis in those days, I think of Job," Eugene Brooks recalled in his introduction to his father's *Collected Poems*. "These incidents in themselves are far from funny, but the dysfunction in lifestyle and attitude between Louis and Allen takes on, in retrospect, a farcical quality."

"Lou would talk to me about the difficulties that Allen had gotten into, how distressed he was about it," Hannah Litzky remembered. "I recall him saying, 'Maybe there's something in the genes that has created all this turmoil in Allen.'"

"I just admire Lou's equanimity in handling Allen," added Leo Litzky, "because, in comparison, I would have had such anger. But Louis . . . I marvel at his control and his ability to try to reason, even when he raised his voice. And he did raise his voice when he differed strongly, but it was always with a sense of reason."

Fortunately, Allen's life became much more settled after his string of troubles in the late 1940s. He moved back home, met and was befriended by William Carlos Williams, and, in general, tried to lead the kind of life recommended by his therapist. As his journal entries from this period indicate, he was far from content with this arrangement, but at least he was staying out of trouble.

Allen Ginsberg's early poetry was derivative of the poetry he had grown up reading – and the kind of work that would meet his father's approval. Allen made a point of showing his poetry to Louis, and Louis would respond with detailed criticism of the work. As rebellious as he could be, Allen also had a powerful need for approval – from his father, his teachers, and his friends, all of whom would see his work. Allen's facility with language and ideas was obvious, but in adhering to traditional forms, he seemed to be lost in rhyme and meter schemes, as well as in confusing symbols and metaphors. Allen realized that his poetry needed to take a different direction, but he had no answers until he met William Carlos Williams in 1950.

Allen showed some of his early rhymed poems (many of which can be found in his collection *The Gates of Wrath*) to the elder poet, who lived in nearby Rutherford, New Jersey, but Williams rejected them as imperfect imitations. Williams was more interested in American idiom and language, with their unique rhythms and sounds. In an attempt to please his new mentor, Allen paged through his journals, pulled out prose passages, and broke them into shorter lines imitative of Williams's poetry. Williams responded favorably and promised to find a publisher for Allen's work. Thus encouraged, Allen abandoned the traditional forms and wrote much of the poetry eventually published in *Empty Mirror*.

Allen's relationship with his father shifted slightly as his friendship with Williams blossomed. Louis was no longer the major influence; Williams, along with Jack Kerouac, had replaced him. According to Edith Ginsberg, Louis was pleased that a poet of Williams's reputation had befriended his son, although he was slightly put off when Williams would visit and he and Allen would huddle together in Allen's room, excluding Louis from their conversation.

With the publication of *Howl and Other Poems* in 1956, Allen attained fame, stature, and influence. As the letters in this volume indicate, Louis was thrilled for his son, and if he felt any envy over Allen's success, he kept it to himself. Louis was never comfortable with some of the language and frank sexuality in Allen's poetry, but after initially criticizing these elements in

"Howl" and "Kaddish," only to see these poems widely praised and anthologized, Louis became less vocal about his objections. He and Allen continued to debate the merits of works by Beat Generation writers, but Louis tempered his criticism of Allen's own poetry.

In time, there was almost a complete reversal of position. While Allen published virtually anything he wrote and submitted, including poetry collections that were issued every few years or so, Louis was continually frustrated by his inability to find a publisher for a new volume of his work. He enclosed new poems in many of his letters to Allen and solicited his son's criticism, and though he was far too proud to ask Allen to use his influence to end his publication woes, some of his letters were thinly veiled appeals. When a publisher finally agreed to publish *Morning in Spring,* Louis relied heavily on Allen's position and experience almost every step of the way, from asking for his suggestions on the selection and revisions of the poems to be included in the volume to seeking advice on the promotion and marketing of the book. Louis's humility during all this is touching, as is Allen's devotion to his father.

The joint poetry readings, beginning in 1966 and promoted as "the battle of the bards," provided Louis with new exposure (and income) in his advancing years. At this point in his career, Allen was maintaining a crushing work schedule, which included extensive traveling for poetry readings and lectures, but he always found time for a handful of appearances with his father. Although Louis clearly had more to gain from these readings, Allen enjoyed them immensely. Not only did he revel in the lively banter over poetry and politics; he also relished the opportunity to spend more time with his family.

Louis might have deferred to Allen in literary matters, but he was loath to concede a single point when they fought over political topics.

"Letters between Allen and Louis contained wrathful political grenades," observed Eugene Brooks, who, along with Edith Ginsberg and Hannah and Leo Litzky, saw many of Allen's letters to his father. The disagreements were almost expected. From the days of their youth, Allen and Eugene had been encouraged to speak their mind about political matters; both were reading and clipping articles and editorials from newspapers when other boys their age were more concerned with baseball scores than with world affairs. Both wrote letters to the editors of the *Paterson Morning Call* and *Paterson Evening News* – and, on at least one occasion, the *New York Times.* Allen filled his diary with his opinions on local, national, and international politics.

The detonation of the atom bombs in Japan, as well as the Cold War with the Soviet Union, had profound effects on Louis and Allen. Both feared for the planet's future, agreeing that science and technology might have created, in the nuclear bomb, a means of humankind's suicide. But they strongly disagreed over the solution to the problem. Louis believed that peace should be maintained through military strength, and that communism (the greatest threat to world peace, in his opinion) would only be defeated or contained by an alliance of countries with superior firepower. There was no reasoning or negotiating with the Soviet Union, he'd argue; the only language the Communist leaders understood was brute force. Allen disagreed. The world, he proposed, was divided by blind devotion to nationalism and religion, with different nations and peoples willing to decimate the world over their differences, rather than to unite and survive in common humanity; the best solution was to extend a hand, rather than aim a missile.

The Cuban revolution brought out some of their most passionate debates. By the time Fidel Castro seized leadership in Cuba, Allen had spent an extended period of time in Europe, Mexico, and northern Africa, where he'd had the opportunity to see and analyze American politics from afar; he had already formed the worldview that he would maintain for the rest of his life. He wasn't buying his father's contention that Castro's government, with its ties to the Soviet Union, posed any immediate threat to the United States, nor did he believe that the Castro regime meant continuous oppression to the people of Cuba. Allen saw Castro as a benevolent dictator committed to improving his impoverished country's medical and educational systems; U.S. opposition to Castro, Allen felt, only pushed Cuba closer to communism and away from Castro's original socialist intent.

Louis, quite predictably, dismissed Allen's opinions as so much idealistic drivel. The Bay of Pigs invasion forced Louis to reassess his stance, but he held to his position. When Allen visited Cuba and was expelled from the country in 1965, Louis found it impossible to resist ribbing his son about how his free speech went over in a totalitarian regime.

The testy exchanges between father and son over Israel and Judaism are particularly interesting, not just for what they say about the two men's individual beliefs but for the ways in which they represent general long-standing debates about dual loyalty, heritage and religion, and Israel's conflicts in the Middle East. As these letters illustrate, Louis became very angry over his son's slightest criticism of Israel's politics, and he badgered Allen about exploring his own Jewish heritage, even though he himself rarely observed the practices of his faith. He did celebrate Jewish holy days and holidays, but he rarely set foot in a synagogue, the household meals were not prepared kosher, and neither of his sons were bar mitzvahed.

"Allen was not brought up with a strong Jewish identification, in terms of the religion itself, but he was brought up with the values," Hannah Litzky explained. "Because my parents were socialists, religion, per se – the observance of religious practices – was not important. Then Lou married a Communist, who, of course, was totally antireligion. There was no observance and no interest, really, in bringing the boys up as Jewish, but there was a very, very strong commitment to being Jewish. That was part of one's identity."

That identification was the cornerstone of the disputes between Allen and Louis Ginsberg. Louis had been shaken to the roots by the Holocaust, and he saw the establishment and continued welfare of Israel as tantamount to the survival of the Jewish people and their heritage. Allen, of course, detested any brand of nationalism, which he believed only led to further division in the human race, more hatred and warfare, and, in the age of nuclear weapons, a greater nudge toward planetary annihilation. Allen enraged his father with his occasional essays or statements to the press about Israel, and Louis responded with harsh letters (including one letter to an editor of a magazine, for which Allen had written an essay), his language as strong and confrontational as anything he would ever say to his son.

Their arguments over the Vietnam War were almost as contentious. Louis, like most Americans of his generation, had witnessed Hitler's conquering of Europe, as well as the Soviet Union's domination of Eastern Europe after the war; the domino theory in Southeast Asia made perfect sense to him. Allen, on the other hand, believed that the conflict in Vietnam was a civil war, and he argued that a Communist victory might not be the worst thing that could happen in that part of the world. As always, Louis boiled over anytime Allen showed the slightest sympathy whatsoever for communism, and on more than one occasion, he waved off Allen's arguments as a matter of Naomi's influence over her son. In several letters, Louis berated Allen as a "pinko" or "commie."

The letters concerning Vietnam are poignant symbols of the country's view as a whole. Louis, like many Americans, hated the idea of warfare, but he regarded it as a necessary evil; one had to stop the growth of communism or face the consequences. However, as time passed and the war dragged on, Louis's stance softened, and though he would never concede the idea that the nation's escalating involvement in Vietnam might have been a mistake, he grew more critical of the government and its inability to resolve the crisis.

At times, the intensity of Louis and Allen's political bickering can be unsettling to a reader, especially in this day and age, when passion for politics has been largely replaced by a sense of cynical resignation, but heated opinion never fractured the bond between father and son. "Allen and Lou would fight with each other like cat and dog," Edith Ginsberg reflected, "but they always wound up in each other's arms."

"Please save all my letters. Some day someone might want to collect them or want to see letters between you and me."

Louis Ginsberg wrote these words in a December 6, 1965, letter to his son, but he needn't have worried: Allen saved *everything,* from correspondence to rent receipts, from his high school term papers to the different drafts of his poems. From all appearances, he saved every letter Louis wrote to him, including those sent to all corners of the world, when Allen was living or traveling abroad. Unfortunately, Louis was not as careful with Allen's letters to him. Many were discarded after reading; others were misplaced after they were passed around from Louis to Eugene to the Litzkys. Both Louis and Allen eventually sold their letters to, or stored them in, university archives, but even so, many of Allen's letters – including those written after 1965 – are missing. One regrets their loss, just as one can't help but wonder about the contents of Allen's voluminous correspondence with William S. Burroughs – letters that Burroughs tossed out after reading.

However, what remains is significant. The letters offer an intimate portrayal of a complex father-son relationship, as well as a running commentary about some of the most turbulent times in U.S. history. These letters chart Allen Ginsberg's intellectual and emotional maturation, his development as a poet, and the evolution of his political views, all within the context of a loving relationship, which, while often tested, endured throughout two exemplary, yet greatly differing, lifetimes.

EDITOR'S NOTE

The sheer volume of the Allen Ginsberg correspondence is staggering, consisting of thousands of letters, notes, and postcards to his family, friends, fellow writers and poets, politicians, social activists and organizers, members of the media, and total strangers. The number of letters increased in proportion to Ginsberg's fame, and it was not uncommon for Allen to complain about being buried beneath the weight of the obligation to answer the mail. Nevertheless, he was dutiful in responding to these communications, sometimes in writing, often by phone. When Ginsberg's selected letters are eventually published, readers will likely wonder, as have Ginsberg scholars already familiar with the correspondence, how Allen found time to write his poetry, let alone the huge volume of essays, journal entries, book introductions, jacket blurbs, and so on.

When reading and editing the Ginsberg correspondence, I kept in mind several facts. Allen had the habit of designating blocks of time for correspondence, and he would write many letters on the same day. As a rule, the letters were written in haste, with little or no consideration of the fact that one day they might be published. Allen, whose spelling was atrocious to begin with, filled his letters with misspellings, horrible punctuation and capitalization, and grammatical errors; on occasion, he would forget what month it was or – usually in the months of January and February – what year it was. None of this is particularly uncommon in a large volume of correspondence – as I learned when I was researching *Dharma Lion* and reading the letters of Ginsberg's literary contemporaries – but it does present an editor with a puzzle and a challenge: Do you publish the letters untouched, warts and all, taking a purist's approach to scholarship, or do you "clean up" the letters, making them more readable for a general, less scholarly audience?

Obviously, my task would have been easier had Louis and/or Allen Ginsberg been alive when I was compiling this book. They could easily have gone over the manuscript and, since this book bears their names, made any minor corrections they wished. Having known Allen and having observed him working on other projects, and having discussed this one with him in great detail, I can state that he certainly would have corrected many misspellings and some of the incorrect capitalization; in all likelihood, he would have tinkered with punctuation. Such was his method, even when preparing previously published poems for his *Collected Poems* and *Selected Poems* or reviewing his published essays and interviews before reprinting them in *Deliberate Prose* and *Spontaneous Mind*.

After mulling over all this, I decided to edit in favor of readability, with as little intrusion upon the original texts as possible. I corrected misspellings (especially of proper names) when it was clear that these were unintended; I kept the original misspellings when it was evident that they were intentional, meant for humor, emphasis, or some other reason. I did not alter any of the prose or syntax, although I did use standard capitalization with regard to proper names and places (unless, again, I felt Ginsberg had a reason for doing otherwise). Finally, I left the punctuation intact, except on those rare occasions when an added comma or period would clear up an otherwise confusing sentence. Ellipses in the original letters are maintained in the text of this book. Whenever material has been cut, either because it was repetitious or of little interest to scholars or readers, or, on a rare occasion, when the handwriting was illegible, I used brackets and ellipses: [. . .].

For the sake of brevity and simplicity, I have used abbreviations in the footnotes: AG (Allen Ginsberg), LG (Louis Ginsberg), and CP (Collected Poems).

Finally, for the sake of readability, I used a standard format to indicate the date on which a letter was written, or, for Allen, the location from which it was written. Since Louis Ginsberg always wrote at home, I indicated his address *only* on the first letter written from a particular location. The reader should assume that until a new address is introduced, all letters were written from the address given previously.

EARLY CORRESPONDENCE

When Allen began his first term at Columbia University in the Fall 1943, he was precocious intellectually, but, at barely seventeen years of age, he lagged behind his Ivy League classmates in terms of maturity and sophistication. Most of his classmates had come from wealthier families and stronger educational backgrounds. This, however, meant little to Ginsberg, who, after his youth with his mother, had great empathy for the underdog and an attraction for people who were different.

During his first term at Columbia, Allen met a strikingly attractive, highly intelligent, and openly rebellious St. Louis native named Lucien Carr. Although only two years Allen's senior, Lucien seemed to be a lifetime ahead of him in knowledge and experience. Through Carr, Allen met William Seward Burroughs, another St. Louis native, a Harvard graduate who, at twenty-nine, became a kind of group elder. Allen also met Jack Kerouac, another friend of Carr's, a former football star who wanted to devote his life to writing. Allen immediately developed crushes on Kerouac and Carr, although he kept his feelings to himself. If the members of this group had one thing in common, it was their open disdain for what they considered to be the stifling standards in American literature and lifestyle. Burroughs was conducting his own private study of the people living on the margins in New York – petty criminals, drug addicts, the homeless, sexual deviants, and other rebellious types – while Carr and Ginsberg (and Kerouac, to a lesser extent) discussed what they called a "New Vision" for literature, in which the individual mind and experience would dictate the language, form, content, and meaning of a work of fiction or poetry.

Such lofty ambitions might have been standard fare on most college campuses, where students were encouraged to stretch the boundaries of youthful preconceptions, but Ginsberg, Kerouac, Burroughs, Carr, and other members of their circle were definitely a cut above the average. Kerouac's literary ambitions alone were awe-inspiring – according to the legend, he had written over 1 million words before he arrived at Columbia – while Burroughs's fierce intelligence, coupled with his natural distrust of all social, political, and religious institutions, provided the group with creative and intellectual sparks not often found in the usual college cliques.

Louis Ginsberg was less than enthralled with Allen's new choice of friends, or with Allen's open rebellion. Louis might have been liberal by nature, but he still believed in an orderly standard of behavior; anything else, he'd argue with Allen, invited chaos or insanity. Besides, Allen and his friends weren't experienced enough in life to challenge the norms of a system that had been functioning so well for so long. Allen was getting an education at Columbia and in New York, but it was not the one Louis had bargained for.

In August 1944, the group – and Carr, in particular – became the focus of a scandal that rocked the Columbia campus and literally changed the course of a number of lives. For some time, Lucien had been stalked by a former St. Louis physical education instructor and college teacher named David Kammerer, whose obsession with the younger Carr had led him to pursue Lucien from city to city throughout the United States, ending in New York. There was little question that Kammerer was deeply troubled – he went to the lengths of breaking into Lucien's apartment to watch him sleep – but he seemed to be more tragic than dangerous.

However, late one evening in mid-August 1944, after a night of heavy drinking, Kammerer confronted Carr in Manhattan's Riverside Park. Kammerer threatened Carr and, largely fearing for his own safety, Lucien pulled out a Boy Scout knife and stabbed Kammerer to death. He then dragged Kammerer's body down to the river, weighted him with rocks, and left him in the water.

Carr eventually turned himself in, two days later, but first he paid visits to Burroughs and Kerouac. Burroughs urged Lucien to surrender to the authorities, but Carr was worried about getting "the hot seat." Kerouac helped Carr dispose of the knife and Kammerer's glasses, and then the two spent what they felt would be their final hours together, wandering around New York. Then Carr went to the police and led them to Kammerer's body.

Allen was horrified and saddened when he heard the details of Kammerer's death. He had liked Kammerer and was appalled by the way his life had ended. He worried about Carr, who was certain to face prison time; in addition, Kerouac and Burroughs were being held for failure to report the crime. The immediate future looked very bleak.

The following letter is very revealing, not only for the details that Allen selected to provide his understandably concerned father but also for what it reveals about Allen's personality and state of mind at the time. Dramatic to the point of hyperbole, yet framing the core of his letter with small talk, Allen displayed a naïveté that would haunt and embarrass him when he was reminded of it many years later. Taken as an introduction of the correspondence that follows, the letter leads one to a better understanding of Louis Ginsberg's frustrations with Allen, and his concerns for his son's direction in life.

Allen Ginsberg to Louis Ginsberg

{New York City}
n.d. {ca. August 1944}

Dear Louis:

Your visit last night I remember only as a rather surprising dream. I was pleased to see you, but felt quite contrite, when I fell back to sleep, that you'd have to travel all the way back for such a short talk.

I have been reading Dickens' *Great Expectations* in my spare time.

The time seems to be out of joint – oh, cursed spite! – but is slowly readjusting itself to normality; or at any rate, it is becoming as normal as it can be under the circumstances. I don't remember what I told you last night. I was at the D.A.'s office, and was asked routine questions about Character – that was compositively unimportant. I also had a long talk with Kerouac. He told me all about the following days – how, says he, the two rode around in taxicabs discussing the ramifications of the deed – emotional, moral, and artistic. Carr cried a little without knowing it and kept saying, perhaps a bit distracted, "He died . . . this is the way the world ends: not with a bang but a whimper."

There were a few heroic scenes, as well: Before Carr went upstairs to his mother, he shook hands with Kerouac, bidding him goodbye for the last time. As Kerouac grasped his hand, he found several dollar bills between their palms. Carr withdrew his hand irritated and flung the money away into the street, then shook hands, turned, and went upstairs. Kerouac added, with a smile, that Carr knew he would pick up the money later.

Celine[1] is taking it all rather well. She saw Carr today, and said that he is chastened and serious, that he is much like old L. Carr when he dropped his attitudes and masks and defenses, and waxed serious. He seems to be, for the first time, openly considerate of others, without consciousness of being what he would have called "Bourgeois," as Celine said. He worried about Jack, whether he would get out, etc. He asked about me, about my interview with ———, and even very solicitously hoped that I didn't get burned.

Celine is the only one to have seen Carr: the attorneys have forbid any other visits. I may, however, be allowed to go next week. If I have time, I shall go, for I really pity Lucien under the circumstances, and, although I would profess to be a moralist, I can't find it in me to condemn him.

1. Celine Young, Lucien Carr's girlfriend.

Celine also asked him, as she put it, a rhetorical question, which he took up: "Why did you do it." He told her in confidence that the reason given was the true one – that Kammerer had suddenly become more violent than ever before, and that Lucien, frightened, had drawn his knife. Lucien told her that for the most part he could not remember what had happened. He said his mind, to use the usual phrase, was blank – and that, as an artist, he was sorry to have lost so much of the experience.

School otherwise is coming along. Chemistry was trouble, as usual. I've about 5 books to read in the very near future, and I've got to apply myself now or be lost, so I've been applying myself for the past few hours.

Any letters from Eugene?

I spent most of the $5 on phone calls, newspapers, carfare, and (the first evening) drinks for Edie[1] and myself when we heard the news. Can you send me a dollar to tide me over to next Friday?

Allen

From the beginning, Louis Ginsberg disapproved of his son's new friends, whom he considered to be bad influences. The talk of Rimbaud, derangement of the senses, a New Vision for modern literature, the "junkies and geniuses" of the subculture – all offended Louis's sensibilities, particularly in the aftermath of the Carr-Kammerer episode. In Louis's opinion, Allen's new obsessions were dangerous invitations to disaster.

Allen countered that literature needed to take a new direction, moving away from the mannered, constrictive approach of the past, though he was not certain what the new approach might be. He had only recently informed his father that he was writing poetry – an announcement that pleased Louis more than Allen had anticipated – and their correspondence was now filled with discussion, sometimes contentious, of literature and what might be appropriate subject matter for it. In his letters to Allen, Louis maintained a balance between intellectual discourse and his duties as a father dispensing advice to his son, yet, as the following two letters – one to his sister and one to one of Allen's favorite teachers – reveal, Louis was growing increasingly distressed about the path his son was taking.

---

1. Edie Parker, Jack Kerouac's girlfriend. Kerouac married Parker immediately after his release from custody. The marriage was short-lived.

Louis Ginsberg to Hannah Litzky

324 Hamilton Ave.
Paterson, NJ
January 16, 1945

Dear Hannah,

Relative to our phone conversation, I'd like you to show this letter of Allen's to Saltman.

Allen, as classwork, is writing a novel whose hero is a fictionalized Lucien Carr, a twisted eccentric. In addition, Allen regards any protest against his use of vulgar words in the novel as questioning his artistic integrity. I remonstrated that (a) Carr is not a desirable protagonist and (b) vulgar words do not necessarily prove artistic integrity.

His letter was an answer to my criticism. [. . .]

Love.
Louis

Louis Ginsberg to Lionel Trilling

February 21, 1945

Dr. Lionel Trilling
Columbia University
Morningside Heights
New York City

Dear Dr. Trilling:

I wonder whether I may take the liberty of writing to you about my son, Allen Ginsberg, who is one of your students.

Allen, whom I am trying to appraise objectively, is a brilliant youngster, precocious intellectually, but lagging, I fear, emotionally. He dramatizes himself as a writer, though he does have some potentialities.

At present, he is making clever but false verbal rationalizations that the immoralist way of life (à la Gide, I think) is a valid one. He thinks merely to rationalize some inner tendency proves a satisfactory way of life, harmonious with what we might term normal values. He seeks to philosophize abnormality into normality. I am not sure whether I make myself clear to you.

Since Allen holds you in high esteem and places great value on your dicta, I wonder whether, if it is not inconvenient for you, I might meet you. I feel that you could exert a salutary influence on Allen, who, by the way, has fallen in with some undesirable friends.

I believe Dean N.M. McKnight[1] has some knowledge of the situation. May I hear from you?

Sincerely yours,
Louis Ginsberg

Louis Ginsberg to Allen Ginsberg

n.d. {ca. 1945}

Dear Allen,

Received your letter. On the whole, it was a clever and even brilliant one; but it was subtly infected with fallacy.

Even if normal values are rationalizations as well as abnormal ones, the latter, as normal values *qua* normal ones, result in a better and safer adjustment to society and a greater integration of the person. According to your blanket statement, you would bracket the rationalizations of a homosexual or an insane person as satisfactory for society and for the person. The homosexual and the insane person is a menace to himself and to society. Danger and disaster lie that way! Your clever verbal solutions are incongruous with reality of life. You are developed intellectually; but, emotionally, you lag.

You exaggerate my own tendencies. I find compensation in the development of my own inner being in accordance and in harmony with salutary, social values. My personality is dominant in my own way; i.e. in achieving a poetic life of modest but definite accomplishments. I fail to discern a sadistic force.

No, I disagree with you – but definitely – that an immoralist can confirm "enduring human values," in chaos, "democratic civilization." You're all "wet," Allen. You simply have little experience in life. Where is your former, fine zeal for a liberal progressive, democratic society? Your sophistry – for that is what it is – is a series of half-truths, verbal cleverness, and dangerous ideas expressed in specious and dexterous verbiage.

---

1. Nicholas McKnight, Columbia's associate dean, asked Allen to refrain from writing his novel about the Carr-Kammerer episode. In McKnight's opinion, Allen's novel was "smutty."

I don't think, at bottom, Burroughs is serious. Even granting, for the sake of argument, that he is, it is the sincerity of a fundamentalist, hell-and-brimstone, bigoted preacher whose ways sow hatred and distortion. He rationalizes his malice resulting from his maladjustment, does Burroughs. He's dangerous not because he rationalizes but because his end product of thought and attitude results, eventually, if carved out in action, in danger and disharmony and chaos. You don't know enough of life to separate his non-conformity from truth or realities. Frankly, I shall be – justifiably – disappointed in you, if you persist in your intimate relation with him.

You are wrong that Trilling, Weaver, and Van Doren will side with Burroughs. Some of his art values they may like better than T. D. Adams; but Burroughs' social values those teachers will reject. I challenge you to present Burroughs' views, art and social, to Trilling or Van Doren!!! I dare you to take them up to Trilling.

No, pleasure is not the final reference of morality. Were it so, chaos, confusion, anarchy would result, not communism or socialism or a better society or a better man. License is not liberty. Pleasure, if it harms the individual or society, is bad. I tell you, Allen, you are living in an Ivory Tower.

Your poems: The one about the rose I don't care for. You don't have enough warrant for the reader to glean that the rose refers to a vaginal one.

I didn't care for Poem II. "No Soap" to me.

Poem III is good. I like it: it has subtle and epigrammatic aspects, well-knit meter, a valid idea.

What about a psychiatrist?

Louis

Louis Ginsberg to Allen Ginsberg

August 8, 1945

Dear Allen,

Received your letter.

Glad you have so much wearing apparel. This solves one problem for the nonce. When you are home, I'll have pictures taken, as Eugene had.

All is quiet here. I have two more days of school; then I'll have a three week vacation to loll about.

When and if you need more money, don't hesitate to write for it.

Your description of a "regular" fellow was about a randy type of somewhat inferior grade. Regularity includes variety of types; and the one you alienated was of rather low grade. (I'm afraid your letter is rather too vulgar to show to Hannah.)

I do think that obeying orders and reasonable self-discipline are essentials in a "regular," which I make coincide with a reasonable or sensible mode of life. The effervescence of your revolt is an ingredient of youth; but if it all makes you anti-social and disoriented, there is a great deal of rue to pay. Don't let yourself get rid of your common sense to make room for your textbooks. A little of the Greek ideal of moderation would do you no harm, m'lad.

The stories of the atomic bomb are exciting. I'm poring over the papers for it all. We may be on the threshold of a new era, though, I suppose it all takes a century or two for the effects to sink into the social body of the common man.

I've been reading a variety of items: essays on Kafka, a book on the electron microscope, the poetry of Hart Crane, essays on modern and modernistic poets, etc.

Feel well – and keep your shirt on!

Louis

Louis Ginsberg to Allen Ginsberg

September 14, 1945

Dear Allen,

Received your letter.

Glad you are O.K.

Sorry you won't be in for the Jewish Holiday. When do you expect to be in Paterson next?

Am doing a bit of reading lately rather than writing, as I am lying fallow a while. Read or re-read Edmund Wilson's *The Triple Thinkers* with interesting interpretations of Henry James, especially his tale, *The Turn of the Screw*. There is also a good essay on mannerism and literature. Have also dipping into Stefan Zweig's autobiography, *The World of Yesterday*. I'll read soon Farrell's new book of essays, wherein he cudgels the genteel writers.

All are well in Newark and send their regards to you.

Love
Louis

P.S. I re-read some of your recent poems. They have good qualities: have good ideas with penetration. However, your verse is at times a bit amorphous and not focused enough into concrete images which sum up and unify and integrate your ideas. I suggest you 1. use concrete images; 2. concentrate more; 3. watch the grammar for greater simplicity and clarity.

L.

Louis Ginsberg to Allen Ginsberg

November 2, 1945

Dear Allen,

Received your interesting letter, that is, what I could decipher of it. In pencil and in scrawls: I was barely able to decode it all.

You say: "In part I agree with Shapiro. The rest, I differ." Me too – with Shapiro and with you.

As for S.'s poem, it is not a poem but clever verse à la Pope.

A fine poem – to continue our discussion – has indirection and allusiveness; it operates on different levels. But too much modern, or rather modernistic poetry, is willfully obscure; it hides in private occult allusiveness, which leads to dadaism and echolalia. This obscurity and cerebral mumbo-jumbo has widened the gulf between the poet and the intelligent reader.

I realize well enough that the modern poet has to cope with difficulties which did not lie in wait for him in previous epochs. The disorder of modern life;; the explorations of Freud, Einstein, Marx; the mechanization and [. . .] of many activities; the pluralism of many conflicting values – all these make the poet shrink into himself. The enormous expansion of science, anthropology, sociology, psychiatry; the influence of the radio – all frighten the poet into hiding in his obscurity. He is afraid of clarity, not finding clarity in life. So he thinks he says something profound when he achieves the verbal duplicity of imitating clever associations. Life may be that way but not the best art.

Rimbaud was an intense seeker but not after adequate normal values. He sought absolute moral values. That's a horse of a different color. Anybody who seeks absolute values gets stalled! He must resign himself to pragmatic values or commit suicide. No one ever will or can find, with infinitely microscopic minds, the designs and meanings in the macroscopic vastness. Pragmatic values have not brought us to chaos; it is the indifference of the masses to those values and it is the amoral cynicism power-ridden moguls and tycoons, aided and abetted by the unorganized masses, that has brought us to the past war.

I don't say that our modern problems are properly faced as they should be; they are solved in a hugger-mugger, bad fashion; but to wait till you get absolute values which you'll never ever achieve – that is infantilism or quixotic incompetence, to say the least.

You in your infinite wisdom are less successful in solving dilemmas than the pragmatic individual, it seems to me. You don't seem to me to be searching for moral and political values. You deny there are any absolute values – then you butt your head against the universe, straining after those absolute values. What a sorry paradox!

When you end by your saying society is destroying itself and therefore you can do nothing to blend personal and societal gains, you are, well, off balance. Your statement reminds me of a lady who went to a psychiatrist to prove to the doctor and her husband that she was sane. "I like pancakes; does that make me neurotic?" she asks the doctor.

"No," he said.

"Well, my husband says I'm off."

"Because you make pancakes?" asked the doctor.

"Yes," she replied. "Will you come sometimes over to my house to taste my pancakes?"

"All right," replied the doctor.

Smiling, as the woman turned to leave, dragging along her non-plussed husband, she added, "Certainly, come to taste my pancakes. I have barrels and barrels of them hidden all over the house!"

More anon.

Louis

Allen met Neal Cassady in 1946. Cassady, a Denver native who would become the legendary hero of Jack Kerouac's 1957 novel, On the Road, *represented a disappearing frontier spirit that greatly excited both Kerouac and Ginsberg. Allen was deeply attracted to Cassady, and, to his surprise, Cassady, a heterosexual with a* seemingly limitless appetite for women, reciprocated Allen's affections, setting off an intense affair that was doomed from the beginning. Allen wanted Cassady exclusively to himself; Cassady was incapable of any kind of monogamy. Soon enough, he returned to Denver, leaving Allen crushed and depressed.

Louis Ginsberg knew nothing of his son's homosexuality, let alone his relationship with Cassady, so he was justifiably confused when, during the summer of 1947, Allen journeyed to Denver and sent home a series of letters speaking of what he termed his "Denver doldrums." As far as Louis was concerned, Allen's depression was attributable to his being away from home for the first extended period of his life; his inability to find a suitable summer job; and the general fragility of his state of mind. As one can surmise from Louis's chatty letters to Allen, father believed son would be fine when he returned to the East and resumed his studies in the fall.

In fact, Allen was disturbed because Cassady, involved with several women, had little time for him; Allen's initial frustration and jealousy evolved into horrible black moods, leaving him emotionally paralyzed. His future was far beyond uncertain; it seemed impossible. Columbia, Allen felt, was not the answer; perhaps psychoanalysis would be helpful. By the end of the summer, he had hatched a new plan: He and Neal Cassady would hitchhike cross-country and visit Burroughs in Texas (where he was now living with Joan Vollmer, his common-law wife, and their son), and Allen and Neal would attempt a reconciliation. The trip to Texas fell through in the worst way, with Cassady again rejecting Allen in favor of a woman, and Allen, now utterly dispirited and desperate, deciding to take a radical route and ship out of the country.

Louis Ginsberg to Allen Ginsberg

July 23, 1947

Dear Allen,

I was relieved to get your letter of the 21st and to know that you were well.

Sorry about that night porter job, but maybe you can give it up soon for something more congenial. That's a poetic situation: a poet alone at night listening to records. . . .

Speaking about the movies, did you know that the Fabians, who own movie chains, live in Paterson? I know Mr. Simon Glass, an in-law of Mr. Fabian's.

Was interested in "Swallow": glad you will appear in an anthology of young poets. Keep on writing: you've got the "good" in you.

I'm enjoying my summer leisure. I read, as I write you, Wilhelm Reich's

The Function of the Orgasm, in which I glimpsed a number of things. The essence of his book is sound enough. His theory of masculine armor is, at least, diverting. I dipped into Otto Rank's *Will Therapy*, etc. but I found the group difficult: too much abstract area. The same author's *Art and Artist* I read more carefully in parts. Here are one or two quotations:

"Whereas the average man subordinates himself, both sociologically and biologically, to the collective, and the neurotic shuts himself off from both, the productive type finds a middle way, which is expressed in ideological experience and personal creativity. . . . An artist willingly accepts limitations that appear in the form of moral conventions and artistic standards not merely as such but as protective measures against premature and complete exhaustion of the individual. . . . He masters the conflict by giving it form and aesthetic shape."

Incidentally, I procured Freud's *General Introduction to Psychoanalysis*, which I am reading carefully. I read it once, long ago, but am rereading it.

In between, I'm writing verse à la the Ginsberg lyric touch. I have had things taken by my old stand-bys like *Spirit*, *The N.Y. Herald-Tribune*, *The Sat. Rev. of Lit*, etc; but I'm trying to break into new places with new verse. Thus, with reading and writing and thinking, if any, I manage to juggle away these summer days.

Eugene spent a couple of days here. He's marking time, as I wrote you. Also, he's taking a play-writing course at Columbia. At least, he obtains stimulation of ideas and social contact.

Hannah is at the shore for a few weeks. Drop her a line: c/o The Lakeshore Hotel, 1217 Ocean Ave., Bradley Beach, N.J.

Keep up your spirits. If you need anything, don't hesitate to write to me. Drop me a line today.

Love.
Louis

Louis Ginsberg to Allen Ginsberg

August 1, 1947

Dear Allen,

How's the improvident genius in the West?

Received your letter of July 27, and am glad you are more comfortable now.

A couple of strictures first. My sententiousness, as you put it – well, you must pardon the solicitude of a father writing to a son who was in the doldrums. . . . I write as I feel. . . .

As for your too loosely used word, "bourgeois," anent Rank's quotation, I used Rank's own words. Awareness of limitations and respect for some of them are what Rank means. You mutilate his meaning by your quaint use of "bourgeois."

So much for my demurring. Now as to Reich. I'll look further into his musculature amor. I guess there is a good deal of that. I'll get, sometimes, Reich's *Sexual Revolution,* though I believe I glimpsed this thesis in his *Function of the Orgasm* (which, by the way, I obtained from Daliels' bookstore in Los Angeles).

Last week I ran down to Belmar for a day where I partook of a hot bath, listened to Hannah's financial problem, shrugged off Clara's complaints, and cheered up my mother. This weekend, I'm going, with some friends, to an island off Connecticut, where, on a small farm, I'll be in an unbutted mood to enjoy, so they tell me, green fields, sunning brooks, and a wood that has aspirations to be a forest.

Did you get a copy of your marks from Columbia? I have one copy. I re-routed to your Denver (Grant St.) address.

Well, here's luck to you trying to unscrew the inscrutable, solve the unsolvable, and approach the unapproachable.

The Passaic Valley Examiner reprinted your poem, "A Lover's Garden," enclosed herewith.

What's new?

Love.
Louis

P.S. Here's a quotation from Benet I like: "A good poet puts you inside a poem rather than puts you on the spot!"

Louis Ginsberg to Allen Ginsberg

August 18, 1947

Dear Allen,

I'm sending you an article, called "The Canceling Out," by Joseph Warren Kuch, in the current issue of *Accent*. He develops a stricture or note or warning or connection with modernistic verse with its "depth psychology." Please return this article, after you have used it.

I bought a copy of the "Accent Anthology," which has a fine poetry section. I'm dipping into it this week.

I just came back from a three-day stay at the island in the Housatonic River near New Milford, Conn. I relaxed in an army life raft on the river, prowled in the wood on the island, and let the gurgling of the river over countless rocks interweave with my thoughts, so that the influences of nature might evoke an answering grace in me. Did you get my postal I sent from there?

All's quiet here. Eugene is in status quo. He expects the results of his bar exams to come out in about a week.

(While writing this, my eye falls on a sentence of mine which you quoted in your last letter: "You must pardon the solicitude of a father who is writing to a son in the doldrums." There floats in my mind a suspicion that you missed the slight sarcasm in "pardon": a slight sarcasm to rebuke your use of your word, "sententious," on your reaction to my worry over your state of doldrums.)

Summer is passing rapidly for me. In about three weeks, Sept.9, high school starts again and pay-days begin again. I've read quite a bit, mostly poetry and criticism, also written a number of poems with more irony and complexity than usual, albeit returning my "lyrical touch," – poems called "Side-Street Bar," "Bus Terminal," "Walking in a Hurry," etc. I hope they will eventually steal their way past the vigilance of some editor.

What have you been writing?

When do you think you'll be home?

Love.
Louis

Allen Ginsberg to Louis Ginsberg

Brayos Motel, Houston, Texas
September 3, 1947

Dear Louis:

I came into Houston today – this morning to be exact – in the hope of getting a ship to N.Y. or a short trip elsewhere to make money. Surprisingly, after all the N.Y. bureaucratic difficulties, I walked in the union hall here and they gave me a job on a ship going to France. So what am I going to do but take it? I leave tomorrow or the next day, the ship is a wheat carrier, going thru Gibralter to Marseilles, on the Mediterranean. I am so disgusted with personal & financial & aesthetic problems that shipping out seemed the only way out. Now, I am going to be 20 days out and 10 days in port & 20 days back so (surprise!) I won't be in time for school's start this term. Now, I've decided not to enter till January for obvious reasons. Financial & emotional are predominant. I can't think really of going back to school & spending money on it till I have the psychoanalysis, which I need much more, and climactically & crucially this year, started at least & securely progressing. I ought to finish school by next summer, and finish analysis at that time, also. So I expect things will work out. Frankly I am not very sorry that I have gotten myself in this position by going out West – my rage or frustration of the other letters was at my own blunders of will in working things out, not in choosing to come out here. The experience has been more salutary than I can describe. I say so because I can't describe it in any but explosive psychologizing and statements of degeneracies of psyche which I have (as a French novel letter might say) "hinted" to you more than once, and made explicit more than once. I really tell you seriously, Louis, that if you want a fine upstanding completely virile son, in me, you'd best take this word to the wise & approve, if you will. Otherwise (and I am not in any sense suggesting an "ultimatum") I will have to just go ahead with what I think best on the matter, which is analysis first & foremost, & school as a matter of course. I have never understood your angle in your fear that somehow, like all the stupid Yiddish boys of yore, I will leave college uncompleted. That is furthest from my mind, to go into the world sans the B.A., even, in fact, an M.A., so don't worry about me becoming a permanent wastrel first because I'm trying to "save my soul" as scientifically as possible. The analysis is important to me, and if you knew (Horrors, alas, too terrible to indite!) my sexual & soul-ful difficulties you would bless my efforts. Forgive the irony. Anyway I shall come back with a little money, at least, and be able to engage the analyst who has agreed to take me.

I have been in Texas just a week, and am rather sorry to leave the serenity of the bayou for the onerous job (messman) I have aboard the ship. But I have been so perturbed (irritation & ennui & floating anxiety & constant self-lacerating introspection) that I cannot continue to stay here any more than in Denver. A 50 day isolation at sea may or may not be pleasant, but the prospect of at last settling this analysis deal – however painful the analysis will be – is pleasant to me, and the only concrete *plan* I have in mind for the next year. So, go. Things happened so happily speedily, that I hadn't more time to consult you, which I would have, if you're curious about that.

Now, what is Eugene's latest? I still haven't heard from him, nothing at all. And the family?

I have been running around Houston all day & am tired & must close. I can't tell you where to write, but will communicate to you from the first port I hit. It may be N.Y., I don't know: if so, I may sign off ship there to follow alternative plans, all depending on how passable the ship work will be.

Love,
Sonny Boy,
Irwin

I won't have time to write. Tell Gene to notify Naomi & Elanor of the prolongation of my absence from the city. Tell them, also, I have gained some weight.

Allen Ginsberg to Louis Ginsberg

{Freeport, Texas}
September 12, {1947}

Dear Lou:

Sorry I didn't get in touch with you sooner but things have been pretty hectic, pleasantly so.

I am in Freeport Texas, 75 mi. south of Houston. You got my last letter? I gave it to a friend to mail as I was rushed & I don't know if it was mailed, though I expect so.

When I last wrote I was signed aboard a ship to Marseilles, but I changed my mind & signed for a longer cruise to Africa (West Africa–French Equatorial–Dakar etc). I am writing on ship now – it is 10:15, and we sail in 6 hours, stopping first at Galveston, where this will be mailed, I suppose, then out thru the Gulf & south.

I don't much suppose, still, you are in accord with me as far as the discretion of my latest deed of prodigality. If you need reassurance, I have (& always had) every intention of getting my degree. My motives in shipping out are spiritual, to be sure (I'm tired of everybody) but are predominantly practical, and I embark mostly for financial reasons. I will come back with a few hundred dollars, I expect (and some souvenirs). I am flat broke otherwise, and I don't want to have to squeeze thru another term borrowing money, & trying to live on $15 a week. Of course I could go back & work part time, but I also want psychoanalysis and that will take a lot more money, & the only thing for me to do, Lou, is to do what I'm doing. Aside from that, it will be healthful & will be a pleasant experience. I've already gained weight & my physique, curiously enough, is already improved; further, I feel finer than I have in a long time, and wait departure with much amiable anticipation, etc. etc.

But I really want to tell you, don't worry, I'm not really unconscious in the sense that I am aware of your consciousness & your anxieties about me, and have anxieties about myself equal & much greater, so you must trust me to work things out. That is all that would be done, anyway, whatever happens.

I heard, at last, from Eugene, a pleasant letter. Incidentally, give him money to redeem the valises. I will (as I wrote him) send you (or him) money to take care of the matter, the first port I reach – in 3 or 4 weeks. As for the typewriter, I will send money to take care of fixing it. It belongs half to me & half to Neal Cassady. He will be in N.Y. in a month & may need it for use, so please give it to him if he calls on you to pick it up. Fix it meanwhile, don't worry about the money, that will, as in God's providence, be taken care of in a short time.

My address is

Allen Ginsberg

John Blair

Ponchelet Marine Corporation

21 West Street

New York 6, N.Y.

They will forward all mail.

I am in touch with Prof. Guttman. Incidentally, will you write to him (or the Dean) asking the college to arrange a leave of absence for the Fall term. I will (barring an act of God) be back in time for the spring semester, and a *June* graduation, which I've always rather wanted.

I enclose some clippings of yours. As you know, I'm not much excited by your "incidental" lyrics, but I think these and all I've seen of yours the last year are way better than the average of those before (except those in the book, which are all pretty good).

Speaking of books, if Cassady shows up for the typewriter, show him my shelves of modern poesy and tell him to take along anything he thinks he can use. He is trying to learn to write, & is talented & perceptive, though not much educated, and I have been teaching him grammar etc. This is how I got half title to the typewriter. Also give him a concise grammar book. Please don't forget this. He will appreciate your kindness.

All my love,
Allen

P.S. I have been reading Henry James. Would you send me the book of short novels I had home? You loaned it out.

Louis Ginsberg to Allen Ginsberg

September 15, 1947

Dear Allen,

I received your two letters, including the one mailed from Galveston.

Your news was a surprise to me, of course; but I took it in stride. . . . It's O.K. Lots of luck to you, Allen.

Before your letters came, I had borrowed two hundred dollars in preparation for your college. I was going to set you off right, though, as to the psychiatrist, I thought you'd have to wait [until] after your graduation, at which time I'd help you out for the doctor.

Do take care of yourself, Allen. Don't dissipate your youthful resources. Save your money; and what additional you'll need, I'll provide later.

I have written to the Dean today asking for a term's leave of absence.

Your typewriter is being taken today for an overhauling.

When Neal Cassady shows up, I'll give him the typewriter and a grammar.

The book by H. James I shall call for and send it out to you.

Otherwise, all is quiet. School started last week and is running smoothly.

Eugene passed the bar last week. He is now casting about for a position with a law firm. He's answering and putting in ads. It may take a little time.

The folks in Newark wish you luck in your venture.

Let your mind be at peace and have no misgivings. (I am relieved, of course, that you are determined to graduate in June.) So, have a good time, build up your health, and soak in experiences for future poems.

Of course, I miss you very much; but I trust all will turn out well; and before long you'll be back.

Love and kisses,
Louis

P.S. Write as often as you can.

Allen did not graduate from Columbia, as he had hoped, in June 1948, and his emotional state remained fragile. Neal Cassady, now living in San Francisco, had married, and he and his wife, Carolyn, were expecting their first child. William Burroughs had moved to Louisiana, and it was doubtful that he would be returning to New York anytime in the near future, if ever. Jack Kerouac was totally preoccupied with putting the finishing touches on The Town and the City, *his massive first novel. Allen, for the most part, was on his own and feeling lonely.*

He continued to spark powerful emotional responses from his father. As part of his psychotherapy, Allen had finally told Louis of his homosexuality and affair with Neal Cassady, and Louis responded with anger, confusion, frustration, disbelief, and deep concern. Louis and Allen continued their heated debate over Allen's interest in what Louis considered to be the seamier side of society. Then, if all this wasn't enough, Allen shocked Louis with the announcement that he'd had a series of "visions," in which he had heard the audible voice of William Blake speaking to him through the ages – a proclamation that alarmed some of Allen's closest friends, not to mention the effect it had on his father, who worried for his son's sanity. Louis had married the former Edith Cohen, moved into a new house, and was attempting to establish a calm domestic life, which had eluded him throughout his troubled years with Naomi, his first wife, but Allen proved to be a challenge to his own peace of mind. His advice to Allen, at home and in correspondence, remained consistent with his advice of the past: Drop the rebellion, move closer to the center, and try to fit in.

Allen, of course, was hearing very little of it.

Louis Ginsberg to Allen Ginsberg

July 11, 1948

Dear Allen,

Exorcise Neal.

Louis

Louis Ginsberg to Allen Ginsberg

July 23, 1948

Dear Allen,

Received your letter and mulled over your poem. It's got some weighty thought, closely packed, but I can't say that I am sure of what you mean. Your piece seems knotty, slightly crotchety, and blurred in places. The glossary helps. The main idea, even if I mutilate it in the simplification, is that your real self is struggling to be free from the false selves or neurotic influences which cling to and hamper it. What I like about your piece is the play of wit lambent about it or through it, and the "sound effects." Your figures are a bit too impacted to take an expression from dentistry: i.e., a bit too inchoate. I do think, though, you are moving toward greater unity and so you lose less strength in diffuseness and bright irrelevancies.

I think the ideal of a poem is that it give a general meaning to the many and a deeper and more complex experience to the few.

Incidentally, I am reading, now and then, in Empson's book on ambiguity. It's rather hard and tedious reading, too arid in spots and too heavily laden with learning. Yet, it has fine insights and is rewarding. I read merely two chapters, but I'll continue on. What he does is, as I take it, to put an intellectual microscope over a poetic line, so that the rich complexity or simultaneity of a line which we felt vaguely is now enlarged and magnified; so that we see the actual merging and fusion of the various hints, ingredients, overtones and nuances.

Nothing new here. Am attempting a reasonable facsimile of plain living, so-called high thinking, with occasional attacks of writing.

Good Housekeeping is holding a poem of mine. Also, *The Western Review*, formerly *The Rocky Mt. Review*, took a poem of mine, called "My Clothes on My Chair." The editor, Robert Stallman – Do you know him? He's done some writing in avant-garde magazines – wrote me the poem will probably appear in the Autumn issue. It is issued by the University of Kansas.

More anon.

Yesterday I wrote a poem whose title is: "Don't Look Now But Your World Is Slipping." It's a kind of mocking, sardonic thing: I'll revise it shortly and send it out.

Love.

Regards to Eugene.

Louis

Allen Ginsberg to Louis Ginsberg

{New York City}
n.d. {ca. 1948}

Dear Lou:

I received your letter, and disagreed with most of it. As you said, it is too incomplete to be judged as a novel;[1] for that reason the section you read did not communicate, except by implication, the purposes of the novel and its concerns.

Thus I was surprised (in two ways) by your deploring of my studying eccentricity. For you followed that sentiment up with the comment that the world was devastated by barbarians with the civilization of man in jeopardy. The juxtaposition of "eccentricity" & "devastation," in *contrast*, struck me as humorous. For it is my point that the whole society is decadent and eccentric, that this has produced Nazism, and that it is the stupidity of society which makes its eccentricity all the more offensive. If you remember the scene in the Rational Café, I contrast the avowedly decadent Rimbaud with the "normalcy" of the Café patrons – sailors, farmers, wives, bourgeois businessman. More important, the perversion of the principal is directly a result of bourgeois "normalcy." Last, the whole society is diseased, and the heroes of the novel know they are diseased (as they must be since they are the symbols of society) and are trying to escape it (which comes out later). There is a correspondence, as there must be, between the emotional disease and the intellectual. Which is why I do not hesitate to pervert my characters (and I paint them worse than they are in real life) emotionally, when discussing principally their intellectual dilemmas.

Further, you are horrified by their emotional unbalance. You shrink from it, half in fear. This to me is a symptom of the smug normalcy of the bourgeois intellectual attitude. You assume we are all sexually stable; while on the other hand, as I have become acquainted with people, I find that they are all perverted sinners, one way or another, that the whole society is corrupt & rotten and repressed and unconscious that it exhibits its repression in various forms of social sadism. The emotional crassness and philistinism of the two "average" "normal" sailors in the Rimbaud part was one illustration of this.

But most of all, eccentricity is only a reflection and caricature of the

1. Allen had resumed writing the novel he had begun several years earlier. He never completed it.

normal; its value lies in revealing the outlines of the normal, in teaching the normal. Above all, personality strikes me as being perhaps the most important consideration in a novel; personality is above good and evil in the sense that having selected a significant personality, I am not sure that the author has a right to impose his standard of values so palpably as to prejudice the efficiency of character portrayal. To disapprove of a novel because the characters are irresponsible or eccentric does not seem to me to be passing a valid aesthetic judgment.

In sum, I am writing a naturalistic-symbolistic novel. Naturalistic because I am trying to reproduce the actual life of a whole community – in its own terms; I am not trying to prettify what is ugly about civilization; I won't hesitate to say outright what it is, and I won't rely on euphemism & presiosite or a censorship of crucial language and detail to make it palatable. What *will* make it palatable is the symbolism of the naturalistic detail – that lack disgusting fact (like the snot in the sailor's beard) is intended as a symbol.

As to the anti-Semitism – the comment was pretty obviously intended ironically. Remember, the hero is primarily above the usual societal mores (and prejudices). But he is not above defensive, mocking opportunism with regard to the [ ]. The point specifically, though, was his sadism at the moment – for the purposes of iconoclasm, breaking idols that he is aware should stand. He mocks here selfconsciously, with a smile. The proper reply is not to rise up in righteous wrath, but to smile back mockingly and say "I can't escape my conditioning." I have not yet forsaken the Jews.

I went downtown to Naomi today, showed her Eugene's letter – she was well. She had been feeling grippy last week.

So far I have been dressing up, and cutting is almost eliminated. I chatted amiably with the dean's secretary, and have started to really get an education, making the most of college, by returning unread to the library all my volumes of Baudelaire and Gide. Under Fritz's advice, I have taken to wearing a black tie.

I'll be in Saturday at 4:30 or 5:30—

Allen

Allen Ginsberg to Louis Ginsberg

{New York City}
n.d. {ca. fall 1948}

Dear Louis:

Your letters on hand. Sorry I can't be in to see you read. I have a class Thursday evenings.

As for scholarships, I am annoyed, but that is Columbia as usual. I'll borrow the tuition, so it will be off your hands in any case. As for working, this letter is presumptuous. As for myself, I went to the employment bureau and all I could get were the usual 75c per hr. jobs. My time is worth more than that to me. I registered for a tutorial position and they told me it might be possible, but no promises. I'm looking around; if I see anything at all feasible, I'll take it.

Next time I take it upon myself to write you a long letter of complaints, please don't be unpleasant enough to reply with three paragraphs to the effect that you got to take your medicine and make the most of it. Somehow, when these things are concretely applied, and psychoanalytically considered, the platitudes are true, and that's a fact. But I wonder what in heaven's name is the meaning *you* attached to them; what kind of concrete applications do these pietistic abstractions have in your mind? Sometimes I wonder what semantic level these Polonious-like tirades issue from. And, further, my problems are as external & real as they are internal and rise out of weariness and disgust. Very well, to be cheery, but in situation like this where it's a question of veritable survival I can't feel very sanguine about pluck and life etc. Tell a man in a concentration camp to make the best of it. This school is hardly a concentration camp, but my feeling that the school offers equivalent external problems (in a lesser degree) on a non-physical level, and that the culture is a huge concentration camp; further, believe it or not, the rain this year will be boiling hot.

Don't send me a check for Monday. I'll cash the blank check on Friday for 1 week's sustenance & 5 (or $30) so that I'll have cash with me at Harvard in case of emergencies. I leave Fri. morn.

Allen

Louis Ginsberg to Allen Ginsberg

October 6, 1948

Dear Allen,

Here is seven dollars.

Come in this weekend, either Sat. or Sunday morning. Eugene said he is coming on Sunday for dinner, as Edith will make a big meal at my house Sunday.

This is water past the dam, but, if you had taken my advice in my letter a few years ago (instead of . . . laughing at it with Burroughs), you would have been graduated already. So, take my advice now: put a tourniquet-knot around your affection for N., tone your letters down properly. . . .

Don't worry about a job; don't be apprehensive.

Work steadily and regularly at your last paper for Barzin.

I'll give you a check for your rent when you come in this week-end.

Love from
Louis

P.S. Ask Eugene whether he called up Judge Rosenstein, please.

Louis Ginsberg's greatest fears concerning his son's welfare were realized in April 1949, when Allen was arrested and charged with burglary and receiving stolen goods as a result of his permitting Herbert Huncke and two of Huncke's friends to store burglarized goods in his New York apartment. Although it was clear from the onset that Allen had been little more than an unwitting dupe in the burglary ring — in fact, on the day of his arrest, Allen had been attempting to move some of the stolen property from the apartment — Allen found himself facing a possible prison term, if he was found guilty of the charges against him.

Fortunately, Columbia University came to Allen's assistance. Mark Van Doren, an award-winning poet and an early Ginsberg mentor, acted as a character witness, whereas Lionel Trilling helped arrange for Allen's attorney. In the end, Allen was spared time behind bars in exchange for his agreeing to seek treatment at the Columbia Presbyterian Psychiatric Institute.

For Louis Ginsberg, the plea bargain was a mixed blessing: He was relieved that his son was not going to be spending any time in prison, but he was still concerned about Allen's mental stability.

Louis Ginsberg to Lionel Trilling

June 29, 1949

Dear Dr. Lionel Trilling:

This letter is to thank you very much for your generous aid to both my son, Allen, and me in our predicament.

As you no doubt know, Allen's mother has had a long series of nervous breakdowns; and she has been in and out of sanitariums for the last twenty-five years. I tried to give Allen what compensations I could; however, I suppose his wounded childhood had secreted from imbalance; or some trauma had precipitated some disorder deep in his psyche. Bad companions in the last few years had aggravated his attitudes; though it may be that his choice of some bad companions might be the results rather than causes.

At any rate, his arrest seems to have shocked him back to sobriety. My lawyer has had Allen cleared of the legalities in the matter; and today Allen entered the N. Y. Psychiatric Clinic [*sic*]. I do hope he will be salvaged for a brighter future, for I think Allen has fine talents.

Ever since Allen entered college, your name has been a household word with us. He has read, and we have discussed, your articles (in *The Partisan Review, Kenyon Review*, etc.). Allen looks up to you with something of veneration.

Permit me to extend to you my deep gratitude for your generosity and your invaluable aid to both Allen and me in our trouble.

Sincerely yours,
Louis Ginsberg

For the next several years, Allen stayed close to home. He served his time in the Psychiatric Institute (where he met Carl Solomon, a brilliant but disturbed intellectual who worked in publishing; Allen would eventually dedicate "Howl" to him); finished school at Columbia; and, in general, attempted to live the sort of "normal" existence recommended by his therapist. During this period, he met and corresponded with William Carlos Williams, who was not impressed with Allen's rhymed verse. "In this mode," he instructed Allen, "perfection is basic." Williams encouraged Allen to write about his own experiences in American idiomatic language, paying attention to the "minute particulars" – advice, ironically, that

Louis Ginsberg had given his son years earlier, but which Allen had chosen to ignore.

This time around, Allen took the advice to heart, extracting descriptive passages from his journals and breaking them into poetic lines. Williams loved the results. "How many of these poems do you own?" he asked Allen. "You must have a book. I shall see that you get it. Don't throw anything away. These are it."

Allen was also being heavily influenced by old friends. Neal Cassady had sent Jack Kerouac an incredibly long, rambling, stunningly detailed letter, written entirely in the stream-of-consciousness riffs so common in Neal's speech. Kerouac was utterly astonished by the letter, as was Allen, and Kerouac, in particular, vowed to let spontaneity dictate the path and style of his future writing.

William Burroughs arrived in New York in 1953, and he immediately moved into Allen's apartment, much to Louis Ginsberg's disapproval. Burroughs had been in a lot of legal trouble in both the United States and Mexico. He had run afoul of the law in Texas, due largely to his taste for drugs and alcohol, but it only got worse when he fled to Mexico, where he accidentally shot and killed Joan Vollmer when the two were engaged in a drunken game of William Tell. Rather than deal with Mexico's unpredictable justice system, Burroughs returned to the States.

The Burroughs-Ginsberg reunion, though pleasant enough at first, fell through when the two attempted to cross the lines of friendship into a sexual relationship. The two eventually parted, with Allen taking off for an extended trip to Mexico. While in Mexico, Allen explored the Mayan ruins of the Yucatán Peninsula, resulting in "Siesta in Xbalba," his first successful epic poem.

Unfortunately, neither Allen nor Louis Ginsberg saved their correspondence from this period. The extant letters that Allen wrote to others – Jack Kerouac, Lucien Carr, and Neal Cassady – are wonderfully descriptive, filled with news and details of his first lengthy journey outside of the United States. Louis, for his part, was thrilled that Allen was gathering material for future poetry.

Allen returned to the United States in the spring of 1954, making his way slowly up the California coastline before finally stopping in San Jose, where Neal Cassady was now living with his wife and children. Even in the aftermath of his disastrous affair with Burroughs, Allen was willing to risk another long-shot proposition with Cassady. With any luck, he reasoned, he would be able to assemble a book of poetry while reviving his affair.

Allen Ginsberg to Louis Ginsberg

{*San Jose, California*}
June 30, 1954

Dear Lou:

I have your letters and poems. I finally got around to looking at the Bodenheim clippings – really very sad. [. . .]

Is Joel all settled now?

I liked "The Blossom" most. I always liked the idea of using a flower for platonic symbolism. "H Bomb" seems most fugitive.

I got my telegram money today. Apparently it was just waiting at WTS for months.

I am seeing about the school idea, first getting in touch with whoever is around here I can connect with, and so wrote a few letters the other day. I'll let you know what happens.

I am meanwhile putting another book together and writing a few poems. They look alright. I'll send some along when I have them in final form. It always takes me half a year or so to be finished with anything over 2 pages. Such deliberation ought to produce something worthwhile, I figger.

You sound quite busy with jobs. I can't imagine what the garden must look like with a fence and no great hedge. Neater and less private I imagine?

I have a few copies of the *Voices* around and will send one for you to put up in my room. The poem is nothing much and is printed with 1949 date underneath.

I am glad you have a new subject in driving. I always thought cars were poetically interesting but I always saw them as symbols of wild flight rather than cooperation. [. . .]

I have no fixed plans except finish book at hand and look up school. I am well off, staying at Neal's house. There is plenty to eat, lots of writing paper. I have some money and no expenses presently and I come out of retirement or reading at dusk and help cook up some great NY dish like steak or sweet and sour, even lotkes. His wife is painting my portrait and there are three children to insure that I get up early and not go to bed too late. Also, there is wire recorder broke but being fixed and San Francisco amusements an hour away. It's a wonderful place and I'll probably move up there for work or school when I'm finished with the book. I've been working daily but hope to get to the all day interest I found when working in Paterson last time. That way finish midsummer.

I may also cook up a few stories for *LA Times* on Mexico. This is being inquired about now.

Nothing new except I go to dentist in week for checkup. Tell Edith [that] Celine, if she's interested, has a new book out, *Guignol's Band*. I saw a review in *Time* which said it was great though as usual strong stuff.

I have no present emergencies or needs. Everything taken care of, laundry, health, etc.

Climate here fine. No threats of winters, bareness. Perpetual spring-summer feeling, though trifle hot.

Love,
Allen

Allen Ginsberg to Louis and Edith Ginsberg, and Eugene Brooks, and Family

San Jose, California
July 10, 1954

Dear Louis, Edith and Gene and Kinder:

I applied at the Railroad for brakeman's job, a good job if it works out and I can do it, which would be difficult but valuable experience and good pay (3–5 hundred mo.) but no hiring going on at present. Will reapply in a few weeks. The situation I am told fluctuates rapidly and I have friends on RR who recommend me (who got Jack similar job). Meanwhile no worry and I can wait beyond summer if necessary without strain.

I looked up Rexroth's connections here. He's away on vacation but sent me name of a Prof. Witt Diamant at San Fran State Coll who runs a poetry institute or club. Moderators are Kenneth Patchen (of all the creeps) (I have been spared meeting him so far but will see him for the sake of my universal conscience), Norman Macleod who is whitehaired and has a speech defect and is sucking around the course to see if he can get a job in the school there, apparently he's taught a lot but in S.F. is presently unemployed, and Robert Duncan, a young Pound student, about 30 and smart but sort of a pathetic type, tries to browbeat these poor nowhere would be student poets at round table workshop type meetings, admission 50c and not worth a nickel. Macleod most simpatico of the trio. I gave him my book unintroduced and he wrote me a letter next day saying he liked it and would pass it on and suggesting a nasty little local magazine named *Inferno* to send some to. But he's a nice guy. Rexroth apparently the only real brain around here except for Winters at Stanford, I haven't met him but will soon. I have a meet to discuss metrics with Duncan some afternoon when I get to town.

I've also seen a lot of Chinatown: the food is more excellent varied tasty and original than NYC Chinatown, it's easier to get to and it's about half as cheap as NYC. They have basic dishes I never heard of, a brand of Won Ton soup new to me and better than original NY style, 40 cent Fried Rice and tea etc. I also hit all the North Beach bars – their Village – and found more life even than in NYC, more bars even anyway, and the same people as NY or their spiritual cousins; a very depressing sight in some respects and I'm glad I'm in San Jose where I can be protected from the temptation to run around to wild surrealist movies, art shows, jazz bands, hipsters parties, cellar lounges filled with hi fidelity Bach etc. All in all a very active cultured city the rival of NY for general relaxation and progressive artlife. Probably a very fine place to live if you like cities. When I get money I'll move there for a while, at least a few months to absorb it all. Spectacular views of the bay, bridges, Alcatraz, whiteroofed city on hills, clean, expansive horizon, ships in the toy harbor (really so huge). Communist murals in the tower (Coit) where sightseers go to observe, but they've decided after much public bitching to let them stay, and they're funny and charming as they are. Also keeping the cablecars, also apparently a big issue here.

I have unnecessary piles of correspondence with Kerouac at the moment a monumental exchange of descriptions of SF-Mexico trip and him sending news of NY. Plus long dissertations on Buddhism which he's been reading in for a year and is all hopped on. In between I work daily on poems but still not really shoveling at the mountain of notes yet.

Eugene sounds positively angelic. Louis sounds happy too. I had a haunting sense that most of my Mexico letters were gibberish since there's no map around, as Edith tipped me off. The parakeet is really a new and shocking development. [. . .] Incidentally I travelled with a monkey for several days on the way out and if you think parakeet crap comes anywhere near the nuisance value of a monkey's bowel movements . . . I should say, you could have done worse. I hope Louis is behaving himself with the animal. I've always suspected him of having a strange unnatural savage fascination with the little dears. It was one of his poetic eccentricities, one of the few he allows himself. Let me warn you about him. If you find the bird dead like some mystical swallow under a rosebush one summer morn I will write Harold.

Regards to all, Sheila. Tell her (again) to dig Gerry Mulligan's music. He must be playing around the Apple (as NYC is referred to from afar).

Nothing new special to report. I visited the Rosicrucian meeting here and met some lady spinster Rosicrucians. They keep seeing imaginary auras and talking about their lousy Karmas (You pay in one life for what you do in the last few) (you keep getting reborn) and they keep having dreams about when they were in Egypt and Atlantis. This is the occidental Rosicrucian center. I sure would have liked to pick up on them in the middle ages but now they're a bunch of mystical bobby soxers.

Everybody appears to be either off their rockers or getting religion. Cassady has some mediumistic cult that has changed him so that he kneels and prays with his children; the doctrine is screwy and absurd, almost on a *Reader's Digest* level, but the seriousness of the search for uplift is real enough and respectable; Kerouac seems all hung up on Buddha doctrine of life as a dream; even Burroughs in far off Tangiers appears to have undergone a humanistic conversion and Jack sent me a letter from him declaring, "I say we are here in *human form* to learn by the *human* hieroglyphs of love and suffering. It is a duty to take the risk of love. I *know* that ultimately the forces of death will destroy themselves." Such generalizations belong in a Nobel Prize speech. As for me sanctity is a worn out suit. I've been reading everything from theosophy to W. C. Fields biography and Eliot criticism. I hear WCW has a new book out. Jack's recommending me some Buddha books so I'll eventually read those too. Nothing like a wide range of information.

Well enough of this prattle. Forgive me if I don't write too often but I'll keep well in touch. It's just that when I get started like this I wind up spending hours instead of writing book.

Love,
Allen

Allen's stay with the Cassadys came to an abrupt, painful halt when he attempted to renew his affair with Neal and was literally caught in the act by Carolyn Cassady, who promptly drove Allen to San Francisco and dropped him off. The move turned out to be fortuitous, setting off a chain of events that totally transformed Allen, personally and as a poet.

Allen thrived in San Francisco's open, tolerant community, with its benevolent attitudes toward the arts and, perhaps more importantly, homosexuality. In no time at all, Allen assimilated himself into the city's bohemian subculture. He attended Kenneth Rexroth's and Robert Duncan's literary soirees, wrote and revised poetry, connected with the younger poets, and, in general, realized a new, stronger intellectual maturity.

He also met Peter Orlovsky, who became his lifelong companion and lover. Although essentially heterosexual, Orlovsky had come from a difficult background and needed someone to look after his emotional and intellectual needs. Allen was more than willing to provide this, in exchange for Orlovsky's satisfying some of his own needs. The relationship, as intense as any in which Allen would ever engage, was rocky from the beginning, and in the summer of 1955, while Peter was off on his own, leaving Allen feeling lonely and depressed, Allen sat down at his desk and, in one marathon writing session, wrote a frank, startlingly honest depiction of all his friends, "the best minds of my generation, destroyed by madness." The first section of "Howl," Ginsberg's landmark poem, would establish his permanent literary reputation.

When writing the poem, Allen had no intention of publishing it; as far as he was concerned, it might be of interest to some of his friends, but it was far too risky for commercial publication. Allen worried about what others – especially his father – would think of such a poem, and he didn't show it to Louis for many months. Fate, however, intervened when Allen read the poem at the now-historic gathering at the Six Gallery in San Francisco. Allen Ginsberg became the talk of San Francisco, and Lawrence Ferlinghetti, fellow poet and publisher of City Lights Books, offered to publish the poem as part of a Ginsberg collection.

With all the attendant publicity, along with Allen's own reports, Louis Ginsberg was aware that his son was in the vortex of a literary storm on the West Coast, yet as the following letters illustrate, he was unwilling to concede much to what he considered to be a wild, rebellious lifestyle translated into art.

Louis Ginsberg to Allen Ginsberg

416 E. 34th Street
Paterson, New Jersey
December 12, 1955

Dear Allen,

Glad to hear from you in your long, meaty, lusty letter.

We have completed our remodeling of the house. Tenants live peacefully upstairs, while we have a newly decorated, glittering apartment downstairs.

News items:

Eugene and Connie bought a house a couple of days ago. A split-level type on one floor, seven rooms, 2 1/2 baths somewhere in Long Island, an hour's ride from N.Y.

Item:

I received a letter today that the Poetry Society of America elected me to a new board membership to the Executive Committee. There was a field of 12 names.

Item:

Clara sold her house and is moving into an apartment near her daughter Johanna's. Sheila lives a few houses away (in Hillside, L.I.).

Glad to hear your readings went over fine. Wish I had heard you.

Read with interest your "Sunflower Sutra." I did not like the dirty words dragged in nor the long, long lines. However, it had feeling and fervor and good concrete details. The ending builds up well.

Eugene comes in tomorrow. After he reads it, I'll send your poem off to Solomon.[1]

No, Williams[2] did not get in touch with me.

Received a note from Jean Witter Byner who likes my verse.

Let me see *Variegations* with your things in it.

Bet you're making a literary reputation! Keep it up! You'll land somewhere in time!

About Dylan Thomas: Waiving aside his women (who is without sin should cast the first stones), I claim that it is stupid for Thomas to wreck his life with riotous drinking. Like pouring sulfurous acid into the innards of a Cadillac. All your vehement, vaporous, vituperations of rebellion move me not one jot. Your attitude is irresponsible – and it stinks!

Love.
Louis

Louis Ginsberg to Allen Ginsberg

December 14, 1955

Allen,

Moreover, I'm not condemning; I'm judging. As rational beings, we must recognize that liberty needs laws for wise direction (as you've heard me say).

1. Carl Solomon.
2. William Carlos Williams.

It's true. You are taking Pope's line, "Whatever is, is right" to read "Whatever is, is wrong." Your rebelliousness strikes out blindly at all things. (What I fear is that you are striking out at your own self.)

Prescott or no Prescott, Thomas behaved abominably to others and also to himself. A fine genius went wildly amuck. What inner compulsions tore deep within him we have still to unearth. Yet we can see, whatever they were and whatever compassion for him they may evoke from us, yet the fact remains that a fine, opulent genius wrecked, ruined, blunted himself, wittingly or unwittingly, it matters not in retrospect.

And for you to condemn the world which lay down at his feet, is, as I have said, a blind, irresponsible rebellion that I have no stomach for.

And where is your blindness? Condemning all things around you – except your close friends who agree with you! Compassion isn't only for very special, extra pals you like.

As for the Machine, the Machine=power. The machine is innocent: it's how people use it. The machine is magnificent means but the ends – there's the rub!

Louis

1956

In January 1956, Allen and Gary Snyder (a new poet friend who had also read at the Six Gallery) traveled to the Pacific Northwest to give a series of university readings. Allen needed a break from the San Francisco poetry scene, and the trip was the perfect respite. He had recently sent a copy of the first part of "Howl" to his father, and Louis's response was awaiting him when he returned to San Francisco.

Louis Ginsberg to Allen Ginsberg

February 29, 1956

Dear Allen,

I was happy to get your letter. It is good to learn that you have escaped any trouble or sickness in the wilds of the Northwest.

I was gratified about your new ms. It's a wild, rhapsodic, explosive outpouring with good figures of speech flashing by in its volcanic rushing. It's a hot geyser of emotion suddenly released in wild abandon from subterranean depths of your being. I'd like to see it in its entirety; and, moving back a bit, I like to discern its music outlines. I still insist, however, there is no need for dirty, ugly words, as they will entangle you, unnecessarily, in trouble. Try to cut them out.

It was interesting what you wrote about Irene. Guess she's been through the mill – as who hasn't? She, too, wrote to Abe and Anna that you have changed for the better with more firmness and developed wiseness – or words to that effect.

Glad to hear of your success at Reed College. The rafters must have shaken. Any sirens try to loop a curl of their hair about you?

All is quiet here. The dust has settled on our remodeling of our house here. We have a tenant, a business couple, with a daughter, just married, who goes to Montclair State TC.

Last Sunday we visited Eugene and Connie in N.Y. They drove us to their new house, not yet furnished, far out in Long Island. Theirs is a beautiful house of seven rooms, with a living room of cathedral ceilings. The house is in a new development which are springing up all about (as I remarked in the car, there's been plenty of kissing going on everywhere). The only fly in the ointment is that it takes about 1 1/4 hours to drive to the house from N.Y.C. On inclement days, Eugene can take a Long Island train. Eugene speaks of building a country practice in law there, while retaining his N.Y. office. Connie is due to have her baby during the middle of May. The house, Eugene reports, will be ready in April, but, as such things go, I doubt it. Maybe it will be ready at the end of May or June.

Everybody in Newark asks about you, especially Grandma. It would please her, if you wrote to her when you are in the mood.

Write me more often now. If you need any money, ask for it.

Wish I could see you. I miss you.

> Love from Edith and
> Your father,
> Louis

Allen Ginsberg to Louis Ginsberg

> *{Berkeley, California}*
> *n.d. {ca. late March 1956}*

Dear Louis:

Not written for long since I've been running around and busy. I'm working full time at Greyhound in the city,[1] but haven't made decent living arrangements, so I only get back to Berkeley a few times a week where all papers and letters are on desk in big mess. I stay over in city on various couches on workdays, since I've been back I haven't had time to really sit down in leisure and figure out what to do about living arrangements, I almost moved back into SF tho I hate to give up this cottage,[2] and was in fact supposed to this weekend but too many things came up and I can't find time. I am really all up in the air.

---

1. See "In the Baggage Room at Greyhound," AG, *CP,* p. 153.
2. Allen had recently moved to Berkeley. See his poem, "A Strange New Cottage in Berkeley," AG, *CP,* p. 135.

Mainly I'm waiting for a ship or some equivalent moneymaking project since I do want to leave here and take off for Europe sometime this year. Meanwhile the Greyhound job brings in 50 a week, Seattle debts are being cleared off this month. I'm also surprisingly enough teaching one class a week at S.F. State College – State is the school that's been promoting poetry workshops, readings, etc. and I am now the local poet-hero so was invited to occupy the chair of guest gorilla at their writing class. I work with another regular teacher who handles all the details, registration, mimeographing of poems to be handed out and discussed etc, and I act as pro in conducting discussions. The class is about 20, half old ladies and half hip young kids who have been attracted by all the recent activity. My teaching technique could shock you undoubtedly and certainly get me kicked out of anywhere else or not be countenanced, I bring in bums from North Beach and talk about Marijuana and Whitman, precipitate great emotional outbreaks and howls of protest over irrational spontaneous behavior – but it does actually succeed in communicating some of the electricity & fire of poetry and cuts through the miasmic quibbling about form vs. content etc. and does this phrase "work" and is that line "successful" and are all those "p & f" sounds too intense, etc. The woman who runs this program is a Prof. Ruth Witt-Diamant who has dug my work – there appears to be, according to Rexroth, a semimajor renaissance around the West Coast due to Jack and my presence – and Rexroth's wife said he'd been waiting all his life hoping for a situation like this to develop. The thing I do in class is get them personally involved in what they're writing and lambaste anything which sounds at all like they're writing "literature" and try to get them to actually express secret life in whatever form it comes out. I practically take off my clothes in class myself to do it. The students all dig it and understand and the class is now grown weekly to where it's too big to handle, starting with 8 and ending with 25.

W. C. Williams read "Howl" and liked it and wrote an introduction for the book; and meanwhile there is the possibility of expanding and making a whole book of poems. We put on another reading in a theatre here in Berkeley, I read some other poems, "Whitman,"[1] "The Sunflower,"[2] and a new poem called "America"[3] – a sort of surrealist anarchist tract – all of which came off very well, so the publisher is now interested in a bookful of representative work not just the one poem. The reading was pretty great, we

1. See "A Supermarket in California," AG, *CP*, p. 136.
2. See "Sunflower Sutra," AG, *CP*, p. 138.
3. See "America," AG, *CP*, p. 146.

had traveling photographers, who appeared on the scene from Vancouver to photograph it, a couple of amateur electronics experts who appeared with tape machines to record, request from State college for a complete recording for the night, requests for copies of the recordings, even finally organizations of bop musicians who want to write music and give big west coast traveling tours of "Howl" as a sort of Jazz Mass, recorded for a west coast company called Fantasy Records that issues a lot of national bop, etc. No kidding. You have no idea what a storm of lunatic-fringe activity I have stirred up. On top of that the local poets, good and bad, have caught up and there are now three groups of people putting on readings every other week, there's one every weekend, all sorts of people – this week Eberhart (Richard)[1] arrived in town for readings at State, there is a party for him tonite, I was invited to give a private reading, refused (sheer temperament), and so the recordings will be played. Tomorrow night Rexroth invited me over to meet a group of Jazz musicians and discuss the possibility of making some form of jazz-poetry combo. There is also another group of musicians, the leader of which used to arrange for Stan Kenton who wants to record with me. Finally I was asked to write an article which I haven't gotten around to do for *Black Mountain Review*, & also contribute to 2 literary magazines starting here. Bob LaVigne, a painter whose work I've been buying and digging, has been putting up wild line drawings to plaster the walls of the readings and painting fantastic 7 foot posters à la Lautrec. Really a charming scene. My big problem now is not having enough time to do all I could, working at Greyhound and not having moved out of Berkeley, so I get little time for actual writing anymore – it will be a relief to get out from under and away on a ship or up to Alaska possibly on a fishing industry job.

Rexroth's house – Friday evenings, open house, 2 weeks ago Malcolm Cowley,[2] I got drunk and made a big inflammatory speech denouncing him for publishing Donald Hall as a commercial shot and neglecting & delaying Kerouac, a funny scene, no blood spilled; last weekend Eberhart there, a long non drunken recollection of a party we'd met at in NY 5 years ago, he remembered the conversation in detail, I'd just got out of hospital and was hungup on the religious experience in the Groundhog poem.

1. Poet Richard Eberhart's *New York Times* article on his visit to San Francisco ("West Coast Rhythms") was one of the most important early articles on the San Francisco Poetry Renaissance and Ginsberg's "Howl."

2. Cowley, an editor at Viking Press, had been working with Jack Kerouac on the editing of *On the Road*.

English publishers want handle *Howl,* that is English Printers (Villiers) and so there is now difficulty in getting it through unexpurgated. I revised it and it is now worse than it ever was, too. We're now investigating Mexico, if necessary will spend extra cost and have it done here tho. Civil Liberties Union here was consulted and said they'd defend it if it gets into trouble, which I almost hope it does. I am almost ready to tackle the U.S. Govt out of sheer self delight. There is really a great stupid conspiracy of unconscious negative inertia to keep people from "expressing" themselves. I was reading Henry Miller's banned book *Tropic of Cancer,* which actually is a great classic – I never heard of it at Columbia with anything but deprecatory dismissal comments – he and Genet are such frank hip writers that the open expression of their perceptions and real beliefs are a threat to society. The wonder is that literature does have such power.

How is Gene's new house? I think I'll begin shipping stuff home – where is there room? – for a box & trunk full of excess clothes & pictures & papers.

Allen

Louis Ginsberg to Allen Ginsberg

March 31, 1956

Dear Allen,

Last night I sent you a note wondering why I hadn't heard from you.

This morning I received your letter breathing much activity.

I was very much interested in your teaching project. It certainly sounds unorthodox, but you do build fires under people. [. . .] You certainly have helped stir things up there. Why not keep it up to see where it ends? Maybe you could work yourself into a decently paying college position so you could write at leisure and let down your hair in the wide margins of vacations?

Glad W.C.W. wrote an introduction. It would be wonderful if you could get out a whole book of your poems. It would do much toward solidifying your reputation. Maybe you are a modern, incipient Whitman? Could be.

When and where could I get the records of your reading? "Howl" as a jazz mass with photographers, etc sounds flamboyant and attractive. Could you get that recording from that Fantasy Co.?

I've read R. Eberhart. His "Groundhog" is the best. He has other good things, but lately I note his poems are too aridly intellectual, not emotional and imagistic as they used to be.

Sorry I can't agree with you about letting yourself go all out, no bars, etc. with expression. Too many writers will not be able to distinguish between filth and realism. To act out inner fantasy is a danger touched with psychopathology and lunacy. There must be a bar sometime. I go for rivers, even strong ones, having banks.

Try not to get drunk; one gets disabled and sometimes injured.

You can send any packages or trunk to me here at our Paterson address. I'll hold it for you.

Eugene's house won't be ready till end of April or so.

Write soon again.

Lots of luck.

Keep up your fine work!

Love
Louis

Allen Ginsberg to Louis Ginsberg

1624 Milvia
Berkeley, California
April 26, 1956

Dear Louis:

Nothing really new since last wrote. Still working at Greyhound, now making $280 a month (small raise) and will stay there perhaps another month or more. Shipping still uncertain.

Have laid off teaching for this week and am revising final mss. for the booklet but not getting very far, tho I set a deadline for this weekend for City Lights & said I'd bring it all in. I don't seem to be able to do any imaginative work till I've slept and read and goofed for a week or more in complete timeless bored meditation. I have a longish absurd poem on America to finish:

Are you going to let your emotional life be run by Time magazine?
I'm obsessed by Time magazine.

I read it every week.

Its cover stares at me every time I pass the N.W. corner of
   Sutter and Montgomery streets.

I read it in the basement of the Berkeley public library.

They're always telling me about responsibility. Businessmen are
   serious. Movie producers are serious. Everybody's serious but me.

It occurs to me that I am America.

I'm talking to myself again.

etc. for 7 pages.

I cover everything from international relations to the dope problem.

Robert Creeley who I mentioned is in town, editor of the *Black Mountain Review*, collecting mss. from me, Jack, Gary Snyder (the Buddhist I went north with), Phil Whalen (friend of Gary's who shares cottage with me now), Burroughs, etc. And also Grover Jacoby of *Variegation* was around again, creeping & peering like an old lady, murmuring about obscurity & his mother wouldn't like THAT or this in his magazine (she supports it & reads it), and took 2 small inoffensive poems about trees, $13.00 worth. City Lights also proposed to me to bring out a series of records of spoken poetry, starting with my book, and we may do something about that if I'm around.

I keep having night dreams about Europe, seeing dockside foggy London, tears and Nostalgia, etc. I would like when I get over there to go to Russia. Apparently it's quite feasible, British consul issues passports and US no longer officially objects. It would be a ball to wander around the actual Moscow and write poetry on Red Sq. and do verbal sketching of the walls of the Kremlin. Do you have any relatives addresses there?

The recent Russian news by the way (last few months of destalinization) is too much – almost miraculous.

What do you think it all means? Rexroth opines it's a new sinister party line to whitewash themselves & start all over worse, but it seems to me they've burnt their bridges behind them in a way – who will the Russians believe in henceforth – they'll have to think for themselves. It must leave a lot of Communists here feeling really sold out.

The Wobbly-anarchist tradition here is still a force among painters and writers, in SF I mean.

Summer's coming on pretty soon, what will you do? I still anticipate shipping out, then a trip cross-country East, stay home about a month and do some arranging of papers and then take off for Europe. I may be there in the Fall then, depending on shipping. If shipping looks bad I'll just take a few hundred dollars from Greyhound work and head East and figure how to go from there. I want in any case to arrange a few years absolutely free to write in Europe and travel. I may be in line for a Guggenheim or something next year, but those are in the hands of successful chic madmen who aren't trustworthy. Speaking of such I met Karl Shapiro, Eberhart took me to see him at Davis College 50 miles north of here where he teaches. Blank eyed, dull, acts like an advt. executive and about as sympathetic, greying groomed temples, artsy craftsy ambitious wife and spoiled avaricious children (I'm exaggerating I suppose) – seeing him in the flesh put the final nail in the coffin. Official literature, the foundations, the colleges, is run by people like him who have no interest in life except what they can get out of it through acceptable channels and all their work is one big psychic asslicking operation. I mean dominated by a desire for respectability & acceptance rather than the bitter gaiety of their own souls. Or whatever gaiety it is. What he Shapiro has wound up with is a lousy job in a jerkwater college after all and the strain of this shows through a brisk international cigarette holding mannerisms. I have not however described the impression of him after these years of knowing of him like a god of some sort, a Jewish boy made good. Not at all just another scared respectable stinker. I mean there was no light in his spirit at all, just money. "India was nasty," he said, and his wife agreed. "Or I didn't like it there at all." Too much suffering, "what can you do but ignore it?" Consequently the themes of his poems is moderation and the virtues of middle class existence, which is for him a refuge form experience: And HE teaches a creative writing course and is admired by a flock of dull eyed professors as the poet (successful) type, and allowed his small eccentricities, like a few jibes about the advertising industry. I longed for souls to begin a REVOLUTION when I saw him. Yop.

Write – love,
Allen

Louis Ginsberg to Allen Ginsberg

April 28, 1956

Dear Allen,

Glad, indeed, to get your letter and to know you are well. I was beginning to get worried not hearing from you so long.

Let me know when you hand in your poem to City Lights. Am eager to see it printed.

Send me the address of *Variegation*: maybe I might have something in my files to submit.

About Russia: I think Rexroth is near the mark. The Reds confess now like Stalin was a butcher (their words) and that untold thousands were framed, murdered, etc. I think Russia knows that its past sins will never be forgotten so they are making Stalin a scapegoat to whitewash themselves. By force alone, they'll never win so they will try ruthless amiability. They still have a party line which allows no deviation so that they are still totalitarian. (In the long run, after a century or two, there may be erosion of their fixedness; so that, in the end, a reconciliation of the West and the East will be evolved for the peace from the world.) Meanwhile, they fish in troubled waters. Even the *Daily Worker* confessed that they are grieved to have been so taken in by evils that they never believed existed in Russia. Yes, who will believe the Commies now?

Was interested in your delineation of Shapiro. His creativeness in poetry seems to have dried up, and he is capitalizing on his previous increments. (I personally believe teaching in a college and writing poetry is ideal, but the duet must resist corroding influences.)

I'll be at home summer, relaxing in the garden. When you come East, ship your things here. Stay here all you want. I'll fix up a desk for you and stake you, if you need it, for a long spell of writing.

You should like our home now. We get an income, which, in five years, will pay off the expenses of converting. Then we'll live rent-free in comfort. It will come just in time. I'll retire in five years with a good pension (we are integrated now in Social Security).

Write more often, please.

Try to come home soon.

Love
Louis

More anon.

For his entire adult life, Allen would suffer deep feelings of guilt over his relationship with his mother. He agonized over the thought of Naomi's living in a sanitarium, and he was tormented by the fact that he had signed the legal papers authorizing her prefrontal lobotomy. (Doctors had told him the procedure was necessary because Naomi was given to violent mood swings and apt to harm herself, and since Louis could not legally sign the papers – he and Naomi were divorced – and Eugene was reluctant to authorize the procedure, Allen, with great misgivings, signed the documents. A reading of such poems as "Kaddish" and "Black Shroud" indicate the depth of Allen's emotional turmoil.) After meeting Peter Orlovsky, Allen devised a new plan, which he hoped would allow his mother at least a modicum of freedom. As the following letters indicate, fate had other designs.

Allen Ginsberg to Eugene Brooks

{*Berkeley, California*}
May 16, 1956

Dear Gene:

[. . .]

My idea on Naomi is this: (tho of course I'm off the scene & don't know what the score is) if she appears to be well enough to get along one way or other on the outside she ought to be put out to pasture with a family say in Long Island. I even have a specific one in mind, a friend whose mother is poor & slightly addled herself – in any case one could be found where she could be boarded for around $100 per month. If it is practicable I would contribute. The main problem with Naomi is that nobody wants or can help her, really. Perhaps we can find a place to settle her. I had not thought of it before reading her letters but they seemed mild enough. It's not necessary that she be sane to live outside, just peace[ful], & the new pacifying drugs seem to do that from what I read in the papers. Write me what you think of this. The family I had in mind was Mrs. Katherine Orlovsky [. . .] I know her son Peter very well, I gather she's living a sort of Russian poverty life on Welfare of about $95.00 a month herself. I'll look up the situation when I get back unless you think there is any use in sooner action, in which case let me know and I'll find out more specifically what I can here from Peter O. [. . .]

My book is being printed in England. There was a long delay while I held on to the mss for revisions, & also I added 3 other poems. It will be quite a volume. I sent Louis a complete mss. this week. I don't know how he'll react to the wilder parts but I am very pleased with the whole deal. I have a feeling he'll be too scandalized to want the family to see it but it really is quite a high spirited & funny & serious collection of statements. I sort of feel unchallengeable on the solidity of the contents & expressions. W. C. Williams has written another introduction and 1000 copies will be made. I'll even make a little money on it says my publisher who's so pleased he decided to give me royalties in addition to publishing it.

[. . .]

Allen

Louis Ginsberg to Allen Ginsberg

May 20, 1956

Dear Allen,

How are you?

I'm awaiting the letter you wrote you sent here.

Last night we went into N.Y. and saw Connie, Eugene, and the new baby boy. He is a 9 lb. chubby, round-faced youngster. His name is Alan Eugene Brooks. (I guess we'll have to refer to you as big Allen, and the little boy as little Alan.) So life goes on.

Shadows there are, too. Grandma fell last week on the kitchen stairs and broke her hip. She was operated on yesterday in the Irvington General Hospital. She is doing as well as can be expected for an 88 year old lady. The doctors say she will be out in about three weeks. (Drop her a postal: c/o Irvington General Hospital, Irvington, N.J.)

How are you feeling?

Do you need anything?

Love from
Your father,

Louis

Louis Ginsberg to Allen Ginsberg

May 27, 1956

Dear Allen,

I saw your mimeographed book of poems[1] and wish it luck in the world! I'm too near it to appraise it fully. My expression, at first blush, is that it is a weird, volcanic, troubled, extravagant, turbulent, boisterous, unbridled outpouring, intermingling genius and flashes of picturesque insight with slag and debris of scoraic matter. It has violence; it has life; it has *vitality*. In my opinion, it is a one-sided, neurotic view of life; it has not enough glad, Whitmanian affirmations. (The fact that you write in such an energetic glow of poetry is one affirmation.) The poem should attract attention and perhaps be a sensation; one will hear defenders and detractors. But it should give you a name.

The poem I liked next was the fine and vivid one called "Sunflower Sutra." You should do more of this style.

I'm keeping the poems by my side in order to get more into them.

Concerning my poem about the grains of sand and necessity, I feel that, no matter how you thrash about, you must, more or less, as a inescapable condition of our predicament of living on the earth, give in in some way to necessity. That last word is an ambiguous one, and there are many ways of yielding. When one makes a truce with necessity according to the most harmonious nature of his being, then there is a minimum of eternal friction. However, I realize no words of mine will fall on your heart as will those of your cronies; so that I must perforce, despite all my love for you, let time tutor you.

Meanwhile I am glad that you are finding happiness and perhaps some purgative cleansing in your writing poetry. I fervent[ly] hope fame and success will come your way.

We saw Connie, Eugene, and little Alan yesterday. They are all well. Till their home will be ready, they are living now at Hotel Regent, 104 St. and Broadway Ave. NYC.

---

1. *Howl and Other Poems*. Allen printed up mimeographed copies of the booklet, which he distributed among friends and family prior to the official City Lights publication.

4 16 E. 34 St.
Paterson 1, N.J.
May 27, 56

Dear Allen,

I read your mimeographed book of poems and wish it luck in the mail! I'm too near it to appraise it fully. My impression, at first blush, is that it is a wild, volcanic, troubled, extravagant, turbulent, boisterous, unbridled outpouring, intermingling gems and flashes of picturesque insight with slag and debris of scoraic matter. It has violence; it has life; it has vitality. In my opinion, it is a one-sided, neurotic view of life; it has not enough glad, Whitmanian afferantions. (The fact that you write in such an energetic glow of poetry is one afferantion). The poem should attract attention and perhaps be a sensation; you will hear defenders and detractors. But it should give you a name.

The poem I liked best was the first and second one called "Sunflower Sta Sutra". You should do more of this type.

I'm keeping the poems by my side in order to get more into them.

Concerning my poem about the grains of sand and necessity, I feel that, no matter how you thrash about,.. you must, more or less, as a an inescapable condition of our predicament of living on the earth, give in in some way to necessity. That last word is an ambiguous one, and there are many ways of yielding. When one makes a truce with necessity according to the most harmonious nature of his being, then there is a minimum of internal friction. However, I realize no words of mine will fall ~~better~~ on your heart as will those of your chories; so that I must perforce, despite all my love for you, let Time tutor you.

Meanwhile I am glad that you are finding happiness and perhaps some purgative cleansing in your writing poetry. I fervent hope fame and success will come your way.

We saw Connie, Eugene, and little Alan yesterday. There are all well. Tell ~~them~~ their home will be ready. They are living now at Hotel Regent, 104 St. and ~~Amsterdam~~ Broadway Ave. R.76.

Grandma is still in the hospital. Have you written her? (Irvington General Hospital, Irvington, ?)

More anon.

Love

Your father,
Louis

P.S. Send me a copy of third of the book published in England, with W. R. W.'s introduction

Grandma is still in the hospital. Have you written her? (Irvington General Hospital, Irvington, N.J.)

More anon.

Your father,
Louis

P.S. Send me a copy or two of the book, published in England, with W.C.W's introduction.

Louis Ginsberg to Allen Ginsberg

May 28, 1956

Dear Allen,

Received your letter re draft card.

I'll be downtown tomorrow to interview the draft board to get you another card. Will write you tomorrow again.

Eugene's present address is: *c/o Hotel Regent, 104th St. cor B'way N.Y.C.* He'll be there about a month after which time he expects to move into his new home in Long Island.

Your ms. looks fine – with new poems and an introduction by W.C.W. it should attract attention and make a name for you. I fervently pray for that!!! (It's not my type of poetry; but there are many mansions in poetry so that, with its exuberant, lusty, gusty vitality, it should draw a crowd!) Best wishes!

Love,
Louis

Allen sent his mother a copy of Howl and Other Poems, *and Naomi's response was probably the last letter she would write. She died on June 9, 1956, and the following letter was postmarked the day of her funeral. Her heartbreaking letter was one of the most powerful letters Allen would ever receive, and it was largely the inspiration for his determination to write a proper eulogy – or Kaddish – for his mother.*

Naomi Ginsberg to Allen Ginsberg

n.d. {postmarked June 11, 1956}

I hope this reaches you.

I sent one before which, maybe, they didn't send out!

Congratulations on your birthday!

Received your poetry. I like to send it to Louis for criticism.

Now what does *he* think of it!

It seemed to me your wording was a little too hard. Do tell me what father thinks of it.

You know you have to have a job to get married. I wish you did have a good job. What did you specialize in when you went to college.

This going to North Pole,[1] who supplies the wearing material? They say when you visit the Eskimos you need a double coat of fur. Are you fit for that flying job? Don't take chances with your life!

I wish you get married. Do you like farming?[2] Its as good a job as any.

I hope you behave well. Don't go in for too much drink and other things that are not good for you.

Eugene and his wife visited me. They expected a child then. I suppose they have it by this time.

I do hope you get a good job so you can get a girl to get married. Eugene's wife is beautiful.

As for myself, I still have the wire on my head. The doctors know about it. They are still cutting the flesh & bone. They are giving me teeth-ache.

I do wish you were back East, so I could see you.

I met Max's daughter, she is charming & married.

I am glad you are having your poetry published.

I wish I were out of here and home at the time you were young; then I would be young. I'm in the prime of life now –

Did you read about the two men who died at 139 & 149 yrs. of age? I wonder how they lived.

I'm looking for a good time.

---

1. Allen had recently enlisted to work on a ship delivering supplies to the distant early warning radar system workers in the Arctic Circle. He left in early July.
2. Off and on, Allen had spoken about buying or working on a farm – a goal he would reach nearly a decade later.

I hope you are not taking any drugs as suggested by your poetry. That would hurt me. Don't go in for ridiculous things.

> With love & good news,
> (mother) Naomi

Eugene Brooks to Allen Ginsberg

> *{New York City}*
> *June 11, 1956*

Dear Allen:

Good to hear from you the other day. I don't [know] where this letter will catch you, but these are the details of the burial.

The day was nice and sunny. We started out from the Hotel Regent at noon. We were a pitiable corporal's guard for Naomi – seven (7) of us. Lou, Abe & Anna surprisingly enough, Max Frohman, Connie and me, and Fanny Freiman, Naomi's high school chum. I guess it was the smallest funeral on record.

Naomi was lying in a funeral parlor in Hempstead, Long Island. We saw the body briefly – she was quite recognizable – her face was perhaps a little sad, although in repose.

After the box was closed, a functionary said a few words. He had to ask her name in the middle of the brief services and even then didn't have it straight.

We followed the box to a cemetery in Farmingdale, Long Island called Beth Moses. I took some brief footage on movies, but not much. The cemetery has a wide expanse; the stones there are low; there are some pine shrubs; it has a rather pleasant look and not crowded, and there is a lot of blue sky.

After a brief prayer by the functionary, who could not give "Kaddish" because a quorum of ten males was not present (a "minion") and engaged in a short discussion with the funeral director, the casket was lowered, and as Lou said, Naomi (mother) was "let down" for the last time.

So ended a somewhat pathetic life.

On the way back, Fanny reminisced a little of Naomi's school days; her poverty and the fact that she always borrowed school notes from Fanny.

We visited Elanor's grave. Elanor is buried about one hundred yards distant.

Naomi's wedding ring was given to me, and I gave it to Connie. I transferred the thousand dollars to your bank account.

Well, today the world is inexorably evil; I suppose tomorrow it will be better. Let me know when you plan to be in New York.

Love from Connie and little Alan, who is thriving nicely.

Eugene

Louis Ginsberg to Allen Ginsberg

June 20, 1956

Dear Allen,

Your letter of June 13 on hand.

It is difficult to write you and tell in a few words a life-full of love for Naomi. Though Fate had severed her physically from me for the last few years, I confess she was in my heart always. There was no day during which I was in a crowd or happy that thoughts of Naomi, torn within herself and cooped up in a desolate room, did not invade my mind. As I saw her coffin lowered into the hospitable earth, I thought that now she would at last have peace and rest, something I had struggled all my life in vain to give her.

Seven of us met at Eugene's hotel room – Fanny Frieman, Max Frohman, Connie, Eugene, Abe, Anna, and I. We were driven out to Long Island to Hempstead where the funeral services were held briefly, a sexton murmuring prayers in Hebrew. When the cortege went to a cemetery in Farmingdale – a plot a stone's throw from where Ed Frohman lies. As Naomi's casket was lowered, the sexton prayed again. The pathos and tragedy of her well-meaning life, the constant struggles within her, the flashes of our happy early moments together – all blinded me. [. . .]

Well, Naomi is now at peace at last. Maybe I, too, will sleep better for knowing she is at last at peace.

Eugene took pictures of the funeral; so you will sometimes see them.

Yes, recently I had written to Naomi and she to me. I was planning, as I told Eugene, to visit her this summer to see whether we might not act on your suggestion. But Fate had other plans and eased her sufferings.

I'm glad she wrote that letter to you.

There is much I long to write, but the tears blur me. Some other time.

When you get back East plan to stay here a spell. We are much nearer and dearer, as you say. You and Eugene are part of her and me, and she will always be a part of me. Be at peace, Allen, because she is at last at peace.

I'm glad you will come into some money, which, together with the money you'll send here, should make a future bulwark for you to lean on when you do writing later.

I'm awaiting your book and hope it is a success. Don't forget, there are many mansions in the house of poetry. If Trilling doesn't like it, W. C. Williams & others will.

Congratulations on your 30th birthday. I did not know whether you had taken ship already: will save your present.

Peace to you, Allen. Keep writing poetry. Come visit me soon.

Love

Your father,
Louis

Louis Ginsberg to Allen Ginsberg

August 4, 1956

Dear Allen,

Glad to receive your letter dated July 29, as I was getting a bit worried. Seems you have a margin of leisure to do plenty of reading. It must feel curious to have daylight at midnight there.

I'll explore to find a brief synagogue prayer book.[1] The Jewish holidays are coming very early in Sept so, no doubt, I'll come upon it soon. Those chants therein have a rhythm and sonorousness of immemorial years marching with reverberations through the corridors of History . . . and laden with the tears of things.

That was a pretty piece of translation, erotic but beautiful.

1. Allen had asked Louis to send him a copy of a prayer book with the "Kaddish" included. Disappointed that the Kaddish had not been read at his mother's funeral, Allen was determined to write his own version – one that combined poetry with the rhythms of the Hebrew prayer.

Interruption: I just called up a friend who will procure the Kaddish in Hebrew and English so I shall dispatch it to you shortly.

Eugene and the baby and Connie are fine. No, the red tape of the VA is still tying up their house. The knot may be broken any time. Meanwhile, they come here every two weeks or so, and we have good times with the baby which seems to like our garden and sleeps under the cherry tree. Once they came in Saturday and stayed over and enjoyed it.

My mother is still in a nursing home, getting over a broken hip and also a broken ankle. All the five families are sharing the expenses.

Edith is still working, as there is still something to pay off on our reconversion of the house to a two family house. I think that about the Spring she will stop working.

Harold is soon finishing a summer college stint in Columbia. He has a room in N.Y. near Eugene, and he plans to take a four-year course in Columbia on his G.I. bill for a B.A. with specialization in journalism. He avers he has the urge to write.

Sheila teaches in Newark. Her husband is struggling to build up his electrical business.

Hannah, Leo and the children are OK, as are Anna and Abe, although Abe continues his inescapable pattern of falling off the water wagon every six months or so and then slowly climbing up again.

As for me, I am enjoying the Summer's leisure in reading, mostly poetry and critical articles. I am writing slowly and unabated. Had a piece called "Hotel Lobby" accepted by the *U. of Kansas Review*. Also am working on a few lyrics re Naomi's funeral.

After three years, our car has a few ailments, such as, new brake linings, carburetor, fuel pump, tires, etc. but these have been remedied and she's now running O.K. Edith drives it well and also drives Harold's car, which he leaves for her during the week.

Keep well and write more often.

Love.
Louis

Louis Ginsberg to Allen Ginsberg

August 13, 1956

Dear Allen,

I was glad to get your letter with your brochure, called "Siesta in Xbalba."[1] It's very interesting with cinematic flashbacks of scenes and people. There is entangled in your lines a nostalgia for the past and for ruins that make a pulpit for mortality. Congratulations! I'll reread it again for more glimpses of your wanderings. Keep up your good work!

Yes, Eugene's poem, as I told him, was one of his best. His lines caught commingled pathos and heartbreak.

I myself am working on half a dozen lyrics about Naomi's funeral, as it affected me. One of these poems, a brief 8 line lyric, called "Burial,"[2] has a condensation and a hunt of the Emily Dickinson touch. This poem has been accepted by *The N.Y. Times*. It should appear in a week or so; and I'll send you a copy, as soon as it is published.

Clara is getting married at the end of September. I'll advise you of her new address, when she moves. Grandma is still in a wheelchair at a nursing home in Caldwell where she is recovering from a broken hip and a broken ankle.

Eugene and Connie and the baby boy are fine. They visit us here often and we go into N.Y. to see them frequently.

Concerning our relatives in Russia, so far as I can glean, they had been slowly exterminated by Stalin's Russia. Any relatives that are living had sought refuge in Israel. I believe there are a couple of nieces and nephews still living. When you are in Newark, Hannah can give any details she has.

When will I see you? It's been a long time! I miss you. I hope you'll stay with me here [in] Paterson for a spell before you cast off for your European travels.

Love from
Your father,
Louis

---

1. Allen privately published a mimeographed booklet of his long poem while he was serving in the Arctic Circle.
2. See "Burial," LG, *CP*, p. 247.

Louis Ginsberg to Allen Ginsberg

September 13, 1956

Dear Allen,

I sent you a letter last week to your Milvia St. address, but the letter came back.

Yes, I saw the account about your book in the *N.Y. Times Book Review*.[1] I was happy to see it. Edith has a copy in her purse, and she shows it to all and sundry; I have passed it around to the Newark folks. I rejoice that your book is coming out. I predict it will make a name for you; you may wake up some morning and find yourself famous. I do hope so.

I'll save any other notices I see of it. I have a couple special envelopes labeled "Re Allen Ginsberg" and am saving all your poems. Keep up the good work – and congratulations!

Send me a couple of your books, or let me know where I can purchase some. I presume Eugene will also procure some copies.

By the way, are you living or getting your mail at the Milvia St. address?

It's good to know you are saving money, as it will stand you in good stead when you relax for an interlude of further writing.

All is quiet here. School has begun and I am in harness again, teaching Tues–Friday nights at Rutgers-Newark.

Edith is fine and keeps busy working.

Grandma is still at the nursing home, slowly recovering. Hannah was pleased with the receipt of a fine letter from you. She dispatched an answer to you. Clara got married last Sunday. She moves to Freeport, L.I. on Oct. 1.

When will I see you? When are you coming to Paterson? I keep missing you.

I keep writing on and off. *The U. of Kansas City Review* took two of them. *The N.Y. Her. Trib* also took two poems. I wrote a couple of poems about Naomi's funeral and am sending them out.

Write again soon. I am eager to hear more good news about your book. Congratulations again!

Love
Your Father,
Louis

1. Richard Eberhart, "West Coast Rhythms," *New York Times Book Review*, September 2, 1956.

Louis Ginsberg to Allen Ginsberg

October 13, 1956

Dear Allen,

I was glad to get your letter, brimming with your literary activities. How does it feel to be a celebrity? I was happy for you.

I bought a number of copies of your book and sold or gave them away to interested people. Aunt Hannah and Eugene, of course, ordered copies. Send me any reviews you get. I'll paste them in a scrapbook I have for you. You should get publicity for your book so that it will all stand you in good stead for your future writing.

I am happy that your poetry is finding such response. The long first poem is a powerful piece with volcanic eruptions intermingled with good and bad qualities, but all marked by exuberance vitality and force, though, sometimes, unbridled. Of the smaller pieces, I liked "In the Baggage Room at Greyhound" with its imaginative and concrete details, "Song" with its tender yearning.

Incidentally, did you dispatch a copy of your book to Mr. Max Herzberg, of *The Newark Sunday News,* or shall I do so? He will probably disapprove of your pocketbook, but the publicity will not be amiss.

Am looking forward to seeing *Ark*: send it on.

When you see the Levys, give them my regards. Tell them to visit me, when and if they journey East.

[. . .]

Eugene finally moved into his new home, and the new furniture is being rolled in. I bought them a new crib for the baby. In a week or two, we'll ride in. It takes about 2 1/4 hours for the journey from Paterson.

Allen, if you wish, you can dispatch your goods to Paterson. I have plenty of storage space here in our cellar.

Otherwise, all is quiet. I'm busy teaching, as usual. I have four more years to go before I retire. How time passes! (Am 61, and I kid that I'm going to have my sex life lowered; it's still in my head, I aver, with tongue in cheek.)

Grover Jacoby took a poem of mine for his *Recurrence;* as did *The U. of Kansas City Review.* Am having another poem "Epitaph" (on Naomi's funeral) in *The N.Y. Times* any day now.

I'm looking forward to your visit here Thanksgiving. We can have a merry get-together here in Paterson and then another one at Eugene's home in Long Island.

Keep well and keep sending me mail. Tell when will your Milvia St. address be good?

Edith sends you her regards.

Love from
Your father,
Louis

After years of fantasizing and planning an extended trip to Europe, Allen finally was able to realize his dream. He and Peter Orlovsky departed by sea on March 8, 1957, and arrived in Tangier, Morocco, at the end of March. According to the plan, they would reunite with William Burroughs, who was presently living in Tangier, and Jack Kerouac, who was already there, visiting Bill and working with him to assemble the collection of routines that would become Naked Lunch. *Allen's plans were sketchy, at best: He wanted to visit his friend Alan Ansen (who had been W. H. Auden's secretary, and who was acting as an adviser on the editing of* Naked Lunch) *in Venice, and he hoped to hook up with Gregory Corso in Paris. Other than that, his only hope was to see as much of Europe as time and money would allow.*

Allen's immense curiosity made him a natural traveler, as the following letters indicate. Allen made a point of visiting all the well-known tourist sites, particularly museums and cemeteries, yet he also enjoyed wandering off on his own and taking in the local color. He would travel extensively over the next five years, and his letters from this period are easily the most descriptive, detailed letters he would ever write.

Allen Ginsberg to Louis Ginsberg

Tangier {Morocco}
June {1957}

Dear Louis –

Long time no hear from you. Things O.K. here. Work on Burroughs mss. about complete now, 200 pages. So I will leave here in a week – Seville, Cordova, Grenada, Madrid, Toledo, Barcelona. You can write me here, mail will be forwarded till the end of June. I'll be in Madrid I think around June 25. After leaving there around July 1, I'll go (thru Barcelona) crost the Pyrenees and thru Southern France to Italy, Venice, & stay in Alan Ansen's place there – he has large apartment. Plans after that are indefinite. Perhaps

Paris the next stop. In fact I think will go from Venice thru Switzerland to Paris – the middle or end of July.

You can reach me in Venice at this address – c/o Alan Ansen, American Express, Boca de Piazza, Venice, Italy. Can start sending me mail there around June 20 or so, Alan Ansen will be there & hold it for me.

Spending lots of time with Paul Bowles & an excellent English painter, Francis Bacon – he has a big picture of a gorilla in a tuxedo under a big deathly black umbrella – in the Museum of Modern Art.

Evergreen Review[1] should be out with my poetry in June, *now;* also, *Partisan did* have a review (bad, I hear) by John Hollander.[2] Can you send it? *Poetry* will have something this summer.[3] Please subscribe to John Wieners' magazine *Measure,* 22 So Russell St, Boston – it should be a very good avant garde magazine & he needs about 47 more subscriptions to make it – also I'd like to have a complete set of them at home, they'll be valuable perhaps – or if you can, request the Paterson Library to subscribe. A good cause. Wieners is going to try rounding up all the threads we've been gathering.

Ansen sends his regards. He leaves here in a few days, too. Peter & Bill also send theirs. Peter's mother send him a clipping from the *Times* of a poem of yours called "Trees." Very good 3rd verse especially.

Weather is fine, I'm reading Melville, *Israel Potter* & *Typee,* and Guide-books to Spain.

Gene back from his trip yet? Have you gone off to Cape Cod or anywhere yet also?

Love, Write
Allen

Allen Ginsberg to Louis Ginsberg

American Express
Venice, Italy
June 26, 1957

Dear Lou:

Received your 2 last letters, including the page from *Poetry* magazine. I guess the seizure works out fine as publicity; except that I am afraid of

---

1. *Evergreen Review* 1 (May–June 1957) reprinted "Howl."
2. John Hollander's review of *Howl and Other Poems* appeared in *Partisan Review* 24 (Spring 1957).
3. The publication of Allen's poetry in this magazine fell through.

what will happen in court – trial set for August 6 – maybe City Lights lose, be out dough, & screw up the whole publishing deal.[1] Jarrell[2] been no help according to Ferlinghetti, who's written him several times asking for official Lib Congress statement but no answer. The issue of *Partisan* is the Spring one;[3] had a big party here again last night, Philip Rahv, one of their editors, was here – lots of PR people around, I don't care much for them, Paul Goodman & Nicholas Calas. Tho Goodman writes good poetry I think. Bumped into him here by accident last week, he passing thru. Guggenheim[4] finally broke down & invited me over but the war still goes on since she excluded Orlovsky. Jack wrote & says he's moved again, to Mexico, his mother apparently didn't like Calif & wanted back to Fla. so Jack spent a lot of loot resettling her & retired to Mexico, says he'll be here next Spring, in Paris. His book is out; at least he got copies – from Viking. I received nice 2nd issue of *Evergreen* here already, with its pictures. Jack's piece in that is the same railroad prose I had around the house[5] – that nearly unreadable mss all black & folded. How does it look to you in print?

What New Directions check? I seem to remember a check – from them? – back in Tangiers. Is that what you refer to – or was it a check you sent here to Venice? By the way, Grove is issuing a record, Part I of "Howl" included, with Snyder, Whalen, Rexroth, Ferlinghetti etc.[6] By coincidence, the sound editing was done by Jerry Newman at Esoteric – who wrote me a few days ago – asking what about his money. That's the $17 bill I sent from Tangiers to be paid out of my account. I think there's still some money left with Gene to take care of that. Please ask Gene to do it this week, it's long overdue & he did me a favor, about 50$ work for $17, cost of the tapes. Send check to Jerry Newman, Stereo Sound Studios, 238 East 26th St., NYC. I guess hold on to the New Directions, I'll see it in Paris or when I remember. All that running around in NY paid off;[7] Grove sent me a nice get back. Very funny Mexican whorehouse scene by Jack in that too, I

---

1. *Howl and Other Poems* had been subjected to a seizure first by United States Customs officials and then, later, by the San Francisco police.
2. Randall Jarrell, poetry consultant to the Library of Congress.
3. John Hollander's negative review of *Howl and Other Poems*.
4. Peggy Guggenheim, socialite and art patron, had an on-again, off-again relationship with members of the Beat Generation.
5. "The Railroad Earth."
6. *San Francisco Poets* (Evergreen Records, LP no. EVR-1, New York).
7. Allen acted as an informal literary agent for many of his West Coast friends' work. In New York, he haunted editors and publishing houses, badgering them about the merits of his friends' prose and poetry. His efforts paid off: Many were published in such magazines as *New Directions* and *Evergreen Review*.

letter with the magazine and a check for $50, unexpectedly, "in payment for anything we owe you now or will owe you." They said they were selling (4000 copies) all over S.F. including City Lights store, so police apparently haven't got wise to that yet. Taking the $50 tomorrow and going down by train to visit Florence, for a few days, and then a week in Rome. Be back, then, in a week and a half, so may not write till then. Looking forward to this trip; almost couldn't make it but for the Grove Surprise. Be great to see all the Giotto & Fra Angelico in Florence and all the Coliseums & Vaticans at Rome, like a week of historical visions. Things are working out pretty great for me here in Europe – I didn't think I'd see so much of Italy & Spain. Will return to Venice for another month perhaps, and in September, or before, figure a way to get to Paris for an extended stay. It's the most expensive place in Europe, unfortunately. Corso says he has a free apartment there now. If so things will be easier, he invited us to stay with him. But I'm afraid the apartment won't exist when we get there, Gregory is quixotic. Burroughs now in London, he has some liver trouble & they have good free health plan there. We'll meet again in Paris. Read some of his mss. to Rahv last night who dug it as an Orwell type prose & said he'd publish some of the less obscene portions. It'll be quite a day for Bill when he gets into print, he needs it, psychologically, more than anyone, with all the horror of life he's gone thru, endured & survived. Venice still charming & had enough leisure here to get familiar with the alleys & some canals; Orlovsky jumped fully dressed into the Grand Canal the other day, a joke; and we've all been bathing at the Lido, the beach here. Best swimming I ever saw was at Nice. The main American meet place here is Harry's Bar celebrated in Hemingway's *Across the River {and into the Trees}* – if you want to get an idea of social life in Venice, look it up. Rain in Venice is beautiful – "a great huge rain 2 weeks ago ended the heat wave. Strange town in that as I can tell. Just a big pleasure palace on water. I don't care for Venetian painting as much as Florentine, I find, now that I'm familiarizing myself with the actual painters and schools – but there are some great things here – Giorgióne, who was just a name to me, but who is like Keats in poetry and temperament. Last week we took an hour's ride by bus to Padua, saw the famous Scrovegni chapel which is covered with a cycle by Giotto, scenes from life of Christ – best Giotto in Italy so I've heard. Getting very museum hungry, which is the reason for the Florence trip – the Uffizi Gallery there has Giotto, Boticelli, Da Vinci, Angelico – all the greatest.

I wander around St. Mark's Plaza here often surrounded by the mad buildings, feeling great & fortunate to have all the time here. I had gone on the Maid of the Mist years ago when hitchhiking to Niagara & remember how beautiful it was & blinding: tho I never got far into Canada. Edith been wanting to go to Thousand Isles for a long time. Did Gene go too? I'll write Grandma a note at Irvington General. It's amazing how tough she is, surviving all those breaks. What does she say? Regards to Connie. I sent Sam a postcard. How is grandpa's life with Alan around? Or that not begun yet? Regards from Ansen & Orlovsky. Glad you subscribed to *Measure,* they need it. I get less and less sympathetic to *Partisan* tho, they seem very slow on the uptake, the recent issues I've seen are dull, they have no good poetry, just academic Hollander or Kunitz. Re natural speech. It's undeniable that every so often the rhythms of poetry are refreshed by exposure to everyday speech, words & rhythms – as with Wordsworth & Eliot & Williams & Whitman. Normal speech has great rhythms – it's not a question of abandoning rhythm at all, it's a question of being conscious, as in WCW, of the beauty of the rhythms of regular talk; and of constructing perhaps from that regular talk, artificial rhythms which are at best more closely related to regular talk than the fixed rhythms of past poetry. But aside from that . . .[1]

Allen Ginsberg to Louis Ginsberg

c/o American Express, Venice, Italy
August 10, 1957

Dear Louis:

Just got back to Venice yesterday, received all your letters, one rather delayed, but safe, including the small check from New Directions, another with *SRL* clip & poems.

I've already seen #2 of *Evergreen,* you'll get it eventually. The *Partisan* issue as I said was the Spring issue. Ran into Louis Simpson (in the Sistine Chapel–Michelangelo's *Last Judgment*) (of all places) & spent part of evening with him there, he was friendly, diffident & apologetic, said he'd written a satirical poem on "Howl" which would be published in *Hudson Review.* If you ever do see that, send it on, tho it's not worth subscribing to the magazine for. Said he didn't know the book was having legal trouble & wouldn't have added his satirical 2¢ if he'd known. The trial should be over now – due Aug 8 – I hear from Whalen that some famous SF lawyer – maybe Bartley

1. The rest of this letter is missing.

Crum or someone like that – has taken over the defense, for free. I don't know who & am somewhat out of touch.

Has Gene & Connie's baby come yet? Let me know what happens.

How is Grandma?

Glad you are in touch with Moore[1] – she's a great poet, tho I suspect an eccentric person (voting for Eisenhower & never marrying) – what else did she say about your work? Her judgment is very reliable, in respect to the precisions she admires.

I read Sartre's article & was interested when I read it, also in what he said about Algiers – that he felt honest in objecting to Hungary since he'd been also objecting to French doing similar thing in Algiers. Haven't heard of Djilas book.

Enclose the clip of "Concert" – thought the 2 first lines of stanzas 2 & 3 the jazziest – the two couplets. The tigers practice "Gentlemen in Hotel Lobby" is also fine, sounds like some highclass phrasing from *Hudson Review*.

Your July 6 letter arrived here only last week.

Left here July 28 or so, train to Florence, I think I sent you postcard perhaps from there – stayed 3 days, saw Michelangelo's *David* and a lot of his sculpture, saw a whole churchful of paintings & frescos by Fra Angelico, and spent a day & half at the Uffizi Gallery – that, the Prado in Madrid, the Louvre in Paris, and the Hermitage in Moscow supposed to be the biggest & finest collections in the world. Botticelli's *Birth of Venus* & *Allegory of Spring*, great halls full of naked Greek statues, Venus de Medici, Rembrandt & Fillipo Lippi, Da Vinci, all the great Florentine painters, Giotto & everything else. I got a student's card to get in free & so took my time & saw everything I could. There's a great Square in Florence – one side a huge impossible castle & tower, the other side a vast porch for lounging filled with Renaissance naked Patroklos's & Perseus & Davids & Sabine women being raped 20 feet tall, in between a great alleyway of the Uffizi galleries, in the middle a huge wild fountain with great bronze drunken satyrs – a very striking place – the spot where all the medieval stiffness & religious fear gave way & the Renaissance burst through with huge naked idealized realistic human bodies – *David*'s nakedness being Michelangelo's great historical statement. Never been more anticatholic than since I took this trip. From Florence went on to Rome by train, lived cheap in Student

Dormitory for four days, rushing around madly – arriving at nite ran down a mile to the Coliseum in moonlight, place so vast, as Orlovsky said, stones so huge they can want nothing but death, & in the moonlight awful with spotlights shining thru arches like an artificial light in Hades. Next day went to St. Peter's, a little disappointing & filled with cheap bric-a-brac, then went out of town to the beach & ruins of Ostia, an afternoon. Next day, fountain of Trevi, & gravesite of Keats and Shelley – both in same yard, very sad, I plucked a clover from mad Shelley's grave & will send it to mad Corso in Paris. After, the ruins of the Forum, Capitoline & Palatine hills, right in the center of Rome, the greatest thing there. Spent all afternoon wandering there & came back later to write a little. Next day went to the Vatican museums, saw Michelangelo – and they've painted drapery over all his naked bodies in *Last Judgment*. Then to their great collection of classical statuary – and there again, everybody has a figleaf. I never saw the Church in such vulgar & ugly relief. After Florence & its classical openness, & after seeing the statuary in the Forum & various state museums, to go in Vatican & see them desecrating the very significance & point of ancient sculpture – idealized human bodies, but real ones – they even put a figleaf on poor old Laocöon & his prepubescent sons. How they get away with it I don't know: I mean, it's so opposite to what you see everywhere else in Italy, it stands out like the piece of dirtymindedness that it is.

Began running out of travel money in Rome & so threw caution to the winds & decided to hitchhike around Italy & eat up my trainfare & extend the trip, so took cheap train to Assisi, where St. Francis came from – great beautiful mountain town, overlooking classical old familiar (from paintings) Umbrian valley. Had read a lot about Francis up North last summer & was all prepared historically for the scene & really had a ball there, we came into town unshaven & dirty & eating milk & salami & fruit on the way, invaded the Franciscan monastery, met all the English speaking monks & argued about St. Francis & looked at his tomb & relics & robes & climbed up hills to see caves where he'd hidden & secret hermitages he'd spent winters in, all in hot summer sun, with small bagful of food & rundown heels & needing a haircut & a broken straw hat, wound up sleeping 2 warm nights right out on the front lawn of the monastery & waking up at 5AM going in church to see the Giotto cycle of frescos there (daybreak the only time you can really see them in the dark church, the sun comes right in) and arguing more with the monks about figleaves in Vatican & how St. Francis would have at least shared his hut with pilgrims (more than those poor old Franciscans do – they wanted money) & in fact behaved like mad Franciscans & read poetry to them & had them trooping out at night peeking to see if we were really sleeping outside in front of their holy refuge. This is about the best & funniest time I've had since been in Europe.

Then began hitching up to Venice, very bad, and so spent several more nights very pleasantly sleeping in the fields, warm summer nights, full moon, great landscape to wake up in, plenty to eat — fruit & cheese & bread & ham all cheap, tho my feet began hurting. Finally got back to Florence, went back to Uffizi & saw the Square again & found a long ride all the way almost back to Venice, about 50 km. away, so bought ticket partway back & sneaked in Lavatory & got the rest of the way home & arrived in Venice tired & without a cent but had a great perfect tour of Italy. The New Directions check & Orlovsky's govt. check waiting when we got here. Also passed thru town of Perugia, saw museum & square there, and Giotto in Padua again.

No definite plans. Will stay here another few weeks at Ansen's and rest up & read and write. Out of money except for Orlovsky's monthly check. Next move will be trip to Paris, Ansen coming along also, in September, meet Burroughs there, & try to peddle his mss. Jack now in Mexico again, says he'll try to meet us there sooner or later. I'd like to go settle down in Paris for at least a half year, really dig in there and live in the city, from everything I hear it's the best place in Europe, also the most expensive. I will try to borrow a thousand from Gene. I don't know if he has it or wants to lend it but will see — maybe with new baby he has too much expenses. Anyway I'll write him & try arrange some monthly stipend like $80 & go to Paris and stay there. Can come back next spring and get job, shipping — or else if luck is good, may have Guggenheim 2 or 3 thousand by then — applying for that this month.[1] Though I doubt that'll really come thru. Talk this over with Gene. If you have enough money to go halves with him & can do so, please do. Though I don't know what your expenses are now with Grandma in the hospital again.

I'll be here in any case till probably the end of month, so can be reached.

As ever,
love, Allen

Regards to Edith

---

1. Reference to award from the Guggenheim Foundation.

Louis Ginsberg to Allen Ginsberg

August 26, 1957

Dear Allen,

Received your last letter of Aug. 10.

How are you these days?

From all the experiences and sights and sounds you detail, new poems must be smoldering deep in you for utterance. What new poems have you written?

Have you still the clover you plucked from Shelley's grave? If so, send it home. I always dreamed of visiting the grave of Shelley and Keats, as those were, of old, my first inspirations and ardors.

I don't suppose you'll visit Israel. I was wondering whether the sight of those Biblical hills would stir any faint vibrations or reverberations slumbering deep in the subterranean psyche of your blood and heritage?

As I wrote you last, Eugene & Connie have a new son, Peter, named after my father. We kept little Allen [*sic*] here for a week and had a delightful time with him: a blue-eyed, golden-haired, sparkling and intelligent youngster. Little Peter looks broad-jawed like Naomi's family. We are visiting this week, and I'll report to you further.

School starts in another ten days. My summer money has run out or I'd send you some money; but, perforce, I'll have to wait for my first check on Sept. 13. I'll ship off something and send it to you. (Should I send my personal check or the bank's cashier's check or a money order?)

Are you in touch with Rexroth & Williams?

Wondering why I don't hear from *Partisan Review*? I sent a subscription check and *four* letters, but still they have not responded.

Keep writing – and love from your father,

Louis

Allen Ginsberg to Louis Ginsberg

Ischia {Italy}
September 1, 1957

Dear Louis:

By the time you get this I'll be back in Venice, probably preparing to start off for Paris, via Vienna – stop off there a few days. Not seen any mail for over a week, since I been traveling. As I think I wrote, *Time* mag. called up for an interview from Rome, and as they were summer vacation short-handed they readily agreed to my proposition that they pay my way down there & they gave me two days living expenses (35 dollars) as well as plane ticket round trip. I've stretched the money out for ten days already and came down further to Naples – went to museums, saw large collection of Pompeilian [*sic*] art in the Naples museum, including a whole roomful of interesting & sometimes beautiful Pompeilian pornography. Also walked a lot around Naples which is a beautifully situated city – slums honeycombed onto steep hills that come down to high waterfront rich boulevards and a great blue wide bay overlooking Capri a few miles out, and overlooked by vast slope of Mt. Vesuvius. The second day here I climbed up Vesuvius & spent an hour looking at steam coming out of the rocks in the walls of the great crater on top; and then slid & walked down the side thru pulverized lava sand & down lava fields into beautiful grape growing country (picking & eating delicious blue grapes along the road) and down further to the Bay of Naples and the ruins of Pompeii – spent the end of the afternoon walking thru those deserted & strange streets. Still quite a bit of statuary and painting left there including a lot of naked Venuses & satyrs & drunken Bacchuses, mythological figures all over the walls, including a set of priapic illustrations in a ruined ancient bordello. I stayed over in Naples at the youth hostel, very cheap & charming collection of traveling young Germans & South Africans & 2 motorcycling Vietnamese. Then took boat to Capri & spent day walking around steep cliffs overlooking azure sea and also went swimming. Stayed overnight, in hostel, very cheap, & drank fresh milk & made cheese & salami sandwiches & ate tomatoes so I dropped very little money there, tho hostel & restaurant prices are high. Then took early morning boat back to Naples & railroad for an hour up the coast & by foot for 4 miles into the country by more grapefields & lakes, to the ruins of Cuma – site of the Caves of Cumaen Sybil – one of the most beautiful and least visited of the local archeological sites – high dark echoey caves and underground stairways and passages, a whole hill honeycombed with dark prophetic rooms, and on top of the hill a calm shady broken temple where I ate picnic lunch alone & took a nap. Then returned to a small town near Bay of Baia ("Lulled by the crystalline streams of Baia's bay" – Ode to West Wind?) called Pozzuoli and took another cheap fisher ferry boat thru Baia Bay to Isle of Ischia, where Auden has settled every summer for past 10 years. It's a big (15 miles circumference) island with several cities, blue Mediterranean sky & clear bright sun showering on the translucent azure-type water. Found a hostel here, spent last evening arguing furiously & angrily with Auden on the merits of Whitman at a cafe table in "Marie's Bar" in town of Forio, outdoors under grapevines drank a lot of wine, woke this morning, had breakfast (huge peach, half quart of milk & large sugarbun) and went swimming. Yesterday also took buses around the island and climbed Mt. Epomeo, which is in the center of it, a high rough craggy mount, ex volcano, with white spurs of windworn rock jutting out crazily on top. More German tourists all over, afoot & on donkeys. This island very interesting, since it has great variety of landscape, mountain-scape, seascape, & cliffs, little peninsular mountains, and every type of civilization from grape-peasants living in caves to hut dwellers, fishermen & strange English high society types wandering around in red shorts & sunglasses. Mostly it is an Italian resort island, contrasting with Capri which is famously international. I'll leave here tomorrow morning (Monday) on 5AM boat, catch Naples–Rome train, be in Rome by noon, catch plane that afternoon and arrive in Venice early tomorrow evening. Now sitting in the afternoon, relaxing with lemonade in shady cafe table, writing letters, everything very slow & calm – I've been on my feet most of the time till today, tramping, strolling & climbing.

Auden stays in all day & comes out to cafe in evening & sits with a tablefull of dull chatty literary old fairies & they seem to vie with each other in making deprecatory home-made sophisticated small talk. I tackled the whole table on the Whitman issue & wound up tipsy calling them a bunch of shits – Auden seems to have a longwinded rationalistic approach to his opinions – I doubt if he respects his own feelings anymore – I think his long sexual history has been relatively unfortunate and made him very orthodox and conservative and merciless in an offhand way – he sounds like an intelligent *Time* magazine talking. Ansen has the same peculiarity – approaching such questions as capital punishment and literary censorship as if they were complicated bureaucratic problems in which they have no right to have private feelings but only series of factual logical considerations – a sort of fetish of objectivity – which strikes me as no objectivity at all but a sort of abject distrust of people & their own lives. I quoted the first line of Whitman, "I celebrate myself," etc., and Auden said, "O but my dear! that's so *wrong* and so *shameless*, it's an utterly bad line – when I hear that I feel I must say please *don't* include me" (re – "what I shall assume you shall assume") – said that he was an orthodox Englishman, not a democrat (in this context). It all boils down to some sort of reactionary mystique of original sin. Auden is a great poet but he seems old in vain if he's learned no wildness from life – sort of a Wordsworthian camp. Said he "intensely disliked" Shelley. He thought my own book was "full of the author feeling sorry for himself" and saw no vitality or beauty beyond that as far as I could see. All this gives me the conviction, or strengthens the conviction I have had, that the republic of poetry needs a full-scale revolution and upsetting of "values" (and a return to a kind of imagination of life in Whitman's *Democratic Vistas* that I've been reading in Venice). In all this scene, with the great names like Auden & Marianne Moore trying to be conservative, and Eliot ambiguous & Pound partly nuts, Williams stands out as the only beautiful soul among the great poets who has tearfully clung to his humanity and has survived as a man to bequeath in America some semblance of the heritage of spiritual democracy in indestructible individuality – heritage established and handed down by Whitman & perhaps Emerson, I don't know I never read him. Hart Crane seems like the only other live soul – he too generally described by academicians [as] improper, sloppy, or immature. But I think they struggled toward freedom with great knowledge & in great solitude. Auden thought Whitman "dishonest" for writing an anonymous review of his own work. I think it wd. improve Auden's present lax poetry if he had to return to such anonymity. Well, I've filled out four pages & so will close & mail this. Wrote p.card from Capri.

Love
Allen

Allen Ginsberg to Louis Ginsberg

{Venice, Italy}
n.d. {ca. early September 1957}

Dear Louis –

Arrived in Venice again, leaving for Vienna in 4 days & trying to clear up all business. No news yet on outcome from trial; tho *Time* mag man in Rome said there was to be some report in Sept *Time* & *Life* also. Wrote you 2 days ago from Ischia. Be in Vienna 3 days & go straight to Paris.

Received your letters – Aug 26 and a long delayed one enclosing Brazil letter from June 9. Saw & commented on its "Hotel Lobby" before. Yes? Last poem about washerwoman very good. *Measure* Wieners wrote he thought it be a good idea print both of us. Send him that, maybe other sharp ones.

Write henceforth to American Express Paris France. Mail already sent here will be forwarded.

Been writing some poetry & lots of prose notes. Correspondence mounts & is being bad problem now. Too much publicity at this point; I'm beginning to think – "Howl" too slight to support so great a weight of bull. Article in *London Times Literary Supplement*[1] too, sort of favorable.

I may send you a pile of papers to dump away in my trunk – want to lighten my knapsack & clippings & letters getting heavy.

I guess you spoke to Gene. Wrote said he was doing poorly, sent $50 which came in handy, said he might be able to send another 50 in couple of months. If you can send me a little later this month it would help a lot, but only if you can spare it. The money problem will somehow solve itself – I'm not too worried yet – and, wonder of wonders, when I got back here yesterday, I found a check for a whole hundred dollars from City Lights – the first money he's sent me. Seems he sold out 3rd edition, 2500 copies, and is even printing a fourth. So that means I'm due some more money from him, another one or 2 hundred, before end of year. So there is a steady unforeseen income for a little while. At this rate I should be able to hold out in Paris till Xmas at least when Jack will pay me 225$ & Peter has 50 a month.[2] Tell Gene I have the City Lites money, so things are OK.

At any rate I want to stay in Paris a while & think I can do it with City Lites new source of loot.

1. "The American Way," *Times Literary Supplement,* August 16, 1957.
2. Allen had lent Jack Kerouac the money, which he was very slow in paying back; Peter Orlovsky received fifty dollars' disability a month from the Veteran's Administration.

I enclose the clover from Shelley's grave – happy to send it – you'll be here in a few years & see all this yourself – Europe a great experience like going to college. I may not get to Israel at this rate but you never can tell. I almost went to Istanbul last month.

Reading Whitman's *Democratic Vistas* which struck me as excellent & original & unique statement of American possibilities – as near a "program" for a new race of poets as anywhere I've seen.

Love to Edith – here's the clover – tho just like any clover anymore I guess – I cried when I saw Keats stone tho.

Love,
Allen

Allen Ginsberg to Louis and Edith Ginsberg

c/o American Express
Amsterdam, Holland
P.M. September 30, 1957

Dear Folks –

Lo & Behold! I'm in Amsterdam visiting Gregory Corso. Never thought I'd be in Holland. Anyway I was in Paris a week, but it was too expensive to stay there and I couldn't find a place where I could cook in. Well I have a room reserved there beginning Oct. 15 – it has a cook-stove, gas, & heat tho it's small & expensive ($30 a month). So I'll stay here for 2 weeks & return to Paris then. Sleeping on Corso's floor till then – nice big room with a rug. Amsterdam is very quiet, canals with huge fantastic weeping willow trees hanging down into them, food is very cheap, there are art & poetry bars, a literary magazine & movements here, modern huge museums filled with 50 Van Goghs, and old museums with Rembrandt & Vermeer paintings. Rode thru by train & saw low green fields & canals & windmills & cows – long plain, huge sky, everything still & green, except for windmill turning furiously in the unseen wind. Been here two days now.

Everything else fine. *Evergreen Review* wrote & asked to publish my long Mexican poem,[1] so that will bring in some money. They've also put out a record, which will bring in a small amount – tho the record is I hear very

---

1. "Siesta in Xbalba" appeared in *Evergreen Review* 1, no. 4 (Winter 1957).

bad – have you seen or heard it? I guess they sell them – ask Gene to pick one up in N.Y. A California company will put out a full size good record of "Howl" tho, sooner or later, says Ferlinghetti. I haven't heard news of the Trial recently, perhaps it's over now. *Time* is supposed to have a story soon. I wrote to my *Time* connection lady & asked her to ask Luce to send us all to Moscow to find out about Russian poetry. Maybe on a fluke, they will (send us). City Lights has sold about 5000 copies & is printing up a 4th edition now, so more money is due me in several months. I saw a review of Jack's book in daily *Times*[1] – Sept 5 – which speaks for itself – a great triumph for Jack, finally. Have you seen his book? Amazing how well things have worked out. I never thought any less of my own poetry and Jack's prose than the reception it's finally met with, but it is amazing to find my own valuations accepted by the outside – especially in *The Times*.

Gregory sends regards. I'm writing an introduction to his book upcoming for City Lights[2] – he says to tell you he's lost his *Everlasting Minute,* but he "still thinks about the lost." His own book should be very fine. Says it's alright because he lost it some time he lost all his old boyish poems in the Miami Greyhound terminal "with my poems went his" unquote.

How is your writing now & what's the date of your book? Properly pared down now you should be able to make it soon – when I get back will see what can be done to find a sympathetic house to put it out – though it's difficult working with N.Y. hardcover – as you see everything we have done (except Jack's novel) has been done thru more offbeat informal avenues. N.Y. is hard, closed, commercial, ingrown, mechanical & not intelligent as far as publishing machinery.

Paris is beautiful – the only city I've seen so far that would tempt me to expatriate & settle down. The rest of Europe has been interesting, and each city has its one, two or three marvels or charms, but Paris has universal interest and permanent charm as a living place. I'll try to stay there for a half a year and then come home, unless I get enough money for a trip to the Far East. Went up the Eiffel Tower which is much vaster than I thought, spent several afternoons at the Louvre and at Notre Dame, lived several nites near Place Pigalle, lived a week in a hotel on the Seine overlooking the great Facade of Notre Dame & the bookstalls along the river, everything as

---

1. Gilbert Millstein, "Books of the Times," *New York Times,* September 5, 1957. Millstein's glowing review, comparing *On the Road* to Hemingway's *The Sun Also Rises,* was one of the great "accidents" in modern literary history. The usual book critic was on vacation, and Millstein inherited the Kerouac review. The *Times* review launched Kerouac's career and, to a certain extent, set the Beat Generation phenomenon in motion.

2. Gregory Corso, *Gasoline* (San Francisco: City Lights Books, 1958).

charmy and arty & free & grotesque as advertised – the very faces on the street look like they've stepped out of paintings by Lautrec & Van Gogh. The streets look like impressionistic streets, the cars & faces look like Gershwin & Gertrude Stein & all the millions of Hemingway & legendary cafe & boulevard & movie recollections of Paris I've stored up since I got to college. Best place in Europe so far. I'll be back there in 2 weeks, so write me there – tho till then I can get a letter here at American Express Amsterdam, Holland. Will try to get to The Hauge before I leave. In Rotterdam already. All new & modern, having been destroyed in war – not [. . .] modern – futuristic looking even. Love to Gene, Edith, Connie –

Allen

In mid-October, Allen, Peter, and Gregory took up residence at an unnamed hotel at 9 Git-le-Coeur in Paris – known by Beat Generation scholars as "The Beat Hotel," not just because of its ancient ramshackle conditions, described in the following letter, but because the establishment housed so many writers, poets, artists, and musicians associated with the Beat Generation. This would be Allen's headquarters for the remainder of his stay in Europe.

The trip to Europe had done much more than simply give Ginsberg the opportunity to experience European culture and tradition; for the first time in his life, Allen was seeing the United States through the eyes of others. In talking to Europeans, and reading their newspapers and magazines, Allen felt the stripping away of any American ethnocentricity he might have possessed. He had always been, by nature, critical or skeptical of American politics and social practices, and his trip to Europe only fortified his beliefs, setting off a series of lengthy, often angry exchanges with his father, especially on issues pertaining to Russia or communism.

Allen Ginsberg to Louis Ginsberg

Paris 9 Git Le Coeur
Apt 32
October 19, 1957

Dear Lou:

Back in Paris – received all your letters, clippings, $10 – it had been held here, several letters anyway. Holland trip was very good, saw a lot of Rembrandt & Vermeer, met some interesting people, Gregory wrote an article on American Poetry for their equivalent of *Sat Review* – a magazine *Litterair Paspoort*[1] – we got interviewed by newspapers & made enough money off the land to stay 3 weeks. Back here, my room was ready, it's a small furnished room size place, rather damp in rain, leaks in fact, with paper thin wall so I can't talk after 10 PM on account of nextdoor working couple, one weak yellow light bulb, a small sink with hot water Thurs, Fri & Sat., discolored plaster, charming view of roofs and chimneys & small round table covered with oilcloth. Big sagging bed, all three of us, me Peter & Gregory sack out in it, Gregory looking for a room or a girl with a room. The $10 came in handy, I was broke when I got it, so I stocked up on groceries that will last till next check comes in for Peter from Vet Admin. All in all a typical Paris *vie de foreign boheme*. Not uncomfortable, a little crowded, – but my room, costs $35 a month, is apparently a rare thing to be able to find – awful housing shortage, everybody huddled like rats in rotting old picturesque buildings without hot water. Day we arrived back, there was strike, no gas or electric, metros not running, candles selling for 35c ea. Landlady says she'll give me a cheaper smaller room where I can make noise as soon as one is free, in a week or so. Main thing is to have gas, which I have, to cook on, which I do – long as I have that can live almost comfortably no matter how little money, – potatoes, bread, vegetables, very cheap, & meat not bad. So cook fine spaghettis & lentil soups, big pots. I live in the Left Bank, near Place St. Michel, near one of the famous bridges that crosses over the Ile de la Cité whereon Notre Dame is – I'm only a few blocks from Notre Dame & see it every day – out of my window I can see the river, down the side of the street, & the booksellers stalls in the rain, & I'm 10 minutes walk from the Louvre, and 10 min. in other direction to St. Germain, the place where all the hip & existentialist & foreign intellectuals have their cafe area – Sartre lives upstairs from Cafe Bonaparte – on the corner, the celebrated Cafe Deux Magots & Cafe de Flore, hundreds of tables full of odd respectable looking literary & theatrical types. Landlady just burst into the room looking for secret radios adding to her electric bills – fortunately it was the people next door, & Gregory was gone. So she was pleased, & undoubtedly will get us the cheaper smaller room where we can make more noise.

Got the record from *Evergreen,* it certainly is terrible, in fact it stinks. Fortunately I can put a full 12 in LP out thru City Lites that will come off better I hope. Grove screwed up that deal, took wrong tapes, wrong

---

1. "The Literary Revolution in America," *Litterair Paspoort, Number 110* (November 1957). According to Bill Morgan, Ginsberg's bibliographer, Allen "wrote much of this article."

sections, wrong people. I got news of trial from S.F., the *Chronicle* there had it in headline on first page. He's[1] sold 5000 & has another 5000 in print he says. He'll send me more money when there is some, he's quite honest, he sent me the last hundred at time I didn't even know I had it coming. I wouldn't shift publishers in any case, since no NY publisher would go to court, as he did, nor would a NY publisher manage to print & sell 10,000 copies cheap, as he can do. Like I say, all NY has is prestige, but not much of that – since it's mainly a money-prestige racket they're in, not the poetry racket as City Lights is. *Evergreen* took some more poems, also some of Gregory's. I finished short intro to Gregory's book, which should come out in a month or two.

Did you see review of Jack's book in daily *Times* Sept 5?

Re Williams.[2] I don't know what the answer is. I don't think he's antisemitic since he has Jewish friends & attacks Pound's antisemitism. He's anticatholic as far as politics, and with that I agree with him – though those who attack him in letters for antisemitism also attack him for anticatholicism – as if he had no right to speak frankly what he thinks. What it boils down to I don't know. I'll ask him what he means by shylocks when I write next. However he's not anti-Semitic as you know full well from his treatment of me & other Jews. Louis Geldman's letter seemed pompous. Why does Geldman care if W. attacks Catholics in politics? Just to have official type arguments, arguments, arguments, that can be written in letters to editors. That level of official type sensitivity seems obnoxious, & is not however a particularly Jewish trait, Negroes, Chinese, Americans, Russians all have it.

November 6, 1957

Sorry to be so slow in writing, I had just about finished the last page when I came down with the Asian Flu, full scale, & have been in bed for 10 days, had a bad case & relapsed several times before it was all over. I couldn't do any writing & even if could, had no money for stamps to mail them so have just been in bed letting things slide for the last 2 weeks – a pleasant rest once the severe coughing & ague discomforts passed. Have been absolutely broke since the 20th of last month & living on lentils & Gregory Corso's charity – he fell in with a rich girl fortunately at the time we all went broke. Finally Peter's check arrived today, rent's paid & we're all stocked up on

1. Publisher Lawrence Ferlinghetti.
2. William Carlos Willliams.

groceries. Orlovsky is preparing to leave in a few weeks & return home as his family seems to be in trouble & he has to take care of his various brothers in their various stages of bugginess.[1] Fortunately his return coincides with Kerouac's new fortune so Jack sez he'll pay me my several hundred in a month. Ferlinghetti sent me a pack of books to sell here, so I'm making a little loot distributing my own book & the rest of his series & some *Evergreen Review*s to stores here. I'll write later as things develop. I am swamped with usual unanswered mail.

I hope Gene has not been doing badly in the Stock Market, what does he say. European papers reported Little Rock about same space as US papers, it's just that the impact here seems more shocking, since Europeans have more better personal relations with Negroes than Americans have, northern or southern. If nice white girls go out with big black nigger looking spades & nobody takes notice & parents aren't upset but rather interested. I saw a lot of that in Holland particularly.

Sputnik I & II greatest story since discovery of fire, has everybody here delighted.[2] The side issue of America taking the Fall finally is too bad but seems inevitable, like the future is not ours, American, any more, as we used to think. At least so it appears from this side of the Atlantic. I would say America seems to have goofed in her mission – too much materialistic self indulgence – as if the whole $$ machine has been running to satisfy the taste of the menopause set. I noticed story in *Time* last week about how whole auto industry now definitely geared for external fashion style – and this the largest US industry – now no longer run with relation to use, scientific principle, or high quality long lastingness – now the whole accent is on trashy & yearly to be changed style design – billions of dollars spent on bad poetry so to speak.

Things really seem very bleak & at the same time with the moon ahead very exciting. What does the *Daily News* have to say lately? I was wondering what kind of pathetic cries are issuing from the editorial pages of the nation? Ike is supposed to speak tonite – write me what the subconscious political or social scene looks like. I mean it sounds like death from here – even Gregory, who's never been interested in politics in his life, is beginning to worry about America.

Saw the Chaplin picture, *King in NY*, it has a badly constructed ending,

1. Peter Orlovsky's brothers, Julius and Lafcadio, suffered from serious mental disorders and spent much of their lives institutionalized.
2. On October 4, 1957, the Soviet Union launched *Sputnik I,* the first unmanned orbital satellite, into space; *Sputnik II* was launched on November 3. The "space race" had begun.

but it's a great picture – would cause riots in America if they showed it. Despite report of it I'd read attacking it as humorless, it's very funny.

I mean, as you can gather from above, the position of America seen from Europe, in light of recent events, seems really unlike what I imagine it must seem in America – the normal order of things, a new crisis or two, etc. Seems more like it appears in surrealist poetry or Whitman's more pessimistic moods in *Democratic Vistas*.

Been indoors mostly so have seen little of Paris life. So far I did get up beautiful Eiffel Tower & been in Notre Dame & seen the bohemian Quarter & walked a few streets & met a few people, but no large scale interesting social life yet. Jean Garrigue was in town & visited me when I was sick, Jack has been writing, his book is a best seller & he expects $20,000 on New Year's Day, he'll establish a trust fund so he'll always have some money, & he may yet get a lot more from movies. I'll write.

Love,
Allen

Louis Ginsberg to Allen Ginsberg

November 20, 1957

Dear Allen,

I read your letter to Edith.

Hannah's address: 11 Pomona Ave.

Gregory Corso: what happened to that affair in which Corso was supposed to marry the daughter of a mid-West official?

Glad to hear *Esquire* will air the S. F. group. Let me know what it appears so I can get a few copies.

I'll be awaiting the books you write about. Maybe, it will titillate an old codger like me, apart from beauty, perhaps, of some lives. If you run across a cheap but good etching of, say, water, let me know.

Spoke to Eugene over the phone today. They're driving down for the Christmas week to Connie's folks. When they come back, we'll run in to see them.

Otherwise, things are quiet here. Tomorrow I start my Christmas (Hanukkah) vacation. I expect to pore over literary quarterlies, read odds and ends, and, if I get an inspiration, do a little private writing. I'll also work over my ms. book, when I'm in the mood.

You must be soaking in the spirit of Paris. How do you like the sights and scents there?

No doubt, Edith and I will come to Paris, but not this coming Summer. Probably, next Summer. We're getting our noses above financial waters and have started saving; but by next Summer, we'll have, I expect, a sizable amount to undertake the trip.

Grandma is now at the Jewish Home for the Aged (it was formerly the Old Beth Israel Hospital on W. Kenney St., Newark). She is more satisfied there and has adjusted herself pleasantly there with old cronies.

Love from

Your father,

Louis

P.S. About the burden of your multifarious correspondence, I suggest you send out only postcards, except to a selected few.

Will write you a longer letter during the coming, leisurely week.

L.G.

I note by the papers that Ben Hecht has written a play about Maxwell Bodenheim. It will have its premier as an off-B'way play on Jan. 14. If I can make it, I'll do so. At any rate, I'll look for the drama reviews about it.

Are you saving all the clippings about your work that I send you? Gather them together. If they're too bulky there, send them here and I'll store them for you.

Also, mull over them. Consider, with candor, all the good and bad criticism and then let your heart of your own deep-seated literary conscience guide you. You – and you alone – should map your course.

Love again!

L.

P.S. again

Joel Gaidemack just called up. He met Kerouac in the Village Vanguard.

They made a date to come into Paterson mid-January to visit me. Joel said Kerouac is going well financially and talked to Joel quite a bit about you, naturally.

More anon.

Love again.

L.

Allen Ginsberg to Louis Ginsberg

9 Rue Git Le Coeur
Paris 6, France
November 30, 1957

Dear Lou:

Everything's fine, received your $15 & also a check from Gene, tell him I got it; been living on that all month, crisis mostly passed, expecting money from Grove now – they sent me proofs on 15 pages of Mexican poem. Also got a check from *Partisan,* & they took 2 sizable poems of Gregory's also, finally. Have better room downstairs, same price or cheaper since the Franc is worthless. I fried a chicken for Thanksgiving, by time you get this Xmas be near so Merry Xmas. I wish Grove had not issued that record, it's so lousy. They took wrong tapes against my faraway advice. I'm supposed to make another LP for another co. I wrote Honey last week. Spend or waste a lot of time answering strange letters, everything from Jesuit appeals to Christ in me to young poets who write on toilet paper.[1] Citadel Press putting out an anthology of "Beat Gener[ation]" material, wrote for permission to reprint "Howl" & also a piece of Burroughs.[2] Seems Carl is out & was advising them. Also letter from *Chicago Review* wanting to assemble SF material. I've written a lot I find but nothing typed up in final form so don't have much to send out; lately been working on Requiem or Elegy for Mama, should be long. Spending days going to museums here & covering Paris touristically. The Eiffel Tower is grand, much huger & more dreamlike than I imagined, the high mansion apartments clustered only to

---

1. Poet and editor LeRoi Jones (who later changed his name to Amiri Baraka) contacted Allen in Paris by letter written on toilet paper.
2. Gene Feldman and Max Gartenberg, eds., *The Beat Generation and the Angry Young Men* (New York: Dell, 1958).

its toes, it rises way up over the city like giant. Haven't seen copy of Jack's book yet; the main thing about it is the method of prose for me – his recording of the time was very good as I remember except that he avoided sex then. The *Times* review by G. Millstein struck me as right tho. People keep seeing destruction or rebellion in his writing (as most reviews here seen same in "Howl") but that is very minor element, actually: it only seems to be so to people who have accepted standard American values as permanent. What we are saying is that these values are not really standard or permanent, & we are in a sense I think ahead of the times – tho not too far ahead – Sputnik has already changed the content of the editorial pages I read. We're not of course talking in political terms. The week before Sputnik I remember in *Time* the cover story on American car design & styling. Did you see it? What it wound up saying, was that this largest industry was now geared to try sell its product not on basis of use or durability but on basis of a cheap Texan 10c store style. Whole industry competing to turn out flashiest (& purposely impermanent) design, to change yearly, bring customers who want outclass neighbors. When you have a whole economy doing that & everybody involved in some version of moneymaking *like* that – this just is no standard of values. That it seems to offer a temporary security may be enough to keep people slaving for it. But meanwhile it destroys real value. And it ultimately breaks down. Whitman long ago complained that unless the material power of America were leavened by some kind of spiritual infusion we would wind up among the "fabled damned." It seems we're approaching that state as far as I can see. Only way out is individuals taking responsibility & saying what they actually feel – which is an enormous human achievement in any society. That's just what we as a "group" have been trying to do. To class[ify] that as some form of "rebellion," in the kind of college-bred social worker doubletalk of most of the reviews of Jack that I read, misses the huge awful point. None of these reviewers even knows how to write, much less sound off, about their idiotic mature standards of values. But this is off the point, Jack's book probably lacks a good deal of character development, I think that's probably true. I think he wrote in in about 20 days back in 1951 as an exercise in immediate fast-writing without revision.

Sputnik – I am impressed how far the Russians and Chinese have come & will come. People starve there but communism has tried & succeeded in improving material living conditions. The present governments of Russia & China will undoubtedly change in the next hundred years. And with their populations they'll run the world. I'm not (don't misunderstand) apologizing for Trials & Hungary etc. But the impression I get now is that after all those countries & some form of communism are now permanent & world-dominant. In the US I had impression that they would simply disappear someday & leave us alone. To be cont.

Was looking at your poems – they all say what I've been saying last page – "speeding around/their vacuum," "the blast of seconds," "arrive too late." We seem to be in agreement. Will mail this now.

Going to Russian Embassy to see if I can con them out of a free trip to Moscow.

Love,
Allen

The popularity of On The Road, *along with the publicity surrounding the lengthy* Howl *trial, made the Beat Generation an international story. All of a sudden, newspapers and magazines rushed to the presses with stories – usually poorly written and almost always missing the point. Over the next two years, the Beat Generation would be both the darling and the scourge of American popular culture, a status that did not sit well with either Jack Kerouac or Allen Ginsberg, who were more concerned with the literary than the social. Kerouac, in particular, hated the crush of publicity. Allen thrived on the attention, and he was thrilled that his work, along with that of his contemporaries, was in constant demand; however, he soon grew weary of trying to explain what seemed obvious to him.*

Louis Ginsberg reacted to Allen's fame with mixed emotions. He was thrilled that his son had gained international repute, but he was often angered by what he felt were the group's sanctimonious attitudes. His arguments with Allen (through the mail) intensified, and when reading these letters, one feels a slight shifting of position between father and son: Allen was clearly more famous than his father, and his opinions were being solicited all over the world, and from this point forward, Louis often found himself making reluctant concessions, not necessarily in his opinions, but in deference to Allen's position. Louis would always be able to hold his own in arguments with Allen, but in doing so, he would be confronting the considerable aura of his son's fame.

Allen Ginsberg to Louis and Edith Ginsberg

9 Rue Git Le Coeur
Paris 6, France
January 14, 1957, {1958}

Dear Louis & Family:

Everything OK here, got your last letter. I'd seen the *Reporter*[1] in the Ben

---

1. David Perlman's "How Captain Hanrahan Made 'Howl' a Best-Seller," an account of the poem's legal history, appeared in the December 12, 1957, issue of *Reporter*.

Franklin American Library here. Also an article last weekend in the *London Observer*[1] reviewing *Evergreen Review* & SF & attacking "Howl" by John Wain, a member of British "Angry Young Men" group – said "Howl" was no recognizable form of poetry that he could see. The more the merrier good or bad, copies sell, & "the vision of justice is the pleasure of God alone," as Rimbaud says.

Letter from Prof Parkinson in England (a Berkeley prof whom I knew & who visited here over Xmas) inviting me to stay & visit London at his place & also maybe make BBC recording for a series on American poetry he's giving for them – I may go over there in February if Jack ever sends that money. He mentions it (the money) in every letter & said originally he'd pay it Xmas, then January when he got royalties, now he says Royalties don't come till February &'s left me flat broke waiting. I wrote him I needed some of it meanwhile to live on, so I should get it next week, I hope. Meanwhile broke but not desperate. Don't send money, Burroughs arriving this week.

Orlovsky succeeded in convincing US Consul he was broke & needed at home or he would flip over here, so they're sending him on the Mauretania in three days – he leaves Friday. I'll give him some books & papers to bring out to Paterson & deposit in my trunk – mostly literary letters etc. I guess you'll see him & get a report on Europe when he calls.

Gregory Corso was here the last few months broke & sleeping on our floor, he went off to Frankfurt to try sell encyclopedias & failed at that, but wrote today that he's contacted a German Literary magazine (through Dutch magazine that printed a long article of his with pictures of both of us – I'll send it sooner or later) – the German editor of which, Walter Hollerer, is a poet who visited SF & had my book already & gave Gregory some money & said he'd find a translator for *Howl* & Gregory's *Gasoline,* also invited me to read at Frankfurt University & found a publisher who would be interested in a German anthology of SF material – so I may get to work on that if it really materializes. I don't know what will happen – I may pay a week or 2 trip to Frankfurt & find out if it's all serious & give reading and go to work on the anthology. No collection so far has been solid enough, if I spent a little time & contacted enough poets I might be able to assemble a book which would be useful permanently & be peddled in the US as well as Germany & Moscow. I saw Jack's agent here & made arrangements with him to get my book offered to foreign publishers & gave him a Moscow

---

1. John Wain, "Revolting Attitudes," *Observer,* January 12, 1958.

address to try. Russia published 6 times as many books per year as the US – you know that? – & wants US material, pays high prices in dollars on a Swiss bank – this info I have from one of 41 China trip youths I met here & talked to.

Burroughs due in town this week sometime also, so we may both give reading in Frankfurt if he feels like more traveling. I got a cheap room for him in the hotel here, rooms are hard to find, so he may want to settle down now it's possible.

New Year's I was broke so someone drove me to Montmartre Pig Alley Pigalle & I wandered around all night & walked at midnite thru Paris past all the whore streets & carousing areas of bar & walked back to Left Bank under the noisy stars.

I've been reading Shakespeare – *Timon, Pericles, Coriolanus* – trying to finish all the obscure plays I'd neglected; also some Balzac & Dickens and various French modern poets. Also bought French translations of the Russians Yessenin & Mayakovsky – the latter particularly great – a major world poet like Lorca or Eliot – first great voice of the new Oriental Age to come – sort of a Whitman of Russian aspiration which made use of Democracy. It's a tragedy he isn't known in America, his scope & power. Here is a case of an aluminum curtain, culturally, much worse than our ignorances of Soviet Sputnik science power. Russia is here to stay, as a great nation, in one form or other, despite changes of leadership or fluctuations in democratization there. Or stay a few hundred years anyway. I'm writing a long political poem. [. . .]

Thanks for sending Wieners – I'm glad he's publishing your poem. I'd wondered what had happened to him, hadn't heard anything since Venice – seems he's moved to SF. I hope you sent him real sharp poem. Lot of things coming up – article on Zen in *Mademoiselle* quoting "Howl" I hear from Jack, and SF issue of *Esquire* in April, the anthology, from Citadel, *Evergreen 3* with 15 pages of mine, *Partisan Review* with poems by me & Peter too & Gregory & *The Chicago Review* – the plague is on! I'll write soon as I've made plans for England or Germany in a week,

Love,
Allen

Allen Ginsberg to Louis Ginsberg

> *9 Rue Git Le Coeur*
> *{Paris, France}*
> *March 2, 1958*

Dear Louis:

Back from London & settled down in Paris, writing a lot lately, running around, have to make tape for Fantasy label L.P. record,[1] have French translator, made (did I tell you?) half hour BBC poetry tape, for which I'll be paid several bucks a minute when (& if) they use it – mostly uncensored so there's some doubt in my mind, tho they said they would play it, have girlfriend here lately too, (did I say? – Indonesian girl, been seeing her on and off the last few months – nice calm piece of Asia) (giving me new ideas also about Asia and miscegenation & the white race complex) (horrors) – cooking big stews here again, money is alright, got your $5, also some money advance on the LP record, & money also due from here & there, I seem to be alright – tell Edith thanks too – I'll write later – don't send more money, now, I am doing alright, more surprised tho, we'll see later. Parkinson, who is advisor on Guggenheims, says he thinks I'll probably get one. He's one of the committee of three that this year gave out Shelley Memorial prize, & said they would have given it to me ($1000) except it was assumed I wouldn't need it on account of Guggenheim. I hope that's so, tho I won't natch believe that till I see the loot. Anyway, settled here in Paris for awhile again, I don't know what next, would really like to go to Berlin & get on the scene there & see East-West culture-conflict but I have writing to do here & Bill Burroughs don't want to come along for the ride as he's consulting an analyst here for last minute patches to his psyche, & won't move. In any case I'll be back this summer, July probably, stay awhile, I have no plans, if come back then will get a room in NY for awhile or roll out sleepbag on wall to wall carpet, Harold no worry stay where you are. By the way, what's new – show this to H. & tell him to drop me a line, what's happening. Anything I would be interested in? I mean, write (truths) Harold. God knows I've done enough confession, in public, worse.

Continuing on East-West affairs. Been having revelations all week, in fact. By the way, did you dig Heisenberg's announcement of Unified Field Theory – everything variants of one basic Glook, & nature of matter itself

---

1. Allen Ginsberg Reads *Howl and Other Poems* (Fantasy Records no. 7006).

finally hypothesized? I've only seen a few newspaper releases but it's bigger I guess than Einstein, A-bomb or Sputnik. Or Fire for that matter. Won't the Apocalypse come this century? Everything accelerating so fast, I begin to think so (tho don't mean St John's *Apocalypse* – Mr. Unknown's perhaps).

Read analysis of new Class & various articles & it seems important & true & excellent analysis. Also read (in London) Khrushchev & Mao Tze Tung's speeches & dicta on Literature: they say, boiled down, the writer must write for people, the Party is the People, the writer must write for Party, the Party must control writer. Obviously mind-murder brainwashed culture & thought control – even in their own propaganda. No question on that – that's why Mayakovsky (& his suicide & Yessenin's) so interesting, & his work so crucial. They offered an alternative vision of communism, just as Whitman offered an alternative vision of democracy in America.

Suddenly realize I am answering your Jan 25 letter again. Where's your other, excuse me while I look for it.

Yes I have it, to continue.

First re question of slow inner change. Yes it takes centuries, but I think we haven't got centuries to wait. I don't see America changing, basically yet & it won't it's as set in its neurosis (so to speak) as could be. I don't remember all I wrote last time but to sum, the neurosis is money-ego-acquisition-competition-materiality, coupled with an immense selfdeluding selfishness that allows Chinese Exclusion Act, which was a piece of unmerciful criminality helped set the world afire (by hindsight) so that (to go on a tangent for a second) America is filled with mad moralistic religious white Europeans who (like Dulles) are waging a "religious war" against communism like a crusade of force. But I better begin slower, please don't get mad at wild language. But I don't really know where to begin, I don't remember what I wrote last & I've thought beyond that since, a lot of my perceptions seem to be crystallizing after having seen London & gotten an idea of the enormous difference of opinion they have with US there, & of the complete US ignorance of what all the European yelling is about – I had in US always taken it for granted that the US could really basically do no wrong & might blunder but was on the right track – but one thing I do feel (I'll try explain later) is that we have to understand that we are capable of awful deeds (blind like any neurotic is blind to his own aggression & can only see someone else's hostility, not his own), have done some really horrible things, & *have* to be responsible for our own salvation's sake – and there isn't much time. I mean the world is bigger than we are finally, & is changing so rapidly, the changes of history are accelerating as rapidly as the changes in science. U.S. could – I'm afraid will, soon be like England (or in ruins) in a decade or so – no one seems to realize that there, except in a way unconsciously & not knowing why, that's what all the crisis in US is about, the sudden seriousness also hysteria – in a way, at this point, actually, I think, there is as much to be feared from a sudden rash mad reaction in America, if not more, than from Russia – in a way it's a good thing that we can't have our way. Our way, in any case, be impossible, we have no way, really, at this point, just hostility & defense & confusion – no idea what needs be done.

What needs be done & what needed to be done for 50 years, it seems by hindsight obvious, was a raising of standard of living over the whole world, & shift to cooperative socialism, an abandonment (perhaps) of money itself, of the whole profit motive, as the socialists said, to each according to needs.

The US (& capitalist Europe) on contrary tried to, basically, keep down development of communism – instead of organizing & feeding it. I think, finally, we are in great part responsible for the development of totalitarian dictatorship in Russia & China.

It may be there was no way to industrialize those countries without maniac totalitarian singlemindedness. It's our own pressure on them that's contributed to that necessity for brainwashed mechanization rather than slow peaceful socialist mechanization. But mechanization was inevitable & necessary there – didn't we care?

These things, tho sweeping, seem just – and not particularly idealistic since we're faced with a holocaust which we won't win, they hate us now – with some good reason.

The aftermath, I mean the process of incomprehension of the need for peaceful *or* forced violent change, the incomprehension on our parts, still is apparent. We still don't recognize Red China. Dulles still makes mad religious speeches praising Christian enterprise & *capitalistic* democracy as against not totalitarian communism, but communism itself.

I think it is basic, that we have been against communism itself, as well as totalitarianism. Tho this is sort of a problem of chicken or egg which came first. I don't mean to say it's only on account of our adamance that totalitarianism developed there. But it developed in the void & hostility that we left with it.

The money we've spent for armaments would have democratized the world. We are not interested in democratization of the world at that high price. We did not do it.

This year 40 billion armaments & 4 billion foreign aid. Of that 4 billion

3 billion go to maintain the futile Chiang & Rhee governments, & various military subsidies. About 1 1/2 billion goes to actual useful aid. We'll destroy the world and ourselves that way.

Our economy is based on armament now. What would we do if that were ended? Total economic collapse. The only way out would be to produce for need not for profit & that['s] impossible without total collapse of capitalism. So we are faced with continuous armaments, continuous war threat, denial of the necessity for production for worldwide use.

I can't fit all the pieces together in one letter, light & dark, the enormous virtues of individuality in America, I'm just randoming now, but I mean it's not a question of black & white who's right & who's wrong, it's a question of what in fact is happening & why.

Now one huge threat is the Middle East & North Africa. We've given France enough money to continue a suicidal war there. Bourguibe cannot stand, pro West as he is, with the pressure of our betrayal put on him. France will war, and lose, perhaps by the time she's lost, Tunisia & Morocco and Egypt will be all lined up against her, and us. Why do we support France's economy for war there – for that's what our last week's loan did. It's all over the French papers & English papers, tho I doubt if that interpretation has fully penetrated the US consciousness yet. But there is no misinterpretation in North African – or Chinese & Russian newspapers – they have us down red handed – & we are. Well we support France there so she stays with Atlantic Pact, so US armies can defend Europe. But land war is already obsolete with Sputnik & meanwhile all North Africa is righteously offended, & this is going inevitably screw us up. It's serious. The French political scene itself's a madhouse. I won't go into that. They're afraid to stop the war for fear the army will come back & start military invasion of France, their own army – it's gotten to such a mess here. That and other weird reasons – tho everybody here knows they can't win & are only fucking up N Africa.

Well this letter is getting too long. That it boils down to – the old line socialists in the US, with all their idealism, had a really prophetic awareness of the horrible possibilities & immense changes & needs ahead. The US has been mad as a hatter & everybody thinks they've got rich, so everything is OK & the radicals were goofy & eccentric. The richness is false, it's been based on armaments, the rest of the world has been starving, we haven't shared the wealth, mad dictatorial developments have developed all around us, they threaten to outgrow us, outproduce & outfight us if necessary, we still dream that we are the king of the earth, not realizing the yellow race probably be the rich majority in 30 or 40 years – just a few years ago people were talking of the American Century, as if we were Rome – & we were a Rome – I think the Fall is on – "Babylon is fallen, is fallen" –

Whole problems of US consciousness – like disinclination to intermarry among races – automatic acceptance of competition for personal material gain – the possibility of eating well when millions starve in Asia (this decade still) – the whole American fear of sex – the longing (my generation of college boys, the Silent) for secure job & comfort home first above all things, honor, love, honesty in work – ache where to begin or end. I've departed from your letter & run on – sorry if this seems out of joint with what we, even I, usually take for granted in US – it seems to me – having seen now personality & opinion over Europe & North Africa – apt comments.

The strange thing to me is I realize how mad a lot of this sounds in America – yet in another form it's only what everybody has been saying all along, thinking it was just ideas, not the wild stony hand of fate coming smash down on real buildings & cities. It's happened in Europe already, that Apocalypse.

As you say, monolithic governments founder – starting already in Russia with increased democratization. But I am afraid the brainwash mechanization will be in a sense permanent & they, even without force dictatorship, in years to come, will still be robot states, the people sacrificing (as in US heretofore) their individuality to comfort, they'll be satisfied with cars & refrigerators & thought control television. The U.S. has set the stage for that historical development alas. Undoubtedly China in a hundred years will wind up with 2 parties – both believing the same thing as in America now.

France gave up Morocco & Tunisia because she had to. She had a huge war & lost not to give up Indo China. Don't know why they thought they could give up Tunisia & Morocco (which surround Algeria) & yet keep Algeria.

We gave up Philippines, very good, I approve. Though not sure how much we did for them. They seem to be slowly turning Red, or having communist trouble. England gave up India – wise England – she was right. It was time. Russia never gave up anything & probably never will now till

1. She doesn't need them (as she did, Hungary, then, for what she thought was defense, I presume).
2. Dictatorship collapses
3. U.S. quits war pressure
    any one of the three will do, or combination.

What I'm trying to say, it's not a question of choosing sides on black & white either or, who's better who's worse. For myself, for that matter, neither side is right – I'm trying to dig what happened, & not choose side. Whose side can I be on? Sides are an illusion. I'm saying, about America, she thinks in terms of side. She always has, since the days of the Chinese Exclusions Act. But an individual is not a side. I mean I feel far from the interests of both sides, actually. America better for me, tho. But I don't forget that China better probably to a once starving now selfsatisfied Chinese bureaucrat.

Back to Algeria, your paragraph. The French scene is quite mad, and not what appears in the newspapers. Various reasons for holding Algeria – sugar, wine, & the vast petroleum, as well as the million Frenchmen. She worked out quite nice agreements on same line with Morocco & Tunis, but was afraid US would get the oil, & the million Frenchmen who run Algeria wanted to keep running it. Do you know that those million are so mad, there is a movement to secede from France, & wage all out war against Algeria & win it, by the extremists whites? Well, the initial balking in giving Algeria her freedom was bad judgment, the Algerians didn't want to take that. So they appealed to UN & fought. UN declared it internal matter. So the Algerians rebelled. They killed Frenchmen. And Frenchmen killed Algerians. The French atrocities are so horrible (much worse than Hungary & on larger scale) that newspapers are censored here in France. Last week *Le Monde* I believe & Sarte's *NRF,* or whatever the name of his magazine, was banned, for carrying official report on atrocities. The Algerians fight among themselves – the FLN extremists (who are running the war) against moderates who want to cooperate a little. The French do same vice versa. The war stretches on tho its conclusion is inevitable. The hatred, mutual, has now grown to such proportion that NOW THERE IS NO SOLUTION IN ALGERIA. Plain dead and blank fact. The whites won't give in without (everybody says here) invading France and taking war. The Algerians at this point don't want the whites anywhere around them, with good reason. Nothing but mad Frenchmen at war – as they were at war for years in Indochina. Plain case of screw up with classical Marxism background. And when Algeria gets free there will be bloodbath among Arabs – and whites too if there are any left – but, the real horror, what the stalemate is really leading up to is alignment of Egypt, Tunisia & Morocco against France – and, since France backs the US – against the USA. So by our loan to France we continue the war – by allowing the war instead of insisting on UN mediation. If we throw the case into the UN everybody in the world would be in our corner – even Russia. But that's the last thing Russia wants now, for US to do something sensible. Russia gains from Algerian war – alignment with North Africa. So why don't we throw it in the U.N.? God knows what mad capitalistic Eisenhower & American ignorant & indifferent reason there is for that. It's a real horror! Yet when I mentioned it to you, in same breath as Hungary, your reply was, well, France after all had interests there, and 1/10 the population so it was . . . natural . . . or understandable. . . . What I'm trying to point out is that the sense of news & significance of events that filters into your consciousness now in America is filtering thru newspapers, radio & TV – you have the same sense of things that I have, when I'm in America – but that sense of things is not necessarily in proportion – in fact the interpretation of things thru media of mass communication in US is very weird & provincial – nobody knows what is happening – nobody *can* know what is happening – unless thru eccentricity – it's sort of a mass hypnosis – or self hypnosis – or, in a sense – a brainwashing. And it's this sort of thing that people mean when they talk of mass brainwashing in Russia. Russian opinion is molded in the same way ----- more consciously, centralized, from the top – but in the same vast way – and what in these letters I am trying to say is that America, individuals in America, take things for granted because they have to, under the vast sprawling mechanical organization of things there, money, motives, richness, comfort, illusion of freedom – take things for granted that will wind up in national suicide, & that means not so much bombs on NY as – well I lose the thread.

Re Korea – I don't know what the story is, was. Rhee still calls for war & is a dictator. Presumably it would be easier for me to get along (non politically) in South Korea than in North. But Rhee's an old reactionary capitalist – and apparently did also cause the outbreak of hostilities, and I *don't* believe the U.S. interpretation of the story that I believed then, and I don't believe Russia's. And probably the North Koreans are communizing & mechanizing & raising standard of living – which is important. I don't know. I'm saying here – without knowing much facts – that North Korea is not black & white – and that our interest in it was not to preserve anybody's liberty or good government – but to protect what we thought was attack on our containment line of defense. And the Chinese & Russians attacking that line. I mean they don't even like Rhee now in Washington, he's a liability – and is fomenting war – it's even in the US papers, that.

As for our backing of Chiang & nonrecognition of China, that's impossible. So many angles on this. Britain recognizes her, sensibly – we are simply too HOSTILE. Canada wants to but we put pressure not to. No South American country does but they want to trade. We put pressure. But mutual trade at this point is necessary for Chinese and SA economy – would lead to more prosperity in China & thereby relaxation of dictatorship, would hasten the process. Why this policy? Some sort of containment? Allegiance to China lobby? Or finally, deeper, I dunno? fear of economic competition. It's on this level now that Russia & China think they have us, perhaps they do. But what do you think the Chinese think at this point? We may object to their dictatorship – they object to our aggression & encirclement & opposition. And here is a case where we are aggressive. It would take ten mules to pull the admission out of the consciousness of one average American that here is a case of our classical capitalist imperialist warmongering sanctimonious neurotic aggression. And yet Dulles makes speeches denouncing China as irreligious & immoral. No wonder they hate Dulles – you would see the raging attacks on him in brainwashed prosaic Chinese poetry. (I have a book of recent Red Chinese verse – sample: "Old America, your volcano/will soon erupt; if a Truman or/a Marshall dares to start a fire/Negroes will rise/and tear the electric chairs to pieces. . . ." Only good image in the book tho, the rest just rant & prejudice.)

A point you bring up re both Korea & Hungary – Russia's defensive psychosis. I think that a great deal of Russian moves can be clearly see[n] to rise from this, just as many of our moves do. I think this is generally accepted, now since Kennan's lectures – this was partly his analysis. Applies in part of Korea, Hungary, etc. As ours does to France – Algiers, Spain, Korea, Mid-East dictators we support, etc – purely fear reasons.

Russia's reason for Hungary undoubtedly that she thought it part of her land defense line against containment policy. And undoubtedly fear of liberalization politically spreading to other Iron Curtain countries. Breakup of defense line. And breakup of internal control.

Well enough politics, I tried to answer as much as possible sensibly without waving red flags – tho some are inevitable – I mean red flags of psychological conflict between us, I'd rather we came to peace & harmony, it's time, we're both growing old. I've already got beerbelly like you.

What happened to me, partly is – talking now about "poverty vow" etc – no it's not really serious – I mean I use money & eat & sensible etc. – tho not as sensible, so to speak, as most Columbia Graduates – but I was after something I had intuition of & believed in, i.e. beauty & poetry & freedom, which meant real things to me – giving strength & humor in mad situations I found myself in search process – hospital, jail, strange beds, moneyless, undignified, dependent on family at times, goofed up – but what it basically represented, in a way, was attempt to find own values & strike out on own – rather than conforming for safety's sake – for life is too short and the price of fear-motivation & the wastage of that is too great – I didn't clearly realize how wild a step I was taking – forced to take in a way – since in most situations, normal work situations, I found myself so completely out of step – felt the world was crazy (which it is, always has been) – in office or factory – the sight of all these people living in such spiritual poverty, with, mostly, fake loves, even in a sense fake babies – by fake I mean incomplete – compromised for some sense of safety-comfort-routine – what was expected, rather than what they wanted – the sight of hundreds of people in offices, ships, schools – leading lives which are doomed – or lives which I felt were doom for me ----- I mean it's as if the whole system were out of joint – for simple reason (false personality thru adjustment to what's customary so therefore no self knowledge, therefore no knowledge of other selves therefore inability to love, therefore, finally, it makes no difference what happens to neighbor long as I got mine, therefore, China starves, therefore, in the end *that* America must Fall, for the love of God): that is to say, I could not adjust to Newspaper, because that was superficial & lies (the last 5 pages of explanations, tho just intuition then) not ships, carrying goods for war, nor offices & advertising for that's just Evil, nor Law – too slow & compromised for me – nor teaching – since the things I felt most deeply were things it would be strange to teach – I'd get kicked out telling kids to go out have ball get laid dig life love bums forget money dodge draft – which is the message (in vulgar terms) of language & education, for me – so I wind up without the basic social values of the culture, but with my own – which are the ideal & necessary values, perhaps, if Whitman is right in *Demo Vistas*, if we are to survive competition with brainwash machine of Asia – but wind up completely sort of disconnected with the flow & rushes of organized life around me, the flow of money (40 billion to armaments – the whole economy – that or prestige cars to prop competitive ego) – so much of the machinery of life unnecessary, a waste – I even had a few moments of comparative mental release a few (8) years ago in Harlem[1] when I was so completely free of my own guilts, struggles,

---

1. Reference to AG's "Blake Visions" of 1948.

competitions, the forces that molded & strained me, that in the moment of peace I thought I saw a living God – an experience so natural, & yet so out of context of the civilization & the emotional world it creates – that the experience frightened me – and anyone around me. But it was a great sense of the unity & mercy of nature – & a creative freedom of the will – a creative freedom of the will which, in a sense, every government is scared of from China to America around the world – because it is not dependent on the armor, myths, lies, rationalizations which hold the structure together – for this brainwashing is necessary in Russia and China – and even in America, in its own weird form – but at any rate this sense of freedom is the enemy of both capitalism & communism – but I've lost the thread of discourse again – so end finally with poem:

I sit in my room
and imagine the future
talk to eternal genius
Sunlight falls on Paris
Love chokes me to death
I am alone, there is
no one whose love is perfect
eye mercy & mouth to kiss
World! World! World!
man has been mad, man's
love is not perfect
I have not wept enough
my breast will be heavy
till death, the cities
are spectres of cranks
of war the cities are
work and brick and iron
The smoke of the furnace
of Selfhood makes tearless
eyes red in London but
who knows of the sun?
meadows cankerd & canned
meek crowd underground
christs parish creeps
No street woman is loved
under a lamp or neon

nor women in house loves
husband in angel unity
nor boy loves boy with soft
fire of breast politics
for radio streams ago
electricity scares night
mad light on TV screens
laughs at dimmed lamps
in empty rooms no dream
of man's joy is made movie
tin dreams of eros
factory makes bad cars
mind eats its flesh
in starvation and no
man's fuck is holy for
man's work is mostly war
India starves forever
China slaves & starves
on American machinery
America chews fat steaks
of capital Britain cooks
her Jerusalem too long
France & to oil & dead
salad of war in Africa
selfhood devours Arabia
white & negro warring
against the golden nuptial
Russia manufactures feeds
millions but no soul yet
dreams of Mayakovsky's
rainbow over machinery
and backtalk to the sun
& it rains in February
as once on Baudelaire
I lie in Paris alone in
red underwear, symbolic
of desire for union with
man in eternity, I
hear cars on the street

I know where they go
to death but that is OK
It is that death comes
before Life, that no man
has loved perfectly, that
none see the giant sun
ray down from a vast cloud
streaming light on cliffs
tanker size of ant heaved
up shining in the mindless
Vast panorama, Dover and
from the cloud a seagull
appeared flying thru light
bearing its message of ants
in myriad English meadows
dolphins streaming thru Mediterranean
steaming & shrieking in Andes
cemeteries littered with tombs
Asias million rivers, glittering
under mindless sun, mankind's light.

Well this is not very good, first drafts,[1] not ending right, I wanted an image of vast mindless sun at end, I saw it over Dover that way, too much rewriting at this point & most of the images too generalized. Hard writing lately, tho I do a lot.

Well I've spent practically all nite, Louis, writing, for gods sake don't try replying in equal length, I just started battering away at typewriter & wound up with almost everything I was thinking about, about politics anyway, regards to Edith, I wrote such a big letter this time this should cover hers too.

Edith, winter in Paris very balmy, today spring like, I took walk thru Luxembourg Gardens, huge park near students center full of naked statues of Greek goddesses & Roman politicians, trees not budding yet tho, soon. [. . .]

Love
Allen

---

1. See "Europe! Europe" (AG, *CP,* pp. 171–173) for final version of this poem.

Louis Ginsberg to Allen Ginsberg

March 6, 1958

Dear Allen,

Received your long letter of March 2 with its torrent of words, containing, in its outpouring, many glittering, good perceptions and also some brilliant misconceptions, intermingled with rationalizations, all breathing a semi-religious fervor. It was a formidable, good letter.

I'll answer only parts of your letter, and those largely of more or less personal nature.

First, I'm pleased, above all, that your mind is working on to a fine, creative ardor and that you are busy writing. Second, I'm glad that you have a good chance for that Guggenheim Award. Let me know any good news at once.

Yes, I read about the Heisenberg announcement, but the information that filtered in here was too meager, though its implications were astounding.

I must demur – it breaks out though I didn't mean it to – about your glossing over Russia's instigation of North Korean invasion because they thought we were attacking on a containment line, defense. The fact is the U.S. *had withdrawn* her troops and was leaving that area defenseless. Then N. Korea attacked. "Truman's War" some called it; but it was a U.N. action to stop aggression. You accuse the Communists, no matter what evil attacks they make (and they vow to conquer the world) by claiming they feared us. I don't accept that. The facts are otherwise. Russia never gives in a point. It has broken every promise it made (re unification of Germany, elections in Poland, Yalta, Dulles aside (I hold not much brief for him) some of the Communist propaganda has nilly-willy seeped into you (however much you vociferously disclaim it) when you say that the U.S. is guilty ("of imperialist warmongering sanctimonious neurotic aggression.") I'll buttress my views later with other letters.

But to go back to personal matters, which I originally intended to. "Beauty, poetry, freedom." Noble ideals of noble natures. But in a world so out of joint and in a world where changes and evolutions move with vast centuries-old inertia, the individual who seeks to wrest these *at once* is either a sublime saint or a neurotic fool. It can't be done at once in one lifetime. *Portions* of beauty, poetry and freedom, though, can be rescued.

I myself love beauty, poetry, and freedom. But I do what my nature allows me. True, in the beginning, when I loved a woman who grew incurably psychotic, I was handicapped; yet in my handicap I used the handcuffs as bracelets by letting my spirit feed in creative poetry and also by providing the best I could for Naomi. I did more than I could, but the odds were against me. (Some day I suspect – as they are even beginning it now, – science will show that Naomi's illness was rooted in a molecular or atomic maladjustment of her brain or nervous system.)

(I hope you never know what it is to love a woman as I did and then have to lose her.)

Later, when Naomi was lost, I rescued some stay of comfort and home by remarrying, hoping, in our house, you would let down better roots here. Yet, I presume, you had to follow, as you do, your own inner compulsion of your nature according to your own lights.

That great confession you speak of – that mystic message (which I now and then try to adumbrate in some of my poems) is an ideal the world moves very slowly to. It will take centuries. (Don't forget the physical man is millions of years old in development, while his mind has just begun to dawn on him.)

When you come back in July, as I hope (it's been so long since we saw each other) I'd like you to live here with us in Paterson. The double bed will hold you and Harold (he expects to stay here only till October, as he expects to live in N.Y. (There he will resume college in the Fall.)

We bought him a metal clothes chest which stands in the cellar; and we'll get one also for you for your clothes. You'll find it comfortable here. We might fix up the cellar to be more attractive so you can store all your impediments.

More anon.

Love from
Your father,
Louis

P.S. Save this letter and also some of my better ones. I'm saving some of yours. Maybe – who knows – parts of our correspondence might be published when we both are dead and gone.

L.G.

Louis Ginsberg to Allen Ginsberg

March 10, 1958

Dear Allen,

To continue –

Well, the French-Algerian situation is a bad mess. (See enclosed article.) There are two sides or more. Neither black nor white.

BUT to say, as you do, that this French situation is worse than Hungary – here I reject vehemently your analogy. Hungary was, is, a black & white situation. The Hungarians desperately rebelled against a totalitarian terror, but were butchered by thousands of Russian tanks. That the Russians did not want to see their empire or satellite slip from their hands is no justification for the Russian bloody terror. To me, the Hungarian situation is the litmus paper touchstone: anyone who condones or white-washes that Russian brutality is just either confused or mixed up or blinded to the facts. I accuse you, Allen, of those charges re Hungary. (I'd love to see Mark Van Doren's face when you fob off Russia's terrorism and bestial actions in Hungary by your earlier rationalization.) Please remember. I vehemently reject your whitewashing of Russia's action in Hungary.

You have a right to your opinion, according to your lights; but I retain my energetic insistence to differ with you, not only on the Hungary situation but on your whole Beat Generation's views that everything that is, to paraphrase Pope, is wrong. Everything, according to your views, is all wrong, all in ruins, all warmongering, all immoral – except you (plural; i.e., the Beat Generation). Nobody wants "beauty, poetry, freedom" but you (plural). All husbands and wifes [*sic*] fornicate selfishly; all is false; all civilization messed up, all progress in the wrong, false track; all doomed. Everything wrong except your Beat Generation. Well, all I can say is "Save me from that mixed up, confused view of the Beat Generation which maintains it has a blueprint on all Truth, obviously handed down to them in a mystic, blinding revelation from Heaven.

Your poem which I mulled over has, to me, flashes of insight and rich lines of compressed felicity, intermingled with false assumptions; viz. "no woman loves man with angel unity." Well, mortals are not perfect angels, but, as mortals, many marriages possess true love. And so on. (I do wish you'd use sentences and punctuation so as to clarify many of your statements.) And cars: Are they all evil? Have they no use, beauty, expediency, value? Your mystic, visionary view in the poem is brilliantly myopic. Has fervid energy. A creditable performance.

Love from
Your father,
Louis

Louis Ginsberg to Allen Ginsberg

April 10, 1958

Dear Allen,

Well, Allen, how is the whirlwind of crises eddying about you there in Paris? Are dilemmas backing up against your door or flowing over your windowsill? Maybe you can block 'em off, for a while, with a nice girl? How is *chery la femme* [*sic*]?

What are you writing these days?

I'm having my Easter vacation now, though it is somewhat marred by teaching at Rutgers College two nights a week. I read the papers and draw my own confusions (as is my wont); I read the magazines and books for new viewpoints or stimulating vistas; so that, in that way, I can mend the hardening of my platitudes and prevent the shrinking of my latitudes, checking intellectual arthritis, etc. In other words, am having a good time at my desk. My thinking I do on a brainy day.

Are you making any plans for coming back in July? I hope so. I've been missing you a great deal.

Afterthoughts on some notions in your recent letter.

Dulles may be guilty of wrathful vacillation, ostentatious piety, aggrieved intent; and Eisenhower, guilty of dynamic inertia and earnest smugness and sanctimonious *status quo* and backing aggressively into the 18th century; but that is much better than the bestial brutality and the cynical barbarism of Khrushchev, who smears bloody many countries with merciless crime; kidnapping ideal words to cover cynical despotism. Eisenhower may be a "big dumb cop," but at least he is not bloody.

I take the Liberal position: "the greatest happiness for the greatest number," happiness being variable, according to the nature of the individual – *and* the individual may be free to be happy according to his lights and disposition so long as his freedom does not mar or obstruct someone else's freedom and happiness.

The Beat Generation are rebels with cause (of a disordered world) but without a Cause; all, to them, is all wrong; only *they* in their specious humility and arrogant piety are right; they go to extremes and throw out the baby with the dirty water in the washing-basin.

More anon.

Love from your father,
Louis

Louis Ginsberg to Allen Ginsberg

April 16, 1958

Dear Allen,

Glad to get your last letter.

Yes, you may keep the pictures I sent.

You're right about fame. Only time will tell. Meanwhile, as you say, the genuine writer must go ahead and listen to the dictates of his own conscience.

Re my poem "Distances": It is true that, in fact, you and I say the same thing: that society is disordered; that money and lust for power undermine men and nations; that mass media routinize, tranquilize, homogenize, with a steamroller, many groups into a gelatinous conformity and amorphous mediocrity; that man's inhumanity to man, what with the menace of the atom bomb, leaves gulfs between man to explore. I say I agree with you *in part*.

Where I disagree with the Beat Generation is that it sees no good and positive values anywhere at all, at all. As I wrote, the B.G. throws out the baby with the dirty bath water. The B.G. sees no leavening influences, no positive values in our modern times. It disengages itself from all action, yielding only to its own undiciplined series of blind "kicks" – bright-colored beads without a string of purpose. The B.G. is nihilistic because it recognizes no values except those "kicks"; it rebels against *everything*. "Whatever is, is wrong," it fulminates.

I go, *in part*, with you in criticizing the ills and disorders of society. But I see also positive values. I see men and women trying to make a better world (the A.D.A, the Socialists – not fantastically arrogant blind Commies – the U.N., the Brotherhood movements, Lehman, Stevenson, etc.). I see the joys of regenerating nature; I see joys in contemplating the harmonious order and wonder of the universe. *I see a joy in having a son, like you, develop his gift of poetry to experience the ecstasy of writing poetry;* I see a thousand and one *leavening influences feuding with evil influences.* I see the delight in wrestling sanity and order from an absurd universe (Camus). I see science curing many ills. *There is honey in the world besides wormwood.*

I read Gregory Corso's book of poems, *Gasoline.* I can't honestly say I understood all of it, but some parts I found interesting – poems like "Vision of Rotterdam," "Birthplace Revisited," "Mexican Impressions." Somehow, I'm fascinated by his line, "I pump him full of lost watches." As you wrote in your introduction, it is like opening "a box of crazy toys."

Otherwise all is quiet here. Spring has finally come with full energy and lavish sunlight; our garden is burgeoning. My night school classes at Rutgers make inroads on my time, but I have another month – and then I'll be free to do more writing and reading.

Here is a poem I dictated over the phone to the Poetry Editor of the *N. Y. Times.* The poem starts off rather in a mediocre way, but, near the end, a few lines rescue it somewhat.

Love from
Your father,
Louis

P.S. I read almost 1/3 of Kerouac's book, *The Subterraneans,* but I had to drop it. Lost interest. For me, it is formless and mutilated in its English: wretched, abominable English sentence structure that makes a hodge-podge and mish-mash. Suppose here and there, a telling, vivid phrase floats among the flagellation and confusion and wreck of the English language, yet, on the whole, it did not communicate to me. Maybe, behind it all, hides "his confessional openness," as you say; nevertheless, it's not my meat; confusion compounded with wretched English. I'd flunk any pupil of mine who mangled the language like that. Sorry, but this is my honest opinion.

P.S. Why wait to come home till Summer? How about coming home earlier. I miss you.

L.

Allen Ginsberg to Louis Ginsberg

{Paris}
n.d. {ca. late April 1958}

Dear Lou:

Can't write much, have been preparing mss. for an anthology Grove is bringing out of young poets 1948–1956,[1] looking at old poems of mine & figuring what's best. Will go to England around May 1, give reading there for some small poetry group, $20 pay, Corso go along too for kicks maybe read or record for BBC. "Transmutation"[2] is very good, that's one of the best of your poems recently, I guess a lot of the material you've used before but here all adapted well together & has considerable power. 4th line cater I like 6th line also, 8th line, last 3 best & sharpest for me. Great you could do that on phone.

Happy that you found Corso's book[3] interesting. I was always really impressed by that lost watches[4] too (and similar phrasing in other poems). It's his particular weird gift – an almost surrealist phrasing that makes strange sense. The line means, as I understand it, in context, since he's revisiting unhappy scene of garbage Dirty Ears loss poverty, and sees the same poverty still there, tho he's escaped it, when it's image raises up to attack him (Dirty Ears aims a knife at me), he realizes he's now free, escaped on the road of his own beauty desire thru time, time has passed, he's no longer a kid involved with same ugly conditioning, he's escaped free of the tragedy of Lower East Side, he's aware of death & time, he no longer attacks back with a vicious gun or knife, but pumps him full of lost watches – lost watches being time gone by, realization of mortality, old forgotten contemplations (as the hours of watches on ships) – while Dirty Ears, still caught in the environment, doesn't realize the immense change – the lost

1. Donald M. Allen, ed., *The New American Poetry: 1945–1960* (New York: Grove Press, 1960).
2. See "Out of Any Dearth," LG, *CP*, pp. 257–258.
3. *Gasoline* (San Francisco: City Lights Books, 1958).
4. See Gregory Corso, "Birthplace Revisited," *Gasoline*, p. 31.

watches, then, basically, as human consciousness – achieved by Gregory, denied alas to Dirty Ears who's still hung up. What I like about that is the language and images – the most unpoetic, garbage cans, Lower East Side realities, Dirty Ears, stairways, hand on gate (fantasy of returning a big Italian successful heroic hoodlum – which is, hoodlum of poesy) – all so realistic, and yet thru strange combinations capable of expressing very lucid and eternal thoughts. That's really making poetry of everyday life, the strangeness of the commonplace, writing about real things. He has a peculiar imaginative second-sight. There's another example in the poem "Italian Extravaganza"[1] – the weird almost frightening beauty of "small purplish wrinkled head" – followed by the last two lines, comparison of the small coffin, a cause so small & real, and the 10 immense black Cadillacs of sorrow, almost pathetic the great display from the funeral home. Yet all done without abstraction, in simple images.

In the poem "Coit Tower,"[2] the language is at its most imaginative – the situation is here he, the poet Gregory who was in Jail in youth, is looking down on Alcatraz from a hill: "And I cried there in your dumb hollows O tower (Coit Tower up on Telegraph Hill) clutching my Pan's foot (imagination, life, & consciousness & experience) with vivid hoard of Dannemora" – that seems a line worthy of Dylan Thomas's "Fern Hill." (Dannemora Gregory's prison.) I've cried reading that, his grief & understanding seem so great (underneath his facade of childish egotism).

The sun poem[3] is an experiment at pure wild images without direct sense, just fantastic combinations – they do make a kind of mystic sense actually, since the mind has its own secret language, as in dreams, we're not always aware of the significance of certain compelling phrases – from another poem there is the line "Rose is my wise chair of bombed houses" – which I don't at all understand – but it's a line that haunts me like some of Kubla Khanish mysticdoms. That's poetry. It takes a weird gift to imagine up a wise chair in a bombed house. . . . Spring started here too, a few trees in flower tho it's been chilly last week – I have a cold. Re Jack's prose, well I like it of course, my reason being that it has the same syntactical structure of fast excited spoken talking – this is an interesting event in prose development, and it's no less communicative to me than heard speech, mine, yours, his, – when you speak *you* also talk a little like that, especially when you're moved, excited, angry, or dizzy with happiness etc etc – heightened

1. See Gregory Corso, "Italian Extravanza," *Gasoline,* p. 31.
2. See Gregory Corso, "Ode to Coit Tower," *Gasoline,* pp. 11–13.
3. See Gregory Corso, "Sun," *Gasoline,* pp. 25–26.

speech in other words. Normal conversation does not necessarily follow formal syntax, nor need it as long as it's communicative. So written prose. Perhaps you find it uncommunicated or uncommunicating because you expect to see a different *written* order of syntax. But it actually gets across very well, what he's describing, faithful to his own way of talk. It's obvious from *On Road* or *Town & City* that he can write normal prose, simple & straightforward. So if he writes experimentally one has to give credit for it being you know at least sincere & even intelligent, an approach, a try – most people don't even try – and it isn't as if he hasn't personally sacrificed a lot to pursue his sense of craft – that book was written long ago without a hope of publication – as *On the Road* was written 8 years ago. I do find it interesting though – I know the girl he writes about – who took off her clothes & flipped – I heard her story about it – that was the way she spoke, the syntax even, her style of speaking – a very common style – he's caught her very well – and if you add his interpolations & private thoughts which he records semi-simultaneously with her monologues, & their conversation – you have a very complicated but very real structure of events to try and get down on paper. Hemingway tried simplification & reduction (and was attacked for being too inhumanly stripped down) – Jack trying (as Proust & Céline) to include all the little private thoughts you normally wouldn't mention – so he arrives at a complicated sentence structure. It's not trying to be English sentence structure. It's trying to be American actual speech – and thought – reproduction. So it shouldn't be judged by standards of a high school or college grammar course. It's not meant to be grammatical *that* way, it's meant to be right *another* way. Nor can one say that standard English syntax is the fixed and only standard way of transcribing human thought – all languages have different syntax structures – the Latin ones are one group – the German type inflected is another – and many primitive cultures have approaches to syntax that are almost incomprehensible to us (but make perfect sense to them – no verbs for instance in some languages, no adjectives in others). And there is Chinese syntax which I'm told is of a totally different order from ours. Syntax is only a tool to speak with, there are many syntaxes, & many variations possible to our tongue, common in use even, in talk – English grammar is only the formal way tied to fixed habits of feeling & communication – Jack, broken free of these fixed habits of thought, has to think & write his own way, find a mode. Look at the sentence I just wrote – it's crazy, but it followed the spontaneous convolutions of my thought very flexibly – would I change my thought to fit the sentence structure better, or alter my thought & pare it down neat &

leave out the hesitations, changes, and halts, interruptions, to make it fit a school copybook? I'd wind up writing gibberish if I tried to halt in midstream & box it up neat to fit some imaginary standard. The ideal is for me a sensitive prose or poetry syntax or metric that is practical & follows the changes actually going on in the process of thinking or writing – where a normal metric or syntax works, fine – but where it doesn't apply, why? I no longer worry about that so much – just go my way – that's all any man can do – live – and do what he thinks practical. And real. See now take that last bit, and real, added on to the sentence. I thought it up next and added it – you can follow my actual process of composition – what I mean is there directly no less and no more – I just thought to say, and real, and added it in, just like that. What freedom – and why not? Language is to use not dictate our thoughts. But so much of our lives & feelings are tied down to the limitations of what we're taught – this is the importance of striking out into variation & experiment – this is not nihilism but courage – not really that – Joy! Well I'll end on elevated note. Love to everybody – wrote Gene tonite – will try Warsaw yet see under skirt of Iron Curtain perhaps. There is no Beat Generation it's all a journalist hex.

Love
Allen

Louis Ginsberg to Allen Ginsberg

April 23, 1958

Dear Allen,

I received my copy of *Evergreen Review No. 4*. Did you get your copy? If not, do you want me to send you mine? It contains your long poem, "Siesta in Xbalba." It seems to me a bit too long. There were a number of passages I liked; such as (p. 30) your dreaming back to a gathering at a party; and also, the feeling of ancient times shifting and intermingling with present time (p. 34) (p. 36); and, also, a passage prefiguring your future travels (p. 41). In the same issue, Ferlinghetti gives a review of the trial[1] of your book, with excerpts of comments – all of which, though I read it before, was interesting.

----

1. Lawrence Ferlinghetti, "Horn on Howl," *Evergreen Review* 1, no. 4 (Winter 1957).

I see Ezra Pound was released from the asylum and will go to Italy. The way I look at him is this: in youth, he was a catalytic agent, deanimating the doldrums of feeble poetry. Later, his verse became too cryptic and fragmentarily occult for me; so I became bored with him. Then, when he broadcast anti-Semitism in Italy and supported Hitler in the latter's abominations against the Jews, I despised Pound. Now I say, "Good riddance with Pound and the hell with him!" (I suggest that you do not comment on my attitude toward Pound, as my mind is made up.)

Recently I was invited as a special guest at a luncheon and a reading by Robert Frost at the Paterson State Teachers College. (We did not eat with Frost, since he came in late, just in time for his reading.) I enjoyed Frost: his homely, sage-like wit and wisdom flavored his deceptively simple lyrics with ambiguities and revealing double-meanings. It was all a rare treat.

I sent away for *The Reporter* in which the enclosed article was called to my attention.[1] It's about your Beat Generation. (It did not arrive yet, so I'll send the clipping in my next letter.)

Well, you see, your poetic efforts are in the limelight, whether praised or condemned; nevertheless, the publicity gives you power. Not only the off-beat and the eccentrics but the sleek men in the "Brooks Brothers" suit in All hail O America looks to see what you are doing! Is not all this some cause for affirmative joy, Allen?

Just received your last letter.

About Jack's prose. Syntactical grammar *follows* and is deduced from the best speakers and writers and is not fixed or foisted on communication. It assists in clarity of communication. See Proust's sentences with other sinuosities and interpolations and simultaneities, as well as Henry James' language, wherein, like a coiling serpent, his sentence squeezes out nuances and shades of meaning.

I will half-allow you your explanation of the fluidities and looseness of syntax wherein the stream of consciousness intermingles and interfuses with the outer, formal thought; but here, nevertheless, there must be enough

1. Eugene Burdick, "The Innocent Nihilists Adrift in Squaresville" *Reporter*, April 3, 1958.

clues and transitions to communicate. I feel Kerouac's pell-mell, tumultuous chaotic style does not yield communicative clarity. Carried just one degree more, and Kerouac's style becomes the confused outpouring of echolalea or the obscure outpouring of a disturbed person in a sanitarium.

Another thing: art is inescapably artifice; the arbitrary imitating fluidity for the sake of clear communication; otherwise, you have a clueless chaos. All art is arbitrary and fix form to simulate flow; else, you have the unstaunched disorders from a dictionary. All art is arrangement (see W. C. Williams). I feel that Kerouac, in his latest book, is too much disjointed and chaotic for me. The masters in writing have used the sentence but have varied it and given it such flexibility that in their own unique way they *seem* free and yet communicate. Limitations in art provide opportunities for exciting adventures in expression. Even Liberty needs laws for wise direction; else, "could a river be?"

More anon.

Love,
Louis

I received an invitation from the nominating committee to be on the Exec. Board of the Poetry Society of America; but I had to turn it down, since I teach at Rutgers those nights they meet. Well, I guess I'll teach at Rutgers for two years more; then I'll retire from all teaching (I'll be 65 then) and devote most of my time to writing.

Another thought: the English sentence is a marvelously flexible structure: by its various participles, phrases, subordinate clauses, etc., a writer can obtain variety and subtlety and relationship of thought. What Kerouac does – and you often do – is to keep on tacking short sentence after sentence at an interminable succession; until you destroy your ideas. Because all your ideas are of the same importance like a child's continual repetition of "and" and "and," you blur your clarity and damage your communication. Personally and frankly, I think it's a bad way to write. What saves Kerouac is his vividness of a phrase jumping up out of the text. I'm inclined to feel that, in his last book – as one writer declared – Kerouac is a vivid eye recording impressions but not connecting them with his brain.

You are not so bad as Kerouac but your method of obliterating the sentence structure blurs your clarity. No, I don't buy your method of interminably tacking on sentence after sentence *ad infinitum*.

As I said in the other paper, art is arrangement and selection and maneuvering of words for the best effect. Your method you think is real: I think it's an easy way out. You are saved by the vehemence of your ideas and the vividness of your phrases or the felicity of your words – but you move against obstacles that *damage* rather than *strengthen* your utterances.

Louis

Allen Ginsberg to Louis Ginsberg

{Paris}
May 24, 1958

Dear Lou:

Thanks for letters and articles, the J. D. Adams a fine harvest. Strange to be there. Thought that the sentence he quoted from Kerouac contradicted his remarks on the prose, it's a good sentence by my lights, for reasons aforementioned – & the sharp picture of the junky girl. While in England, read the same sort of article in last Sunday's *Observer* by John Wain, an "Angry Young Man" attack on me & Jack with lots of quotes, which satisfies me fine, as long as they keep quoting. Had a fine time in England tho as usual wound up broke & hungry at midnight at pavement on Piccadilly one evening – rescued by one David Archer, who fed us & gave us a little money for poetry's sake – he published first Dylan Thomas & Barker & Gasgoyne – showed us around London literary society & so got great glimpse of remnants of the Thomas era & his friends, & George Barker saw much of in Soho pubs – also I passed out a few anti A-bomb leaflets for fun, they were having a lobby of Parliament led by surrealists, & anarchists. Saw more of England than last time, also, as I probably wrote, went to lunch at a ladies club with Edith Sitwell & had tea and a walk with Auden at Oxford – better time this time, he lone & sad away from Ischia, more approachable & friendly – in fact heard that at a party later he said he'd been out of sorts & had acted evil with me at Ischia – so I gave him a copy of Artaud poems (great modern dead Frenchman) that he'd never read – madhouse poetry sort of. And met all the teddy boys and bebop hoodlums & angels around Soho – one particular fellow named Adam, with a *Mad* comics What-Me-Worry? face & porkpie hat 17 years old, works in the complaint department of a pajama factory & spoke six languages & was translating a small play of Brecht, a lower class East End kid, speaks an exaggerated US bebop hiptalk swears & wears teddy boy clothes – weirdest character I found there. So it was a great trip & the readings were OK.

Still here in Paris, doesn't look like Warsaw trip will materialize so thinking about heading home in a month or so. Have to raise fare back still, I don't know how but expect it will turn up by magic so to speak sooner or later. Getting nostalgic for home & NY & see everybody – so be back this summer sometime – July probably. Burroughs in psychoanalysis here so may stay longer; and Gregory will stay on, he has no home to go to anyway & likes Europe. Or maybe they'll come back around summer or fall too, nobody has any definite plans. Gregory working on an anthology of young US poetry for some Germans who offered him a house in Goettingen so he may go there soon & settle down for as long as he can hold on. Discovered another writer living downstairs from us, 20 years old & very sharp kid, finished a novel with interesting prose, tho kind of unjelled novel, but brilliant for someone so young, sort of Salinger like.

Nothing's happening in Paris – I mean about the Revolt, politics, except a few day potato shortage – not seen the massed cops & missed what small riots there were – appearance of everything the same as before – everybody shrugs and laughs at the politics that seems to be going on somewhere else. Very safe here. No action at all.

3rd stanza of "Pond"[1] very good, I didn't dig "Love Song" too much; "The Quarrel" seemed the best, very funny tho, or was it age, interjection & repeat. The sharpness of the poem is somewhat lamed by the seems-to-me trite inversion "no more will I flout you" & dull rhyme that follows, & flat moral. I thought the poem excellent but found the end not excellent as the idea & phrasing of all the rest. What you think? As Williams once said, "in this mode perfection is basic." Enclosed find the clippings. "Quarrel" is one of the best of your poems, can it be fixed up?

I'm writing a little but not well or anything, mostly automatic rambling. I wonder what NY will be like on return. It'll be hard to keep some kind of non commercial, non hypocritical social, non bullshit balance – pressure all the time to do this or that, for money, or position, or ego. But it should be a great happy ball & I'll meet a lot of strange people. I think need for making money

1. See "Pond," LG, *CP*, p. 318.

some kind of interesting way to be a good path – might take up acting, bit parts or something. I won't be reading much. Hear there's a great deal of it in Village now. Well, later. I'm snowed under as usual with letters & trying to get them all at once. Paris lovely & green right now and weather warm, I bought some white sneakers & new bluegrey teashirt & French Levis. Still torn corduroy black coat. Did you ever receive the *Genet* book I sent by mail 2 months ago? Or was it seized by the Customs? I'll send Henry Miller next.

Love
Allen

Louis Ginsberg to Allen Ginsberg

June 4, 1958

Dear Allen,

I was glad to receive your letter dated May 24.

Found your account of English trip interesting, what with the inter-mixture of weird characters and poets of fame.

Thanks for your strictures on my poems you returned. I must say they (the poems) are not of my best. It's puzzling that some of my best poems – poems that won prizes, etc. – keep going on the rounds without any acceptances. I have faith in them, though, and feel that eventually they will see light of day.

Here is a clipping of a review of a book on *The Beat Generation and the Angry Young Men.* I ordered the book and will save it for you. I'm saving, in a bookshelf in the cellar, all the Allen Ginsberg data, clippings, etc.

Also, here is a comic with reference to the Beat Generation!

This Sunday we are having our annual Ginsberg Picnic of the whole family. Expect about 35 people. Wish you were here.

In July, when you are ready to come home, write me whether you need fare home. Between Eugene and me, we'll gather the funds. Let me know what it will cost. Or, could you work your way by boat? I'll speak with Eugene about the latter.

Did you receive my birthday gift of ten dollars to you to arrive on June 3? Happy Birthday again!!!!

All is quiet here. In three weeks, school is over. Tra-la!!
I miss you.

Love from
Your father,
Louis

P.S. I see, out of the confusion and turmoil in France, de Gaulle will try to bring order from chaos. It seems to me – as are many things in life – it was a choice of the lesser evil.

Write soon again.

P.S.S. Yes, I received the Genet book. Rather scabrous. I didn't care for it much. Sorry.

Allen Ginsberg to Louis Ginsberg

9 *Git le Coeur*
Paris 6
June 4, 1958

Dear Lou:

Your letter & 10$ on June 3. Thanks, I went out had drink at ritzy bar on Champs Elysées, I seldom otherwise get to.

Well looks like the whole French scene is permanently cooled, and everything worked out alright, with de Gaulle who, if he continues as he presently announces – some kind of large concession to Algerian democracy – will solve the whole problem. Cops still all over the street but no real opposition – the left wing has nothing to complain about since de Gaulle's program is more liberal than that of the socialists (who supported the war – great shame) – and the communists here still grumbling but they have no other program than a civil war for the same goals which he proposes to get bloodlessly. . . . The lesson, if any, or among the lessons, is that the left wing here sort of bankrupt & the right wing lunatic, & the moderates sensible – if de Gaulle can be called a moderate – tho he's more an independent who just kept out of the whole idiot tangle – as if maybe 500 people created an entirely artificial war situation which lasted for years and years & involved the whole nation, with both sides wrong, Algerian Rebels

& French Army – all cleared up in a few days with some simple sensible arrangements. I hope de Gaulle tackles Russia with the same lucidity – break the East-West deadlock which seems a similar piece of artificial lunacy on both sides as I've been trying to say.

Spent day typing up some Burroughs mss. for *Chicago Review* – they offer to publish him complete at last if no one else will – so he's recasting material in form acceptable to US censorship.[1]

Everything here fine, lots of people around. I'm casting around now for some way to get home, soon as I can. Problem is boat ticket, or get job on ship. Haven't figured a way yet but something usually has turned up & will again. As I think I wrote I should be back in July sometime. Earlier if an opportunity rises earlier . . . ship out of Rotterdam or something like that . . . What'd Eugene do for birthday, spend day home or go to Paterson?

Got $20 for BBC rebroadcast of some poems, and made another tape of "Sunflower [Sutra]" there, with Gregory also, when there, so have more coming in . . . also sold some poems there & will try to get something in the *Paris Review* here – the editor came by yesterday looking for material, so that looks possible. Said he had wanted to ask before, but Donald Hall edited poetry & was against the idea I guess – now try to bypass him – this being one revolution I'm in favor of. Was told some conservative gent wrote *Partisan* (a man who edits a new criticism art magazine & writes art for them) & protested their publishing Gregory (& presumably me) on the ground it vulgarizes the mag. All sorts of attacks in English papers also, rather like J. Donald Adams attitude. Almost like a dream (fortunately not nitemare) to see these types who have always been anti-Pound-Eliot-etc-experimental now come out with same sort of protestations against work I'm living through – rather like a pleasant dream in which the world shrinks as I get older – and what suspicions & intuitions I had when younger confirmed by subsequent experience. Adams always did bug me. But all the publicity is fine, and will only bankrupt the squares in the end, as far as I can see. Not that Squaredom will ever exhaust its maniacal energy. I begin to see why Pound wound up paranoiac. *Pogo* at least has sense of humor.[2]

---

1. The selections from *Naked Lunch,* published in the Fall 1958 issue of *Chicago Review,* set off a furious controversy. The magazine's editors intended to publish other excerpts in the Winter 1958 issue, but officials from the University of Chicago, which sponsored the magazine, refused to allow it. Six of the magazine's editors resigned in protest, and a new "underground" magazine, *Big Table,* published by former *Chicago Review* editors Irving Rosenthal and Paul Carroll, printed the excerpts.

2. The satirical cartoon strip had poked fun at the Beat Generation.

I notice new style by younger writers 20–24 yr olds – in *Measure* &
elsewhere – a sort of clipped laconic syntactical change – avoidance of
angelic bullshit I indulge in – speech pared down to very hip conversational
stoicism almost – almost incomprehensible, since they never finish sentences artificially, just break off with a dash or . . . when first idea of the
phrase is written down – and move on to the next perception – difficult
reading – but there is I think-beginnings of another "generation" of poesy –
and a new style. I'll write later.

Love,
Allen

I've been reading thru Vachel Lindsey's complete poems – some Negro
rhythms very original & great – "Santa Fe Trail" I like.

1959

Allen Ginsberg to Louis Ginsberg

Allen Ginsberg
c/o City Lights
261 Columbus Ave
San Francisco, California
May 12, 1959

Dear Louis:

[. . .] Busy organizing poesy activities & reading. Spender[1] heard me read "Kaddish" & objected to the intrusion of personal material. But then he dropped in on Parkinson's office in Berkeley & said he hadn't been able to forget it & had begun writing (for the first time in years of dryspell) poems with personal material. Then he came by Parkinson again and asked him to ask me to send it to him to print in *Encounter*. Took him about a week to hear it & get the point & accept the possibility of that kind of poetry – very good to hear that he did finally see. Unfortunately the poem's already promised out.

Horrible in-group article in *Partisan* by Diana Trilling[2] – rather self-smug & bitchy & all balled up psychologically. She's trying to be sympathetic too. Rather embarrassing her mistaking that "Lion for Real"[3] poem as a "love" poem to [Lionel] Trilling. I dedicated it to him as a sort of ironic gesture since he's the Analyst or Professor who sees "no value" in the experience of the Lion which is supposed to be God, not Lionel Trilling as she apparently mistook it. Rather ugly mistake, I must say.

1. Poet Stephen Spender.
2. Diana Trilling's essay, "The Other Night at Columbia" (*Partisan Review*, Spring 1959), was a report of a reading by Allen Ginsberg, Gregory Corso, and Peter Orlovsky at Columbia University on February 5, 1959.
3. See "The Lion for Real," AG, *CP*, p. 174.

I got a check for $450 from Kerouac's Agent for my part in collaborating with Jack on an article for *Holiday*. Good deal. Now I have some money and can come home slowly & see the Grand Canyon. Half of it's Peter's who also worked on the article tho.

The weather here is beautiful – you ought to visit here some day – bright blue sky like North Africa on a nice day.

Here are some portions of the "Kaddish" that are ready, I don't think you've seen these. They are extensions of the rhythmic organization I began in "Howl [Part] III." This not the final version but near it. The Caw Caw Caw section is like a fugue with two parts that meet & harmonize in the last line – which is a very weird line. Built on the structure of a fugue, like Bach. The "With your eyes" section is an extension of the stanza shape-form of "Howl [Part] III," used sort of as a stanza, it builds up 3 times & the third it diminishes back down. I sent these sections to *Yugen*.

We are doing a benefit reading to finance *Measure* mag here for another issue. Wieners is a good kid, but no money & not a businessman.

What's happening with you, & Gene? I sent him a postcard. Love to the family, to Edith & to you,

Love
Allen

Staying here at Phil Whalen's apartment, eat at Chinatown cheap in evenings.

Louis Ginsberg to Allen Ginsberg

May 14, 1959

Dear Allen,

Was glad indeed to hear from you.

Thanks for your sending me the section of "Kaddish."

I like it very much; it is nostalgic and poignant; some lines are heart-wrenching, what with not only you but me being at that time in the middle of the anguish. Some of the lines are poetically magnificent and imaginatively vivid.

I do object to one line: about the "beard about the vagina." It's bad taste and offends my sensibilities. Also, to a lesser degree, I have

Dear Louis—   March 20, 1959

Got your letter & poems, which I return as per instructions.
They are all fine. What happened with Indiana? I 'm o.k., I will
be here another few weeks, then start home slowly, overland. I went down
to Stanford Univ. the other day to be subjected to a research
experiment with a new drug— LSD-25 (Lysergic Acid)
which Huxley described in his books Doors of Perception & Heaven & Hell.
It was astounding— I lay back, listening to music, & went into a
sort of Trance state (somewhat similar to the high state of Laughing
Gas). and in a fantasy much like a Coleridge a old of Kubla Khan—
saw a vision of that part of my consciousness which seemed
to be permanent & transcendent and identical with the origin
of the universe — a sort of identity common to everything —but
a Clear & Coherent sight of it. Rather beautiful visual images
also, of Hindu-Type Gods dancing on themselves. This drug seems
to automatically produce a mystical experience. Science is getting
very hip. It's a very safe drug— you ought to Contact someone
at Rutgers who's doing experiments with it & try it— like a
Cosmic Movie.

The line about the "beard around the vagina" is probably
a sort of very Common experience & image that Children have who
see their parents naked & it is an archtypal experience & nothing
to be ashamed of — it looks from the outside, objectively, probably
much less shocking than it appears to you I think—it's a universal
experience which almost everyone has had tho not many poets
have referred to it but it can do no harm to be brought to Consciousness

Caw Caw I still rather like since it's the Climax of a sort of musical form, a fugue — two themes (Caw Caw & Lord Lord — representing realistic bleakness- pain materialism, versus Lord Lord which is mystical aspiration) that alternate and in the last line merge into one cry. I've read it aloud here & it sounds alright,

I'll be here till around June 1 (I'm going back to Stanford then for another bout with the Lysergic acid) and then see if I can find someone with a car driving east — would like to see the Southwest & Grand Canyon on the way home.

The Jet plane ride here (5 hours) was like a movie of Topographical Geography.

This Saturday all the poets get together to give a reading to raise money to resuscitate Measure magazine & so that it'll be on its feet again at least for another issue.

Partisan asked me to reply to Diana T's article but I am busy with other worlds so I'll shut up & let things take their own course. Hope you are o.k. & having nice springtime

Love, Allen

reservations about all those "caw caws," though you might have something there.

Eugene is O.K. as well as his brood. They were here one afternoon, and we enjoyed the antics of the children.

Nothing much new about me. Pupils from Clifton H.S. and Barringer H.S. in Newark are doing terms papers about my poetry; the Rutgers Alumni monthly is doing an interview of me shortly. I sent on the ms. of my third book of poems to the Indiana University Press about two weeks ago to Mr. Bernard Perry but have not yet heard their decision.

I miss you and hope you are having a good time.

Write me more.

Love from your father,
Louis

P.S. Yes, I read Diana Trilling's article in the *Partisan Review*. Frankly, I did not think it was so bad as you make it out to be. Too bad about her mistake about the Lion poem.

Allen Ginsberg to Louis Ginsberg

{San Francisco, California}
March 20, 1959[1]

Dear Louis —

Got your letter & poems, which I return as per instructions. They are all fine. What happened with Indiana? I'm OK, I will be here another few weeks, then start home slowly, overland. I went down to Stanford Univ. the other day to be subjected to a research experiment with a new drug — LSD-25 (Lysergic Acid) which Huxley [2]described in his books *Doors of Perception & Heaven & Hell*. It was astounding — I lay back, listening to music, & went into a sort of trance state (somewhat similar to the high state of Laughing Gas) and in a fantasy much like a Coleridge World of Kubla Khan saw a vision of that part of my consciousness which seemed to be permanent

1. AG misdated this letter. It was actually written on May 20, 1959.
2. Aldous Huxley, novelist and early pioneer in psychedelic drugs.

transcendent and identical with the origin of the universe – a sort of identity common to everything – but a clear & coherent sight of it. Rather beautiful visual images also, of Hindu-type gods dancing on themselves. This drug seems to automatically produce a mystical experience. Science is getting very hip. It's a very safe drug – you ought to contact someone at Rutgers who's doing experiments with it & try it – like a cosmic movie.

The line about the "beard around the vagina" is probably a sort of very common experience & image that children have who see their parents naked & it is an archetypal experience & nothing to be ashamed of – it looks from the outside, objectively, probably much less shocking than it appears to you I think – it's a universal experience which almost everyone has had tho not many poets have referred to it but it can do no harm to be brought to consciousness.

Caw Caw I still rather like since it's the climax of a sort of musical form, a fugue – two themes (Caw Caw & Lord Lord – representing realistic bleakness-pain-materialism, versus Lord Lord which is mystical aspiration) that alternate and in the last line merge into one *cry*. I've read it aloud here & it sounds alright.

I'll be here till around June 1 (I'm going back to Stanford then for another bout with the Lysergic Acid) and then see if I can find someone with a car driving east – would like to see the Southwest & Grand Canyon on the way home.

The Jet plane ride here (5 hours) was like a movie of Topographical Geography.

This Saturday all the poets get together to give a reading to raise money to resuscitate *Measure* magazine & so that'll be on its feet again at least for another issue.

Partisan asked me to reply to Diana T's article but I am busy with other worlds so I'll shut up & let things take their own course. Hope you are O.K. & having nice springtime.

Love,
Allen

Louis Ginsberg to Allen Ginsberg

May 24, 1959

Dear Allen

Glad to get your letter of May 20.

I showed your sections of the KADDISH poem to Eugene who liked it, especially the last two parts. I think, on reconsideration, that the line "Caw Caw and Lord Lord" are good: the unity of the assonance and the contrasting implications of the two names do hover above the grave.

However, I still have reservations about the "beard. . . ." It still offends my taste, and I object to it. Definitely. But the decision is yours. . . . In words, begin responsibilities. . . .

The other day I read an item in the *N. Y. Times*. It seems that a group of Americans, including some teachers and their wives, were surrounded in Kremlin Square by some Russians. Amid a host of various questions, suddenly was asked, "What do you think of Kerouac and Ginsberg, of the Beat Generation?"

Irrelevant, to me, was the answer by the Americans: "They are not high on our list." My own comment is that it is wonderful that your name has spread to such far-flung regions. I am happy about it.

That was an interesting experiment you had with Lysergic acid. I have heard about it. I think Waugh mentions it in one of his narrative books. Well, the fantasy in which you floated and on which you were borne on some mysterious waves to some transcendental first source is a mystical experience. My own opinion is that the drug chloroforms the consciousness and that the subconscious into which have poured and have been deposited sensory impressions during your life floats up and swarms up into a heterogeneously intermingled surge. Yet, these are all but sensations originally sunken into the mind from THIS LIFE. Science knows of no other.

The only other explanation, according to Jung, might be that these floating impressions might be some archetypal remnants from the racial subconscious sleeping in the genes. About the latter, I should like to consult some scientific expert on human biology. Meanwhile, why not enjoy the sensation and extract some poetry from the illusion?

I have not heard from Mr. Bernard Perry of the Indiana University Press. He has had it about a month now.

If you see Wieners, give him my regards. He is holding a poem of mine, called "Still Life,"[1] about the atmosphere in 324 Hamilton Ave. when you were in college, Eugene was away in the army, and I was surrounded by ghosts. . . .

Regards, too, to Ferlinghetti. Have him send me a catalogue of his new issues; I'd like to order some that interest me.

Take care of yourself.

Love from
Your father,
Louis

Allen Ginsberg to Louis Ginsberg

{New York City}
n.d. {ca. late October 1959}

To My Father in Poetry

As often, on the phonograph, in youth
I heard your voice half tremble near a rose,
some image of eternity . . . the nasal hall
of ancient colleges . . . and heartbreak knows

at last what Hebrews in a row
moan in a Synagogue thru endless time
. . . up to the wall, here on the New York street
full of Puerto Ricans . . . and your aptest rhyme

can not bring back that knowledge to the mind
that has forgot . . . What lightning on the jagged mount?
What woman weeping in a long grey hall?
I can't account

For all my hatred of the forms you used
knowing full well the bags of intestines & eyes
the lungs and sputum classrooms of the grave
all the experience that brought you to your sighs.

1. See "Still Life," LG, *CP*, p. 253.

Father, I read you in an ancient book
and as you prophesied I know you best
and love you most when the last page is turned
and hear the echo of your soul in my own breast
and night is quiet, and I have forgot the rest.

notebooks 1958

Dear Lou —

Here is a strange deformed rhymed poem I wrote in 5 minutes one night last year after reading thru the book of Jewish poetry. Thought it would please you, tho some of it is awkward & obscure.

Love,
Allen

Everything is fine, working thru some notebook material on that politics poem —[1]

Louis Ginsberg to Allen Ginsberg

October 23, 1959

Dear Allen,

Thanks for sending me the poem of yours called "To My Father in Poetry."

A minor demur: Why should you hate the forms I use? The house of poetry contains many mansions, among them regular forms and free verse ones. Poetry is where poetry is. To exclude regular forms which the bulk of the best poets of times present and past have used only mutilates the fundamentals of poetry.

As to the main idea of your poem, it is a valid and seems a true one; namely, there is something to the fact that my soul does echo in yours. (Little did I know, when I wrote my poem, "To My Two Sons,"[2] about thirty or so years ago in a dinky, dilapidated room with tawdry furnishings in James St., near the Newark Library, that my lines were prescient and prophetic of a dark note in our future years!)

1. Most likely "Europe! Europe!" (See AG, *CP*, p. 171.)
2. See "To My Two Sons," LG, *CP*, p. 144.

Glad to hear you are busy working at your poems.

We enjoyed our stay with you at your place. Frankly, I feel that, however dingy a place it might be – even less dingy than the one I had in James Street memories ago – what really counted and counts is the glow of creative poetic activity that illuminates the place and transforms it to a happy habitation for the soul's endeavors.

By the way, did you see Eugene's poem in today's *N. Y. Times*? I'll save a copy for you, in case you missed it.

Love a-plenty from
Your father,
Louis

Louis Ginsberg to Allen Ginsberg

Saturday morning, November 21 {1959}

Dear Allen,

I obtained some copies of the *London Times Lit. Supplement* and saw your poem.[1] Congratulations! I am proud of you. The poem is a feature!

My own poem, I was surprised, did not appear in the issue. Could they have taken it for a subsequent regular number?

Let me give you my reaction to your poem. First, what did not appeal to me. There was no punctuation nor any sentence structure to guide the reader; then, no transitions to help the readers, for heterogeneous images crowded nilly-willy upon each other in unrelated fashion. Then, too, some parts of it were obscure: the metaphors were, for me, not clear. What does "Death to Van Gogh's Ear" mean? I realize that your mode is semi-surrealistic and has a validity, but, candidly, it is not my cup of tea.

Besides, some lines, as "nobody publishes a word that is not cowardly robot ravings of a depraved mentality," are not true. Really, nobody publishes anything worthwhile? Only you?

Now, on the good side. You have mixed in the smoke and fury some startling, imaginative images flashing out! True poetic genius! Bravo! I like also such a sage statement as government will fail but not the country. Then again, your fiery indictment of the God of money

---

1. "Death to Van Gogh's Ear," *Times Literary Supplement*, November 6, 1959. (See AG, *CP*, pp. 167–171.)

is a good and valid one. All in all, your poem, in general, is a lusty, fiery, energetic, modern outcry and diatribe, a slashing, burning jeremiad against the false god of money! The poem should add laurels to your world-wide reputation.

I look forward to seeing you on Thanksgiving Day, Thursday.

Pride and love from
Your father,
Louis

Louis Ginsberg to Allen Ginsberg

December 27, 1959

Dear Allen,

What did the doctor say about your illness? Let me know, as soon as it is convenient for you to phone.

I missed you after you left.

It was good to exchange ideas with you. While our methods in writing poetry may differ, we both aim at the central ideal of greater awareness, deeper insight, and richer delight in the astonishing phenomenon of life. You use the outpouring, torrent-like, telescoping, run together semi-surrealistic line; while I use the compressed, controlled traditional (fundamental) line. But both aim at the flashing revelation of the metaphor with its lightning of delight.

About your view of old about Hunky[1] [*sic*]: I am not unaware of a certain nobility of your concept of love (a central and divine principle of the world). Yet such is the inertia of society and its laws (made for the greatest good, the greatest number) that, as a father, I don't want my son to get hurt. I like a statement Roosevelt once made: "I sometimes compromise in certain matters in order to be present in the future to be able to decide on a greater matter."

When you'll have a son, you'll see the feeling I have.

(Parenthetically, does the fact that one writes a book entitle him to break fundamental laws? May one steal or rape because he has a good command of

language or writes a book? I'm thinking still about your attitude to Hunky
once.)

Love.
Your father,
Louis

P.S. I was lonesome for you, after you left.

---

1. Herbert Huncke, the Times Square hustler and petty thief befriended by Allen, William Burroughs, and others. Allen's association with Huncke led to Allen's arrest in 1948, and while Louis Ginsberg found it difficult to forgive Huncke for his role in Allen's arrest, Allen had no such problem, and he continued to see him (and help him), from time to time, over the next three decades.

1960

In mid-January 1960, Allen arrived in Chile, where he and Lawrence Ferlinghetti participated in a writers' conference at the University of Concepción. Not surprisingly, Allen decided to take advantage of his being flown to South America, and, for the better part of the next six months, he visited Chile, Argentina, Bolivia, and Peru. Years earlier, William Burroughs had told him of a hallucinogenic drug called ayahuasca, or yage, supposedly the most powerful hallucinogen naturally available, and Allen was eager to visit the Amazon region and try the drug himself.

Allen Ginsberg to Louis Ginsberg

{Santiago, Chile}
March 8, 1960

I'll be in Peru in 2 weeks so write me there c/o US Embassy, Lima

Dear Louis:

Got your letter & poems, now back in Santiago staying with a poet Nicanor Parra. My checks from City Lights have been (as usual in traveling) delayed or lost in transit and so am waiting here another week till my mail gets straightened out, then I'll fly up to La Paz, Bolivia. My planeticket expired, so I am giving a lecture at Univ of Chile this Friday to make up the $40 necessary to extend the planeticket. I'll be gone another month then, between Peru and Bolivia. Everything is fine here, I crossed over to Argentina and saw a lot of Andes and some very marvelous lake landscape – tho didn't go far beyond the Argentine Barriloche town on the border. I eat lunch here daily in the poet's cafe & meet a lot of famous old Chilean literateurs & veterans of ancient literary latinamerican wars, notably one Pablo de Rokha. Will visit [Pablo] Neruda this week too. Parra is professor of Newtonian Mechanics & had studied at Oxford, a very intelligent and sympatico man, & good poet – City Lights put out a book of bad translations of his work. "Kaddish" is getting translated here too, so I'll probably have a second book out here. Meanwhile all's well & I'm getting familiar with the scene somewhat like SF & my Spanish is improving. Conditions for writing letters are very difficult – am downtown usually daytimes, and nights there are no lights to write by, so will not send many letters for a week or so. I'll write from La Paz next probably. I'm fine, hope you're well. I must say the communists here are very strong and much more interesting than in the States – mainly because here there are outstanding labor & hunger problems, the masses are poor, and the Reds seem to be the only active party interested in actually changing the situation. Saw Eisenhower on the street here & heard a speech he gave to American Colony in a theater – he got mixed up in middle of a sentence answering a student union open letter & talked weird.

OKOKOKOK LOVE
Allen

Louis Ginsberg to Allen Ginsberg

May 14, 1960

Dear Allen,

Received your card of May 5 and am glad you are well.

I miss you here and wonder when you will get back.

Still, I feel that your sojourn in S. America should be salutary for your health, seeping in the quiet rural atmosphere and being away from the hectic N.Y. scene.

Ellie Dorfman[1] writes me often and keeps me informed of the garde scene. She sent me Don Allen anthology *The New American Poetry* in which you are, of course, included.[2] Have you seen the volume?

Meanwhile, your name is accumulating more fame. The April's *Reader's Digest* had a condensation from a *Life* story; and a book, *The Beat Scene*,[3] will

---

1. Elsa Dorfman, photographer and friend of both Allen and Louis Ginsberg.
2. The anthology contained a large selection of Allen's work: "The Shrouded Stranger," "Malest Cornifici Tuo Catullo," "Sunflower Sutra," "A Supermarket in California," "Howl," "Sather Gate Illumination," "Message," "Kaddish" (an excerpt), and "Notes for *Howl and Other Poems*."
3. Elias Wilentz ed., *The Beat Scene* (New York: Corinth Books, 1960).

appear soon. I presume you know about it. I am saving all the Allen Ginsberg data for you.

Nothing new here. I am busy, at this time, with heavy school chores; college examinations are in the offing; book reports. Still, I see the end of the tunnel. I have set the date of my retirement on January 31, 1961. In other words, I have one more term – which will mark forty years that I have been at CHS.

Edith is working, as you may know: she gets bored staying home. Harold is the perennial scholar, living in N.Y. and attending Columbia. Eugene and Connie are OK. Tomorrow we shall run in and visit them. Otherwise, things are running in the same old way.

I may have Dave Haselwood of Auerhahn do a book of poems for me. I have enough poems for two books. In a few weeks, when I can concentrate on it, I'll pick out some of my best poems published and unpublished, in and out of my *Morning in Spring* ms. So I may have two volumes ready: one Auerhahn will get out and the other will be making the rounds till something fortunate strikes. What think you? Ellie Dorfman seems to be my unofficial agent or mediator or go-between.

Write me a long letter and tell me how you are and when you plan to come home and what you are writing.

> Regards from Edith.
> Love from your father
> Louis

Louis Ginsberg to Allen Ginsberg

May 21, 1960

Dear Allen,

Glad indeed to get your card and to read of your insatiable zest for travel and adventure. You might as well take it all in and absorb it while you are still unimpeded and are on the scene.

Did anyone send you a copy of *The Beat Scene*? The articles and the prose exposition are not the best, but the profuse pictures – you're everywhere – make the book interesting. I'm saving you a copy, as well as other material that crops up about you.

How does it feel to be world-famous? I am very proud and happy about it!

All's quiet here. I have a few more weeks of paper work for my teaching; and then I'll get down to the business of sifting my poems to get out the very best volume I can for Dave Haselwood of the Auerhahn Press. He writes to Miss Ellie Dorfman that he keeps looking forward to issuing a volume of my poetry.

We miss you here and talk about you often. Hope you get back soon and tell me all about your adventures. Hope you'll stay here with me for a spell.

Absorb the peace there and let it heal you.

Love from
Your father,
Louis

Allen Ginsberg to Louis Ginsberg

Huanuco, Peru
c/o US Embassy
Lima, Peru
June 2, 1960

Dear Louis

Forgive my spareness in writing, but occupied traveling, what quiet hours I get I try to write in journals or poetry. Now stuck in a small town on way to jungle & writing letters finally – wrote Eugene Birthday letter too today. Enclosed a lousy photo from Lima newspaper. I had given a good poetry reading here & will have a small book of translations published here too – so they take pictures of my beard whenever they can.

I'm delighted you accepted Haselwood's offer – it's a very good deal, and I'm getting a book out with him too, later. Give him the best book you can – I mean the cream of crop. If many copies sell, that's all to your credit. If few copies sell, you can *always* reprint the good poems in a hardback book. So there's no point *not* putting best foot forward. I got a ton of letters from Ellie Dorfman – I wrote her back but I'm sure not what she wanted to hear. [. . .] But the point of Haselwood press is, that good & discriminating poets do see it. I hope I get back in time to see your mss. & make sure you don't hold out your pearls. – Not seen *Beat Scene* but am so far away it's only a nightmare, all that bad journalism. I'll see it when I get back.

The solitude been very good – this afternoon took a nap & heard in a dream some very strange Divine Music. Being "world-famous" is a minor childplay compared to the beauty & terror of what I can guess of the nature of the universe. That is to say, most of my conscious activity is concerned with that obscure part of the mind which connects with the Creator. I am more & more convinced I'll wind up studying mind-control in India for a few years, later. Meanwhile been writing a lot & studying Inca & pre-Inca archeology, & gotten interested in funerary urns and ceramics which is an extensive field here & not much known. The ceramic (pots & pottery sculpture including representational portraits 2000 years ago) arts here were as highly developed as any civilization in the world before Christ's time. I'll bring back some samples.

Give my regards to Hannah & family, & Clara and kids, & Grandma, if she's in any condition to remember. And Abe, if he's in any condition etc.

I got copy of Don Allen's anthology – it's pretty good but there are some gaps – the *Creeley* selection is poor & the poems difficult so Creeley's charm doesn't come thru. The Kerouac section is too small and scanty. And Gregory Corso's selection is not his best poems, like "Bomb" & "Power." Have you seen Corso's new book?[1] – Did *Reader's Digest* repeat that story about Edith Sitwell? I saw a letter she wrote correcting *Life,* but R.D. probably took no note of that. – Well, delighted that you're done with school next year. Maybe if we all have time we can drive down to Mexico or fly.

I repeat, please select the very best for Auerhahn – they can be reprinted in a collected works, or a hardback volume later if you're not satisfied with Auerhahn sales and splash. But the book *won't make no splash* if you give him secondary work & hold *out* your gems for some future fantasy – publisher – because publishers are (1.) hard to get (2.) stupid. Have a ball with *this* book. Forget about tomorrow.

Enclosed the clippings of poems 1. "Golden Morning" – *All* golden is trite for you, i.e. you've used that trick. Why not make an image, leaves golden, or *sun* golden, etc. [. . .] 2. "Autumn Leaf"[2] is one of the best poems – almost perfect I'd say except for possibility that the particularization or individualization of *The Leaf,* a leaf, is slightly lacking – some local color – perhaps in place of "a fragile, wafted" – a red veined leaf, a brown dry – some visual focus on the *image* of the leaf itself. I dunno. However the poem is quite exquisite. 3. "The Kiss" less deep – tho reminds me of Donne style.

I'm running out of paper. Enclosed two poems. Love to you as always. I'll be seeing you soon – another month to finish with the jungle & a few

1. *Happy Birthday of Death* (New York: New Directions, 1960).
2. See "Autumn Leaf on a Pool," LG, *CP,* pp. 225–226.

things I want to look up there – local witch-doctors & herbs. I'm all OK and feel fine & sitting at table in bar downstairs from my 40¢ a nite hotel room in small town.

Love,
Yr Son,
Allen

I'll be back in Lima in 2 or 3 weeks – write me there.

Louis Ginsberg to Allen Ginsberg

June 10, 1960

Dear Allen,

Glad indeed to get your letter and to find out how you are.

You say nothing about earthquakes. How far are you from them?

Yes, I've resolved that I'll put my best foot forward with Auerhahn Press. I wonder why Haselwood wants my book? He was in touch with Ellie Dorfman by phone urging her to solicit my book. As I say, I'll pull out my best poems from my mss. and from uncollected and published and unpublished poems and present the very best I can. School is over in two weeks so that then I'll bend my attention to it. Ellie seems to want to get into the act by helping me select poems. I hope you get back in time to give me advice. I'll try to hold it up a bit, though I hazard a guess I'd like to have it all complete by the end of July.

Being world famous does put at rest one's more surface or even hidden strivings of the ego and satisfies the age-old infirmity of man: i.e. fame. With that aside, the true inner being may then, unmolested by more worldly agitations, sink deeper into the core of himself to search out a link between him and the universe, sink into some archetypal submerged, subliminal region (cf. Jung), when Time was young. . . . Do not the Inca ruins and urns give you a queer feeling of some mysterious imminence, as if Time were immutable, immovable, while it is man who changes and who thinks Time makes those felonious marks on him and turns him to dust.

The family is O.K. On June 19, we give our annual Ginsberg cook-out here in our garden. Sorry you will be missing in body; no doubt, all will want to know about you. Everybody is O.K. Abe is working, though for how long, it is problematical.

[. . .]

Regarding Don Allen's anthology, I think you came out perhaps the best. Maybe I'm prejudiced. But your "Howl" and parts of "Kaddish" are strong and moving. I like Madeline Gleason, Ferlinghetti, Doyle, and a few others. But most of it, frankly, I thought fragmentary, pretentious, chaotic, fustian rather than Faustian.

Really, some of those youngsters think the world began when they opened their eyes and that with them begins poetry!!!

I have taken a "Sabbatical" from college teaching, so that next year I shall not teach at Rutgers. The authorities wrote me that, whenever I wish to go back, they will give me classes. As for high school, my retirement date I have set as of Feb 1, one more term. This will complete just forty years of teaching at dear old Central High.

Write me more, when you get a chance. Did you receive my birthday bill for you?

Love and kisses. Write more often.

Your father,
Louis

Allen Ginsberg to Louis Ginsberg

Allen Ginsberg
U.S. Embassy
Lima, Peru
June 21, 1960

Dear Louis:

Wrote two weeks ago or so – by now I've crossed over Andes & spent 10 days in Pucallpa, a small town on a huge river big as the Hudson – The Ucayali – which winds 1000 miles up to the Amazon – so took a small steamboat 6 days ago and, sleeping in hammock with mosquito net on passageway on deck, spent the week traveling up to the Amazon thru huge flat area of jungle – on riverside small grey thatchroof huts and every 20 or 50 miles a small cluster of houses and every 100 miles a little town, frontier towns, of several thousand gents. Cost of boat trip including 3 meals a day is $6.00 which is cheap – am now on last day of trip & just a few hours ago entered the Amazon proper – big wide flat brown shining water wide as a big lake with sticks & greenery floating on surface, balsa rafts and canoes paddling near shore – we dock at Iquitos this evening & I go find hotel, stay a week, & then fly back to Lima, to catch plane home a week later. Iquitos is the river port at western-Peruvian end of the Amazon. From Iquitos one can take another steamer down thru Brazil & the Atlantic, 2500 miles, for $50 – but I haven't the money or the time, & have to get back to Lima.

While in Pucallpa my main purpose was to look up a local Curandero or witch doctor & try a native herbal brew named Ayahuasca which reportedly gives visions – similar to peyote, Mescaline & Lysergic Acid – Well I tried it 4 times and with remarkable results as far as I was concerned subjectively – I certainly saw "visions."[1]

What the drug seems to do is activate the unconscious without putting the regular consciousness asleep – so that you can both be awake *and* dream real solid dreams at the same time – a neat trick, but quite possible. The local Indians use it for curing illnesses, finding lost objects, communicating with the dead, religious visions, etc. and I'm sure they can do all that, from what I've seen. It was like stepping into a voodoo movie & finding it was all *real*.

Anyway the main dream or vision I had was of the condition of my own death, i.e., how it feels like to die – and I don't think I've ever (except once before having "visions" in Harlem) been so terrified before in my life while awake. It seemed that Death was a *Thing,* not mere emptiness, a Living Being – and my whole life was being judged & found a vanity, as in *Ecclesiastes,* – and I saw as in X-ray my skeleton-head settling in final position on pillow to give up the Ghost – a *familiar* feeling, strangely – with the realization that I had known all along, but avoided consciousness, of the fact that I am flesh and that flesh is crass. The main after effect, aside from a desire to widen further the area of my consciousness, and realization that my life so far has been relatively empty, was resolution to bear children sooner or later before it is too late. The question is to be or not to be – and also, what *Thing* is beyond Being. I saw something – a sort of great consciousness which was familiar, but unhuman – as if in one being were united an Elephant & Snake & Mosquito & Man – and all the trees – nothing like the terrible hidden God of Moses or *Revelations,* it felt like. Whether this is vision or Hallucination makes very little difference – I passed thru several hours of intense suffering awareness of the Worm at my Ear. I thought of

---

1. See William S. Burroughs and Allen Ginsberg, *The Yage Letters* (San Francisco: City Lights Books, 1963); "Magic Psalm" (AG, *CP,* pp. 255–256), and "The Reply" (AG, *CP,* p. 257) for Allen's immediate writings on the *ayahuasca* experiences.

you and the whole family – everyone I knew passed thru mind at one time or another – with tears & love – realization that sooner or later, I, or everyone, enters a great solitude and give up everything – which was painful to realize, which is why I said my life seemed a vanity, for I as yet had thought of it as semi-permanent & had not considered the inevitable. It also seemed that until I were *able* to freely give myself up, entrance into some great Joy (in life or beyond life) would not be seen – but that there is some kind of Inhuman Harmony yet to come. But this is speculation. In any case the universe did seem like one Being.

Well that's enough of that for awhile – I wrote a great deal this month, huge ranting wild poems, psalms, notes, sketches, drawings, a whole book actually – I'll have to reread it in a year & see if it's still hot. But poetry doesn't seem enough – "in the vast strange & middle of the night."

Also bought a lot of native pottery – hand-painted ceramic ashtray types – for souvenirs, which I'll bring home – and a hammock & mosquito net.

I thought of poor Williams, living so long on the edge of death – "for this is the first – and last – day of the world" – he wrote. Had a dream of him entering Non-Being with huge snowy = feathered angel wings. And saw you Louis as a sort of Elephant-nosed seraph or Diety with old human eyes. Well the Indians in the jungle certainly don't lack a huge metaphysical inner Civilization, half the town of Pucallpa drinks ayahuasca every week & has its own secret life aside from radios & movies of the A-Bomb. So that's I suppose the proper poetic climax of my trip down here – it's been almost half a year & I am nostalgic to get back to N.Y.C. & see everybody & see you.

Love,
Allen

Regards to Edith & Eugene – I wrote him June 3 or so.

Louis Ginsberg to Allen Ginsberg

August 8, 1960

Dear Allen,

It is only today that I received from you a letter you wrote in Peru on June 2.

It was a very interesting and intriguing letter with much food for thought and speculation.

Especially did I note your mention of a native brew called Ayahuasca, similar to peyote and mescaline and Lysergic acid. The phantasmagoric imagination that flowed around you and in which you had a vision that you were as the grass that passes away, as does all transience, must have been a vivid and startling one.

As I told you, it is my belief, supported by my scientific readings and also by those of the psychiatrists, that every vision of phantasm which floats through our minds when they are excited or enlarged or intensified by some means, as a drug, has its roots in something concrete, something that senses saw in waking life which then sank down deep in some remote subterranean region of our brain or our subconscious. When reason is allayed by a drug, these images merge and fuse and recombine to weird or imaginary shapes to assail us.

Or, it may be in our germplasm, in our chromosomes, and genes, the ancestral memories of ancient primitive times, according to Jung, are still clinging there; so that, when our subconscious is astir, as a pool is stirred by a thrown rock, primordial memories are roiled up.

However, I do not believe – though our enlarged imagination may simulate a revelation – that we actually glimpse the Oneness or the Primal Source from which all nature and beasts and flowers and trees and fish and men draw their being. I suppose we may speculate that all these growing and living things are but manifold and multitudinous pulses of this creative process.

Yet, as a poet, seeking to enlarge frontiers, you may, in your fired imagination, sink yourself in fantasies in which you seem to be at one with the universal. In those moments of ecstasy, your soul on fire merges with the Absolute. Then, when you think of the inexorable transience of things and the irresistible forces which will overcome you, as it does all mortal things, then splendid moments of beauty stir us and inspire us to cherish those moments and, as creative poets, we try to capture them and fix them in symbols of art that perpetuates them so that they may transcend mortality.

I, too, dwell upon the above thoughts, though I must say that you, perhaps more venturesome than I, try to explore them with enlarging and heightening drugs. When next I am at my doctor's, I'll ask him about Lysergic acid and some other drugs.

I am reminded, in this connection, of what Malraux said, I think, "The most unique quality of modern literature is the eruption of the unconscious within the conscious mind, which is not able to understand and control all that has forced its way up."

In any case, I believe it is our duty, as creative artists, to let ourselves be used by forces deep in us, forces which we do not fully understand but which seem greater than we are or which are the fountains of our beings, while at the same time, living a double life, we also move among mortgages, box-tops, teeming streets, eating places of our daily routines, not forgetting the irreconcilable paradoxes and predicaments and animosities strewn over the world.

Reinhold Niebuhr claims that, as humans, we cannot resolve all big conflicts but we should resolve those little ones we can. Meanwhile, we can hoist above us the bright dream of a social conscience, which, as Romain Rolland claims, craves a world where lovely things will not seem out of place and where the chief human impulse will be not to destroy.

Further, brief bits of ephemeral clusters of atoms, our minds can still ponder on the mystery that, though we seem transient motes of insignificance, we still can wrest some significance from this absurd welter of the world. And, as I wrote in a poem in my new book, we are greater than any sun because we really know how small we are, even if the biggest sun does not. Again it was Malraux – one of my favorite authors – who wrote: "The greatest mystery is not that we should be thrown up by chance between a profusion or matter and a profusion of stars, but that, in that prison, we should be able to get out of ourselves images sufficiently powerful to deny our own insignificance."

A few of the above ideas in this letter I have smuggled into a recent, rather long poem of mine, which I'd like you to read when you come next into Paterson. The poem is called "View from the Grave". (Remember our conversation we had last when you asked me what I think, at my age of 65, of death?)

Lots of love.

Keep writing. And come to spend a few days with me, while my flesh is mine, so we may ruminate or wander into poetic thought.

> Your father,
> Louis

On September 13, Allen sat down and put the finishing touches to "Kaddish." The poem had been a mighty struggle, beginning almost immediately after Naomi Ginsberg's death, when Allen had begun researching the Hebrew text and making preliminary notes, continuing through the early writing in Paris, and extending *through various additions and permutations thereafter. Louis Ginsberg had seen and commented on earlier, incomplete drafts, and when Allen showed him the final draft, Louis was once again stunned by the power of the poem, even if he did have a number of reservations about what Allen had included.*

Louis Ginsberg to Allen Ginsberg

September 18, 1960

Dear Allen,

I read your "Kaddish" with tears. It's a magnificent, heart-wrenching poem!!!

My revisions:

First take out on p. 17 references to "my affair." It's too embarrassing and will prove troublesome to me

p. 4 "fear of Louis" ambiguous: and "paranoiac fear"

p. 13 delete "homosexuality" – why give power to calumniators?

p. 24 Remove "Louis found himself a girl" too embarrassing to me

p. 35 Take out "homosexuality" – You'll be exposed to sensation mongers: Why court trouble?

p. 39 "long black beard around vagina" – delete: too obscene for reference re: mother.

Louis

Louis Ginsberg to Allen Ginsberg

September 19, 1960

Dear Allen,

I was in a hurry and hastened revisions.

Here they are fuller.

p. 4 It would be clearer to say "paranoiac" "fear."   NO[1]

p. 13 Delete "mountains of homosexuality." Why give grounds for attacks on matters extraneous to literary merit?   NO

---

1. The "NO" here and subsequent ones were written in Allen's hand in the margins of the letter.

p. 17 By all means, omit the part of "the dentist"s wife writes love letters to Lou . . .' to "on sleep – what it seems." It's too embarrassing. Do omit this section.

p. 24 Omit all of 1/2 page from 1st line to "idealism." It's too embarrassing for me. (Also, first part sounds like incest: Why bring attacks on yourself)   NO

p. 35 Near end, omit homosexuality. You'll invite slander, irrelevant to consideration of literary merits.   NO

p. 39 Omit "long black beard around vagina": Too vulgar.   NO
Otherwise it's a great poem.

Love
Louis

1961

On January 1, 1959, Fidel Castro led a successful overthrow of the Batista dictatorship in Cuba, setting off a furious international debate, not only between the United States and the Soviet Union, which had their own reasons for watching Castro's new regime, but in Central and South America, where communism was favored by intellectuals looking for a means to elevate the oppressed masses. Allen Ginsberg was extremely interested in the Cuban revolution, and he made a point of meeting Castro when the Cuban leader visited New York in September 1960. Oddly enough, however, he and Louis spent little time arguing about the revolution and its international implications.

All that changed in 1961, when father and son exchanged fiery letters, which would continue for years to come. Louis, a socialist sympathizer, had spent years arguing with Naomi, a Communist; he was not about to listen to his son voicing the same old arguments. Allen, for his part, felt that his father was caught up in a combination of Cold War nationalism and a patriotic fervor whipped up by the recent election of John F. Kennedy. (Louis Ginsberg favored Kennedy; Allen Ginsberg did not.) Allen's letters reflected his continuing development of a worldview spawned by his travels to Mexico, Europe, and South America: He had visited the Mayan and Incan ruins, and he feared that the survival of the planet was endangered by the presence of nuclear technology and political leaders willing to wage wars — including the final one — over strange territorial, philosophical, or political disputes.

Louis Ginsberg to Allen Ginsberg

February 24, 1961

Dear Allen,

Thanks for the leaflets.

I'm all for the Franco one; that is, protesting against the Franco dictatorship and for the two Spanish sailors.

Concerning the Cuba one, I have my reservations. It doesn't print the other side. Visitors tell of being in manipulated throngs chanting pro-Soviet and anti-American slogans in whose frenetic atmosphere it was as dangerous to dissent as "Amid a hostile throng of benighted, hate-mongering white citizens, KKK groups in the South." The fact remains that the Commies have poured in arms into Cuba and that the Commies call the tune in Cuba: there is no freedom of the press, no freedom of speech in Cuba. That some of the workers have been given new homes is quite true, but they have been mostly showpieces for visitors (re Wallace once in Russia). Further, the people, as I say, have been robbed of free speech so that it is dangerous in Cuba to dissent.

Last night I ran into N.Y. where I attended a meeting of the Poetry Society of America. I was one of two discussion leaders. First, the anonymous poem is read; then I took to the podium and delivered my strictures on the poem. Then the other discussion leader (a Miss Farrar, daughter of John Farrar and a teacher at Barnard) delivered her comments. I had a good time and met many people, some of whom mentioned you. (I caused a couple of lifted eyebrows, when I said, though your manner is not mine, I was proud of you for your achievement.)

Well, as I wrote you yesterday, I am now in semi-retirement with a Rutgers class here in Paterson on Monday and Thursday, due to the sudden illness of a teacher.

Spring is coming, and I am thawing out . . .

Keep well.

Your father,
Louis

Allen Ginsberg to Louis Ginsberg

{New York City}
March 2, 1961

Dear Lou:

Tho it's true that some of my information comes directly from Heaven a good deal of it comes from earth, particularly on the Cuba scene for the reason that I have been in Cuba, I speak and read Spanish, I know a lot of S.A. poets & intellectuals here in NY, I spent half a year talking about these problems in S.A. This year, I have met Castro slightly & had chance to talk lengthily to govt officials visiting here, I know and have talked at length with people who have visited Cuba (LeRoi Jones, Marc Schleiffer, Wright Mills, Dr. Halper and several others) and I have done a lot of reading in the matter including Castro's speeches before the revolution, Che Guevara's writings, Mills', Huberman and Sweezy's *Anatomy* book, Sartre's and Francois Sagan's essays – in other words I have done partial investigation of subject; in addition had chance to test and partially confirm my paranoia about mass media reporting of Cuban facts day to day with people from [*New York*] *Post* & United Press [International]; in addition have a first hand experimental working knowledge of the possibilities of factual distortion and opinionation replacing fact in the mass media and now have a 3rd eye so to speak in reading X-ray thru newspapers on account of the genesis and development of Beat myth & drug myth. In addition I am involved both thru jazz and poetry world with the Negro intellectual colony here thru James Baldwin, LeRoi Jones & Bob Kaufman all experienced Negroes who have connections with Castro & African nationalist groups and so I get a view of their world which has been new to me the last 2 years and quite different from the idea of the Negro world I knew previously from the outside.

I don't think the *Times* article which I read before was very helpful as it tended to make them all seem eccentric futile and crackpot; a good many Negro groups have decided on direct action (like the sit-in movement in which now I am also involved in sense of meeting M. L. King and receiving their propaganda & meeting sit-in students lately) and this action is a healthy thing, both in North and South including the U.N. protests; and any attempt to discount it as *not representative* of US Negro thinking or northern hip Negro thinking is a mistake fostered by complacent white liberalism and *Times*-type conservative press. You should read the Negro newspapers to see that.

Lumumba was elected premier by an elected Parliament which he had a majority in; and one of the long struggles has been to reconvene Parliament all along to reaffirm his position, and that has been blocked by Kasavubu, Mobutu, the U.N., the US CIA, the Belgians etc. He "insisted" on uniting the Congo – and there is where I found him heroic and a martyr since the main impulse to secession and the main form the secessions took were according to Belgian-American economic-influence boundaries; not tribal warfare which was important but which did not determine the process of secessions. Kasai and Katanga which seceded are and were strongholds of Belgian influence which has been so often denounced by U.N. and by

Russia – and only after Lumumba's death gently chided by the U.S. finally – after it was too late. And the leaders who seceded who are Belgian "puppets" quite literally are now in power running future of Congo. The "U.N. addressed many letters to them," the Belgians, telling them to get out; but they are still there and that was [what] Lumumba was yelling about; and the U.S.A. refused to back Hammarskjöld in this particular aspect of Congo problem all along; and Hammarskjöld in his speech last week complained about that; but all the USA has eyes for psychologically is the Cold War and getting the Russians out; and possibly preserving Belgian interests there. Rockerfellers now own 22 1/2% (controlling interest) in Katanga Mining Co. The "imperialism" here is more outright than you want to see or Stevenson can deal with. But it is the same old problem which you deplored when it happened 50 years ago but see as normal part of scene when happening right now. The myth of political instability and warring tribes is one which may or may not be true but I would say it is fostered and used consciously as the excuse for Belgium etc to retain control. Let the UN pacify warring tribes in a united Congo if they want to. But past & present policy has led to destruction of the socialist left-wing radical unified nationalist leadership, and left Congo now in control of the worst types who started the economic secession movement – Kalonji and Kasai, and Tshombe in Katanga. According to the *NY Times* Lumumba did not receive unnatural help from Russia until the secessionist movements were backed by U.S. & U.N. refusal to protect sovereignty of Congo. Your facts are wrong here, as far as I know. Lumumba originally asked for US troops to quiet his army which was rebelling against continued white Belgian officership; then asked for UN, which said it was an internal problem when Katanga seceded as result of Belgian influence; and then asked for Russian help which he got; and from then on the Cold War was on and Congo was in it.

The Cause is that we granted Congo nominal independence but when Lumumba wanted to make it stick with economic take-over as in Cuba, we felt economic interests (uranium) threatened and entered a policy which ended in his murder. I see him as a sort of tragic hero caught in Cold War.

Originally all sorts of excuses were used to denigrate him (tho before independence he was built up in US press and "responsible") and make him irresponsible, power-hungry, unable to control army, unable to stop warring tribes, communist dupe, etc. Now that he is dead and the conservatives have power and the tribes are still warring and the black army is still committing atrocities just as under his rule, and Kasavubu and

Mobutu are fighting with the U.N. and the Belgians are still in control of Katanga all these excuses have been reduced to what they were – a series of rationalizations and excuses blown up in headlines and snide editorial comments to full blown "Reasons for Maturity" but only old gossipy second-hand typical US hysterias.

No, I am saying that the German people were guilty or better directly responsible for Hitler's scene, and the US people are now in same position, and unless we do something now to liberalize and radicalize the US govt all future blood is on our hands and we can't keep on forever blaming the Russians for everything that goes wrong as in Congo. The problem in Congo is Russian interference coming in to combat and screw Belgian and US interference. You want to see it as all Russian interference with the US as having clean hands. Well we don't.

As for your info on electrical workers union it is not I think accurate. The *Daily News* generally distorts news anti-Castro direction. Obviously, I'm not taking it as fount of truth. I'm saying, *even* in the Daily News (partly because they are so hysterical they can't see they're undermining their own arguments) there was an extended series on anti-Castro forces in the US which the *News thought* made them look good; and that included a proud account of Electrical Union leaders sabotaging Castro govt with bombs before they were purged. That's been reported elsewhere too. The bombs didn't begin after they were kicked out. The resentment was over communist influence in govt I think; partly, because unions were being subject to general Revolution rules etc. It's complicated. Castro revolution is now destroying freedom and Reds have too much influence tho not nearly so much as reported here and not in the nasty *way* it's reported here since all over S.A. the Reds are considered part of the spectrum of parties and when the left wins they assume more importance; i.e. Reds are pariahs as per US psychology does not apply there and only in the USA is it considered absolutely necessary to hate the communists as part of "liberalism."

There is a publication of anti-Castro material on larger scale in Cuba – on larger scale percentagewise – pamphlets and Catholic newspapers too – than there is pro-Castro material in USA. [. . .]

I don't personally care whether or not Castro paid for Fair Play committee ad. If he did I don't think it was a great conspiracy. If it's a conspiracy how do you know it's not a conspiracy to embarrass Fair Play? Circumstances of this *Times* ad deal might well be investigated. I'm all for that. Except that US Congress, UN-Amer Activities Committee, etc – is the context wherein it will be done. But the point is:

Do you think the Fair Play committee is a communist front? Do you think its direction is Red?

I don't care whether it is or not. The communist front fear is a product of McCarthyism & hangover.

However, I do know a lot of people involved with Fair Play committee and they are not communists. So that's that. So if Castro paid for an ad, that's fine, so what. It's ridiculous the attempts to destroy radical protest groups like SANE and Fair Play thru accusations and proof of communist influence. Of course there will be Red influences and various fuck-ups. However the dominant tone of Fair Play is not only non communist but anti-communist. Same with I. F. Stone. You think he's a communist? Well he's not.

The Ad business is an attempt to cripple a useful organization. It seems to have worked in that your response to Fair Play issues is to reply with questions about the ad.

I don't approve of Justice Dept being swept out illegally, I don't approve of the executions, I don't approve of the communist influence, I don't approve of the nationalism, I don't approve of the anti-Yankee fervor, I don't approve of the ban on marijuana.

I do approve of the social reforms, I do approve Castro's sincerity, and I do think that had not the US interfered here as in Congo something very great would have been worked out in Cuba. The fault of the Cuban Revolution is now with the USA and not Castro and if anybody gets hanged better it should be Kennedy at this point rather than Castro.

And if Stevenson defends a more anti-Castro position, the position that Kennedy took which is no different from Nixon's, then I say the End has come openly symbolically for US Liberalism.

Only way out of Cuba situation is Kennedy invite Castro to White House (YES YES YES); offer financial aid for reconstruction of Cuban economy on socialist revolutionary lines, take off the economic & military pressure which is driving Cuba to dependence on communist world, and ask for free elections and free press as exchange. But we are so far from doing something practical like that, and as a result we're building confusion and propaganda chaos and war. And I won't stand still and accept continued propaganda on yr negative anti-Red basis on Cuba. The issue is not the Reds, the issue is the fact that Cubans have 30 years less life span expectancy than USA.

I think the situation will calm itself because now Brazil & Mexico are taking independent stands from US to recognize and have trade with China

& Russia, U.N. recognition, etc. – so that Cuba's actions will seem less eccentrically leftwing than before.

OK – Later – enclosed more I. F. Stone – this time pessimistic.

Love, Allen

P.S. I notice that everytime I open my mouth on Cuba or Congo I get accused of being a Red or Red-dupe and if Castro reacts to this in the same way I do I see nothing strange in his present anti-US hysteria. These Red accusations and obsessions are basically used to obscure the issue – which is that he and SA are declaring economic, psychological and political IN-DEPENDENCE from US domination. If we fight that independence naturally they'll have to get help from Russia and China and naturally they'll get to be prejudiced in favor of the communists in these situations. And naturally you'll become more and more convinced that they're a bunch of commies. Whatya expect? They'll finally *become* communists, if this keeps up.

I'm complaining that the USA is not radical enough. What would you say if I went to Jail for a cause? I don't intend to, but don't you realize how comfortable & secure the liberals are in USA that jail for causes is no longer something to be considered? Yet down in So. with the sit-in movement, that is the way of protest.

For years, Allen had dreamed of visiting India and the Far East, and his growing dissatisfaction with American politics acted as a catalyst in his decision to take another extended journey outside of the United States. On March 23, 1961, he and Peter Orlovsky boarded a ship bound for Paris, where they hoped to spend some time with William Burroughs at the Beat Hotel. Burroughs, however, had left for Tangier. Allen was reunited with Gregory Corso in Paris, and after spending a few weeks hanging out together, they decided to pay a visit to Burroughs in Morocco.

Allen Ginsberg to Louis Ginsberg

c/o U.S. Consulate,
Tangier, Morocco
June 12, 1961

Dear Lou:

Sad to hear Max had died – and whom to write condolences to now? I saw less of him the last few years but when I did we were pretty close & I always felt for him, in thought, and that apartment in the Bronx was landmark always – was there last year again looking at it knowing I'd not see it much evermore, it was a mellow place for Max-Elanor there. Eugene must be sad too.

Say hello to everyone at picnic – I wrote long letter to Honey yesterday, details on Paris, for Ruth & her.

Glad you had poem in *Second Coming* and *Liberation* – I also had prose piece in *Second Coming*[1] – I hear it is out. I haven't their address. Can you send them a card or note telling them to send me a copy of the issue with my & your writings and also remind them they owe me money which I have not received & which I need – so tell them to send it here to above address. They said they'd pay me I think it was $50 & that payment is overdue by now if the piece is out. Have you time to drop them a note? I could but I don't have the address.

Glad you are getting *Liberation* as it is a sincere magazine compared to most – interruption –

[This section of the letter is written in Gregory Corso's hand.]

Hello everlasting minute, I could have become king of Israel if I wished it so having met the daughter of heir apparent Moyse [*sic*] Dayan in Greece – what with a little bit of wooing and dignity I coulda been her husband and in turn everybody's king when she became queen – but I thought best against the idea and continue on this seemingly wanderous crusade of gods knows what, perhaps towards Louis Untermeyer's anthology – whatever I've been seeing your noble work in the European *Herald Tribune* quite often, and am always nodding my head yes upon reading a poem of yours, there's no poet like you really, and in a way you're like me, in that I

---

1. "When the Mode of the Music Changes, the Walls of the City Shake" appeared in the July 1961 issue of *Second Coming Magazine*. See AG, *Deliberate Prose*, pp. 247–254.

acknowledge what you say right away, you leave me with something I have
already known – maybe we is on the same muse-ical show, and the radio is
just different – but anyway there ain't nobody like us because we is very
funny kind of poets, I mean the first of their kind, we stand to Shakespeare
like Sitting Bull would to Christ; happy – Great to see yr son, perhaps the
funniest kind of poet ever, surely funnier than Max Eastman, again – he looks
great and has an attitude toward life – things with such certainty and
gentility to be around my golden friend again, send me a new book of poems.
I tried my hand at prose, wrote a novel, one month time, very careless exercise
of youth-fantasy done, though, in grammar-school style – I really enjoyed
writing it, and feel it in to be for it is unique; yet something there is when I
write poesy does not touch me with uncertainty – But surely you must have
something of great certainty if you haven't had a book out since ELM; you
must have a lot of good poems – I do hope you have them published soon and
get another book of yours, I'm tired of reading *Ever Lasting Minute*; I've had
enough, I want an end to it; the book is magic for sure – OK; I will write a
nice letter to you about my trip to Greece and all the temples when I find
myself in a less silly mood, goodbye and love, gregory

Gregory just came upstairs, read your letter & sat down at typewriter so
that was the result – he's very funny – I live on top of a roof, a little tile
room in hot Mediterranean clime, and that leads to a glass enclosed sun-
shack, and that leads to a little terrace overlooking rooftops and Tangier.
Bay and parapets of Spain (as last time, I'm around the block from hotel I
was last time) – all this costs $20 a month – Gregory has a slightly larger
room downstairs for $14 a month – Peter walks around the Arab streets &
keeps diaries – Burroughs around the corner in his old room just finished
novel (*The Soft Machine*)[1] now cuts up newspapers & photographs to make
collages in spare time (weird juxtapositions of news stories, Kennedy
stepping off airplanes onto Queen Elizabeth's forehead) – everybody busy
– I'm typing up journals and answering letters – the weather is great – lots
of young beatniks suddenly in town swinging with the poor Arabs buying
old clothes & smoking pot (it's legal) – Paul Bowles takes us to his favorite
cafe on mountain-cliff overlooking vast blue crawling hide of the sea & we
sit silent watching the universe, everybody tranquil – Gregory & Peter & I
at nite on roof discuss Galaxies – We eat 50¢ shishkebab meals in dark Arab

1. William S. Burroughs, *The Soft Machine* (New York: Grove, 1962).

fry restaurants – sometimes go to European quarter and get highclass French meals for a buck – cheaper than Mexico here – in fact this place is more interesting & weirder to live in & happier than Paris at the moment for me – so everything's fine. Since independence Tangier no longer is international freeport trading post & so's more tranquil less paranoiac less Europe-Arab conflict, calmer few people less business less tourists less surface confusion, more calm to live in & cheaper. You can get $180 Yugoslav boat here from NY – ought to come for a few weeks sometime.

Anyway as I say glad you read *Liberation*, seems more active radical than the old-time-radical-now-liberal-weeklies. I agree generally with Finch, the guy who resigned, more than the other editors in disapproving of Castro dictatorship; & Finch's ideas on that are based on more specific and accurate information than generally circulated in U.S. – excellent detailed accurate info in previous issues of *Liberation* attacking Castro by Cuban Anarchist-pacifist groups who are persecuted there. Do you ever see I. F. Stone Newsletter? That's the best glances political comment & reporting I see from USA – I get it regularly, someone put me on a list. Enclosed if I have sample around.

Now this above (disapproving of Castro police state) not to be taken as change of opinion on my part as to complete vileness of U.S. Govt. & U.S. *people* in last year regarding Cuba. Nor if I were Castro am I sure I'd be able to do any better with Cuba than he's doing, given the US for neighbor.

All last year I was complaining about the CIA and I think by now what sounded in me to be eccentric has been put into perspective by events & some general public consciousness, realized – the whole complaint I had then is now the general US complaint. What sounded in Castro as Mussolini-hysteria – his screaming about US attack – has also been justified by event.

I wondered how you reacted to the Cuban invasion[1] & if that made sense of what you had taken to be mere communist propaganda before., i.e. accusations by Russia and Castro that US was preparing military blow at Cuba. This was dismissed as paranoia for a year before it happened.

According to Gallup poll at invasion time 80% of US people, on basis of U.S. mass communication data – including *NY Times* etc – thought that Cuban masses were against Castro. I remember Leo thought so, too. I disputed that point wildly & was put down for it, as a "dupe." I was merely

---

1. On April 17, 1961, Cuban exiles, advised by the United States and promised military support, invaded the Bay of Pigs. The U.S. military support never materialized, and the rebels were easily defeated. The invasion intensified the hostility that Cuba felt toward the United States.

reporting fact and amazed to realize that all the liberals even were completely misinformed to the point to mind-control or brainwash on the facts of the case. Now the fact is no longer ambiguous and it is generally reported in US press (*NY Herald Trib, Times* etc) that majority of Cubans are behind Castro. I keep warning, this total reversal of public information is the result of illiterate manipulation of information reaching the US public and until people stop believing the newspapers in the US they will have as inaccurate information and opinions on the cold wars as they have on the Beat Generation, to give an example close to home.

What was really shocking was that the old-line liberals & socialists like yourself after 20 years of McCarthyism are completely out of contact with any kind of perspective on what's happened to America.

Put it this way – to my generation, the Cuban scene is similar to the old Spanish Civil War scene – with many of the same stresses and interior conflicts –

I don't see any way out except full public investigation of CIA activities in Guatemala, Iran, Cuba, Formosa, Korea, Laos, Congo, etc for the last 10 years – total reversal of policy of secret manipulation of foreign policy and hiding or withholding news and info from public – the extent of which nobody knows fully but what I already know has made me gasp with horror and has justified the worst Russian tirades in the U.N. –

I also see last week's banning of Communist Party as formal police state action by the U.S.

In fact at this point I think the U.S. is too far gone and now useless to complain since I don't see the people of the U.S. awake enough to take their own life up again & begin to swing politically in some imaginative free expression.

The reason I kept yelling at you is in a sense you represent the intelligent liberal symbol in my mind – the people who are supposed to be depended on to be able to defend themselves from right wing police state – the stable progressive old school – and I see you inundated by History, by a USA that wd have been inconceivable in Roosevelt's day, by a US that is suicidal and unable to straighten out in time to prevent itself from being blown up by the communist world, and that will steadily lose ground & degenerate & get more right wing every year, no matter what party is in power.

The only way out for America now as far as I can see is socialism, return of government power from oligarchic holding companies & Military power groups that run things – industry *and* information-propaganda (We do NOT have a free press. Period.) (Actually about 8 people in the USA determine policy for majority of newspapers & TV and Radio) (That's why it's possible to have such massive factual misinformation as on Cuba) (i.e. one year of constant information totally at variance in factual data & attitude from British, French & Moroccan papers, to say nothing of Russian or Chilean) – and shift of US economy from present monopoly capitalism to some relaxed socialistic form wherein a shift can be planned from conspicuous consumer & military production to world-integrated useful production for undeveloped countries (This be Toynbee's suggestion too). Which means a lower standard of living for US and a more meaningful life maybe, at least be of some use to the rest of the world instead of a mockery and horror of fake democracy gone nuts. More and more from outside US everybody digs US as approaching some vast crisis which people inside USA are almost completely unconscious of, as if everything was well in the refrigerator and history be escaped.

I.e., to French socialists, the "world struggle" is not the Cold War at all but struggle against "power" monger groups in US & in Russia both, and it makes very little difference if the US power group loses, in fact it might be preferable for the Red power group to win since at least it's a power that's still ALIVE in the sense that the U.S. is dead from the neck up and more retrogressive & less promising of flexible development than the Red power groups. I could imagine the world developing & relaxing (maybe) after a total Red victory; but after a TOTAL US victory I wd see nothing but medieval scenes of Cuban Guatemalan horror sort of, a McCarthy-Kennedy-Max Lerner state, I'm not making sense.

Anyway, what I'm saying is, some new sense of a serious fix is coming into consciousness on the American scene, is it not? Something's got to give, I hope it's the right wing not the left – at least there's the beginning of some open fight – Republicans calling for war on Cuba and Democrats beginning to draw back from that & be neutral.

It simply is a shame that there is no real progressive party because now there is a progressive scene possible, i.e. historical demand for reversal of US policy on Latin America so that we encourage peaceful socialism – which neither party is willing to admit – outside the USA and even inside if necessary.

Anyway I be here a while, I don't know how long. I should get loot from City Lights for books soon. "Kaddish" was taken by my German publisher & will be translated; also in Italy I think it's arranged. I'm writing a little.

What details did you hear about Max — Ask Gene to write me maybe? It's too late at nite, I quit — getting fatigued & not said anything clearly.

OK —

Love

Allen

Louis Ginsberg to Allen Ginsberg

June 27, 1961

Dear Allen,

I was glad to get your letter dated June 12.

Regarding Max, I gather that his last few years were one of a semi-sad resignation and loneliness. He died alone of a heart attack. I surmise the only one to send condolences is his sister, Edith, who lives in California, but I do not have her address.

I wrote a note to the editor of *The Second Coming* and asked him to send you the issue containing your prose article, together with a check. They sent me a copy of the article of yours.

I sent it to Dr. Mones who visited me. We both discussed your article. We thought it was brilliant with magnificent passages. I liked especially "Cornerless mystery, mystical illumination, spontaneous, irrational juxta-position, sublimely related fact. One must verge on the Unknown, the pattern of the poem discovered in the mind. The only poetic tradition is the voice out of the Burning Bush." Splendid.

My only reservation would be that the mystical outwelling and gushing forth from the subterranean subconscious should have irrelevancies combed out and selected so as not to let the smoke, so to speak, choke some of the fire.

Tell Gregory that I enjoyed his passage to me. Tell him I'll write to him soon a separate letter.

I am glad you're enjoying yourself with your cronies. Wish I were with you to ruminate on the galaxies on the roof-top. Lately I have been reading about the macrocosm (as well as the microcosm). I wonder ever that enigmas are ferried where by those countless gyrating galaxies that are speeding outward, away from the us: the enigma is that the further away from us, the faster they are rushing . . .

Enclosed find a review by Dr. Charles Angoff in the Philadelphia *Jewish*

Exponent. He liked your *Kaddish.* I keep scrutinizing the press for other reviews. Incidentally, I bought fifteen copies of your book and have distributed it to relatives and friends.

All is quiet here with me. I keep pounding my typewriter, not wishing to rust on my laurels, and now and then have poems punished in the papers and magazines. Will send you some new poems that have been accepted but have not been published yet. My own book of poems is still in the hands of my literary agent who tells me it is being read, but I have no word yet.

Cuba. Yes, the U.S. did made a boo-boo, which set us back. Yes, the CIA did blunder, and there is protest against it here with universal criticism. Yes, we did the wrong thing in feebly helping the Cuban anti-Castroites. But we were on the horns of a dilemma: To maintain our policy of nonintervention plus to help the liberal refugees stem the Commie tide, which in Cuba is sending ammunition and pouring Red propaganda throughout Latin America. It will be a good lesson from which Kennedy will profit.

I do not believe that 80 percent of the Cubans are for Castro. Between the lines, I think it is half and half: the half against Castro are suppressed by a terrorist police state.

There is one idea in your letter that I am vehemently against. You say that "it is preferable for the Red power to win since it is alive." Listen to this: Top former Commies like Djilas, etc. assert – which I believe – that the ills that the Reds seek to cure are less evil than those which the Commies introduce. The fact that they are strong or alive proves nothing. So was Hitler alive. At present, all the satellites – Hungary, East Germany, etc. – are restive and suppressed with revolt squelched by brute force. The Democracies, despite their blunders, have more free speech and human liberties, however less than one hundred percent. The Democracies advance, three steps forward, two steps back, but they advance. Should the Reds win, there will be no relaxation but little volcanoes of rebellions will erupt all over the world, for the spirit of man and his freedom, though temporarily suppressed, is in the end inviolable. Despite the CIA, many voices in America are rising in protest and demanding changes; and those changes are beginning to be made under the Kennedy administration. We have a long way to go, but the way of the Commies leads to a dead end of suppression of human liberty and a totalitarian police state which the wave of the future will in time engulf. I am sad to think that you are fooled by a poor perspective and illusory symptoms. You remind me of the hapless Lindbergh, who saw in the Nazis the wave of the Future.

More anon.

Yes, we had a delightful annual family picnic. All asked for you. Joel fell in love with a school teacher in E. Orange. She lives in the same apartment house. They are getting married at the end of August. Eugene and Connie were there with their treasure-trove of three children, all bright as a whip. Relatives were there of assorted kinds. (I am pondering a poem called "Family Barbecue," where they are all ranged around the grill and table, balancing joys, envies and jealousies, etc.)

Give my regards to Gregory, Peter and Burroughs.

Love from
Your father,
Louis

Allen Ginsberg to Louis Ginsberg

c/o U.S. Counsel
Tangier, Morocco
August 3, 1961

Dear Louis –

All's well – how are you? I came back from trip to Marrakech (see photo other side) and will stay here a short while before pushing on. The Harvard Mushroom professor[1] came to visit also, & is bringing Burroughs to Harvard to experiment in consciousness alteration – all is going very well. I think I'll go with Gregory & Bill to England for a month, first & see what London is like to live in. I think of you often, with love & everything is *all* right with me [. . .]. I'll write soon – finished proofs of a new book, the old *Empty Mirror*[2] 1951 which 8th St. Bookstore publishes next month. OK, Love Allen

1. Timothy Leary. Allen had met Leary the year before and, under Leary's supervision, had taken psilocybin, a hallucinogenic drug discovered by Dr. Albert Hofmann, who had also discovered LSD. Leary's controversial experiments with psilocybin and LSD eventually led to his departure from his job at Harvard.
2. *Empty Mirror* (New York: Totem Press, 1961).

Louis Ginsberg to Allen Ginsberg

August 8, 1961

Dear Allen,

Glad to get your short letter today and am glad that you are well and that you are writing.

Empty Mirror is a fine title for your new book. When will it be out and who is publishing it? More power to you!

I have had a quiet summer. Have done a little writing, but not much. A poem of mine appeared today in the *N.Y. Times*, but it's a rather old topic for me. Have had poems accepted in assorted places, but they are not out yet.

Haven't heard from my literary agent for more than a month. They wrote me on July 1 that Harcourt Brace had turned it down after holding it three months. The ms. is being read now by another publisher. Hope for the best and expect the worst. Some day lightning will strike.

In the Fall, I am having two classes at Rutgers here in Paterson: Freshman composition class and a course in advanced composition, called Language and Literature. Had an offer from Montclair State Teachers College to give a night course there, but rejected it, as I'll be busy nights with Rutgers.

Edith is fine and busy working in her office.

Eugene and Connie are OK. They are expecting a new baby in a couple of weeks. [. . .]

Am enclosing a review of your book by your friend Paul Carroll in *The Evergreen Review*.[1]

I think of you often and hope I shall see you soon as I miss you. However, so long as you are well and happy and busy at poetry, I take pride in you. Keep up the fine work.

Will send you soon a sonnet to appear in a school magazine called *The Clearing House*. The poem is called "On Reaching the Age of Sixty-five."

With love and pride from
Your father,
Louis

---

1. Paul Carroll, untitled review of *Kaddish and Other Poems, Evergreen Review,* July–August 1961.

Louis Ginsberg to Allen Ginsberg

August 15, 1961

Dear Allen,

Thanks for showing me the letter from *Olympia Magazine,* with a hint that I write about a father's view of you.

Frankly, I think I am too much involved with and too close to your writing to make an objective report. My candid view, as you may know, is that you have done work of a high order, with exuberant vitality and with magnificent imagination – all of which makes me proud of your eminence. I have some reservations about one or two aspects: namely on your going overboard in some matters and also on your undisciplined and ungrammatical outpourings. I am well aware of your able and even eloquent defense of your method, as delineated in your article called "When the Mode of the Music Changes the Walls of the City Shake," in *The Second Coming Magazine.* I believe in controlled abandon, while you have a bit too much of the abandon. That virtue has its defects. An uninhibited flow of the mystic subconscious should be followed a bit more by conscious scrutiny.

Be that as it may, in general, I hold that poetry is where you find it; and that, in the house of poetry, there are many mansions. While you denigrate good regular meter which has permanent values, I take a larger view and maintain that free verse with excellences, such as yours, has strong validity as poetry.

I'd rather wait a while before writing an article on your poetry from a father's objective viewpoint, though I doubt I can really be objective, for I am prejudiced in your favor. At any rate, if, in time, I do write such an article, I'll submit to you for your comments.

All is quiet here. No news yet. [. . .]

Love from
Your father,
Louis

Allen Ginsberg to Louis Ginsberg

{Tangier, Morocco}
n.d. {ca. late August 1961}

Dear Louis –

Thanks for the reviews – here – things going well – changes & thoughts – I
go probably to London for a month or so with Gregory & Bill–Peter left to
go travel to Istanbul alone & try out his soul – I'm answering letters today –
12 so far, I wonder how I can get out of this Allen Ginsberg trap – I'm
halfway out now I think – so all be well –

Yes I did think that one poem was really great, about your father, & I feel
the same way about you about your brow – all strange & beautiful &
awesome – I'm too bemused now to write much – so will keep this short –

I finished proofs of old *Empty Mirror* book – looks sharp & spare &
prophetic now after a decade, better than I remember –

I wrote to Honey too – how are you & how pass the days? – got any
advice? – That James Dickey review[1] is really exactly the summary of all
that I was getting away from at Columbia – it's just humanly & spiritually
closed door forever, it sounds like. [. . .]

How's Gene? I still haven't heard from him, send my love – What *is* his
address –

Love,
Allen

Hello Edith?

Allen never made the trip to England. Instead, he boarded a ship for Greece on
August 24. He and Peter had quarreled and split up, and Allen was feeling
lonely. With any luck, Allen wrote his father, he would spend some time in Greece
and hook up with Peter later in Israel. For Louis, who always felt a vicarious
thrill when hearing the details of his son's travels, the idea of Allen's traveling first
to the native land of democracy and then to the land of his Jewish heritage was too
good to be true.

---

1. James Dickey's untitled review of *Kaddish and Other Poems*, which appeared in the July 9, 1961, issue
    of the *New York Times Book Review*, underscored Dickey's generally negative response to the Beat
    Generation.

Louis Ginsberg to Allen Ginsberg

Saturday, September 2, 1961

Dear Allen,

Am glad to hear you are in Athens, Greece. Take a look at the Parthenon whose columns, as I glimpse them through literature, are bathed in a light that never was on sea or land. Then, too, the classic clarity of air that illumes the islands . . . The Acropolis, too, must look with calm disdain on the frantic gestures of modern man. Maybe you can take notes inspired by "the glory that was Greece," the glory that is till suffused through History.

In case, as you hinted, you might go to Israel, there, too, you will find hallowed light where the momentous still shines through every moment in the current times of Israel; in the Judean hills of Israel, something timeless leaned down into time, which the centuries has sanctified as the heritage of the Jews; so that, apart from religion or institutionalized religion, there is a heritage there, which, if you believe the validity of the "subjective unconscious," flows deep in the subterranean psyche of all Jews, whether he knows it or not. So I believe.

Received your SOS for one hundred dollars this morning. Banks are closed Sat. – Sunday – Monday (Labor Day), Early Tues. morning, I'll go to my bank and obtain a cashier's check for one hundred and dispatch it to you air-mail. (Eugene is providing 50 and I, 50.) Let me know when you get the cashier's check. Allen, send the loan back to me when you get your money.

Hope you are feeling fine. Soak up impressions like sponge so that you can, undoubtedly, squeeze them out later for new poems.

I'm still waiting for Godot. The last I heard from my literary agent was two months ago. Am keeping my fingers crossed.

Speaking of religion, it has been defined as the active reverence for a dominant moral ideal.

Or, as Einstein has it, "as the awe and wonder at the harmony of the universe."

Or, as the adoration of the First Cause.

So be it. But the inquiring voice within asks: who made the First Cause?

Also, while there is great hominy at the balancing and gravitational equilibrium of the galactic systems and the island universes in the un-fathomable reaches of space, yet, yet, astronomers tell us that even these systems have entropy and expire and lose their power; or there are vast collisions or, as in supernova, there are explosions. Then down to earth, a mindless force seems oblivious of man; nature, like a mother, is all bosom but no heart; cancers, malformations, still-births, monstrosities, wars, volcanic eruptions, natural and various kinds of catastrophes all attest to disprove that "God watches the fall of every sparrow."

The truth, as I divine it, is that man's knowledge cannot plumb the enigma, that we must pause in a general doubt; that nature, in the words of Shaw, is the life force which tries to attain a greater power of contemplating itself. As an ardent agnostic, one can hold, at least this that man, however doomed to be overcome by trampling forces indifferent to his fortunes – man at least can have this power of comprehending in his pinpoint of consciousness, in his infinitesimal speck of his mind, the infinity of the universe, even if he expressed it or explained it darkly with complicated errors and intricate fictions.

More anon.

Love from
Your father,
Louis

P.S. Tuesday Morning.

Just as I was going down to the bank to send you one hundred, I received your letter of August 31, telling me not to send the money, as you received your three hundred dollars. All's well that ends well.

That photo of you in front of the ruins was fine.

Keep well. Love. Keep writing.

Louis

Allen Ginsberg to Louis Ginsberg

{Athens, Greece}
n.d. {ca. fall 1961}

Dear Louis:

I am getting plenty of Greek "glory" but it don't seem to stand up against the unhuman sense of things that is making my skin crawl lately. The light thru Parthenon columns is a great white-blue solid color – like looking thru eyesockets of a skull. I traveled all week, Delphi & Olympia, walking all day thru idyllic valleys – that's the best thing I've seen so far & made me actually happy for a day.

I hope to be in India – Bombay – by Jan 1, & will visit Israel before then for sure.

I tried quitting smoking yesterday & have held out so far 24 hours tho my chest feels empty & my throat strange & I am almost drunk with dizziness & awareness of something missing. The withdrawal-symptoms of nicotine are fantastic.

I'm in Athens for weekend to pick up mail, then off on a few more side trips – Crete, Hydra (Islands) Mt Athos (strange monasteries) – I'll keep sending you cards if I'm not in place for regular letters. All's going well, I've been drawing & filling notebooks with scraps of description & thoughts etc. Nothing special – I don't know what for even to write poetry lately. Interesting turn of events. [. . .]

I would attempt to explain more what I am thinking about, but lately words & language themself seem to be a kind of mistake – I would like to try to reach some level of consciousness involving another part of my brain than the cortex (I think it is) which reduces all experience to "structure" "meaning" and words, language, logos. I got there with some drugs often, & it was a different universe – much richer & more "real" tho extremely painful as it involves the death of any idea of self, etc.

Spent all day wandering around in cafes downtown Athens, & in the park, talking with people & getting information on Islands, travel, India, etc.

Enclosed find a bunch of clippings to store – maybe some are duplicates.

O.K. – Love to you & love to all –

Your son,
Allen

Allen Ginsberg to Louis Ginsberg

Athens, Greece
October 16, 1961

Dear Louis –

Closing up accounts in Greece, finishing *Iliad,* probably move on toward Middle East the end of week – here are some papers, reviews etc. to file, including yr. cut out poems & a poem on snow by W.C.W. you might be interested in –

Everything fine, back in the $ for awhile, rcd. from City Lights.

Wrote Honey (rather intemperate incoherent letter on US politics as usual) – things seem to get worse & worse & will not get better till people in the U.S. *do* something to change U.S. life & govt. to make it more human & *socialist*, and end the puritan-Catholic-Jewish Middle Class materialism & conformity. Greece, France are in the same hole – Countries racked by lousy governments, stupid wars, the people completely indifferent, inactive, supine, believing everything they read in the papers is real & inevitable, all political parties corrupt & no one able to get enlightened groups together. [. . .]

Always the same choice between Kennedy & Nixon & not one *human being* in the government able to say shit to the Cold War and get on with more pressing problems of evolution & *world* prosperity. The whole human race at an impasse and everybody willing to pour out their filth and frustration on someone like Bertrand Russell who at least makes sense & takes individual action. Whole idea of individuality has become a disgusting joke in U.S.A. & that's the only place there is hope – or was hope – for a humane alternative to mass mechanization under communism.

Greek intellectuals all in same boat, they have police state super McCarthyism supported by U.S. bases – none of my bohemian artist friends here can get passports, half the intellectuals on prison islands, folk music concerts canceled by police with fire-law excuses, newspapers full of pre-election hysteria, shootings in the suburbs at left wing (non Commie) rallies – and not one candidate willing to declare independence of both U.S. and Russian threats. Same scene North Africa, South America. West Berlin & Adenaur is just the old Nazi middle class turned Catholic now voting for Adenauer & wanting another war. East German communists are also creeps & thieves but no worse than West German scene: any U.S. propaganda on West German side is (I tell you) crap.

So much for today's editorial. I'm alright – I hear people on E. 2 Street are all flipping & LeRoi Jones been arrested for picket line activity in U.N. –[1]

Allen left for Israel in late October.

---

1. The bottom of the letter, including signature, was torn off.

Louis Ginsberg to Allen Ginsberg

October 26, 1961

Dear Allen,

A man was here to say that you owed the Internal Revenue about twenty-five dollars. He asked you to fill out this form. If you can't dope out the form, send it to Eugene, our lawyer. Sorry.

Here is a poem I wrote a few years ago, called "My Mother at Eighty-eight." [. . .]

Otherwise, there is no news here.

I received five copies of your new book, *Empty Mirror,* and will read it shortly. Have you received any response about it? Am saving all clippings about you in a box.

How is Israel? If I were there, I presume that, somehow, I would receive a tug somewhere deep in my subterranean regions, in the deeps of Jung's collective Unconscious where genetical vibrations stir from our Jewish historical lineage. Write and tell me how you felt.

Love from
Your father,
Louis

Allen Ginsberg to Louis Ginsberg

{Haifa, Israel}
November 2, 1961

Dear Lou:

Received letter here, answered Treas Dept one – asked them for more info on why I owe them loot. I'd already written & got no answer. Poem on your mother last 2 lines very funny & bleak too. No, probably no reviews for *Empty Mirror,* minor book in long run. I wept on ship pulling into Haifa, old holyland blues, I'm a sucker for anything like that. Having a nice time, it's like being at vast anarching Family Circle meeting, everybody hospitable, have places to stay here & Jerusalem & Tel Aviv – I've been keeping to myself a lot tho, no public scene, avoid readings and newspaper interviews, I have tho seen literary cafes & met painters & some poets etc. The great thing is all the old-world socialists have made their utopias here – the kibbutz atmosphere is like Camp Nichtgedeiget[1] – NY state summer camps. Lots of "lectures" à la Sam Freiman or better – it's very charming. Intellectual life tho is very tame, painters & poets all in-group professionals, they make a good living, nobody does anything astounding – the Prophets be out of place. They even have artist's villages (mainly commercial art dreary – the few good artists complain) – Also lots of complaints by the old timers that Israel's getting too middle class & Pioneer spirit slowly fading – except for Arab threat which is huge incentive to energy & growth & flexibility. Arabs here not treated very well at all, basically an insoluble problem until people forget their differences & identities – which neither Jews or Arabs are capable of doing. You'd probably enjoy visit here, I do a little, tho I found the first week a little depressing – Spent a few days in Galilee near Bible-spots, a day in Tel Aviv & most of time in Haifa so far. But still haven't gone out to see the land and countryside & kibbutzes yet. I'll be here a month, then get ship from Eilat, which is port on Red Sea – ship to Orient.

I see by enclosed that LeRoi Jones is in soup again. It's discouraging. Don't feel like writing letters today so will end here –

Love
Allen

I sent a package of books from Greece – just store everything in basement when it arrives.

Allen Ginsberg to Louis Ginsberg

{Haifa, Israel}
n.d. {ca. November 1961}

Dear Louis:

Still here in Israel, stuck, can't get out thru Arab States toward India & can't get a ship from southern Israel part of Eilat. I sent to *Playboy* magazine asking for $500 on promise of a small article on India, which I guess they'll O.K. so then when that comes thru in a week or so I'll fly out – toward

1. A camp in upstate New York, heavily political in tone, where the Ginsbergs camped when Allen was young.

Teheran in Persia or Mombassa in Africa – and trans-ship from there. Am anxious to get to Ceylon near the new year – as Paul Bowles will be there & has a house & knows the country – also Gary Snyder is there by then & we're to travel together.

The main beauty of Israel (aside from democracy as I mentioned) is that it is a haven for persecuted Jews. Many are here by necessity and not all are happy to be here just by necessity – after that it is another thing, to live for future. And living for future is not necessarily fun here as it's not for some kinds of people as interesting a place as N.Y. or Paris or even Mexico City or Athens. I don't personally feel much historical connection in my bones after all – I feel it more in the *Idea* or *Ideal* than I do in the reality while I'm here – that is to say, this place is just another small country while & when you're here for real – unless you have a pronounced tendency to be Yiddish which I don't – as a matter of fact I feel a more pronounced tendency to feel at home among Indians & Arabs in Mexico or Tangier – and that *Oriental* atmosphere is slowly disappearing here, to the dismay of many Sabras – disappearing to be replaced by a materialistic polyglot modern second rate industrial country. That is the significance that's attached to the slow decay of the idealistic socialist kibbutz scene – which now has a minority place & in a sense is no longer the soul of the new nation. All I'm saying is that unless you have a pronounced single-minded dedication to an *exclusive Jewish* frame of reference in life, this place is not so exciting. Granted it's fine as a refuge for the persecuted, and granted also that the persecuted themselves are not so kindly to their own Arab minority. But it's like being in a Chinese place where all the Chinamen are hung up on being Chinese and that's all they talk about – can be maddening too. It demands an *exclusively* Jewish mentality, whatever that is (everybody here's always arguing that) and I find that a definite limitation on my own mentality which is Jewish enough but a lot more than that. This is XX Century and I still say the old order of Identity is a big nationalistic hang up on every side. It would be something if there were any folk songs to preserve, but here they *invent* second rate folk songs so they can "cherish tradition" –

Thanks for the poems – Glad you hope to travel. I'm off to India soon I hope – Please forward the enclosed letter? – "Upstairs and Down"[1] is very modern, have you tried *New Yorker* with that?

Love
Allen

1. See "Upstairs and Down," LG, *CP, p.* 245.

P.S. I mailed 2 packages – slow mail – one envelope full of old letters, please store those unopened, they're all mixed & no mss. in it. The other a square package of books, guidebooks to Israel & Greece included. Open those & put them on shelf & skim thru them, they might be interesting.

I heard from Eugene & am in touch with him.

OK,
Love
Allen

Louis Ginsberg to Allen Ginsberg

November 17, 1961

Dear Allen,

Glad to get your postal from Tel Aviv. That was a fine panoramic view of the ocean front of Tel Aviv. I guess you have much leisure to browse around and to ruminate and even make notes on new poetry.

We all are O.K. here. This Thanksgiving we are having Eugene and Connie and the children, together with some others, for a regular feast. Wish you were here.

Nothing new otherwise. No news from my agent yet. He's trying.

I received a sudden summons from the Paterson State Teachers' College to do some substitute work. A teacher fell seriously ill so that I was asked to complete the part of her program until the end of the term, another two and a half months. Starting on Tuesday, Nov. 21, I'll give three courses: advanced composition, a short story course, and also, guess what? – a creative writing class. It looks challenging; so I hope I shall enjoy it, though it will require work on my part, much reading.

I gather you had a favorable review of your *Kaddish* in *The Nation*.[1] If you have not already received it, I'll try to procure a copy for you.

More anon.

Love from
Your father,
Louis

---

1. The review, written by Robert Hazel and published in the November 11, 1961, issue of *The Nation*, was actually a review of *Empty Mirror*.

Allen Ginsberg to Louis Ginsberg

{Jerusalem}
November 25, 1961

Dear Lou:

Got your letter. No haven't seen *Nation*. Enclose an article in Hebrew.
Met some interesting poets, met Buber & Gershom Sholem who is
Caballa scholar, seen rabbis dance in Synagogue, now getting India visa
& trying to figure how to get there. [. . .] I will leave here around the 4th
or 5th or 6th; today is the 25th. About 10 days. How're you, nice to get
your letter. Having weird dreams about arriving in India and early
impressions of life, like leaving wombs, tho that's a little literary all this.
Lots of Politics discussed all bound up with questions what is a Jew,
nobody here knows, and also a lot of guilt about Arab population among
poets & intellectuals & almost everybody, who talks, who I talked to. I
met lots people, Tel Aviv & Jerusalem where I passed last week. Too
much American money, too many cars, the "old spirit" giving way to
television in 2 years, same confusions as the rest of the world, except
teetering on Arab brink but no worse than US & Russia – all *Time* &
Newsweek talking about US bombshelter & that appearing weird here, &
that type news is received with raised eyebrows. Happy Thanksgiving.
I'll be here for Hanukkah, but that's not a big holiday. The Orthodox
Jews have voice in Party politics & keep buses from running on Sabbath,
also handle divorces, so that Jews and Arabs can't marry which is not
democracy nor a satisfactory situation for the majority of people who are
annoyed at theocratic intransigence & ugly character; same time the
Hasidic Karta orthodox group don't even recognize the State because it
has nothing to do with the Laws of Messiah, & they throw stones . . .
threw stones at an ambulance on Sabat, and someone lost an eye. A
Cannanite group says forget about West & go back 2000 years & be
Levantine. I'm going to bed.

Love to you
Allen

Great courses you're giving. Well you have good experience, just encourage
them to reveal their souls!

Please mail this letter enclosed. I can't send mail direct to Morocco from here. Terrible block! Also have lots of travel complications in figuring how to jump from here to India.

Louis Ginsberg to Allen Ginsberg

December 9, 1961

Dear Allen,

Glad to get your long and interesting letter of the Nov. 29.

I dispatched that letter of yours to Paul Bowles.

I observed your adimadversions on [Henry] Miller's sex descriptions: I am not offended by his writing on sex, but many of his pages are – to me – tasteless and unillumining. As for goofy happiness, James Thurber is much admired there in America. The more I read him, the more I like him.

I didn't go to the Newark Lit. Club, since I had to attend a faculty meeting of Rutgers.

About Israel: I have already written you about the sense of belonging to Israel because of an inherited historical heritage in the bones of the Jews. Also, the fact that Israel is the only country in the world that longs for the inflowing of all Jews in the face of a refuge from all forms of virulent and covert anti-Semitism. True, Jews, as all people, have a common bond of humanity which humanitarism progress will enhance in coming times. Besides, all types of nationalities contain universals, each adding their contribution to the general. A rose differs from a marigold, though they are both flowers.

I read with much interest the clippings. Will file them.

I am keeping busy here. I took the Paterson State College work, because, though I prefer retirement, I need to save up money for traveling later. Seems my pension just about almost makes ends meet. In my creative writing class, we are getting out a mimeographed magazine, containing the best term's efforts.

Am enclosing my poem, yet unpublished, which was read at the last meeting of the Poetry Society meeting. Also a clipping of a poem, "Concert," which appeared in the *N.Y. Herald Tribune*.

My literary agent reports that some publishers like my poems but are afraid to take a financial chance. So it goes . . .

Keep well – and keep writing to me.

Eugene and Connie and the kids are fine, though the kids are always having dripping noses from colds. We'll visit them next week before the Christmas holidays, as is our wont.

> Love from
> Your father,
> Louis

Allen Ginsberg to Louis Ginsberg

> *Tel Aviv {Israel}*
> *December 27, 1961*

Dear Louis –

Fast note – I'm leaving tomorrow (exactly two months here now) by ship for Mombasa, E Africa – that's in Kenya – I'll get a few days sniff of the Mau Mau & catch the first ship I can on to Ceylon. [. . .]

I'll probably be there around the 3rd week of January. Spent Xmas in Holy Land, but not much happened & I couldn't manage to get across into old Jerusalem because of the bureaucratic mistake on my passport making it impossible to pass Jordanian Customs – so missed the party. Israel's Customs had absent-mindedly stamped Israel visa onto my passport instead of on separate paper as is customary to deceive Arab border officers. When he realized what he'd done he looked unhappy & then spread his hands. 4000 miles travel nullified in half a second's goofing.

I'll write soon as I get to Mombasa.

> Love,
> Allen

Please tell Eugene change of address, when you next call him.

As he had hoped, Allen reunited with Peter Orlovsky during his stay in Israel. His plans to visit India, however, were slow in reaching fruition, mainly because he and Peter were having difficulties in securing passage on a ship that would take them to Bombay. They finally took a ship from Israel to Kenya, and they spent a month exploring Africa.

Allen Ginsberg to Louis Ginsberg

> *c/o East African Airways*
> *Jubilee Insurance Bldg.*
> *Kilindini Road*
> *Mombasa, Kenya*
> *January 21, 1962*

Dear Louis:

Fast note: Been in East Africa for about a week – Mombasa & now in Nairobi – seen lions and giraffes from bus living in cheap Negro-Arab hotel in Nairobi. Will travel further inland to Lake Victoria this week probably.

I have ticket for Bombay, India, on a ship that leaves from Mombasa on 15 February – about 3 weeks from now. You can reach me here till then (don't mail anything here after the 5th Feb) – I'll send you Bombay address later.

Today I sent a huge skin drum and a smaller drum to Paterson by slow boat mail. The drum cost $10 here and is worth a hundred or more in N.Y. Treat it gentle when you get it – you can even use it as a coffee table till I get home to bang on it. It should reach you in about two months. One big drum wrapped in cloth, and another box with small drum & a wooden percussion instrument too.

Also today went to huge political rally in Nairobi Stadium, Jomo Kenyatta main speaker, vast thousands of Negro audience, Peter Orlovsky and I were literally the only white people in the crowds – a weird dreamlike experience. I'm writing in haste – very exciting & curious human scene here in Kenya – spent several days last week in Tanganyika too – all independence fever here. I'll write –

Love,
Allen

Louis Ginsberg to Allen Ginsberg

January 30, 1962

Dear Allen,

Received your letter from Mombasa.

Sounds exciting about the lions and the tigers. Will save the drum when it comes.

Here is a letter from the revenue officer, saying you owe $25.00. If you can't pay it, let me know, and I'll pay it.

As I wrote you in my previous letter, which you may not have gotten, I turned down, at the last minute, the regular position at Paterson State College. Two composition classes at night plus three composition classes by day plus a drama course would loosen a tidal wave of papers that would smother me.

Had another poem taken by *Ladies' Home Journal*. *The Outsider* wrote me and asked for a poem. I sent them one called "Still Life"[1] (which you may recall about you and Eugene away and me in the movies in the empty apartment where a ghost rattles the lock . . .)

No other news. Write soon to

Your father,
Louis

P.S. I miss you.
    Love and kisses.

---

1. See "Still Life," LG, *CP*, p. 253.

Allen and Peter finally found a ship that would take them to India. They arrived in Bombay on February 15, 1962.

Allen Ginsberg to Louis Ginsberg

c/o American Express
Dadabai Naoroji Rd.
Bombay, India
March 16, 1962

Dear Louis:

I've been last 3 weeks traveling with Gary Snyder and his wife[1] & Peter from New Delhi, sightseeing here, up to the foothills of the Himalayas – up to about 6500 feet, old towns called "Hill stations" which the British used to use for summer resorts to escape the heat – it's spring here now & we saw some great views of the high Himalayas – 200 miles all along the horizon ranged high as clouds a series of flat snow peaks going down to Nepal & into Tibet – been 100 miles from the Tibetan border & had great trip. Maybe go back later in summer if the heat here proves as bad as they say it is. Health is fine, India no less healthy than Mexico & I'm used to that now so everything hunky dory.

India is really great – don't know where to begin there's so much to see & do. Next move a trip thru an area called Rajasthan & a city Jaipur full of Arabic-Persian influenced castles & towers built by oldtime Maharajas – and lots of elephants & monkeys there too.

The tax collectors letter made sense to me. I have no way of paying him from here. Will you please send a check for $25.59 to U.S. Govt [. . .]

Add a note saying you are sending it to cover 1960 Income tax for Irwin Allen Ginsberg as per request of Mr. Mullen's letter of Jan 29, 1962.[. . .]

In the meantime you should by now have received or will be receiving $20 sent to me by American Express – use that to make up the money you're putting out. Has that $20 arrived yet? Is it in a form you can cash & keep? If it is not, send it on to me here, and I'll send you the $25 as soon as I hear from you. O.K.? In other words I'll see you get your money back promptly, one way or another.

Meanwhile I've sent you 2 packages yesterday from New Delhi. One is 9

1. Poet Joanne Kyger.

small Indian & Tibetan style brass & copper statuettes – religious figures mostly. If any of these please you or Eugene, take them for mantelpiece. The rest please put away for my return with the rest of my papers and Junk.

The second package is some books & pamphlets & some personal papers of Orlovsky, a bagful. Please put his papers in the basement unopened, and read or store the books for me. Gregory wrote that he picked up his box of mss. Put Peter's away safe – some collectors & libraries are already asking for letters & mss., they're worth loot some day & so should be kept safe from harm. They're his private notes & letters so best not go thru them. The books are mostly about India.

English Penguin series offered me 1/3 of a paperbook – 25,000 copies to be printed – so that's going OK. Also I have an Italian translation set for Jan 1963. And a German *Kaddish* next year, and a Hebrew-Israeli selected poems volume being done this year. Dribbles of money come in so I'm OK especially as living is so cheap here – We go from city to city living practically rent-free in Hindu & Buddhist Pilgrim's rent houses. I've been eating cheap vegetarian food which costs 20¢ a meal. Interesting to try no meat for awhile. It's a general custom here, and "intrapersonal" relations with cows & chickens are much improved in this part of the world. Tho the diet is boring – I take vitamin pills to supplement it & eat lots of fruit & nuts. Not bad.

I sent Eugene a big Tibetan wool blanket to use or save for me, plus some extra clothing I want stored for return.

If you want any kind of Indian blankets, rugs, paintings, statues – if Edith wants a silk Sari – let me know and I'll try to ship it across to you. Prices are very cheap. I don't have enough to pay for very expensive items but if there's anything definite you would like, send me some loot & I'll shop around for you & ship it. Kashmir shawls for instance. I saw one fantastic huge (8 feet by 8 feet) brown shawl of exquisite *warm* thin Kashmir weave – so delicate it can be pulled thru a ring – warm as heavy wool blanket – light as a hand towel – rare – but costs $150.00 – If I were richer I'd send it. If anyone wants something like that, I can arrange. Be a great life-long present for Kashmir shawl lovers – etc. or a baby elephant?

OK – Later – Love –
Allen

Vekselman[1] I don't think knew your father, I'm not sure.

1. In a November 2, 1961, letter, Louis had encouraged Allen to look up Israel Vekselman "the son of a woman who is my father''s sister. He might recall my father, Pinkus Ginsberg.'

Enclosed poem "Age 65" – you sure sound peaceful & that's sad happy thing to read.

Say hello to Harold & Olive & congratulations on their baby.

Sounds best not to teach so much but take it easy & write poems – What else to do – why work when it's not absolutely necessary. Nice they offered you a steady job.

Say hello to Claira & Honey & Leo & Abe. Tell them I'm letting my hair grow down to my shoulders, I'm eating vegetarian and I'm wearing Indian Gandhi-style shirt & pants made of white handloom cloth. I look exactly like an Indian native. I'll send a photo sooner or later. The way I look, nobody notices me here, whereas if I drest U.S. style everybody would stare & ask questions. Anyway my long-hairomania has finally found a practical use.

I'm sending little brown envelope of clippings by slow cheap mail – stow away when you get them.

Louis Ginsberg to Allen Ginsberg

March 20, 1962
Spring today

Dear Allen,

Received your letter from India today.

I also have on hand a check for you for twenty dollars from the American Express Co. Will cash it. Then I'll send $25.59 to the local Revenue officer in payment for your 1960 income due.

Yes, the big drum arrived. We are keeping here in my sun-room: a good conversation piece.

Glad to hear you are widely translated. Send me copies of all when they are available. Am happy you are so successful!

(Incidentally, an article by Rexroth in the current *Nugget*[1] mentions you. He says that "you are slave to your public image, but you are very good poet and have exerted a liberalizing influence in current poetry."

Send photo of yourself: it should be intriguing.

Enclosed find two recent poems from *N. Y. Herald-Tribune* and the *N. Y. Times*. The latter has a new policy: about four poems a week with "names,"

---

1. Kenneth Rexroth, "San Francisco: The Cool Frontier," *Nugget*, June 1962.

like I. A. Richards, Stephen Spender, and I think R. Lowell, etc. *McCall's Magazine* will have a poem of mine out in a few days.

Oberfirst Associates reports no news. If nothing happens with my book, they are considering putting it out themselves. They have published books of short stories and anthologies, I'll see.

In a week, when I get paid from Rutgers, I'll send you a small money order to get a shawl for Edith.

I am teaching two nights a week at Rutgers; the rest of the time I have an abundance of leisure to read and write and am enjoying myself. A new rather avant-garde magazine called *Poet and Critic* took three poems of mine. Also the *Book Review* of the *N. Y. Times* reprinted a short poem of mine called "Microscope."[1] Am going to the March meeting of the Poetry S. of A. where I am to be a critic of the mimeographed poems.

Eugene and Connie are OK. The kids are thriving, except for periodical colds. They are all coming here this Sunday, and I'll regale them with news from you.

It was a long time since I had heard from you so I was getting worried. Try to write more often.

Otherwise, all is status quo. Abe, following his pattern, fell off the water wagon, but he is recovering. Harold and Olive got a four-room apartment in a project and are happy.

I'll store safely all those things from your friends. Kerouak [*sic*] admitted his paternity in his case, defended by Eugene, and has to pay twelve dollars a week for support. Eugene had him sleep over his house a few nights so he could get Kerouak sober in the courtroom for the trial.

I send you my love. I miss you.

Your father,
Louis

Allen Ginsberg to Louis and Edith Ginsberg

{Bombay, India}
April 21, 1962

Dear Louis & Edith:

Arrived back in Bombay a week ago after trip thru Ajanta Caves & Sanchi

1. See "Microscope," LG, *CP,* p. 369.

(ancient sculpture) and Ellora rock-cut cave temples & been staying in comfort in house of rich friends & gave a little poetry reading here with Gary Snyder, who is sailing back to Japan today. So I'll stay here a few weeks & catch up on mail & fill out income tax & read books. I got all yr. letters & $15 check. One letter says buy a *shawl* & the other, a *sari*. I'll get a shawl, I *guess* that's what's wanted. If you want a sari, fine, I'll get one too. Do you want a sari too Edith? India is lovely, & the hot season is just beginning – so I'll see what that's like in Bombay. I'm reading lots of classic Indian poetry & legends & philosophy. Not tended to my mail yet so I'll answer yr. letters in a week or so. We did some climbing – up to 9000 feet in Himalayas – met the Dalai Lama of Tibet for an hour's interview – saw all sorts of Tibetan refugees – been traveling 3rd Class trains sleeping in luggage racks & eating Indian style with my hands. So, after a few weeks here next stop probably be Calcutta & then to Himalayas for summer.

Love
Allen

Louis Ginsberg to Allen Ginsberg

July 27, 1962

Dear Allen,

The inevitable happened. Yesterday, My mother – your grandmother – died, and today we buried her.

She had been fading for the last year; and a few days ago, a stroke half paralyzed her. Yesterday morning she died; and because Saturday is a Jewish holiday, we had to bury her today, Friday.

As the pallbearers carried the coffin to the grave, dug out beside my father's, I fancied I heard the faint echo of the hoofs of Emily's horses as "their heads were toward Eternity." I had something of the same notion when Naomi was buried (and you mentioned the notion in "Kaddish").

So, now my mother joins Naomi in a deep rest and peace on which nothing more can disturb them.

We all spoke about you and wondered when we would see you.

Take care of yourself.

Love from
Your father,
Louis

Allen Ginsberg to Louis Ginsberg

American Express
Calcutta, India
August 5, 1962

Dear Louis:

Received your letter July 27 about Buba dying. I'm sorry I was not there to comfort you if there is any comfort or if any is needed, but I guess the whole family must have had a mass vision of Time, all gathered together at once to see the last word spoken on all our childhoods. Are you alright? Give my love to Hanna & Clara and Abe, I am missing a great deal not to be at 11 Pomona this week. I guess there's no way to roll back the picture. July 28 I was writing poem in Journal:

> "Now I am brooding on a pillow
> with my arm resting on my head
> eyes closed open on gulfs black time
> (water buffalo herds, wide streets,
> the liquid image of Olive Oil
> popeyes in and out of a second
> mixed up with the vast blankness)
> This is myself in the flesh. Whom
> am I to trust? I feel companion
> to all of us now before death
> waiting inside life. One big
> place we are here. Others have
> left before us – Where could they keep
> themselves absent now – but
> what tricks they had to play to
> escape from the fat bodies –
> to take that step at last, cracked
> open from head to foot, choking, blind
> swallowing themselves entire like
> the snake that does remain
> to them the old reminder of
> before the solitary Question
> one became one was familiar –
> That poor hopeless being in the dark

knowing its own whole universe
a big selfish lie become so
painful it must vomit all its
memory away – and let that
reptilian vastness recreate itself
apart from eye or ear of any dreaded
touching any more – Who am I in bed
with my eyes closed, so familiar
from before –?"

Well this went on for several pages recalling ghosts of people but I'll leave it off for now. Yes Emily Dickinson's horses are amazing Prophesy, that is at moments the Symbol of their destination takes on a cosmic inevitability and a strain of unforeseen light enters the mind. It is to that area of unforeseen awareness I was directing my attention, almost scientifically, trying to widen my own conscious till it be continuously in fuller contact with the source of the uncanny light – because it is there, always constant or "eternal" at moments of crisis – recurring – Also deeper awareness, at a depth as a day to day experience may lead to some difference in evolution of human society. I don't know if poetry can carry all that weight once the awareness becomes more than a transient poetic flash, tho that's all we mostly experience, except I guess as age comes nigh or life freaks us into abnormal awareness. The "reptilian vastness" above is the sense of non human or non egoistic radiance that is underneath Time.

So how's Eugene? I sent him a package of 2 Tibetan Tankas last week which should arrive in 6 weeks.

What kind of mind was Grandma in the last weeks? Did she have anything special coming thru? Or was she too weak to remember much? And what do you feel like now orphaned so old – I guess you were used to your mother as a permanent fixture of life – but I guess you must have been prepared? OK Lou, I'll close & write later, I received Cuban pamphlet which I had seen in *Encounter*. No plans except leave Calcutta & continue travel India when money is sufficient.

Love
Allen

Are you OK? Too many memories crowd in. I wonder if it's worth writing them down or is it more sand. Love, Allen.

Louis Ginsberg to Allen Ginsberg

August 13, 1962

Dear Allen,

A few months before my mother died, she kept asking about her grand-children. I showed her clippings about you and told her about your international reputation as a poet. She seemed pleased and remarked that the poetic ability of ours descended from the literary strain of our forebears.

The last month she faded rapidly, like a candle going slowly out. Then a stroke laid her low until she died shortly after, without pain, more like a gentle falling asleep.

At the burial, as the casket was toiling its way slowly down into the impartial hospitality of the open grave, there flashed through my mind, like a rapidly running movie, some incidents in her life: her coming to America, her marriage, my childhood and its scenes in Newark, my starting to write on 15 Ave. (Often she insisted, though tired, in wrapping the laundry bundles, because, she told my father, I was too busy upstairs writing poetry), her efforts at consoling you and Eugene at the various summers in Belmar while Naomi was away, etc. etc. All in a flash, as the coffin slowly sank, her body emptied of her countless errands, dust to dust, bestowing her immortality to her children and grandchildren . . .

About that unearthly light granted to earthly creatures: it is a transcendent experience, as we call it, visited on saints, lunatics, drug users, flagellants, poets, etc. It does give one a feeling (I have had it at times during some of my poems) as if one has been lifted to the heights where some luminous stream of empirical light streams from secret sources to find all things porous and open to its influence, knitting near and far, linking the moment to the momentous, in a moment when the timeless dips into time, like a sudden holy sanctification. True, all true in effect; however, I find no scintilla of scientific evidence to prove that we explore sources outside of our own being's or body's senses . . . What radiance there is beyond Time we conjecture: but in truth, the sky is black in outer reaches of space and we see light because of thick atmospheric dust on earth . . . There is blackness in the universe except for the unimaginable brilliance of the millions of suns, some exploding or dying through aeons, as our own sun eventually will, so scientists tell us, dooming our own earth to inevitable extinction. Says Schweitzer: "The universe is a riddle: it both creates and destroys." Meanwhile, man is different from all other creatures: he is not indifferent to the indifference of the universe, but tries to snare a meaning from a seemingly meaningless universe, trying at the same time to heighten his awareness and intensify his contemplation of himself and his surroundings.

Otherwise, all's well.

Here is a review of your book from the current issue of *Poetry*.[1]

Am also enclosing a condolence card of a Rutgers student of mine, a staff writer on the *Passaic Herald-News*. (Please return it.)

Write soon to

Your father,
Louis

Allen Ginsberg to Louis Ginsberg

American Express
Calcutta, India
September 10, 1962

Dear Louis:

You all right? Everything fine here. I send back your borrowed $50 in a week. I been busy last 2 weeks reviewing proofs for a new City Lights book *Reality Sandwiches*[2] which will be poems 1953–60 uncollected, mostly published in scattered magazines here & there. So been working & happy. I'll leave Calcutta & go to Benares the end of the month but keep writing me at this address till I notify you otherwise. Everything settled down in NJ now. Grandma's gone? How's Gene? I sent him some Tibetan paintings.

I go back to work now – mail unanswered a month & piled up. Also probably prepare a selection of poems for Penguin books in England to publish in one of their series. Received friendly message from Yevtuchenko[3] a few weeks ago. I suppose the Cold War is really over all but the shouting. Will require compromises by both sides & cessation of propaganda & paranoia both ways. No way out other than that or blowing up the world. (B. Russell[4] makes most sense of anyone. I hear his scientists at Pugwash have come up with a little black box that solves the problem of bombtest

1. George Oppen, untitled review of *Kaddish and Other Poems, Poetry*, August 1962.
2. *Reality Sandwiches* (San Francisco: City Lights Books, 1963).
3. Russian poet Yevgeny Yevtuchenko.
4. Bertrand Russell.

observations. That puts it squarely up to politicians of both sides. If they don't stop now, it means they are in some kind of secret league to screw up the race which I doubt.)

OK I write later

Love
Allen

Allen Ginsberg to Louis Ginsberg

Amer Express
Calcutta, India
September 25, 1962

Dear Louis:

Enclosed find your poems, the last stanza of ."Funeral" looks solid & "Blunder,"[1] "Diners Cards in Pockets" etc very modern. "Spring Rapture" you wrote before & the years thru you repeat this attempt each time a little more information on the sensation, but if it proceeds from a real occurrence, or a series of real experiences, why not make an attempt (not necessarily in any free verse) to write in direct autobiographical detail about one such specific experience – like say Wordsworth *locates* the site of his Intimation – in Mont Blanc poem – or others – in other words I mean instead of generalizing the experience why not try one poem locating it in time (giving your age specifically & autobiographical circumstances surrounding the moment transfigures) and space (your backyard or at seashore where Jersey or NY State or Newark Public Library wherever it occurred) – and throw in as much prose, prosaic, factual material as can be rhymed oddly or interestingly – that be an interesting variation on this poem – because you repeatedly return to the theme making new attempts periodically, very good why not try from a new angle the same theme but throwing in all the personal detail & data that accompanies the experience, or as much as seems relevant to get across the experience as a living experience of a modern man not just a "poetic" experience to be generalized – "leaf & grassblade" looped – *where* – in your garden, in Eastside Park? – or just general leafs – in other words direct visionary data wherever possible to fix & locate. Working in

1. See "Blunder," LG, *CP*, p. 208.

that direction you might come up with a new powerful statement of this old theme you been breaking your haid on for years & years. I take it you're not entirely satisfied with earlier efforts to fix the sensation artistically because you keep re-trying & re-writing that experience. So, if it is locatable, when & where did it first happen, for instance, & where recur, & in what laundrycart or campus in what decade under what tree or on whose lawn near what smokestack or suburb? Don't that make sense?

Received letter from Bertrand Russell he says: "The nuclear technology is faulty . . . it is a problem in elementary mathematical statistics: nuclear war is a matter of statistical near certainty unless we prevent it." He also says "I have a very personal admiration for Blake, & was so powerfully affected as a young man upon hearing Tiger Tiger read out that I nearly fainted." It's a scary letter, that is he does say, as mathematician, that mathematical probability is that there will be an explosion, given the present setup. What do you think? If I thought his figures & reasoning were really correct, I would be inclined to set out to do something. I'm not sure he's exaggerating or not. Yet on thinking it does seem to make sense, that with all the hysteria & hairtrigger network there will be bad trouble unexpectedly. Well here's a real problem for you. What you think? I am not sure whether to *do* something seriously, or not.

I figure to be back in US on visit next summer coming – Creeley wrote me from Vancouver offering 3 week writers conference invitation with round trip fare paid – which would mean a round the world plane ticket – I could stop off in Japan, NY & return via Paris & Moscow to the Far East – Chance to spend a few weeks in Russia on my own (not sponsored by US or Red bureaucracy). So I wrote him OK – so I should be in NY late August or Sept for a month at least. So see you soon. Then go back for a year in Japan.

I see *Time* magazine is this week calling for invasion of Cuba & appears to me the right wing is solidifying in the US do you notice that. This will prevent Kennedy in future from making real conciliation with communism, & compromise, & that looks dangerous to me. *Newsweek* & *Time* diametrically opposed in tone & facts & attitudes now – looks like sheep & goats separating & possibly some sort of fatal decision taken in the US – and the people not aware.

Do if you have a chance look up whatever material there is around on Russell & his peace marchers etc & ban the bomb propaganda in the USA – it seems to be growing serious, the situation, not the marchers – at least I have been more or less ignoring Apocalypse as actual possibility but difficult to do so when Russell writes me directly that there is urgent danger. He says also both governments hiding news & facts etc. Very much like *1984,* the situation, or a science fiction storybook. What do you think?

The other question that presents itself, if there is such danger as he says, is it worth doing anything about – that is To Be or Not To Be. Not that I don't like life & the human race but I wonder – *if* the race is threatened – if it is so important that the human experiment continue. I guess I would want it to be, yes. Russell seems very convinced that it should go on. At this point however he seems to think it depends on decisions of individuals to intervene to prevent Govts. from blowing everything up. Do you think he's right? Or do you think we should trust the Govts & let things drift.

The alternative to drift is individual action warning yr neighbors, waking up Chuck Joelson (yes why not) etc etc – actual individual responsibility, in cooperation with others who feel an actual threat.

I would pay no attention to purely rational prophesies of doom, except that also intuitively I do sense something very wrong – always have – but now this year I have dreams of politics & deathsheads & bombs – i.e. I receive both subjective & objective (Russell) warnings. So what you think.

Of course Russell's anxiety & tension only *adds* to the overload of world fright, & that doesn't help.

Well father, you got any advice? Should we save the world or let it – possibly – blow itself up? I really don't know the answer, or not sure Russell has posed the right question. It's a scary proposition.

Book I sent Ferlinghetti was poems 1953–60 as yet uncollected in a book – poems published in mags but not in *Howl* or *Kaddish* – writings from Mexico & So America & travels – about 100 pages – *Reality Sandwiches* by name – out in a few months.

Enclosed find $50 travelers check made out in your name from Peter – pays back the money I borrowed months back. Immediate financial pressures here are much less – Peter got 600$ from Veteran's Administration.

Regards to Eugene. OK –

I'll write later.

Love
Allen

What do Honey & Leo say about Bomb? I'm not trying to get anyone hung up on it, I'm just inquiring, what do you, & they, think on this subject nowadays – is it a problem?

Louis Ginsberg to Allen Ginsberg

October 8, 1962

Dear Allen,

Received your letter of Sept. 25 today.

Thanks for the fifty dollars, though, if you needed it, you might have held it.

Re your admonitions regarding my poems anent "revelations," you might have something there. (Reminds me of a remark by Gertrude Stein: "There's no there there.") Sometimes, though, I have "located" the matter in hearing music. Ruminating in my garden touches off some geyser released from subterranean, subconscious fissures or clefts. . . . No, my friend, I am not breaking my head: it's my subliminal self that's struggling for utterance till it rushes out in a final, timeless lucidity.

Here is enclosed a poem called "I Met an Alligator," from the *N.Y. Times*. While we were in St. Augustine, Florida, we went to an alligator farm where I looked, eye to eye, at an old, time-beaten, worse-for-the-wear, enigmatic alligator.

When your new book comes out, *Reality Sandwiches*, let me know so I can order a number of copies. Am eager to take a good bite on those sandwiches. No doubt there's meat but will it give one gas? (From the sublime to the meticulous: Sign at a diner and auto station: EAT HERE AND GET GAS.)

Cuba is a thorn in the side. Despite jingoists, Kennedy is keeping calm. I doubt whether he will let Russia mouse-trap us into some real action so Russia can slice a bit of baloney or "salami," as they say, in West Berlin. But why is Russia stuffing with such arms? Why is Russia making a so-called "shipping port" off the East coast of Cuba? Can it be a submarine base or a base to let the Red subversion seep into the fabric of South America?

Be that as it may, the nub of the question is in West Berlin. I foretell that Russia will make a "pact" with her satellite, East Germany. Then, when East Germany attempts to stop Allies from access to their battle-won rights, there will be bloodshed. But Russia will halt there, not wishing to wet her own paws. Then the U.N. will take up the matter. Of one thing I am certain: if the Allies let a hole go in the dike in West Berlin, the Red rivers of Russia will invade all, till the walls or dikes crumble and the whole continent will go under.

Were Stalin living, there might be a nuclear war. As Khrushchev holds now: Stalin's era was one of assassins and cannibals There is a thaw now; not much, but something. There still is some dialogue. It's too bad, though, that the Russian people are not told the truth: they don't know the reasons for the wall in Berlin; they don't know about Russia's breaking the moratorium; they don't know about arming Cuba. In truth, no Russian can leave any of the satellites. The Commies fear to contaminate their people with the truth . . .

From all I've been able to read: from *Time* and the *N.Y. Times*, *The N.Y. Post*, *The Nation*, Norman Cousins in *The Sat Rev. The London Times Lit Supplement*, *The Evergreen Review*, *The Reporter*, and *Atlas*, *The Magazine of the World Press* – from all these I add and subtract and deduce that there will be no nuclear war but that there will be brush fires stopping short of universal decimation.

We are not living but we are encamped in the world, but the dark clouds will slowly roll away. In conclusion, I would say: Keep your shirt on.

Regards to Peter,

More anon.

Love from your father,
Louis

Allen Ginsberg to Louis Ginsberg

Amer Express
Calcutta, India
October 19, 1962

Dear Louis:

Probably the most communicable way to waken latent timeless sensation in reader is by making economical use of the actual data, circumstances & particularities of your own subjective events – i.e. which music, when, what orchestra, what kind of radio, what kind of room, what did you notice then about the furniture, eyes open or closed, what part of the music, what instruments, what kind of gum were you chewing at the time, what your feet feel like, etc etc – all these as the "objective correlative" of the subjective sensation. The subjective feel is otherwise indescribable except thru abstract generalized idea words which carry little emotional reality acrost to the readers mind's eye. "No ideas but in things."

Not only "ruminating in garden" but when, which time were you ruminating, this year, last, what month, etc all the details which are the life of the moment. All those details to be assembled in whatever form possible makes the poem, rhymed or free as you please. As long as the Form doesn't by its very stiffness rule out use of real doggy details. "Alligator" is excellent first half & last half tho it proposes questions is not as poetic as the photo of the alligator in first half . . . impulse wandered off is still half photographic (wandered) & so carries meaning.

Reality Sandwiches, plenty of gas as the last poem is 25 pages of notations on Ether gas.

What Russell (& also I see this week Burdick book) warned was not that "evil men" would start a war but that already the nature of the machinery makes a war inevitable: Russell says "The nuclear technology is faulty. Rockets cover the planet and are on a hair trigger. It is a problem in elementary mathematical statistics: nuclear war is a matter of statistical near certainty." *Newsweek* Oct 22, page 73 quotes Burdick saying his questioning of scientific experts working in the field, they all agree that now "war by accident is not probable or likely, but inevitable." I don't know. All non govt scientists seem to agree on this. The govts have not commented & can't be expected to. You are the only one who can do anything about it, not the govt., now. That is, I wouldn't let no Govt do your deciding for you any more, on this particular issue. That's like asking for it. The good thing about this situation, it will force people to be individuals again, whether they like it or not.

I guess I am so far apart, from yr political views, it don't make much sense to argue by mail. Several letters ago I was describing how this Maj. Weatherley, Eatherley, whatshisname, flipped & got thrown in the bug-house for saying he was sorry he dropped the atomic bomb. When you wrote back that, right, man was undoubtedly neurotic.

No, what I meant was the govt is neurotic, Truman is mad, the USA is off its rocker, the ONE sane statement in it all is this one lone individual saying he was sorry he dropped the atom bomb. When you wrote back the poor man had a hard time & was undoubtedly suffering strain I was sure we were in *1984*. Usually I would start screaming in this situation but now it's too sad & impossibility of basic communication makes even that hopeless.

Suffice to say, I think it would be helpful if the Russians could read the *NY Times* every day, and it would be equally helpful if you could read, carefully, *Pravda* every day. Or better if Burroughs' method were followed, & somebody cut up the *Times* and *Pravda*, mixed them surrealist at random, & dished up the mixture for international consumption. I'm not kidding. Try taking a statement by Kennedy on Bomb tests & a statement by

Khrushchev, cut them to ribbons with a razor, shake in a paper bag, reassemble at random. You'll emerge with a complete coherent international manifesto displaying the subconscious intentions of both parties. Try same with Cuba, Berlin, etc. Why anybody in his right mind should want to take SIDES in this suicidal contest of Stupidity I'll never understand. Leave it, that as far as I'm personally concerned, I don't care if Russia *or* the USA wins the Cold War. As it is fortunately neither can win so they're both stuck, and everybody with them. As for Cuba, I hope the Russians arm her to the teeth & Cuba makes as much trouble for the USA all over South America as she can. If it were left to the USA alone nothing would ever happen, nothing has for the last hundred years. I been there. The only answer for the USA is to LOWER its standard of living. $12 billion spent on advertising in USA every year diverted to South America would solve the problem. Getting involved with further dogfight with Castro only diverts attention from the real problem which is that South America is everywhere a big goddam economic-political mess & the Communists are the only ones that will do anything about it because the Capitalists certainly won't, haven't, and won't act until it's too late. Alliance for Progress was hopeless from the beginning. 50 to 100 billion is needed not 2 billion. Castro said so 2 years ago. And to think that huge minorities in USA want to attack Cuba NOW? And that this minority & *Time* magazine are now swinging everybody's thought so far to the right in the USA that a pro-socialist reconstruction of SA is unthinkable! Then let the Communists triumph!

Love
Allen

Louis Ginsberg to Allen Ginsberg

October 29, 1962

Dear Allen,

Received your air mail letter of Oct. 19. Have read it carefully. Your remonstrances and indignations are not unfamiliar to me.

I agree that there is danger in the atom bomb. But Russia is pursuing salami tactics and provoking us. I suppose you have not heard the latest; namely, Russia had set up or was setting up missile bases in Cuba, while at the same time she was denying it. Kennedy threatened to extirpate the missile bases with forces of bombers, paratroopers. Then, Khrushchev capitulated and promised to dismantle them, crate them, and return them to Russia, all under U.N. supervision. Note: the people of Russia did not know about the missile bases in Cuba as, indeed, they know very little about the threatening postures of their country. No protests are allowed in Russia again Kruc., but here in America, we allowed peace protests against the White House, even while we were mustering our forces and imposing a quarantine!

Today's *New Republic* says, "The challenge presented by the Soviets was real. The President had to act."

If you were here and saw the loud outcries and protests aired publicly by the COP, peace groups, Commies, and a hundred other dissenters as CONTRASTED with the monolithic one party press in Russia, you'd have pause for doubt or you would be bemused.

There is a little thaw in Russia, but K. still thinks he can bury us. K. is telling Little Red Riding Hood that he is Grandfather . . . The corybantic protraction of the Russians once before Stalin who tried to explain away rivers of blood by downright lies may be over, but the thousand and one distortions of the truth by the Soviets at present only needles the precarious world situation.

Now what about the Chinese Communists???

Listen, boy: Why didn't you answer my challenge which I am now repeating for the fourth time: namely, name one country that Russia released from its despotic grasp compared to the forty or so countries that have been and are being released into independence by the West. Do answer, please.

The method you mention about tearing up statements then shaking them in a paper bag, etc would result in chaos – that way is anarchy. I am surprised that you take it so seriously.

I'm shocked that you want Russia to arm Cuba to Death. As you may by this time see, Khrushchev has promised to remove them. Yes, I am in favor of bombing those missile sights off the earth. You have a mental block about the Commies. Could it be a rationalization of a childhood bias? I any case, I am just as indignant as you are, only I'm against Russia, and I don't give a God damn how you fulminate or froth at the mouth, so kindly talk in a low tone and with low voltage and do reply about my challenge underlined in red.

About the first part of your letter, about the "objective correlative" or about "No ideas but in things" and about concrete details: yes, yes, yes. But one forgets himself in the urgency of writing and one's writings do not come up to one's knowledge or aims. Still, I keep trying . . .

Just keep your shirt on and I'll keep mine on.

Love from
Louis

Allen Ginsberg to Louis Ginsberg

Use same address
Calcutta, Amer Express
December 7, 1962

Dear Louis:

Leaving tomorrow to settle down in Benares. Same Calcutta mailing address can be used, till further notice – they'll forward. Cleaning up & packing, not much time for letters and also I want to cut down on correspondence and get back to solitary writing.

Have been spending a lot of time in the burning ghats (where Hindus dispose of bodies in small wood fires) on Ganges bank, sitting at night and talking & smoking ganja (same as marijuana) with holymen. It's the custom here, sort of Tantrik discipline – to see & familiarize self with dissolution of the body & be at home with corpses & hair burning and eyeballs sizzling etc. Amazing how after a few visits one realizes nothing is happening except a lot of old sofas and pillows of meat are being disposed of.

Received both yr last letters with clippings. I thought my last letter to you have been sensible, in any case I've tried to avoid the hysteria that's drowning everybody left & right. I don't have much more to say than what I said there. I read the clippings you sent. The Jurists report seems fair & Castro regime comes off very badly. This is not news to me as you may remember I began complaining against police state suppression of marijuana also at time of meeting Castro people in Hotel Teresa. The argument by Draper is less convincing, since I am generally against compensation for expropriated industries, and that seems to be the main point at issue, in the general argument as to what turned Castro so anti-US. US aid according to the letter set as precondition such compensation. I do remember as the crucial headline during that whole period (leading to the expropriation of oil refineries) that US owned refineries refused to process Soviet oil, & that

Louis and Naomi Ginsberg, in happy times. Their turbulent marriage was marred by quarrels over politics and Naomi's lifelong battle with mental illness.

The Ginsberg family during one of its summer vacations in upstate New York. Both Allen (front) and his older brother, Eugene, would follow their father's lead and write poetry.

Allen, as a student at Columbia University.

Neal Cassady, ca. 1947. Cassady, fictionalized as Dean Moriarty in Jack Kerouac's *On the Road*, was a pivotal figure in both the Beat and hippie movements.

William S. Burroughs, at the Metropolitan Museum of Art, New York. An early mentor to Allen Ginsberg and Jack Kerouac, Burroughs achieved fame and notoriety with such novels as *Junky* and *Naked Lunch*.

The New Visionaries: Jack Kerouac, Lucien Carr, and Allen Ginsberg in 1959, at the time of the filming of *Pull My Daisy*.

Edith and Louis Ginsberg, summer of 1954. Edith's wit, intelligence, and compassion brought stability into the Ginsberg household. Quite often, she acted as a buffer in disputes between Louis and Allen, and her extraordinary tolerance was greatly influential in Louis's coming to terms with his son's homosexuality.

In the classroom: Louis taught English and composition on both high school and college levels. Later in life, Allen would follow his father's example, first, at Naropa Institute, where he co-founded a poetics school, and at Brooklyn College, where he taught until shortly before his death.

Allen and Louis, 1964. By this point, Allen, with his characteristic beard and long hair, had become an internationally known figure, with a reputation as a poet that surpassed his father's.

Allen typing in his Cherry Valley, New York, retreat.

Louis, only a few months prior to his death in 1976.

"Battle of the Bards": Allen and Louis, reading together in 1972. Intially marketed as a kind of poetic oddity, the father-and-son poetry readings became highly regarded and popular events for nearly a decade.

was followed by expropriation, and that was followed by wholesale outbreak of anticastro propaganda in the US and anti US propaganda in Cuba.

Too much technical detail to argue over in letters. As for instance Draper in the clip you sent me calls Castro's call for $30 billion foreign aid to S.A. a "grandstand play." Since you remember perhaps that at that time I wrote in Buchwald column supporting that great amount of money as necessary; and wrote you saying I thought the half million proposed by US was just too minute; and since in the last few months the US itself has admitted the failure of its new frontier aid to SA; I now find myself on Castro side of this argument, not yours, Draper's or the US.

I take it you sent the clipping to propose the argument that it was *not* US intransigence that forced Castro into Soviet sphere. My conclusion through all this time is that US intransigence *is* the main problem. It remains so today. After concluding agreement with Russia on Hands Off Cuba & withdrawal of missiles, I see in *Newsweek* that the US no longer considers itself bound to not invade Cuba. Movements such as this are what whip up war hysteria on both sides – especially as in this week's papers I see reports that US based anticastro raiders are continuing attacks.

The US is not sure how, but wants to get rid of Castro. The real problem is that the USA has no proposition who to put into his place. The US did the same thing in Guatemala as I emphasized before to you in letters & conversation, and if you read this week's *Newsweek* you will see the present Guatemala mess. It's no less of police state than Cuba, and not en route to solving any domestic problems anyway. The only difference is that it's pro US – so there is no agitation in the US to change regime there.

As far as I can see the only route at this point is an attempt at conciliation between all parties.

Anticommunist people I know who've recently been to Hungary Poland etc say things are much better. Newspaper reports of recent Czech party congresses – more destalinization campaigns. Read recent Yevtuchenko volume. The main direction seems to be liberalization. Probably because Bomb inevitabilities make war impossible for everyone.

It's just that I'm not interested in fighting "communism" as such. I don't really see the imperialist tradition of Russia as at present in regard to the satellite countries as anything equivalent to western colonialism, "the satellites looted plundered profaned" etc. I would guess that beginning several years ago &, given peace, the tendency of development will be toward more liberalism & economic prosperity in the satellite countries. By 1960, there's no percentage for the Russians in "plundering" Bulgaria,

Hungary etc. I don't think that's what's presently happening there. The worst place is probably East Germany right now. Once pressure from Adenauer is off & imagine the Russians will kick out the intransigent E German communist leaders & try to get things liberalized & destalinized there.

What I'm saying is the present tendency of Russia is relatively rapid movement against old police state scene & I think that will all work out well in the next decade. If you read Yevtuchenko, & recent Ehrenberg etc – also been receiving letters from Villagers who've been in Russia – the worst now seems to be over in Russia. Hypocrisy not over, but worst police is. China's a different matter. My own feeling is, the only way out (re India) is admit China to the UN & support development of a liberalized communism. See the new Snow book.

In fact I imagine the recent Toynbee analysis makes sense, tho it was much attacked several months ago when it came out.

Continued maintenance of emotional hostility on both sides can't solve the problem. Forcing Castro out no solution.

In other words the Cold War gotta stop on both sides. Actually it is stopping but it is taking time for both sides to adjust emotionally to a neutral non hysterical attitude.

Cessation of the Cold War is the only way to insure liberalization inside the communist countries. I don't think there's anything intrinsically wrong with communism. Trouble is, the US was fighting a Cold War against communism itself rather than abuse of communism by power-heads.

Unless you WANT communism to "Fail." I don't. Rather see it succeed and come out allright, adjusted & with power as decentralized as possible in an electronic civilization the techniques of which tend as in US and Russia to centralize power.

Endless agitation & hysteria about war here, now quieting slowly as negotiations begin. Nobody understands Chinese motivation, which is basically irrational, the Chinese motivation I mean. Only way to end that irrationality it to take pressure off China. See Snow book.

In other words force is getting nobody anywhere. Force and righteous wrath which is just tiresome on all sides. The combination of Roy Howard, Luce & Hearst press is holding US psyche back from recognition of simplest neutral necessities as you can even find in *Newsweek*. *Newsweek* now owned by Liberal *Wash Post* people this year & coming on more & more sensibly.

I don't think either US or Russia all last year were ready for Bomb agreement so I don't "blame" either side exclusively – certainly not Russia –

for failing to agree. The Party Line I am following here was first enunciated to me by I. F. Stone & Walter Lippmann.

The situation is too dangerous (or was a month ago) for anyone to indulge any longer in righteous wrath, "anti-communism" "anti-capitalism" blame on the other side, etc. It's obvious communism is here to stay in Russia and China so the problem is to make communism feasible & easy to live with and under etc. The original Dulles line, which corresponded to the original paranoid Stalin line, was death struggle between the two.

Present China war scene tends to further liberalize communist world scene since it splits up the parties into individualized groups. See clip enclosed. The Indian Reds had to shit or get off the pot finally. Enclosed another clip in which U. Thant parrots the party line I am parroting. Was this featured in US press? I imagine so, or hope you saw it already.

The one place where I think "communist imperialism" was/will be ultimately destructive is Tibet. Loss there irreparable.

That's about it. The main problem everywhere is the emotional hangover, everybody been so degraded, everywhere.

Love – Allen

I will go to Moscow next fall I think.

Louis Ginsberg to Allen Ginsberg

Monday, December 17, 1962

Dear Allen,

Glad to hear from you.

Sounds like a gruesome thing: sitting and smoking and watching dead bodies burn. Ogh.

Am enclosing two reviews of your *Kaddish*: one is good; the other is what you'd expect. (It's not a review of your own book, but you are brought in.)

All's quiet here. The population explosion continues: Olive, Sheila, and Connie are all pregnant. How's that? Edith is beaming, for she will be able to boast of nine grandchildren.

Yesterday we visited Eugene and Connie: they are all OK, and keeping busy. Eugene dabbles in astronomy; also, he is writing some fine poetry, which I am sending off to publications for him.

I suppose you heard of the death of Mrs. Roosevelt. Sad but inevitable. Stevenson said: "She did not curse the darkness but lit candles. Her glow warmed the world." [. . .]

I continue teaching at night at Rutgers in Paterson. Next term I am having three instead of two classes.

I suppose in the long run, time will erode the truculence of the Soviets and the West; and each by osmosis and viability and reconciliations will interfuse some of each others qualities.

However, in the short run, I charge you with being a brain-washed Commie – brainwashed by a rationalization of childhood memories and attachment to Naomi's family or by your inbuilt, blind rebelliousness.

The main charge I have against you, re above, is that you blindly waive aside Russia's conquest and rape of her satellites and cavalierly dismiss it all as not in the imperialist tradition. What kind of perverted logic are you giving me? It's all right for you to foam at the mouth and fulminate in wrathful indignation, not forgetting to splash a few obscenities about, when you are strongly indignant about any of the West's faults. Russia's imperialism, I maintain, is worse that the West's former imperialism, because more modern times and more social enlightenment regarding imperialism now as an anachronistic throwback. Yet here you blindly waive aside Russia's rape of her satellites. Hungary, like a brainwashed Commie, you blink at. What if there is one degree less brutality than formerly: Russia's tanks still menace Hungary and Russia's claws (a bit sheathed in wool) are still deep in Hungary. So "things are better in Hungary," you bleat. What garbage, you give me!

About Cuba, you feebly mention "Russia's withdrawal of missiles" and then pass that off into an obscure corner. No, you have no indignation against Russia's introducing atomic armaments into Cuba. You hail Russia's conciliation. You praise the robber for leaving the house, after he has been discovered and threatened if he doesn't leave. How noble of you and how compassionate and understanding!

To conclude my main point: if you don't see the imperialism of Russia in holding on to raped and plundered satellites, there is no further use of arguing with you about the West vs. Russia.

Yours,
Louis

Allen Ginsberg to Louis Ginsberg

c/o Postmaster, Dasaswamedh P.O.
Benares, U.P. India
January 10, 1963

Dear Louis:

Been traveling the last month & returned to Benares where now living. Note new address above. Yr letters were forwarded here. Hope all the Beings upcoming see the light safely. Happy New Year, late, & Happy Xmas. I spent Hanukkah in Benares the "oldest continuously inhabited city in the world" – and have a large room, 9 French doors, balconies over-looking market and Ganges bank bathing ghat, $9 a month rent. Then took trip to Agra, slept inside Taj Mahal for two nights, Xmas Eve there, sublimest hotel in the universe – Taj Mahal unexpectedly great place – greatest human construction I ever encountered – worth trip to India for that alone – Picture Postcards don't reveal the great vibration of the place – I even scribbled a new poem I was so awestruck – awe's the word – that human beings could have got organized to create such a thing – I haven't seen an H bomb explosion tho that alone might rival the Taj Mahal – Peter says the Pyramids in Egypt do something similar – But Taj Mahal moved me much more than Acropolis or anything in Rome. /// Delighted to hear Eugene's looking at planets & stars again. /// Benares burning ghat, holiest in India is ten minutes walk along waterfront from my room. Well gruesome only at first encounter; actually the scene is so real; is traditional place for meditation; after familiarity the sublime transcends the gruesome at the burning ghats. If you can take that as a human picnic ground you can take the thought of death, and the thought of life, easier.

I didn't know I was on trial. "I charge you with being a brainwashed Commie" etc etc. Oh well. All yr clippings from Cuba etc. depressing. Hard to separate propaganda from legit complaint, etc. At same time I receive yr letter – written in somewhat excessive fury – I also get furious letters from LeRoi Jones, Marc Schleiffer, Irving Rosenthal ("Cuba's alright if you like socialism"), & others who have *been* to Cuba, who think Cuba's great & the fault's with America. I trust their judgment – to a point. Also I trust Draper etc – to a point. To the extent that I have had direct personal *first hand* acquaintance with any specific issue in the Cold War scene – I have found all sources of public information as inexact (in politics) as they have been in poetry. So I don't really judge the way you do. Certainly hostility, as I have been saying last months, will solve nothing. Best thing would be guarantee not invade Cuba by US, and promotion of democratic development in Cuba. Both sides now so hysterical that seems impossible. Present U.S. policy as far as I can judge – i.e. the kind of policy that alas flows from your attitude – which is representative US – seems to me to lead to blind alley, blood, stagnation. I don't think the US had proposed a legit alternative to Castro. Be that as it may as you say there's little point arguing about West versus Russia. I don't feel particularly anti-Communist nor anti-Western. The main problem is not Hungary etc – even the US & Russia are negotiating dropping that from UN agenda finally, haven't you dug that? Main problem is (I see it thus) inevitable centralization of power everywhere (E & W) thru technology. I repeat I don't equate Western & Eastern imperialism because I think they lead in different directions, infuriating as that may sound to you. However I'm living in Asia at the moment & it alters perspective oddly. I have no particular sympathy for Chinese attack on India naturally. The main single political issue, to focus & concentrate all tendencies, is China however, & I don't see any progress anywhere till USA tries to make peace with Chinese communism. That is, I don't see any progress within China till that happens. I'm more worried about that than anything else (this month). But I'm sick of yelling from every direction – not even sick, that's just a cliché – I'm sick of clichés – I mean they make so little sense & are so little helpful. Yr idea of my "inbuilt blind rebelliousness" is probably a cliché, "being a brainwashed Commie" etc, "Russia's conquest & rape" etc. We don't seem to be getting anywhere. /// I think mainly, in these terms – I don't predominantly judge the future by the health of America; that is, I don't see why someone living in Topeka is more to be protected than someone living in Nairobi or Calcutta. That's a side note, & obvious statement; but I think much Russian & US thinking is predicated on protection of the motherland, & its safety etc. Certainly Kennedy's thinking and Khrushchev's. /// It's senseless to fill letters like this with vapid political arguments. I think we should stop. Or keep it to a minimum; aphorisms.

Bought a stove for a dollar & shopping & cooking here to see what marketing & home food is like; no beef no pork no lamb; only mutton and fish; lots of vegetables. Below my window an encampment of lepers – must be about 100 of them that live on this street (sleep in cold riverside street nite in burlap rags) – stay here begging because it's a famous pilgrimage holy street, many strangers give charity, tho not much. Women with baskets of vegetables beating cows off from stealing their turnips – they sit on curb & peddle greens, cows hang around & try steal a bite – it goes on all day till dark. Will take trip end of month to Allahabad see gathering of 100,000 holymen to bathe (yearly) there in Ganges. Live in tents, come from all over India to bathe & bless the riverside. Also we visited Brindaban, birthplace of Indian God Krishna – important to them as Bethlehem to Xtians – met some saints & yogis and talked; they sd Blake was my Guru.

Love
Allen

Allen Ginsberg to Louis Ginsberg

Benares, India
March 10, 1963

Dear Louis:

Sorry not written in so long. Been reading second proofs on City Lights book, probably out this summer; many people visiting in and out the house here, professors, poets, musicians, journalists, Secret Police, holymen, American passers-by, etc; *Esquire* magazine sent out a photographer & later a writer to do a story on our stay here[1] & that took up time & nervous energy; and all thru the last month we been bothered by the local CID (Indian FBI) who couldn't figure out who we were & bothered landlord downstairs, dentist neighbors & me & Peter & finally ordered us expelled from India. We had to go to Delhi & see the higher ups in the govt. to find

1. Alice Glaser, "Back on the Open Road for Boys," *Esquire*, July 1963.

out what it was all about & get it straightened out. Almost too long a story to go through, sort of Kafkian bureaucratic dream – it would have been a nightmare but it was too silly to qualify – Anyway we seem now to be OK. Main thing seems to be that since the war the CID, which on local level is nearly illiterate, is looking for spies and decided we must be Yankee-Capitalist-Communist spies. I don't think it's possible to describe the peculiar provincial stupidness of the Gossip, as it's another world. Fortunately we had friends able to speak to the Govt & explain who we were & why here in India so long & finally the Embassy reluctantly intervened & spoke for us. Meanwhile for a month the plainclothes police were visiting us, wanting to see what we write, peeking thru the shutters at nite, gossiping with neighbors & pestering landlord & visitors. From here to Delhi I got a good look at the functioning of the bureaucracy & now begin to see why India's starving. A great corrupt Kafkian mass toppling in on itself.

Writing a lot & publishing some letters & journals material in small Bengali magazines – nice group of Bengali (Calcutta language) writers staring a sort of renaissance "Hungry Generation" they self-called – publish weekly manifestos – we catalyzed them into action & some of their writings be published by City Lights in translation. Liveliest group here.

Also we went along walking one day with a Delhi-Peking Gandhian peace march, met several saintly types & also the Chairman of British antibomb "Committee of 100" who's walking with them. They seem to be the only quiet sane people around. Everywhere else it's loudspeakers & hate & World War I vintage nationalist propaganda & war taxes on the poor & attacks on Nehru & Gandhi tradition & bureaucratic hysteria. They were digging trenches in Delhi & stoning windows of Chinese restaurants till Nehru called a halt. Meanwhile people downstairs near my house dying on the street of hunger & rotting with leprosy, Communists here also hopeless, dogmatic, moralistic, hate-filled & almost as illiterate as the CID. In fact actually it was the Communists who turned the CID on to us. (Odd later to be walking with peace marchers who were being attacked simultaneously by right wing press here *and* Peking Radio.) Great relief to sit down on the banks of the Ganges at sunset & smoke with naked holymen who've taken vow of silence & are the gentlest people around – no axes to grind.

Spent all our money telegraphing Nehru & training to Delhi & now waiting for more to arrive & then take off more touring. Lots to see before I leave here sometime in May. OK – hope you're well. I shipped home four small packs of books while in Delhi, they shd arrive in a month more or two

– one interesting one, Boswellian conversations of the great 19th Century saint Ramakrishna – with pictures of him in samadhi state – ecstatic trances – 1000 pages of odd conversations. Great introduction to the peculiarities & details of Indian mentality/traditions. Take a look at it if you have time. Also there's a pack of old letters mixed in somewhere, to store away. I now accumulated so many papers I can't keep track. However I assume they should be saved as various agents/universities keep writing me offering to buy mss. & letters etc. I haven't sold any yet (except last year the typescript of *Empty Mirror* – just typed pages without corrections – for $100. (Some agent for bibliophiles at Yale. Said he bought copy of *Howl* first edition I'd signed over to Mike McClure for $25.)

Reading Lawrence's poems & also Salinger who's amusing. Odd to see how *Time* built him up as great American Novelist of Decade & now party line's changed and they're attacking him. I see in papers that Russians are cracking down on the poets again. I suppose that means Cold War beginning again in earnest. I feel more & more a general madness on all sides, mainly sheer angriness & incoherence – I'll sit this one out. Dread coming back to the US and encountering all that electrical hate. Tho the tide of same seems to be rising now in India. Feel sort of comfortable here with beard long hair floppy pyjamas in street looking like anonymous Indian. I suppose it would be unsafe to walk US streets looking like that, stoned by J.D.'s.[1]

Reading Blake again. I'd like to go spend a month in London at British museum reading his original editions, they had colored pictures. What you writing, & how feeling now? I'm tired – answered 2 weeks mail yesterday now caught up. OK. Say what color sari did Edith want? I'll send one from Madras next month.

OK – Allen – love
Allen

Louis Ginsberg to Allen Ginsberg

March 23, 1963

Dear Allen,

I was wondering why I didn't hear from you and was hoping you are O.K.

1. Juvenile delinquents.

Good to hear about your next book to be out in the summer. Will get some copies in due course.

That woman from *Esquire* called up before she left for India and after she came back. She said she'd stop into Paterson to see me, but she hasn't come yet.

That must have been a big Kafka affair with you in India. Too bad you were molested and your time robbed from your work. Meanwhile, you got a glimpse of the tangled inside of the messy outside of India.

What new insights did you get of the caste system?

Send on all your books and papers and mss. I have them all. When the books arrive, I usually peek into them and scan some of them, especially the ones containing poetry. Yes, your own mss. will be worth more money some day so I press you to save them. I understand one or two mss. have found their way into collectors' hands. When you come home here, you can sift and sort and arrange all your things into proper and coherent categories for convenient use in due course.

I read the K. has silenced the group of younger poets, including Yevtuchenko, for speaking out a bit too literally for Russia. That's the way it is with totalitarian nations.

As for fluctuation tides of hostility, well, a sage or elevated writer does not let himself be disabled but looks on, if he can, with an Olympian disenchantment.

I have not heard anything new further from my literary agents, but they persist in being optimistic about finally getting my poems published in book form. I now have ready two mss. books of poems. However, I continue writing slowly and steadily. (There has been a N.Y. newspaper strike here for the last three months so that the *N.Y. Times* and the *N.Y. Trib.* have not appeared.)

Recently I have had poems published in these places: *McCall's, The American Weave, The Fiddlehead* (Canada), *The New Mexico Quarterly, The U. of Kansas City Review, The Plumed Horn.* (The editor of the last named magazine sent me a long interesting letter and asked for more of my poems.) I am enclosing three poems selected from the above mentioned magazines.

Eugene is writing new poems. I think they are very good. He should have some accepted soon.

Everyone is O.K. here. Connie expects a new baby in July; Olive, Harold's wife, expects one in June. So, all in all, we'll have eight grandchildren.

Get any gay color of sari for Edith. If you need any money for it or for you, let me know.

Write soon.

Love from
Your father,
Louis

Allen Ginsberg to Louis Ginsberg

Dasawaudh P.O.
Benares VP India
April 8, 1963

Dear Lou:

Everything OK here, general shortage of money as usual but some expected this week. Our visas now renewed but still some static from local CID. I read text to Khrushchev speech it's worse than it sounded in news reports even. Interesting to see if Yevtuchenko & boys will be able to fight it out at all; i.e. to what extent will pressure be economic-bureaucratic & to what extent strongarm. Amazing to see also how much the party's decisions dictated by sheer Philistine ignorance rather than purely politics/necessity. i.e. for instance Sholokov opined Yev should not be allowed to travel as he was a bad propagandist, not realizing that the immediate impact of Yev was to create sympathy for present Russia generations rather than vice versa. Also not realizing the beneficial (from their viewpoint) impact of Yev's visit to NY on people like LeRoi Jones & procuban militant poets. Also Khrushchev doesn't realize his attack on Jazz going to infuriate pro Red Negroes, i.e. a tactical mistake not realizing that Jazz is "authentic Negro common people's music" so to speak. Since the attack was on abstract paint, jazz, poesy, dedecaphonic music etc. I don't think in the long run the bureaucracy will make it stick – i.e. I think it will be too late for them to enforce (strongarm) their opinions; best they can do is make it difficult to publish play display commercially thru state monopoly, & cut off money to avant garde. All which will (as long as violent punishment not applied, maybe it will) tend to strengthen the avant garde which no longer identifies itself with Govt. Like the irony is Yev did identify self with & try to represent the WE of communist politics – now he'll be driven (unless the social pressure or need for money breaks his spirit) to individualistic position more near akin to his U.S. counterparts, i.e. not identifying self with state. The interesting figure all along is Yessenin-Volpin, a young poet natural son of Yessenin who's always in bughouses, writing obscene poetry "Kill all the farts of the older generation" – that's what got Khrushchev really riled, he spent paragraphs denouncing that & denouncing the juv delinks "trying to start war between father & son." Of course all the square sons of Russia probably line up to shit on Yevtuchenko & Voznesensky so they can keep their jobs in univ. [. . .] I hope to go this winter as my plane ticket will take me there free. All I got to have is enough money to live there & I may be able to sponge unless the pressure is so great that Yev or people I already know will be afraid to have me around, an embarrassment.

Biggest thing that is happening to me here in last year is slow attempt to keep my temper and not flip out with hostility & hatred & disgust every time I get crossed, but cool it & try to pacify the scene. It began with letters to you & insulting scene with backward head of English Dept of BHU (Benares Hindi Univ), continued with trying not to scream at local FBI (CID) creeps that were harassing us, not scream at local communist apologists for Khrushchev speech, not scream at USIS people in Delhi who wouldn't lift finger to help us out of CID mess, not react *back* every time I get frustrated. I think it's the massive accumulation of *individual* frustration angers amplified back & forth from person to person that has built up into war psychosis. There seems no way out but individuals becoming more aware of the irrational/un-functional nature of their *resentments*. Or at least no way out for me. Like living in madhouse getting angry at patients, hopeless. Delhi-Peking peace marchers here now slowly running into trouble on front pages both India & China.

I wonder to what extent it is possible to totally neutralize emotional violence in environment by total impassivity/neutrality/indifference/un-moved awareness in self, i.e. not trying to *force* change on anybody. Difficulty of Russian/American policy is it's all predicated on force; therefore creates counter-force, both ways, an unbreakable circuit except thru complete neutrality, i.e. the temptation to – well this is all so abstract it's meaningless.

Enclosed the two printed poems – I've seen them before often – both awright. The "Radiant Dead" is ok but "the radiant dead is fled" leaves itself open to instant parody. "Is" I guess causes that.

I keep never answering about Caste system because the whole mess of India. . . . I mean is big mess & caste system just small part of it – There is an oldfashioned caste system as described in books slowly & messily breaking down under impact of movies industrial cities, it doesn't *mean* anything anymore, impossible to keep Caste in a crowded 3rd class train for instance . . . a system of rules like Kosher involving fooding, social mixing etc. The Govt has rules against it, which are OK in areas where Govt involved like jobs education etc but meaningless in private affairs – marriages etc.

Love
Allen

Louis Ginsberg to Allen Ginsberg

April 15, 1963

Dear Allen,

Received your letter of April 8.

Sorry you did not "see" my poem, "Remembering Ruined Cities"; it's one of my better ones. Here is one of my "rain" poems, which periodically I am in the force of an inner compulsion to release.

The crackdown on the "new wave" of Russian poets I expected, knowing the ways of the totalitarian Commies. They fear democratic ideas. (Did you know that the Moscow University was closed for two weeks because the students began to ask questions when Russia drowned the Hungarian uprising in blood?)

Personally I think that, with time, the liberal ideas, especially with the ferment of youth, will seep their way into the body politic of Russia.

I can understand your hostilities precipitated in you by all the malignancies, cruelties, and evils swirling about you. I suggest that you gaze down from an Olympian peak of tolerant enchantment and sympathetic and philosophic urbanity upon the blizzard of paradoxes assaulting the nations. Be at the center of calm in the middle of the eye of the storm. Life is sucking honey from a thorn.

I don't mean that you remain indifferent or impassive; but I do mean that you don't permit your hostilities against injustices DISABLE you in either your writing or living.

Your answer about the caste system is unsatisfactory to me. Let it go for a while. Some other time I shall present you with some facts that you are too near to see.

Meanwhile, though I seem robed in seedy or somewhat mangy tatters of homilies, inside, my mind or spirit seems to grow vivid with time, even as the flesh grows weak. I keep poking at and trying to rearrange clichés and phrases in hopes that I shall hit a magic point where those clichés explode noiselessly and, in the flash of illumination, they will transfigure things about me to something new and beautiful and strange and more meaningful!

Keep your shirt on.

Love from
Your father,
Louis

Allen Ginsberg to Louis Ginsberg

{Calcutta, India}
n.d. {ca. early May 1963}

Dear Louis:

Slowly folding up affairs here & be ready to leave in a few weeks, waiting for arrival of ticket & money. May stop off in Cambodia or Burma on way by plane. (I get free stops all over S.E. Asia.) Or perhaps Viet Nam I'd like to see the war there – then be in Japan June–July & Vancouver end of July. Sept in S.F. & then home before Xmas, stay of few months. Same plane ticket continues on thru Europe to Russia & back to Asia.

The many arms – usually on the God Vishnu – of those pictures is associated with a lot of legends & myths. Most familiar one is in Bhagavad Gita. Krishna (who is an avatar or form of Vishnu) shows his friend Arjuna his cosmic form . . . "speaking from unnumerable mouths, seeing with myriad eyes . . . adorned with countless divine ornaments, brandishing all kinds of heavenly weapons, wearing celestial garlands . . . annointed with perfumes of heavenly fragrance . . . lodged as one being within the body of the God of gods . . ." & Arjuna says

"Universal Form, I see you without limit,
Infinite of arms, eyes, mouths, and bellies –
See, and find no end, midst, or beginning . . .
million armed, the sun and moon your eyeballs . . .
At the sight of this, your Shape stupendous
Full of mouths and eyes, feet, thighs and bellies

Terrible with fangs, O mighty Master
All the worlds are fear-struck, even as I am."

These passages from Gita, here the highest literary religious statement of
India, sort of like Dante's Vision of the Yellow Rose at end of paradise, except
here everyone even illiterate knows the Gita by heart or hears it sung weekly
. . . so pictures like the ones I sent are mostly popular like calendar art, that
hangs in barbershops & in cigarette stalls or over cash counter of dank
eateries. If you never read Bhagavad Gita it's worth the short time . . . I think
there's a copy Harold had or I have in *Wisdom of China & India* Lin Yutang
book . . . I'm fond of it as I've seen similar apparitions on Mescaline.

Several weeks ago noticed one of the hundreds of beggars on my block
covered with shit & flies looking like last stage of Buchenwald skeleton
lying in fetal position in gutter of urinal so Peter & I washed him in Ganges
& fed him & hired boy to care for him on street & finally removed him to
hospital. . . . I'd seen several Buchenwald cases like that die the last few
weeks so finally decided to intervene . . . Doctor said it was starvation . . .
Since then have taken care of several other beggars tho not so extensively
. . . if I stayed on here I suppose I'd go into the matter deeper. Horrible
thing is this all happening right underneath loudspeaker blasting noisily
about the evil Chinese.

I wrote whoever I know in Russia (K Siminov & others) to do what I
could to support Voznesensky & Yevtuchenko. Togliatti, I notice, in Italy
attacked Khrushchev art policy. Really a conspiracy of the most stupid
elements of art world and bureaucracy. . . . Voznesensky one poet is really a
Genius the most beautiful writer there since Mayakovsky. Crackdown
presumably because new liberal element threatens a whole political bureaucracy with its roots in Stalin. I don't see how the liberals will win since
probably the mass audience is probably conformist also. Still the issues
Khrushchev attacked is on such obviously weak ground he can't roll back
jazz & abstract art etc. I sent statement saying Yevtuchenko converted me
to Marxism so he was as far as I was concerned the best propaganda they ever
had, if he represented the possibilities of Marxism, that because Sholokhov
said he was callow bad propagandist abroad. I hope you noticed that the
"psychological" accusations against the Russian poets by the mediocre
writers bureaus (i.e. that they are callow, jejune, bad writers, undisciplined,
neurotic, pederasts, eccentrics, social misfits, etc) are the same as leveled
against U.S. beatniks. The situation is roughly similar, tho everything is
brought more to a head in Russia since Govt monopolizes & centralizes all

activity, & the Russian poets perhaps less disillusioned, they still believe in possibility of social progress. . . . I wonder if I'll be able to get into Russia at all . . . probably be very tough scene. . . . One thing, Voznesensky says he interested in poetry as exploration of consciousness, first sign of that I've seen from Russia . . . which brings everybody up to date . . . did you see recent *Encounter*? *Evergreen* #28 brings one *great* piece of composition ("Hotels of the Moon") by Voznesensky.

Meanwhile here I've seen the Delhi-Peking peace marchers again, they just walked thru Benares . . . nobody paying attention to them at all except both Chinese & Indian politicians attacking them.

I only wish people in US would recognize need for a similar anti-Dulles-Luce popular revolt. The issue's never been clearly defined. Best definition is over recognition of China but liberals are afraid to publicly formulate that once for all, & so there's a maddening stalemate in US psychic life. We didn't have one monster Stalin, we only had familiar Babbitt monsters so nobody yet recognizes how really perverse America became, and how much there is to revolt against. It's that very quality of blandness & smartness that's disguised the literal murderousness of US heart & specifically US policy, as in Viet Nam & Formosa. Here goes again.

Love
Allen

Louis Ginsberg to Allen Ginsberg

May 13, 1963

Dear Allen,

Received your letter about your projected journeyings and your planing the starving Indian boy. Very absorbing.

However, your last line was rotten: Your deluded notion that the American foreign policy was murderous. What about the Soviet tanks bloodying Hungary? You're silent about China. I have nothing but contempt for your sanctimonious, arrogant, false assumption that you have the blueprint of all the Truth. I charge you with being a brain-washed fraudulent, hoaxed fool. Now don't send me any more of that crappy garbage.

I sent you the proof of the *Who's Who*. What the hell is the mention of Orlovsky in the account?[1]

Yours,
Louis Ginsberg

Allen Ginsberg to Louis Ginsberg

American Express
Calcutta
May 22, 1963

Dear Lou –

I expect to fly out of here this weekend if all goes well – Calcutta → Bangkok → Saigon (see some of the Viet Nam war) → Angkor Wat (Cambodian ruined city in jungle) → Saigon → Kyoto Japan for a month. Don't send any mail to me in India now – Next address c/o Gary Snyder [. . .] Kyoto, Japan (June 10–July 15) – After that I be c/o Tallman [. . .] Vancouver, B. C. Canada (July 15–Aug 15) – After that c/o City Lights for a month. Tell Gene I got his letter. I'll reply from Japan.

God you sound mad. News from Birmingham sounds good however in that perhaps finally the white-patriotic Southern Demo–Northern Republican stranglehold be broken. But I do think it was a "murderous" combine for as long as I can remember. If the Negroes win out I hope there be a whole cultural change in USA & China get recognized.

I'm in a rush having to fill out Visa tax health police ticket bank forms to leave here after over a year. M *means married Orlovsky why not?* They never had nothin like that in *Who's Who* it'll set a nice precedent. World's overpopulated anyway.

The Indian we were saving – that all worked well & we even contacted his family so after 2 weeks in hospital he could begin to walk again & his brother came for him & took him on train 500 miles away to home. Meanwhile I brought several others from the street to hospital & tried to set up a rescue system in Benares around our neighbourhood – Peter's still there working that out – he'll stay in India to study music the next year – Meanwhile I'm soon on my way. OK. Take care of yourself –

Love
Allen

1. Allen listed Peter Orlovsky as his spouse in his *Who's Who* entry.

Allen Ginsberg to Louis Ginsberg

American Express
Calcutta, India[1]
June 14, 1963

Dear Louis:

I got back a few days ago from nearby Himalaya hill-stations Darjeeling, Kalmping & Sikkim, & found your letters – just sitting down now to answer weeks of mail. Glad the shawl came – I got the check for ten & will get a sari. I have already bought Eugene a terrific Tibetan picture & will have to ship that in a week or so.

June 22

Got your letter from Florida also. Hope this reaches you in time. In any case I think I sent a letter from Darjeeling a few weeks ago. I spent a few days in Florida, mostly passing thru – but never found it too interesting, except the Negro district in Jacksonville. Miami Beach *feels* like Reno a little – the gaudy money hotels. They're a real wow, almost beautiful so much in bad taste. How was visit to Arthur Kline? He was always friendly to me, tho the last time thru I'm afraid I shocked him since I was anti-U.S. policy on Cuba & he is lawyer for refugees. I had the impression he couldn't understand how an American could come by the point of view I had which was obviously eccentric & sort of sinister in his eyes. I told him I was a Red, which probably finished the job.

Gene & I saw Gettysburg hitchhiking years ago, I remember a few hills & some antique houses.

Plenty caste system here, tho one encounters it pure form mainly among the extremely pious Hindus who're not caught up in Gandhi's modernizations. There are 4 castes: Brahmins – who are scholar-priests; Kshatriyas – who are warriors; and then Businessmen; and then Sudra or untouchables. In course of centuries development, these caste lines apply primarily now to formal scenes like marriage & church attendance (untouchable not allowed in some unreformed temples). However social lives are so mixed that it becomes more or less of a formality – at least in the big cities – i.e. Brahmins (who wear white string around their bare shoulders)

1. This letter was begun in India and finished in Japan, probably after Allen had sent the following letter home.

who work as coolies and untouchables who are chairman of the Congress Party; also there are no real warriors anymore. Caste distinction mainly survives among die-hard pious old Hindu families and is extensively observed by masses in countryside & village. Nothing seems to make inroads on it in country because it is built with the economic-social static primitive village life pattern.

The people I know best here are products of inter-caste marriage. The people I meet on street or trains don't observe caste rigidly at all because otherwise they wouldn't mix our trains – so that my *direct* experience of caste system has been very offhand & minor. It does exist on large scale in country provincial scenes where I haven't yet been. But I see marriage advertisements in Bombay papers which mention caste of partner, most of them. It's more like Jewish-Gentile distinction than Negro-white.

Thank you for June 3 birthday wishes & cake.

Not much reaction to poet & critic poems – The one light visuality of "Trains" was good, but ending with the *word* loneliness, rather than an image pure, weakens the vision. "Nude in Art Gallery" has yr. old routine glow in it almost like tears. But you sent some poems this year I thought were more crafty & higher level.

(I got all upset about Laos after reading some communist propaganda accusing the U.S. of consistently intervening to overthrow – neutral government there with CIA "henchmen." I checked in the last 4 weeks stories in *Time, Newsweek,* & *London Times* and find that the *present* official U.S. line seems to coincide with the Red line on our responsibility for the mess. I think more and more, it is not possible to get an accurate picture of local conflicts without absorbing *both* Western & Communist versions of history, (seriously) and canceling & checking one against the other. There is valuable information on the communist record which doesn't appear clearly in the western record, and vice versa.

I am still not exactly pro Cuban but certainly anti American on that scene. I don't see we have anything to offer Cuba but further confusion & violence. My remark about Castro was that his present repudiation of obnoxious party control was refutation of the unfair earlier accepted US propaganda that he was a strict communist. I mean, they made him out to be something he isn't, and ever had me suspicious and I think had most of U.S. sold.

My recollection is that most active anti-US vitriol in Cuba is chronologically result of anti Castro vitriol in U.S. after not before seizure of private property – especially after he started doing business with Russia. It was the economic break-away from U.S. dependence & economic contact with Russia that got US upset. I thought it was a healthy sign & still do, in fact. I wish the US would start trade with Red China. Oh well this is all ancient history. I see by a copy of the respectable *Columbia Alumni Forum* there is now some "liberal" rethinking being done about Korea itself. And also a summary of recent books on A Bomb Hiroshima concluding that in actual fact, the bomb dropping on our part was a mistake since the Japanese already had offered to surrender & various other details. My point in all this is that something went dreadfully wrong in the USA since the war & we did all sorts of really ghastly things that didn't show up *at the time* in the papers – and are beginning to show up now 17 years later when it's too late for anybody to feel responsible – a public situation much like the Germans who didn't really feel directly responsible for their atrocities, or like the Belgians who to this day are unaware of the genocide that went on in the Congo at the time of King Leopold (population decimated by ten million – from 25 to 15 million) – and which got Mark Twain all worked up, but was hardly noticed in America except by Vachel Lindsay (Leopold's ghost burning in Hell) etc.

All I've been saying for years now has been that on a purely political level, the U.S.A. has committed some really outrageous deals. These have "justified" communist fear of U.S. *as much as* Stalin-Khrushchev outrage have justified Western fear. The only way out of Cold War impasse is for change on both sides & reform etc. This seems to be the course of the Laos Compromise.

But if the U.S. public wants to follow a Black & White line, & refuse to see what *we* have done – in Guatemala, all over So America, in supporting French in Algeria & Franco in Spain financially, in Korea, in Formosa with Chiang Kai-shek, all over So E. Asia, Malta, Congo, as result of Dulles containment policy – if there is no *reevaluation* on all these issues as now there is one on Laos (which you can see in all last month's papers), then the progress will be very slow & stay as dangerous as it has been the last 20 years. 20 years completely wasted in 2 way psychosis with Russia & US both behaving with almost unforgivable viciousness. Anyway I think Laos shows the way out.

A good deal of my fury & energy in writing you about politics goes back to that traumatic moment in Newark when Leo told me to see the FBI before I went to Cuba – I felt I was in 1933 Germany with all the solid citizens collapsing with an irresponsible brainwashed police state-control conformity which could only lead to some horrible climax of blood in the streets. Actually it has led to that, only fortunately the U.S. has not yet been on the receiving end. But I don't see how the US can make any progress till it accepts its own share of guilt. But I don't [know] how it can do that till there is a complete re-thinking & re-evaluation of what's happened from Hiroshima day onward. And I don't see that happening until it gets to the surface in mass media. And that won't happen till individuals begin insisting on it and really revolting against a system which has allowed like 4 years of completely obscure confused reportage on Laos, treachery double dealing, half a billion poured down the drain to old creep right wingers – and a sudden about face like this month when all the old unreported story slowly creeps out & there's a change of policy.

etc etc. I'll stop here.

Anyway I went to Sikkim & saw all sorts of Holy Lamas and heard about how monstrous the Chinese were in Tibet. I may go back in a few weeks & be initiated with some of the secret psychic games of the Tibetans. For my money they're the most interesting people on the face of the earth. I got a supply of mushroom drugs from Harvard so I will try to experiment and exchange information with the Tibetan Lamas & maybe East will meet West somewhere on the other side of the moon.

Love
Allen

Allen Ginsberg to Louis Ginsberg

c/o Snyder
31 Nishinoyama-che
Omiya, Kita-ku
Kyoto, Japan
June 17, 1963

Dear Lou:

Traveling by jetplane kind of a gas, you do get in and out of centuries from airport hangars & glassy modern downtowns to jungle floating markets &

900 year old stone cities in a matter of minutes & hours instead of weeks & months. Like space cut-ups or collages, one minute paranoiac spyridden Vietnam streets, the same afternoon quiet Cambodian riversides. I spent a week in Vietnam talking with opium poets & USIS directors & State Department spokesmen & Army public relations sergeants & most of all with newsmen & also the Buddhist priests. Horrible mess as you can read in the papers. Curious scene here [about] the reporters is that they are all young & relatively eager there, unlike most "hotspots," so this a rare instance if you follow the politics war there, one can get a relatively straight account within the limits of assumed anticommunist slant & the euphemisms of ticklish situations (i.e. Diem govt. not referred to outright as Diem dictatorship, but as "Diem Govt which has been called dictatorial" etc.) (i.e. phraseology picked to suggest idea rather than say it outright as is done with Red dictatorships). Anyway I'm glad I saw what little I saw of that. Gave me nervous stomach after a week. Then spent a week in Angkor Wat ruins in Cambodia & now here in Kyoto with Snyder & his wife in neat little Jap house sitting typing on the floor. Big week of Zen meditation in the monastery, I've been going with Snyder & sitting 2 1/2 hours immobile crosslegged the last 3 nites & learning proper belly breathing for that kind of sitting. Hard on the ankles but interesting subjective effects. I'll be here a month & thence Vancouver. Japan amazing after all the other Asian & Arab countries – not much police state, everybody neat & keen stylish & motorcycles & transistors & cameras & civilized, nobody starving in his shit in the street like India & everywhere else practically. Native Japanese quickness plus the fact they aren't saddled with active participation in coldwar so all their energy goes into selfimprovement. Lucky they lost the war. Jap style living very lovely, houses with sliding walls & clean food & mats barefoot on floors leave shoes at door & sense of taste & cleanness in all the woodwork & carpentry & weird little careful gardens everywhere, and all the young people real chic like they stept out of an Italian fashion magazine with girls Jackie Kennedy hair mops & the men hip downswept over forehead like Brando as Marc Antony – just amazing to see all these Asians prosperous – Quitting now, 6:30 PM going out to sit early eve in temple.

Soon – Love
Allen

Allen left Japan in late July. He had been out of the United States for more than two years – a period that had seen him contemplating his Jewish heritage in Israel and democracy in Greece; he had lived among the impoverished in India, and sought advice from a number of the country's holy men; he had seen Vietnam in the days when the number of American advisers escalated, and had visited the ancient ruins of Cambodia's Angkor Wat. Eastern religion, mysticism, and philosophy had given his worldview pronounced Hindu and Buddhist shadings. Yet, for all his travels, he was deeply troubled by the disparity between day-to-day global, post–atomic bomb politics and the unspeakable misery and suffering that he had witnessed on the dusty streets. By his own admission, he felt traumatized, the victim of "a long, sustained state of SHOCK." He had journeyed to India and the Orient in search of answers, and yet he seemed to be departing with even more questions.

However, on July 17, while traveling on a train from Kyoto to Tokyo, he had an experience similar to his Blake visions of 1948, in which he recognized his own mortality as a part of an enormous continuum of human experience: so much of existence involved suffering, but in the eternal scheme, such suffering was temporary. Rather than reach for unattainable answers lost in spiritual riddles, one had to live in the present. Deeply moved, Allen took out a notebook and scribbled a long poem – "The Change: Kyoto-Tokyo Express."

The key, Allen believed, was to love oneself, which, in turn, helped in the quest to love others, and he took this newfound spirit to Vancouver in late July, where he participated in a joyous poetry conference wioth Charles Olson, Robert Duncan, Robert Creeley, Denise Levertov, and others.

Allen Ginsberg to Louis Ginsberg

{*Vancouver, British Columbia*}
Sunday, August 16 {1963}

Dear Louis:

Sorry so silent – wrapped up teaching great spirit poetry course all last 3 weeks – lovely union of souls – plenty pretty girls – I seem to be back on girls again (after all!) – maybe I'll bring you back some baby Ginsbergs after all – I'll write you when I get to S.F. in a few days – driving down – Everything's OK – How are you Louis – Because of Fate, poesy, drugs, loves, etc. I seem finally to be returned back into my body after many years absence – I think the Indian Gurus did it, as well as you – I'm actually *happy*! – Hope you are. Love yr son Allen. I'll write, soon. Back East Xmas.

Louis Ginsberg to Allen Ginsberg

August 23, 1963

Dear Allen,

I bought three copies of your book from City Lights Books. *Reality Sandwiches* seems a more mellow book. I liked among others, "Siesta in Xbalba," with the title's romantic overtones. That is a fine description, in that poem, at the bottom of p. 26, hinting at the passage of Time. Also, in that same poem, on p. 32, I liked your ruminations projected forward of "what vagrant rooms and streets and lights in the long lights urge my expectations. What wild houses do I go to occupy." "Psalm II" is good. I like especially the poem "Squeal," a vivid satire. Another poem, "My Sad Self," has good passages that remind me of your wandering in the N.Y. streets.

"Aether" is fascinating as a poetic speculation à la Rimbaud, with his derangement of the senses. He used poetry to attain the unattainable, to reach the sense behind the senses, the seeing beyond all sight, the vision of the Unknown. Yet man will try to do this in vain. Rimbaud's poem, as well as your poems with hallucinatory drugs, etc., cannot find the vision, but they do widen experience, because, in the words of Archibald MacLeish, "The voice amid the oxications and the hallucinations and Peradics, though strange, is his own voice."

How is your book going? Hope it does well! Meanwhile, congratulations aplenty!

(Say, how about dedicating a book of yours, not always to your own friends, but to your own brother, Eugene?)

Enclosed please find an interview with me about my puns and my poetry which appeared recently in the *Paterson Evening News*. (Kindly return it, after you have frowned over it.)

Give my regards, if you will, to Ferlinghetti.

More anon.

When do you think you will be home?

With love,
Your father,
Louis

Allen Ginsberg to Louis Ginsberg

{San Francisco, California}
August 28, 1963

Dear Louis –

Too much to do here – can't write – better save it for conversation – hope to spend a couple months here at least – have things to type & people to see & old affairs to straighten out & books to proofread – anyway I'll be home by or before Xmas I'm not sure – probably in 2 or 3 months – just want to get everything cleared up that's been accumulating for years – people, mss – I'm in fine shape – never felt better in my whole life – I'll write when I have a breather – Patience – Love – All hell breaking loose in Vietnam – Allen

Allen Ginsberg to Louis Ginsberg

{San Francisco, California}
September 9 {1963}

Dear Louis –

Still too busy to write – Enclosed your poems – I saw another stack of them at Ferlinghetti's office – "Women Queerly Bus," "Bed Pictures," "Mother Burial," "Two Porch," "Meeting Hall" etc were excellent –

Lucien Carr got on a jetplane & arrived here last week to say hello welcome back – He left 2 days ago – Made me realize it don't cost much to phone at nite so I'll phone you in a few days.

Love to Eugene & Connie & Edith & everyone. I'm tied up with all sortsa work – Much typing to do. Also Robert Frank who made *Pull My Daisy* movie has money & plans to film *Kaddish*. He seems to know what he's doing. He's coming out here today – Also I have to sit down with Neal Cassady & reduce his manuscripts to order for publishing – all sorts of old threads being tied up once & for all, with happy endings for everyone –

As I wrote I'll be back by Thanksgiving or Xmas or before. Want to unload [what] I can before coming home. I'm well. Take care of yourself –

Love
Allen

Louis Ginsberg to Allen Ginsberg

October 4, 1963

Dear Allen,

Camus says, "One may fight a lie in the name of a quarter truth."

Louis Ginsberg

Louis Ginsberg to Allen Ginsberg

October 12, 1963

Dear Allen,

I wrote you, I think, some time ago that I had a "kick" on the Symbolists. I had read them, in translation, in college, but recently I re-read lives and works of Mallarmé, Rimbaud, Baudelaire, etc.

Recently I read a book called *Surrealism* by one Yves Duplessis and translated by Paul Capon. (No, the book does not seem castrated or bowlderized.) Aragon, Tzara, Eluard, and Freud are dwelt on; also Jean Cocteau, who died the other day. Some of these writers, goes on the book, throw themselves into the marvelous, hurl themselves into the irrational, and repudiate the real world for the fantasy, finally blurring the difference between the two.

Reverting, for the nonce, to the burden of my last letter, I maintain there are, as in religion, many mansions in the house of poetry. There is a part of the truth in all of them, the traditional, the academic, the Beat, the obscure. Poetry is where you find it. Much, too, depends upon the individual makeup of the poets. Bierce said, "Philosophy is the extension of a temperamental (genetic) make-up or bias of the poet to the incongruities of life." It depends, thus, upon what colored mental and emotional and intellectual glasses you view the ironies and dilemmas of life, seething around you. Perhaps one might maintain an Olympian disenchantment or urbane tolerances and ironic detachment [. . .]

Maybe I write so because I have seen too many clichés and cliques and cults with their demi-gods spouting absolutes.

The Unground man becomes the top dog one day, and then another day he is bitten by a new dog who has his day. Just as in a democracy, there should be a plurality of opinions, so in the poetic world, I hold, there should be a plurality of kinds of poetry. The current fashion of one (still wet behind the ears with "embalming fluid") should not invalidate other kinds of poetry. What I chiefly resent, as I intimated in my last letter, is the unalloyed and pontifical certitudes of empyreal pronunciations by authoritarian gurus and panjandrums, who, with egregious infallibility, lay down the dogmatic, self-righteous laws to all and sundry!

Each to his own compulsion.

"Absolutes in criticism smell of fustiness and faggots."

In politics, I am a theoretic Socialist somewhat deflated by the New Deal, against the 16 Century far Right and against the Totalitarian Commies; in religion, my heart is like Einstein, in awe and wonder at the harmony of the universe, but my head is agnostic and scientific; in poetry, I am a pluralist or an eclectic, seeking the best in all types.

If that be treason, make the most of it − "and damned be he who first cried 'Hold! Enough!'"

With love from
Your father
Louis

Louis Ginsberg to Allen Ginsberg

November 6, 1963

Dear Allen,

Received your postal.

Speaking of masks of Gods, as you were, I thought that in life, one becomes many; in death, the many become One.

"Mind-feelings-moments" is not bad. I try controlled abandon.

Just flew in from a three-day stay in Detroit. Had an exciting time. On Tuesday, at 11 in the morning, I talked and read my poems to about seventy Wayne State U. medical students for an hour; at 3:00 P.M., I read before The Merrill-Palmer Institute child psychology students. In the evening, I addressed and read poems and answered questions at a dinner given in my honor by Dean Dorsey. Novelists, special English students, some city and university big-wigs crowded in. Besides questions about inspiration, modern poets, methods of writing, a favorite question was: how do you and your son get along? What do you think of his poetry? In the main, I told them I approved and was proud. (Besides getting $150.00 for expenses, I received an honorarium, as the phrase goes, $200.00) And all the way, Edith and I had red-carpet treatment. (Incidentally, last in this lecture series, they had Archibald MacLeish and Mark Van Doren; this term they were having me and John Ciardi.)

I have been missing you very much. You have been away too long a time. Could you – as soon as you ascertain it – tell me just when you will be home? All the relatives, their children and grandchildren, all want to see you again so we are planning an evening. Let me know so I can set a date.

Take care of yourself.

> Love from Edith and
> Your father,
> Louis

Louis Ginsberg to Allen Ginsberg

Saturday, November 23, 1963

Dear Allen,

I was happy to hear your voice over the phone last night. It did me good. It has been more than two years since you have been away, wandering over the world – and your name has been snowballing to fame! I hope, when you come home soon, that you will stay long enough for us to talk our way through many things.

Yesterday the shock of the assassination of President Kennedy shook me as it shook the world. Not since FDR has such a tidal wave of incredulous grief hit America. Somehow, the last two days, I have no desire to work at my desk.

It all shows how impermanent are things. Nothing is constant but change. In the midst of life, there is death.

I hope you will come here soon.

> Love from Edith and
> Your father,
> Louis

Allen spent most of 1964 on the East Coast, visiting his family and becoming very active in New York's arts and political communities. He worked with Robert Frank on a screenplay for "Kaddish," became involved in the underground film world of Andy Warhol's Factory, and crusaded tirelessly against censorship, whether it involved the growing battle between avant-garde filmmakers and play producers and the government agencies trying to suppress performances, or the crackdown on satirist Lenny Bruce. Allen also testified in Boston on behalf of the literary merits of William Burroughs's Naked Lunch, *now the focus of a highly publicized trial. In addition, the war in Vietnam was now becoming one of Allen's major obsessions.*

Disagreements between the two Ginsbergs over Vietnam heated up considerably during 1964, and while none of Allen's letters to his father for this year are available, Louis's letters to his son are emblematic of the battle lines being drawn throughout the United States. Not surprisingly, Louis (who had witnessed the rise of Hitler, the Soviet takeover of Eastern Europe, and the Korean War) was inclined to subscribe to "the domino theory" and the Defense Department's stance that the conflict in Vietnam was a necessary evil. His testy letters to Allen reflected the edginess between the supporters and opponents of the war.

Louis Ginsberg to Allen Ginsberg

July 26, 1964

Dear Allen,

I enjoyed our talk last night at Harold's.

By the way, do you think that flexible iambic rhythm has an instinctive appeal or communicates to a subliminal level?

Do you think that rhyme is really "filthy"?

Cordially yours,
Louis

P.S. Those questions, among a hundred others, are brought to mind by an article I just read in *Books,* called "The War Between Iam and the Id." The article contains much mention of you. Congratulations and many more!

Kindly return the article, as I need it for my notes.

Do you know FM radio station WSOU? I have been asked for an interview for them next month.

L

Louis Ginsberg to Allen Ginsberg

September 10, 1964

Dear Allen,

I read with care the statement, "Memo on Vietnam," by David McReynolds and A. J. Muste. (You will, of course, recognize that people see things not as things are, but as people are.)

While the Memo says that the Viet Cong forces gathered other resistance groups, it does admit that some Communists gave it direction and were active in So. Vietnam.

I received through Congressman Joelson a statement from the government to the effect that The Viet Cong forces violated the Geneva Agreement and that, at the request of the South Vietnam[ese], our help was requested.

I'll let you read the fuller statement of the State Department. It depends on what colored-glasses you wear as to what you see. From my life-long experience with Communists, I wouldn't trust them from here to the corner curb, though now both time and its turbulence and general erosion of Absolutes make them a bit more tractable.

Yours,
Louis Ginsberg

Louis Ginsberg to Allen Ginsberg

September 30, 1964

Dear Allen,

Received your notations on that statement from the State Department.

From years of experience I don't believe anything in the *Daily Worker*. *The N.Y. Times* and Stone are more reliable, though I don't consider them as oracles of Delphi.

I'll pursue those comments of yours to see if I can track down the truth.

I wish, though, I had your untainted certitude empyreal declarations. I stand in awe of your omniscience and infallibility. Your humble smugness in granting such unflawed knowledge, italicized by your dogmatic self-righteousness, really touches my heart!

Yours,
Louis Ginsberg

Louis Ginsberg to Allen Ginsberg

October 2, 1964

Dear Allen,

Your letter on hand.

In reply, I assert that even if U. S. reports are unrealistic and bend news to more favorable position, the fact remains that the overriding assessment is that the Commies, the Chinese ones, are bent on gradually conquering North and S. Vietnam and thus, in "domino fashion," sweeping down gradually on demoralized and unarmed countries, eventually exercising a hegemony in all S.W. Asia, menacing Australia and Japan. They are out to conquer the world, in spite of Russia.

That's what Russia did, pouring into the vacuum in Europe. As for deaths, you say nothing about guilt of Commies.

The S. Vietnam mess is a tangled dilemma. You add nothing to it but churn up half-truths and quarter-truths. I'll say what Joelson says: "Your opinions ought to be discussed and are valuable."

I am very busy writing poetry. But when I get a chance, I try to track down some things. How about sources in the *New Leader*?

You say, in a previous letter, that "Joelson ought to be ashamed of himself in passing the buck like this." How do you know that he feels he is passing the buck? How can you creep into his mind and see what is there? Maybe he believes what he asserts. If so, you are, as I said, smugly arrogant and even slanderous.

Yours,
Louis Ginsberg

Louis Ginsberg to Allen Ginsberg

Friday December 25, 1964

Dear Allen,

Thank you for bringing me all those magazines.

Frankly, I find that many of those so-called avant-garde magazines are yawns ticked out in deranged verbiage or display new words of arranging boredom. Also, I see that they think they have invented honesty. I say there is enough genuine feeling for life to be shared by others.

My point, however, in writing to you is this. In your "statement" in *The Burning Bush II* (of San Francisco),[1] you make a few statements that have an extremist flavor. For instance, you equate the Jewish notion of "chosen race" with the genocide of the Nazis. Well, modern Jews do not believe literally in the "chosen race"; they believe in doing good to others and practicing or rather preaching brotherhood, even if they don't come to actually practice it. (Who does except a few great souls?) But the Jews never practiced or preached genocide.

However, the main point of this letter is to call to your attention an episode in your and my life that you failed to mention, in order to help balance your one-sided picture.

Do you remember that, when we lived on the first floor of a building on the corner of Haledon Ave.? One day you came to me and said that a colored boy in your class was hungry; that you wanted to bring him to our house to have a bite, but that the landlord downstairs refused to admit him with you. Although I knew that this Gentile landlord might make things difficult for me (He did later when he gave bad references when I sought to get an apartment), yet, in spite of any dire consequences, I said to you – to show justice and to remove prejudice – yes, bring him to the house.[2]

1. "Statement to *The Burning Bush*, *Burning Bush*, no. 2 (September 1964). See AG, *Deliberate Prose*, pp. 58–60.

2. The rest of the letter is missing.

Near the end of 1964, Allen was invited by Cuba's minister of culture to participate in a writer's conference in Havana. The U.S. State Department was less than thrilled about having an outspoken member of the "beatnik element" appearing in Cuba, but it had little choice but to let him go. Still, the travel arrangements were outrageous, to say the least: to travel to Cuba, Allen had to fly first to Mexico City and then on to Cuba; to return, he had to fly first to Czechoslovakia and then to the United States. The arrangements irritated Allen, but he was also excited about the prospect of visiting Cuba and a prominent Iron Curtain Country, and of drawing firsthand conclusions about the Communist governments in these two countries.

He ran into trouble almost from the beginning. As an advocate of free speech, he was not about to tone down his rhetoric in Cuba. Whether he was being brave or politically naïve – and there have been arguments supporting both positions – Allen stirred up a controversy that would eventually make international headlines.

Allen Ginsberg to Louis Ginsberg

{Havana, Cuba}
February 5, 1965

Dear Louis –

Re'd your letter, it is faster via Mexico. [. . .]

I'm OK – have been keeping day by day notes of what's going on & filled several notebooks already. Work as juror in poetry contest finished & now will relax & stay a month before moving on to Czechoslovakia.

All told "socialist" Cuba is both good and bad. I was here in '53 and the country is much better off, that is everybody eats has work & has shoes and also has education. Economically, compared to other Latin American countries, it's a much healthier place than before.

They get this done thru total organization like a big government monopoly.

The Cubans have a funny Latin humor in creating this huge bureaucracy and so far the general attitude toward experimental formation of the structure is basically "existential" – i.e. the structure is open & constantly changing, & *personal* in the sense that it's run by only 23 people, Castro at the top.

Being a huge structure run experimentally by *people,* the directives & direction is as sane or as neurotic as the people running the joint are.

So far they are quite puritanical. I arrived here in the middle of a big wave of hysterical crackdowns on homosexuals camping in the street & a bunch of professors & students were kicked out of art schools. As soon I opened my mouth & began complaining to journalists about the persecution of homosexuals & saying repressive measures were stupid (they ought to *encourage* heterosexuality but being Catholic/bourgeois that's also inconceivable to them) – and also talking about marijuana & ending capital punishment – waves of gossip & anxiety spread throughout the journalist/literary/Casa de las Americas[1] world. A couple young kids I had met were taken to jail overnight & questioned. I got paranoid & immediately began complaining. Finally I went to Nicholas Guidlen, a poet head of Writers Union, & Haydée Santamaría,[2] [who] are the Cabinet ministers (who'd invited me) and got the young poets out of trouble. But by that time it was a sort of general scandal i.e. the unjust arrests, and everybody began feeling guilty toward me & I got to be quite popular, tho I was obviously an embarrassment to my hosts. There is a heavy bureaucratic bourgeois element, a liberal utopian element, a dogmatic Marxist puritanical element. Castro is very popular & actually much loved. Everybody expects him to get Cuba out of its internal & external mess – like a ship with Castro/Ulysses as the captain. A quasi police state with no constitutional protection, and on the other hand a fantastic optimistic unanimity of agreement to go ahead with the *"Revolution"* which is spoken of everywhere & which has changed everybody's life – So it's a weird scene – all in all rather hopeful than not – despite my own direct experiences with limitations on freedom of expression. If the "dogmatists" as they're called here take over – which would only come if the Cubans experience so much U.S. pressure they get paranoid – it would be Stalinism. If the liberals slowly take over it'll be a sort of Latin Utopia. The Liberals – as at the Casa de las Americas which invited me – feel the older squarer Communists will just slowly die off & the younger generations be alright. So like everything, the scene is mixed. The one

---

1. The Casa de las Americas was Allen's sponsor during his stay in Cuba.
2. Haydée Santamaría was the director of Casa de las Americas.

intolerable element which is screwing everything up is the U.S. threat, continuous attrition & economic strangulation which maintains Cuba in a state of perpetual neurosis & material struggle. If the U.S. would *let go* it would resolve the whole 2 way Cold War here & everything end happy with some sort of democratic socialism like Sweden. The basic emotional tension between the countries is similar to that between over protective over aggressive parent & independent youth in whose consciousness the parent has no dominant place.

OK there's report on Cuba. I'll stay here another month & go on to Czechoslovakia. I'll write soon. Was waiting for someone to take a letter out. Direct mail to the U.S. is stopped or delayed for weeks by the U.S.

Love
Allen

Allen's stay in Cuba was cut short in February, when he was arrested, briefly detained, and finally expelled from the country. He was put on a plane to Czechoslovakia, where a new series of adventures was about to begin.

Allen Ginsberg to Louis Ginsberg

Allen Ginsberg
c/o Peter Pujman
Writer's Union
Vaarodni 11,
Prague, Czechoslovakia
March 1, 1965

Dear Louis:

How are you? Had odd dream last nite that I had a baby, you were in dream somewhere. I called Orlovsky a week ago from Newfoundland on my way here, asked him to call you, did he? I got kicked out of Cuba after a month – probably for talking too much about marijuana & sex & capital punishment. Police & Emmigration people hustled me out in 2 hours without telling the Casa de las Americas, which invited me. So now there's an internal struggle going on, they're all embarrassed. I haven't made a scandal lest it hurt the people there who invited me. They have a hard struggle as it is. So from this you can measure the police-state politics there. I'm still waiting to hear the latest gossip.

Prague is absolutely beautiful, and much more relaxed. They had their terror in the '50s, worse than Cuba. Now they are opening up, which means, technically, decentralization of economic authority (and consequently political & artistic). It is a whole special interesting world. I'll go explore more. I have royalties here, enough to pay for a road trip to Moscow, am living in nice hotel 2 weeks, guest of Writer's Union. I'll go to Moscow – and maybe then Warsaw – on my own as a tourist. More freedom & less hassles that way.

Following tracks of Kafka here – *The Trial* a perfect parable of life here in the '50s everybody says.

His books are just published after years of silence. Also met Jewish community – 77,000 pre war and 3,000 now – went to services last Friday in oldest Synagogue in Europe – met them again this morning – all sorts of Tales of Golem to hear & Rabbi Seou's grave & library full of Kabbalistic mss. Medieval squares and bridges & 19th century nostalgia all over the streets – happy to be here –

Find out by phone from Bronx or Riverside relatives exact address of Moscow relatives & please send it to me fast. I'll leave here in two weeks, tho mail will be forwarded from above address.

Say hello to Gene – I'll write him soon.

Love to you – as ever – & Love to Edith & all –

Yr son,
Allen

Louis Ginsberg to Allen Ginsberg

March 2, 1965

Dear Allen,

Received your postal from Prague.

Called up Eugene and told him about getting a cousin's address (Joe Levy's) in Russia. Eugene will call up to obtain that and will then write you.

We were over to Eugene's the other Sunday and called up Peter Orlovsky. He transferred your things to a new address which I suppose you know (408 E. 10 St.). Peter also told us that you had been escorted to a plane and directed to leave Cuba. What infraction of totalitarian laws did you commit? What law did you run afoul of?

I suppose in Prague you are reconnoitering and soaking up local color. I trust, too, you will bring back here pieces of the "truth."

All is quiet here and we are pursuing the even tenor of our ways. Eugene's kids are thriving. Edith is working and so am I, still at Rutgers, two evenings a week. (We are saving a little money for traveling later.) Now and then I put a glow in the status quo, so some days I live less daily by putting a prismatic fringe of poetry around a few hours. Am having poems published here and there.

Is the Writer's Union stirring with new ferment? I gather that in Russia, the poet Brodsky[1] is still imprisoned, despite planted stories that he is free.

Write me, if you are allowed to, a long letter with details such as may be permitted from behind the Iron Curtain.

> With love,
> Your father,
> Louis

Louis Ginsberg to Allen Ginsberg

March 3, 1965

Dear Allen,

Glad to get your letter dated March 1. Seems like quick service by mail. Let me know when you get this letter. Also, I sent you an air mail letter a day or two ago.

Eugene will get the address of the cousin in Russia and send it on to you.

Peter Orlovsky did not call me. However, Eugene, when I visited him, called Peter and received the information that you had been escorted in Cuba to a plane. I surmised that you forgot in Cuba that you were in a totalitarian regime.

I gathered, from reading previous articles in the *N. Y. Times,* that there has been a relaxation in Czechoslovakia, what with coexistence. One of the by-products of the relaxation is the spread of word of Kafka. One of the symbolisms read into Kafka is the blind totalitarianism of the Stalin iron-fisted, mysterious rule. As you say, the 50's were a parable.

1. Joseph Brodsky, poet and political prisoner, eventual winner of the Nobel Prize for Literature.

Prague has an old Jewish community whose roots sink back deep to the Middle Ages and before. The Golem and other mystic tales were brewed in an atmosphere when Jewish mysticism and cabalistic legends helped the Jews ward off, as if by talismans and conjurations, the prejudices and anti-Semitic evils assailing them.

All is quiet here. Spring is on the way, and we are preparing to help our garden rejoice.

In a couple of weeks, Edith and I will join a group going for a week-end up the mountains in a Catskill Hotel. [. . .] Hope we don't get blinded by the white glare of the sour cream.

It was a strange dream you had. What was I doing in the dream?

Keep well and watch your health!

My love speeds to you across oceans and continents.

Your father,
Louis

Allen Ginsberg to Louis Ginsberg

c/o Ylena Romanova
Writer's Union
52 Vorovsky Str
Moscow USSR
n.d. {ca. March 1965}

Dear Louis:

Received Levy's Moscow address. I leave by second class train thru the snows of Russia to Moscow tomorrow afternoon. Trip paid by my Czechoslovak royalties, it works out fine. I have enough $ for 4 days in Moscow at Introuist expensive rates. I hear also that the Russians will invite me to stay at least a week on their expense & I'll see how long I can stretch that out.

In Cuba I committed about every "infraction of totalitarian laws" I could think of, verbally, and they finally flipped out & gave me the bum's rush. It was half Kafkian & half funny. I had been expecting to stay another month, and one govt. group there was (secretly conspiring) working on that, while the police and emigration people were secretly conspiring to get rid of me. Did you get my letters from Cuba? I think I sent you two.

The interesting thing about the communist countries is the interior balance of forces working one way or the other. One group humane, other group sectarian police state oriented. Same *types* of people as you find in U.S. proposing *soft* & *hard* lines. The essential thing to do is to help out the liberal types here (& in U.S.) – the heavier the Cold War attack, the more the liberals suffer. Like, in Cuba, the more *pressure* the U.S. puts against Castro, the more difficult it is for the liberals to fight police state tendencies.

Prague absolutely beautiful. Old Medieval town, the Golem synagogue, weird castles and cathedrals, Kafka's homes – Kafka just published here this past few years after 15 years blackout – by that you can measure the winds of political change – I wrote Gene – Everyone here official & non-official complains about the Horror of the '50s as if it were a nightmare. They're slowly waking out of it. My visit seems to have done some good. Everybody here adores the Beatniks, & there's a whole generation of Prague teenagers who listen to jazz & wear long hair & say shit on communism & read *Howl*. I gave a reading at Charles Univ. (on the banks of Die Moldau river) with big audience & answered all sorts of sex and brainwash questions. Food good middleeuropean soups & pork & knaedlich – I live in expensive Ambassador hotel at Writer's Union expense & my picture's in all the literary supplements with long strange explanations about marijuana & L.S.D and Hari Om Namo Shiva Indian mantras – and I run around with teenage gangs & have orgies & then rush up to Writer's Union & give lectures on the glories of U.S. pornography Henry Miller etc. All very happy – Love to you –

I'll send you card from Moscow –

Love
Allen

Louis Ginsberg to Allen Ginsberg

March 22, 1965

Dear Allen,

Received your letter, undated, from Czechoslovakia, according to your incidents, but the heading seemed to be from Moscow.

Great news about you and for you caused rejoicing here with Eugene and me. Eugene heard from Peter that

YOU RECEIVED A GUGGENHEIM AWARD! CONGRATULATIONS! What are the details?

We are all well here. Edith and I had a brief holiday up in the mountains with a group, in the Borsht circuit. There were all sorts of things to do, but none of them beguiled me; such as, swimming in indoor pool, ice-skating outdoors, tobogganing, skiing, indoor practice of dancing the frug, alley-cat, and watusi. So I read the papers. At night there was an interesting show with comedians: this took my attention. Otherwise, I lost the battle with food which overwhelmed me.

I was interested in your account of Kafka. I knew that it was only recently that he was being published. A rich and fertile Jewish civilization teemed in Prague.

I see by the literary reviews here that a new vein of novels has poured in upon Russia with tales of horror about Stalin's concentration camps.

Am glad to hear that the young Beatniks have taken you to their bosom. When you read them your poems, which ones do they like? Is sex your only subject you regale them with?

Write me how Moscow is. (I heard that once again the Party Line has been laid down for writers in Russia. What do they say?)

Have you seen Joe Levy yet? The news trickle led to us some time ago that he admitted there was anti-Semitism and that, in fact, he had lost a factory supervisor's job because he was Jewish.

Keep writing.

Once again, CONGRATULATIONS ON YOUR WINNING THE GUGGENHEIM! Write details.

> Love from
> Your father,
> Louis

Allen Ginsberg to Louis Ginsberg

> *{Prague}*
> *March 29, 1965*

Dear Louis:

Been in Moscow a week saw Joe Levy & old pictures & tearful stories of Vitebsk 1905 – Sat around Red Square & wrote poems – drank with Yevtuchenko – saw ballet & symphonies & plays & museums – heard old gossip about Death – Then 3 days also in Leningrad, visited Hermitage & this Street Nevsky Prospect I read years ago in Gogol – Now back in

Moscow in hotel overlooking Kremlin . . . be here a week & meet more poets & then by train back to Prague – I may stop over a few weeks in Warsaw on the way, but Prague address is the best – All well, will relate gossip on return – Love – Allen.

Allen Ginsberg to Louis Ginsberg

> *11 Narodui* – Writer's Union
> *Prague, Czechoslovakia*
> *April 10, 1965*

Dear Louis:

Arrived here in Warsaw[1] several days ago and am settling down for a few weeks, then will train back to Prague. After that if I have any money I'll visit Hungary, Budapest, & see what's happening there. My plane ticket is Prague→London→New York.

I saw Annie & Joe [Levy] in Moscow. He was very sweet & so was she, almost familiar as if family. They weren't very open or talkative (to me) about their political experiences. Probably they told more to other relatives they knew better. In fact Joe told me he thought Beria was in pay of "Scotland Yard."

I spent a lot of time with Yevtuchenko, Voznesensky & others, and got more information from them than from Joe. Also saw Yessenin-Volpin whose work's not published there.

Party line has always been laid down for writers. It's determined by balance of forces between "good men" and "bad men" inside the bureaucracy. Right now it's relatively liberal. Yevtuchenko heard, last day I was there, that long new poem of his would be printed 1,000,000 copies.

Moscow was a big drag mostly. I got around but the weight of the State is too heavy to be comfortable. Warsaw more open, but more small town. Well I'll see who's here. OK – I'll see you soon –

> Love,
> Allen.

There might have been a "thawing" of the Cold War in Czechoslovakia, as Allen reported, but the country was still under Communist rule, and Allen's presence,

1. Although AG used a Prague return address at the head of this letter, it was written in Warsaw.

although not as controversial as his time in Cuba, was proving to be difficult for the country's officials. On May 1, Allen was crowned Kral Majales (King of May) in a huge student celebration in Prague; displeased officials immediately stripped him of the title. Over the next few days, things got worse: One of Allen's journals was stolen, and he realized that he was being watched or followed; on May 5, he was attacked and beaten on the street. Allen made hasty plans to leave the country, but on May 7, before he was able to depart, he was arrested and formally expelled from the country. He was escorted to a plane bound for London, and while in transit, Allen took out a notebook and wrote "Kral Majales," one of the highlights of Planet News, *the collection of poetry that he would publish a few years later.*

Louis Ginsberg to Allen Ginsberg

May 15, 1965

Dear Allen,

Glad to hear from you after a hiatus.

How come they expelled the King of the May? Too much revelry with Pan?

Did you get my message – sent to you three times – that you won a Guggenheim? How much money does it give you?

Here is a clipping about you and me in the local *Paterson Eve. News.*

I am missing you here.

Come home soon with voluminous details and fascinating stories, what with new material for poems.

We bought a new car. Our old one was stolen and then found: we used it as trade-in.

Write more.

Love from your father,
Louis

Allen Ginsberg to Louis Ginsberg

{London, England}
May 21, 1965

Dear Louis – Czech police stole my journals, notebook & later expelled me for anti-state orgies. They were jealous about May King. Now in London since May 7, and traveling around countryside – spent this weekend at Newcastle & visited old poet Basil Bunting & met a lot of longhaired young lads and their wives – England very beautiful May sunshine & I'll go on to Paris a week mid-June & then fly home end June. Allen.

Allen Ginsberg to Eugene Brooks

London
May 25, 1965

Dear Gene –

Sorry so sparse with letters – I wrote Peter more extensively because he's in contact with Lower East Side network –

As far as I know (re your question), I didn't violate any Czech formal (personal) laws. All sexual relations between adults (over 18) are legal. (In Poland oddly it's over 15 yrs.) I had *no* narcotics there at all.

I was May King and that upset the Communist Party. I was more or less guarded in my conduct thereafter. But I lost (or had lifted from my pocket) one of my notebooks from previous visit (Feb 18–Mar 14). The police kept it, more or less illegally I believe – as far as law goes – and used it as they wished – 10 days after I got bounced. I kept quiet to see what they would do, & they opened the recriminations. The problem for them was to get rid of the "legend" I left behind & justify their own gaucherie in kicking me out. Fortunately everybody in the Writer's Union & all the students know the whole story. I had also been attacked & beaten in the street by a supposed police "provocateur" several days before I was bounced. I reported it to U.S. Embassy in Prague (before I was expelled) about being attacked on street & loss of notebook, so they were all primed for further difficulties & so was I.

I checked in at US Embassy here to get word from Prague about my notebook – the Prague attaché said he thought it would be easy to get back. There's nothing against the law in Prague (as in US) in keeping private thoughts or diaries. He thought it wd be easy to recover, but that was before Czech police printed extracts in *Mlada Fronta,* a youth newspaper May 16. London Embassy hasn't yet word on it. I wonder if they're putting me off.

There's nothing in the notebook I would be ashamed to have published (with the exception of a few names of people whose conversation I reported sketchily) – so there's no *threat* there. The main thing is I'm afraid the

Czechs will try to *keep it.* And there are a few good poems in the book. I may have to look up international law when I get back, unless the embassies prove more efficient than they've been so far. That's the sum –

Allen

I'll be back in NY June 15–20 – I think.

Allen Ginsberg to Louis Ginsberg

{London}
June 1, 1965

Dear Louis –

Prague scene *too* complicated long story to write. I'll be home in 3 weeks anyway – many details in the newspaper are correct & many are incorrect. I spent the last week in Liverpool, where the Beatles come from, listening to new rock & roll groups – it's a jumping city like San Francisco – tonite a party at my publishers, and I give a reading June 3 in London & June 6 at Cambridge University. Then to Paris for a week, see Gregory Corso who's finally at peace there – then I'll fly back to New York around June 21. OK – Love Allen

Louis Ginsberg to Allen Ginsberg

Monday, September 27, 1965

Dear Allen,

Received your letter dated Sept 23.

Glad you are OK. and keeping busy. Nothing like killing time by working it to death.

Pleased you understand about the *Call* interview.[1] You well describe drawbacks and blockages and filter agents which communications are distorted and mauled. So it goes. Yes, even communications between

---

1. Regina Smaridge's interview with Louis and Edith Ginsberg ("Childless, Lonely Old Gruffer") appeared in the "Home Magazine" section of the September 18, 1965, issue of the *Paterson Morning Call.*

friends and lovers and father and sons are also mauled and distorted and garbled. More anon.

Wish you were here. This coming Sunday, Eugene is making a party in Plainview on my 70th birthday on Oct 1. The family and some friends will gather. Wish you could be present, too, as I shall miss you very much. However, I send my love to you across the continent. I am happy that you are happy in fulfilling your inner nature and destiny. This quotation could apply to you as well as to me: "When a material object has left me with the imprint of Beauty, the office assigned to me by nature has been fulfilled." D'Annunzio.

I am fine and in good health, and my mind is teeming with ideas for new poems. Will send you some new poems, when they are published. (My third book of poems ms. is still going the rounds. Each time it comes back, I replenish it with new poems and take out some weak poems or those that seem so at the moment. The rejections seem a bit warmer so I am hoping that sometime here – or hereafter – a good publisher will take them.)

Edith is fine and so are all the others. Sheila had a new baby boy so Edith is all agog.

I just started my seventeenth year at Rutgers evening sessions teaching. I enjoy it and it keeps "my hand in," as the phrase goes.

I do a little more reading of my poems than in the past. In Nov. I am reading at the Newark, N. J. YMHA before a little book club. On the 8 of Nov., I fly (with Edith) for the third year to Detroit, Mich., where at the Wayne State U. I am to give two or three readings of my poems. The loot there is good.

I keep ever more busy at my desk, reading all sorts of magazines and writing slowly but steadily, trying to put a prismatic fringe about the status quo or a nimbus about the commonplace. All in all, nothing is happening except some new poems and my watching forces of creation concentrating on myself perceiving myself more aware of those forces composing a miraculous commonplace. More anon.

I ruminate a great deal on Determinism and Free will. I came across this thought on the subject (Nehru): "Determinism is the cards you are dealt; and free will is the way you play them."

Write again with letters and not postals for am eager to hear all about what you are doing and thinking, even if, at least, in politics, we agree to disagree.

> With love from your father,
> Louis

The two Ginsbergs continued to disagree vehemently about the war in Vietnam. Demonstrations and protest marches were springing up on college campuses across the United States, with some of the country's most notable ones taking place in the Bay Area, where Allen was staying. Activist Jerry Rubin, leader of the Vietnam Day Committee, planned a series of marches and demonstrations, only to be countered by members of the Hell's Angels motorcycle club, who threatened to disrupt the marches and beat up the demonstrators. The confrontation and potential for violence provided one of the sternest tests of Allen's leadership, but, as the following letters prove, he was up to the task.

Allen Ginsberg to Louis Ginsberg

c/o City Lights
261 Columbus, S.F. California
November 6, 1965

Dear Lou:

I guess you'll get this on your return from Detroit.[1] Nice time? I'll probably go thru there on the way home by car. In a month or so. I'll be here till Dec 5 or so, and then drive south to Los Angeles & see Max Levy & Tillie in Riverside, & stay a couple weeks with friends in Los Angeles, then head thru desert country & stopover at Albuquerque to see Creeley & on south & north or wherever, thence to NY, in Jan or Feb.

I met some poets from Artist's Workshop in Detroit – group of young people jazz musicians & painters & poets founded an avant garde group, integrated with Negro musicians & hired a house for center for readings & theater & art showings. They seem to be flourishing except that John Sinclair the young kid who was the organizer was trapped by cops into selling them some marijuana a few months ago & sentenced to 20 years. Some of that group had heard your last reading there at Wayne.

Spent ten days at Big Sur by oceanside, & practiced singing Tibetan & Hindu mantras. I'm getting good enough to put out a record soon. Maybe blast that ecstasy thru the jukeboxes. Have you heard the new wave of pop-folk-rock on the radio? Bob Dylan's recent records are genuine poetry; also one called "The Universal Soldier" ("He's fighting now for Russia, he's fighting for Japan, he's fighting for the U.S.A./Without him Caesar would

1. Louis and Edith Ginsberg had recently traveled to Detroit, where Louis gave a series of readings at Wayne State University.

have stood alone, and Hitler wouldn't have had his way . . .") – amazing to hear preached to kids on radio – also another song "Eve of Destruction" is very strange – unexpected – message to hear on normal airwaves – political rockandroll prophesying end of earth.[1]

I took some LSD for the first time in several years at Big Sur – very beautiful afternoon on magic earth, the ancient ocean and titanic cliffs & old sun solid in the atmosphere, great masses of kelp life-forms washed up on beach, & the tiniest flower on the path a violet jewel. All the young people out here are experimenting with it – by all I mean a huge number, maybe 10% of college kids, and those all the ones interested in poesy or politics or art. It'll have an effect. I wound up on my knees praying for Johnson going into the valley of the shadow on Gall Bladder table for operation. What seems to be happening is a slow shift of consciousness of the species to something more ample & tolerant – have to cope with the massive hatreds & wars ranging the planet & the threat of bomb annihilation hanging over it all.

I took part in the Berkeley Marches – read poetry at the teach-in with Louis Simpson & Duncan & Ferl & McClure – then Gary Snyder & I on the sound truck leading the march with mantra-chanting – Buddhist hymns to calm the crowd – everyone afraid the police would get violent. Stopped on Oakland border – reminded me of Hague & Journal Sq. days, refusing Thomas permit/protection to speak and the eggs etc. Next day we all marched again to Oakland border – I was in front row when Hell's Angel stomped up wearing swastika & tore down Peace in Vietnam banner. We all – 6000 people – immediately sat down calmly & watched. The Oakland police had last year encouraged the Hell's Angels to "have some fun" with the free speech demonstrators in Oakland, so I heard rumor. I know some of the Hell's Angels here & gather from them that the police this time were treating them well for a change & had sort of tacit agreement to let them thru the lines to attack. The leaders of the Vietnam Day Committee are mixed – some hepcats, some Marxists, some Progressive Labor, some liberals – mostly neutral types not partyline. The majority of the 14,000 that came out and marched are Spiritual rather than political, i.e., not Marxist oriented but the opposite. New generation change-of-consciousness youths who listen to the Beatles & Bob Dylan. There's lots of local attacks on them for being pinko cowards etc; but there are so many & all so independent that the

---

1. "The Universal Soldier" was written and recorded by Buffy Sainte-Marie. Barry McGuire's "Eve of Destruction," one of the hits of 1965, punctuated a long series of folk songs protesting war, including Bob Dyan's "Masters of War," Phil Ochs's "I Ain't Marching Anymore," and Pete Seeger's "Where Have All the Flowers Gone?"

generalized attacks show in relief the vast gap between actual event & massmedia reportage, & the students get more insight that way.

I'm giving a reading with other SF poets here to raise money for the next march, & then I'll be on that Nov 20, & then a week or so after head out for L.A. My main function seems to be trying to keep everyone calm & sing mantras to avert Disasters. A calm-belly'd OM outbreathed over loudspeakers does create a tranquil atmosphere in contrast to hate speeches.

Missed the comet here, did Gene & boys see it? I got up before dawn but it wasn't visible thru the smog that's settled down in bay like a thin brown haze covering the planet.

Also tried a new drug DMT which smoked lasts a half an hour, somewhat like the magic theater of Steppenwolf or Laugh Gas apocalypsis of mind-consciousness – all visual phenomena separating out into a wall of colored wave forms like Einstein might chart & the somewhat horrifying discovery that it's all empty transient phantoms, including people. Fits with Buddhist metaphysics & Chaung-Tzu. i.e. the foundation of phenomena, empty. Felt like science fiction, the waves of disappearing colored vibrations alternating with solid Ginsberg reality as I breathed the smoke in and out. Much pondering over the years from 1950 when I first took peyote in Paterson backyard, I got no conclusion except that all perceptions are equally valid, but that none including usual consciousness have any but transient existence. Which is classic enough. But to experience it directly with senses is awesome. Where it's all coming from I can't imagine, except glimpses of it all as projections of desire in a void where there's nothing to stop desire from rising, if it insists.

To bridge the gap between this area of perception of phenomena & the waves of rage & blood that climax in Vietnam – I don't know where to finish that sentence.

Meanwhile the Army has taken over monopoly control over LSD and related drugs, so I understand from Leary & from the ex-head of a pharmaceutical house in LA who explained the situation. The Army sd come to him to ask him to develop an LSD that would immobilize people – alter a few of the LSD molecules a little so it would be a bad kick or be usable for victimizing people – he quit the drug business.

Sorry I missed your birthday party but I figure you'll have plenty more. See you soon –

Love as ever

son

Allen

Allen Ginsberg to Louis Ginsberg

{San Francisco, California}
November 19, 1965

Dear Louis:

Been even more involved in Berkeley March than I expected; all the poets here got together to give a reading & raise money for the Vietnam Day Committee. The last march a swastika-studded band of crazy motorcyclists The Hell's Angels attacked the march & were threatening to turn tomorrow's into a riot; all the newspapers played up the threat, the Oakland police opposed the march & so everyone was afraid the police would let the Angels through as they did last time; all the VDC Marxists began talking counterviolence and a dangerous situation was developing. I went down 70 miles to San Jose College to get on a platform with some representatives of the Hell's Angels last week and did what I could to head them off; then the other night Neal Cassady & I and Ken Kesey went privately to their house, had a party with a lot of marijuana and LSD, sang and danced & talked to them till some kind of communication began getting thru.[1] They're paranoid, the police state conditions here fall heaviest on them as they're stupid and brutal tho sensitive, all products of the last Korean war, they think the communists are going to come here and liquidate them, that the march is a communist march (both last opinions they picked up from the *Oakland Tribune* & UPI and AP and SF Hearst *Examiner*) and so the only way to defend the country and themselves is to attack the marchers (mostly apolitical teahead pacifist bohemians) with chains. At San Jose State I began singing Buddhist hymns, tried not to debate or argue but to inquire & explain. The audience mostly hostile, laughing & cheering – 1000 young healthy Americans – when the Angels promised to come out & attack the march. I got up and asked if they really wanted to see wounds blood unhappiness on the march and a great youthful roar of Yeah! came up out of the crowded cafeteria where we were gathered with news photographers & TV Cameramen. "You want to see Unhappiness?" "Yeah we want Unhappiness!" This a specially conservative provincial school with secondrate teachers, not like the larger Universities, but the temper of the crowd was so Sick I was – surprised – the corruption of US consciousness now advanced to a point enough to make even you ashamed.

---

1. See "First Party at Ken Kesey's with Hell's Angels," AG, *CP*, p.374.

At the party a few nights later we did better & the Angels promised nonviolence & anyway the Oakland Mayor got a court order he had to protect the march and so called out the State troops & national guard – to protect a political parade! – This sickness is the same sickness as your constantly reverting to calling me a communist – the same screams of the crowd "Pinkos cowards Commies Draft dodgers etc etc."

I'm not an absolutist and naturally everybody has different opinions and sees things different but even THAT role-playing is over inasmuch as at this point it is necessary for everybody to compromise and come to one mental place where the diversity can exist, lest the earth be destroyed by this vast bomb which is not the Atom bomb but the egotistical rage & frustration which you see daily in the editorial columns & screams of parade attackers. Free to his own opinion etc. but the US has carried that too far in Vietnam at this point and now it's not Johnson or McNamara at fault, it's the whole USA and how this country will ever get out of its Karma, how it will ever get out of having to *pay* for all that suffering and blood, I don't understand.

As you remember a year or more ago we differed on other matters but one thing we did agree on, you agreed on, that the Vietnam war was a farce and stupid policy. Since then we've totally changed policy – at the time we were only advisors to a So Vietnam Effort – the rationalizations are now all different, it's our war now even if the So Vietnamese don't want it – (and if you can find any scrap of printed paper saying the So Vietnamese DO want it you'll send it to me despite that every day you can read exactly the opposite in the Foreign press or even in the UPI dispatches – that Vietcong would win an election because the people are so sick of the USA – that So Vietnam army no longer interested, many deserters, that there's no Govt except one general who likes Hitler as an ideal etc) –

but now I don't understand how you changed your position to correspond to this last year's Govt change of tactics???????????? You began against the war, now that it's got serious thru US escalation you're suddenly for it? In 12 months? Now you're saying it's not a civil war? It's Chinese Absolutism threatening world peace? It's EVERYBODY'S stupid absolutism threatening world peace including yours Louis Ginsberg and now you got blood on your hands.

And if you don't like that sit on it. You're just like the Germans under Hitler and all your talk since 19Alpha is the same hypocrisy. They were trapped in history and so are you. And if I get my head busted tomorrow in Oakland walking along singing with my fingersymbols it'll be a piece of the same Television-hypnosis hysteria you carry in your heart that did it. That's what Karma is.

Okay enough of my own hysteria on you. I was kinder to the idiot Hell's Angels than I am being to you. But you're supposed to be more responsible so the frustration I feel is – ugh, I give up. This kind of screaming at you certainly doesn't change your mind because it backs you up into a position where you have to defend yourself. And that, as usual in our letters, only brings violence back from you in answer to my own violence.

But I see why LeRoi Jones gives up on the US whites.

This prophesy Merlin shall make for I live before his Time: the next great war crises for the US will be in South America. For the last 8 years since everybody including you got conscious of the fact that there was a severe economic problem there, and that the answer would be either Communism or US sponsored total reform, the US has been putting in small amounts of minimal reform, not enough even to make up for the *increasing* social degradation, and pouring in large amounts of military energy there, cultivating right wing juntas etc. Dominica a perfect example. In ten years there'll be a large scale war with US on one side and nationalist communists on the other side. And the reason it'll be all communist (at worst) is because the US refused to let the steam escape any other way. And at that time it'll be the same Paranoid U.S. cry, "It's US or Them Folks hurry up and get in the barroom brawl." Exactly as now in Vietnam. Even though even you know (or knew a year ago) that North Vietnam was trying to ESCAPE from Chinese domination and was taking the Soviet side of the sinosoviet dispute. The one consequence of the war you're approving will be to FORCE on the Vietnamese, exactly the thing you think you're trying to prevent. You'll force them to side with China. And then you'll blame China for having paranoid world-conquest ambitions. Meanwhile the Idiot masters of Communism and Capitalism will be rubbing their hands and gathering police state power everywhere. The Pentagon & McNamara etc are MIRROR IMAGES of the Chinese bureaucracy. But I must say it's disgusting after years hearing you complain about flip flops in the party line to see you doing a total flip-flop in your opinions on the Vietnam war. Which should show that the old party line you were so angry about was not an EVIL thing, just a thing of subtle belief & exposure to Imagery, as your flipflop has been.

And don't say it hasn't been a flipflop because we discussed this for the last years and you were always very Dubious of the Vietnam war, and there's been nothing since (including the Stevenson last conversations) to change one's mind except a continuous barrage of overhearted imagery in the papers & a lot of pictures and soft soap on Television.

And if for 10 years I've been screaming like a paranoid nut about Mass Hypnosis – this is a perfect example of it in action.

I also saw it in action at the first Vietnam march, attacked physically, attacked by "patriots" as sedition – attacked by HUMPHREY as seditious – and now suddenly in the last week now that war-dissent has become respectable in the newsprint of Reston, Lippmann & The Courts – suddenly legal and healthy. But there were a few dangerous days last month when those who organized the march were preparing for sedition trials. And if the wind had blown that way, I could not have depended on you to know the difference.

And that's why I always get so bugged! My OWN FATHER caught in the same mass hysteria and sadism that is dragging planet to radioactive shit. My own high minded ex-socialist liberal family!

Well enough of my vomit. I'll write in a few days. I spent the last week running around from VDC to Hell's Angels to newspapers to insure the march would be peaceful so I wouldn't get my skull bashed on the streets.

"Apollinaire: now is the time for prophesy *without* death as a consequence."

as ever
Allen

I wrote you card, OK for poesy society, maybe March OK.

Suture Self.

This is a disgusting letter to write you. At least it's better than the Napalm you're paying for and approving. And justifying to yr son. Oughta be ashamed of yourself at yr age. But this tone of letter leaves no room for someplace to agree in. Forgive me. I'll be more calm when the parade anxiety's over.

P.S. Honey's article was well prosed but not cogent. Generalizations removed from reality; as, well, we didn't do no good with Diem 1956–63; and not much better since; but we *will* do better. Or Geneva accords not good basis because quote international lawyer Diem repudiated it unquote. That's like a southern lawyer saying coloreds can't vote because Gov. Wallace set certain legal standards for voters. *Sophistic* legalism.

Louis Ginsberg to Allen Ginsberg

November 23, 1965

Dear Allen,

Received your long letter interspersed with sorrow and hysteria and emotional attacks.

First, let me applaud your efforts to bridge with love the hostility of Hell's Angels and the Peace Movement. It is a noble gesture.[1]

Second, let me inform you of my attitude toward South Vietnam War. It was true that I am against our fighting there, despite the fact that the Commies from the North a few years back came down like wolves on the fold and murdered the village elders and ravaged the country and despite the fact that the Commies ravaged the South there. I say I am against the war there, BUT we cannot just walk out. The Commies – it does not matter whether of Ming Ho or Mao – believe that they can take over the world by force: if we walk away without negotiation, they will regard us as paper tigers and continue with their infiltration and guerrilla tactics and overrun other countries and take over Southeast Asia. They say so.

Why do you deny you are a Communist? You admitted this in your *Who's Who* statement that you are a "theoretical Communist." You always took the side of the Commies, even though, later, you tried to admit some deficiencies there, such as restriction of free speech. Whether you are subconsciously rationalizing your mother and your Aunt Elanor, your red-colored spectacles always took the Commies' part. You blindly failed to see how Russia took over by hook or crook Romania, Czechoslovakia, Hungary, Estonia, etc etc. You never called the Russians the greatest Imperialist powers, even though they are.

When Stalin, as it leaked out gradually, terrorized Russia with so-called spy trials; and when Stalin, it is now admitted in Russia, caused wholesale butcheries, not one poop or whisper came out of you. It is not a sickness: it is simply your inability to see the evils of Communists. You failed to see the prefrontal lobotomy Stalin and Russia performed on the Commie sympathizers.

As for Pinkos, cowards, Commies, draft dodgers, etc, while it is unfair to

---

1. See "Demonstration or Spectacle as Example, as Communication, or How to Make a March/ Spectacle," AG, *Deliberate Prose,* pp. 9–13; and "Coming to Terms with the Hell's Angels," AG, *Deliberate Prose,* pp. 14–18.

link them all, still there are all sorts and conditions of types, including Commies, who are against the U.S. So, too, those who favor not leaving South Vietnam without negotiation also are infiltrated and infested with the Rightist reactionaries and the Rockwells.

As for my being responsible for napalm, I am against the use of that, and I recoil from it. I did not see you, when you always take Russia's part, I never heard your outcries against Russian purges or the bloodbaths or the Russian butcheries. These, too, according to your faulty logic, are on your head, because you always defended the Commies. The blood of the youngsters in the Hungary revolt, with the Russian tanks crushing them in blood-spattered streets, are also on your head, because you kept white-washing Russia!

Unlike Russia, we have free speech here. Look at all the dissent and opposition to the war; look at all the parades defended, in the main, by the police and by the courts. All is not hysteria. If there are Hearst papers, there are many other papers (which I read) which are revolting against the war. I agree that there should be compromise: Russia at this stage of history would like, in a small measure, to compromise, but China is Absolutist and demands that we leave all South Asia to her. This is dangerous. We must negotiate with sincere intentions ON BOTH SIDES.

I never said – you put the words in my mouth now – I never said that the war is a farce. I do think it is foolish to fight so far away and in the wrong place to make a stand; but, once there, even by an error, one cannot retreat or walk away without being called cowards, without having one's honor besmirched, without having North Vietnam and China gloatingly prove that "the law comes from a gun" and its guns are the law of the world.

No, I say again, it is not a civil war; that is a figment you are guiled with. I maintain the Commies infiltrated and used guerrilla tactics to ravage and despoil and murder countless peaceful South Vietnamese.

You must ride yourself on your congenital Red viewpoint. Even if you are under the delusion that you are fair-minded, my conversations with you over the years have proved to me you are Commie-oriented.

We see things not as they are but as we are.

The U.S. may be wrong in its mounting such a massive war, but remember: a three-quarters truth or a half-truth are better than an eighth-truth. To walk out of South Vietnam, I reiterate, would leave the field to the lying, butchering, Absolutist Commies.

As for LeRoi Jones, because of the wrong done to his blacks, he, too, is an Absolutist. He has exchanged his heart and put hate in the hollow. He is a madman. Even his wife he now discards; he sneers at white workers who are killed fighting for the blacks in the South. He is a madman and will get his comeuppance.

Please don't talk to me about my so-called liberalism with its flaws: you yourself, with your Commie-tinged viewpoints, have condoned most of the Commies' depravities for the last thirty years.

Your emotionalism – while it is nobly aimed and shows a great and kind character – nevertheless is blind to many aspects of reality. The old party line of the Communist Party was and is an evil thing, a Procrustean bed that lopped off limbs and minds. You yourself being a theoretical Communist do not appear to have clean hands, despite your blind nobility.

There may be mass hysteria on parts of some Americans, but many newspapers are questioning the government in free dissension. An example is the fact that the Democratic Governor of N.J., while he deplored Genovese's statement that he wanted the Commies to win – yet the Rutgers College and the Governor declared he had a right to his opinion. The goons and the reactionary Rightists are a small part of America.

In conclusion, I charge you, as a Communist with blood on your hands, because, in the past, with a few exceptions, you have condoned the blood baths of the Russian Communists. You are and have been caught in the prefrontal lobotomy and emotionalism of Russia. What about Russia's planting missiles in Cuba? What about tanks squashing youngsters in Hungary? You, by association and condoning, are guilty. Remember: Hell is paved with good intentions!

Your holier-than-thou attitude, with your noble intentions, does not prove that you have a Heavenly blueprint of the Truth.

You may be a great poet, as I believe you are, but you still can have false ideas and false facts, despite your noble intentions. T. S. Eliot and Pound had Fascist ideas.

As ever,
Louis

Allen Ginsberg to Louis Ginsberg

{San Francisco, California}
November 29, 1965

Dear Lou:

Before we got on to whether or not I "am" a "Communist" or whether there's any point to your continuing this line, which you do seem to continue despite the fact that it seems only to be playing with words – capital letter Communist I notice this time – in fact we won't get back to it (unless you later still want to play that game more) because it's just too silly to go on with. Or at any rate I'm not playing this game.

Your attitude to the war as you put it is that "The commies from the north a few years back came down like wolves on the fold and murdered the village elders and ravaged the country . . . the Commies ravaged the South there. . . ." This is a specific set of interpretations of the events which are loosely presented, and inconsistently presented, in U.S. mass media. But in detail they have been contradicted, many times, even in the U.S. press, and I think you have seen those contradictions too often to set that forth as the actual event, much less the cause of the war.

Also "Ho or Mao believe they can take over the world by force . . ." I think that in this context, it's not far from statement of official U.S. policy, it also is statement of your sense of things, it's also statement of Hell's Angel's understanding; and I think it's a paranoid – Paranoid in the sense that the Birchites are more extremely paranoid on same line – interpretation. In the same sense of Paranoia, it's the Mao-ist interpretation that the "Imperialist powers believe they can take over the world by force." It's a paranoid mirror-image, as I was saying in last letter. Both lines of interpretation can only lead to mass destruction.

I rarely "take the side" of the communists but I think basically you misinterpret my resisting "the side" of the US mass media as some sort of favoritism. "You never called the Russians the greatest Imperialist powers" etc. I don't think there's any benefit in thinking or acting to resolve the conflict or even understand the conflict by switching the terminology of conflict to "calling the Russians the greatest Imperialist" etc. That seems to lead nowhere but to self-righteousness.

When time came on specifics to speak & act I wound up in conflict & bounced out of the *mildest* of Red police states. I mean after all that . . . well let's not get back into it. Still I did not *at the time* "whitewash Russia" on Hungary; I remember quite distinctly that I was outraged by Russia then. You don't remember that because you were probably more outraged or outraged in a different way. 1962 we had correspondence & I pointed out that at least Hungary situation was not dead end as Latin America say Brazil, and had improved. At the time you denied this. Subsequent U.S. reporting follows my interpretation that the satellite countries in E. Europe are slowly decentralizing; U.S. now pursuing that line by recognizing & trading with them (inc. Hungary) to encourage the decentralization of military state.

I don't remember proposing to you leaving Vietnam without negotiation. Tho at this point I don't see what there is to negotiate. We could have negotiated when (when I came back 63) there was still some hope for a noncommunist S. Vietnam. At this point I think the population of S. Vietnam is so hostile to the USA (it was already 80% hostile according to Eisenhower at the time of possible elections following Geneva, which is why we didn't want elections and still don't). If they are hostile it's the result of our own actions and I don't think you can project that on to Ho. We have free speech here, but the mass media is sufficiently screwed up that to this day you think the So. Viet. population is *on our side.* That it's a Chinese maneuver to take over. That the war is not a civil war but controlled and directed from the North. That if it weren't from the North there'd have been no war.

I've said over and over, and you've read over and over, that Ho Chi Minh was attempting to take Russia's side against China, because historically Indonesia & China were always in conflict. And I've pointed out that it was Dulles policy "neutralism not acceptable" that is pushing S. Vietnam policy into a position so untenable that the effect of our policy is to GIVE China all of Vietnam. Because the only chance we actually had of containing China was to build up neutral pro-Soviet satellites.

"No, I say It again, it is not a civil war: that is a figment you are guiled with. I maintain the Commies infiltrated and used guerrilla tactics to ravage and despoil and murder countless peaceful S. Vietnamese." Well this is the crux of the problem, exactly what kind of war *was* it from 1954 on; what kind of war did it become until a year ago; what kind of war is it now. I think you are accepting very loose thinking in the above.

I mean you are making it sound like "Commies" – presumably from China or agents of China – ?? – started it all? If that were so, just like that, I wouldn't disagree with you. But Experience *there,* as well as reading, makes it sound so different that your interpretation doesn't really hold very well.

Now the above interpretation you give *is* really "officially" the basis of US policy; and it is the same as right-wing generalization; and it is the superficial stereotype of the war you might read in a provincial columnist or editorial. But it is not the interpretation of Lippmann, or *NY Times* news stories *or* editorials, or Pulitzer Halberstam, or I. F. Stone, or the *London Times,* or the French press, or anyone except a minority propaganda group within the US.

Jones, LeRoi, and myself flip our lid because finally it seems the misunderstanding runs so deep it will lead to bomb war and violence. He's not a "madman." Really.

When I said theoretical communist, it means what it says. I don't see any future for Capitalism as a theory. Actually I'm probably a syndicalist. The mass media have got to be taken out of private monopoly hands. Giving it to the State would make it as bad or worse, more centralized. Union ownership probably be best . . . i.e. Lucien [Carr] & coworkers determining U.P. policy line, not Roy Howard.

Enclosed a few — need I say non communist? — articles, one by Morganthau & one by Scheer. Scheer gives background history & is very simple and readable & should clear up genesis of the conflict. It covers points raised in the article you sent me, such as whether or not Geneva accord was legal, and exactly what was Geneva accord, and who is the VietCong, etc.

The march went alright — no violence at all, we'd persuaded the Hell's Angels to stay away by getting them high on LSD.

Also enclosed an anti-Marxist leaflet I wrote as directions for the marchers. Anti-violence, which the Marxists here were, just like you, thinking was necessary in the situation. In that sense you're mirror images of each other. I'm not playing that game, to the best that I can escape it. Trouble is, we're playing it with each other, at our age.

Love,
Allen

Please read the enclosed Scheer, check it with your memories of the *shifts* in U.S. emphasis and reporting, and try to follow the whole process from '54 to now.

Louis Ginsberg to Allen Ginsberg

December 10, 1965

Dear Allen,

I have read the enclosures of your last letter.

Your own delineations of a parade are eloquent and poetic and full of loving-kindness. I think it is a fine declaration and should be widely broadcast. I sent it to Eugene.

That article by Hans Morganthau I perused carefully and I find it plausible, though fine-spun and sophisticated statement. He is articulate and cogent, on the surface. I would be inclined to give him more heed, had I not heard him refuted and rebutted by Dr. Scopalini (or a name to that effect) in a televised teaching debate in Washington. Dr. Morganthau was even forced to admit openly that he had been in error in previous pronouncements.

The pamphlet called *How the US Got Involved in Vietnam* by Robert Scheer gave me pause. The pamphlet does contain damaging statements to the U.S. line. I'll peruse it and check it more carefully. I'll say now that, despite its damaging matter, it seems to me to be all one-sided. Nothing on the American endeavors are good.

(It reminds me that never have I heard you make a statement favorable to America. Also, why you deny you are communist oriented when you admit in your *Who's Who* article that you are a theoretic Communist? Also, in accordance with your red-spectacled viewpoint, you never admitted that the Commies were wrong when they raped Czechoslovakia, Poland, East Germany, Romania, Hungary, etc. etc. These points will have to wait for your debate. I want to air the Vietnam situation.)

My own viewpoint, condensed, is this:

1. We should not be in Vietnam because it is not practical, being too far afield from our country.

2. The Commies are wrong in infiltrating and descending like a wolf on the fold (Scheer ignores that).

3. We should get out of Vietnam *only by negotiation.*

Am enclosing an article in today's *N. Y. Times* about educators backing the U.S. policy.

The pamphlet by Scheer I am sending to some knowledgeable friends in the State Department to get further enlightenment.

When I am downtown, I shall get *The New Leader* to see what they say. I read the *New Republic* and other tracts and so get a wide variety of viewpoints.

Yours,
Louis

1966

In December 1965, Bob Dylan presented Allen with a gift of six hundred dollars, which Allen applied to the purchase of a reel-to-reel Uher tape recorder. Allen had been eager to "sketch" America through a series of spontaneously composed poems written while he was on the road, and for much of 1966, he toured the country in a minibus, recording his impressions on the Uher. Some of his finest work – including his classic antiwar poem, "Wichita Vortex Sutra," and many of the poems included in the award-winning The Fall of America – *was a result of these recordings.*

The Vietnam War was now at the forefront of the American consciousness, and Allen and Louis Ginsberg continued their debate on U. S. involvement in the war. Louis, horrified by the nightly news reports on television, and by the headlines in the newspapers, slowly modified his stance on the war: He hated the war and its destruction, but he saw no way out of Vietnam – at least not in the way it was being proposed. (In this respect, he was not much different from a large percentage of the American population.) Although Allen's letters from this period are missing, one can surmise, from Louis's responses, that Allen was continuing with his insistent demands for the United States to withdraw from Vietnam immediately.

This year also saw the beginning of the Allen Ginsberg–Louis Ginsberg joint poetry readings – or "the Battle of the Bards," as they were often called. The readings brought father and son closer together, even as they debated poetics and politics from the stage. Both Allen and Louis enjoyed these joint readings, and they would participate in dozens of them in the years to come.

Louis Ginsberg to Allen Ginsberg

April 6, 1966

Dear Allen,

Are you taking care of your health?

Newsweek, dated April 11, '66, has a paragraph about the "Battle of the Bards," on page 63.

Abe Greene, assistant editor of the *Paterson Eve News,* suggests a reading by you and me in Paterson. It's just in the thinking stage. Would you be agreeable?

Love from
Your father,
Louis

Louis Ginsberg to Allen Ginsberg

April 9, 1966

Dear Allen,

When Mr. Abe Greene of the *Paterson Eve. News* asked me for suggestions, I wrote that a reading might take place, as a cultural event, in Paterson, in the hall of the YMHA. Perhaps Jos. Zimmel might promote it. We'll see: it's just an idea that is growing.

I spoke with Eugene about his appearing with us in "A Night with the Ginsbergs – Poets." To my surprise, he did not seem to relish joining in with us. He raised objections. Said something curious, i.e. that, as a lawyer, the resulting publicity might expose him to annoying, unwanted phone calls. (!)

How do you figure him out?

Come in Sunday, April 17, if your engagements permit.

Hope the weather is balmy.

Love from
Your father,
Louis

Louis Ginsberg to Allen Ginsberg

April 12, 1966

Dear Allen,

Your array of facts gave me pause, but there are other facts. Your formidable array of facts on hand but you neglect to mention:

I. While the U.S. was pondering neutralist election, H. Chi Minh and his cohorts (democrats? Baloney!) infiltrated thousands of Commies who butchered thousands of leaders of villages and terrorized thousands of villages.

Just as with South Korea, so in S. Vietnam the Commies infiltrated with terror. (As they are now infiltrating into Laos & Cambodia.)

II. The Buddhists want no fighting but they want *no Commies.* You ignore this fact.

III. While I {am} against the military, sometimes they can hold a country together, otherwise the country would fall to pieces and the Commies would fall on a dismantled and fragmented country to devour those pieces ravenously. The military is a temporary expedient. *The military agrees to hold elections shortly.*

R.E.D. The cause of all the conflict is the forceful, ravenous infiltration of Communists, even as they did in S. Korea, not speaking of Czechoslovakia, Hungary, etc. etc. The Chinese call it war of liberation; I call it foul aggression. (I'll send you clippings, too.)

Louis

Louis Ginsberg to Allen Ginsberg

Wednesday, April 27, 1966

Dear Allen,

Paterson is waking up.

The Paterson YMHA phoned me to ask or to invite you and me to a joint poetry reading in the Fall. A Belle Krass asked me what the cost would be. I told her I would consult with you and, meanwhile, requested her to phone you to find out whether you would desire to join in such a reading. Did she call you?

Of course, as I said, your own celebrity summons you for enough readings. I gather, however, that the added father-and-son reading gives further piquancy. Also, the fact that we are of two schools adds bait, so that the press licks its tongue with "the Battle of the Bards."

Hope you will like to join in this Paterson reading this Fall. I suggest a fee of about $200.00 for each of us.

What say you?

How was your Princeton trip?

Tonight, I am driving down to New Brunswick where I am to give a reading and talk before the Literary Club of the Rutgers University evening college. The classes have been circularized so that I expect a good crowd.

Come in soon.

Love from
Your father,
Louis

Louis Ginsberg to Allen Ginsberg

May 23, 1966

Dear Allen,

Congratulations on that magnificent spread about you in this week's *Life*!!![1]

I rejoice in your brilliant eminence as a world-wide poet.

You should feel fulfilled and happy indeed.

Some of your observations quoted in the text are admirable and deep: you tap roots of profundities.

Other comments you make I disagree with: that is because of my nature, the way I have been put together.

Take care of yourself.

Love from
Your father,
Louis

P.S. One minor error: I am not an atheist. It is more complex a matter. On the battlefield of my mind, there is a perpetual contest going on between my head and my heart, between an agnostic and a religious, though not an institutional one. When I think of the butchery of six million Jews, I am an agnostic. When I think of the infinite order of the universe, I am religious in the sense that Einstein meant: awe at the wonder of the universe. Behind it all, though, there is a deep affiliation with the racial and historical memories of the Jewish people.

L.

---

1. Barry Farrell, "The Guru Comes to Kansas," *Life*, May 27, 1966.

Louis Ginsberg to Allen Ginsberg

May 31, 1966

Dear Allen,

Congratulations on that splendid interview in the current *Paris Review*![1]
Your discourse had many fine and rich insights. Some of your satori and
visions I had already been aware of.

I was especially interested in your remarks on spaces between words.
"There be a gap between two words which the mind would fill in with the
sensation of existence." Very good, indeed. Are you aware of Arthur
Koestler's *The Art of Creation*? He remarks that "the creative process comes
from the collision of apparently unrelated areas . . . from an intersection of
different frames of reference in which one matrix is crossed by another."

Lorca has the idea of the imagination leaping as on horseback over two
different fields of thought.

I was also interested in your description of states of illumination in which
Blake gave you momentum or flashed revelations. It is all stimulating and
inspiring. Some thoughts of others float into my mind in that connection.
Shelley said, "Beauty is the perception of the infinite in the finite." Also the
poet discovers the timeless in the temporal . . . or the poet links the fleeting
and ephemeral with the permanent and the eternal.

Was interested, too, in the idea you adumbrated – though not express in
this interview about your theory of the nakedness of the spirit and the holiness
of every human feeling. Am I correct about the latter? What I want to question
is whether everything in the human is holy? Since we are part animal and part
human, nature plus nurture, are there not some parts to be chained and
confined? For instance, what about the feeling of brutality and savagery in the
Nazis who butchered 6 million Jews and others? What then, do you say, about
what should be suppressed? What feelings of man should be suppressed?

Congratulations again!!!

I miss you and at times feel lonesome for you; but I want you to come to
visit me only when you have an inner compulsion to do so, but not from
some sense of obligation or duty.

Love from
Your father
Louis Ginsberg

1. Thomas Clark, "Allen Ginsberg: An Interview," *Paris Review*, Spring 1966. Reprinted in AG,
   Spontaneous Mind (New York, Harper Collins, 2001), p. 17.

Louis Ginsberg to Allen Ginsberg

June 20, 1966

Dear Allen,

How are you faring on the coast?

This is to let you know that I have settled on a date with the Paterson YMHA. Our joint poetry reading will take place on Sunday night, on October 23, '66. Kindly confirm this date. O.K.?

The YMHA plans to advertise our reading in all the colleges nearby; so that a good crowd can be expected.

All is quiet here.

What is so rare as a day in June? A night with June! Just for the fun of it.

> Love from your
> father,
> Louis

Louis Ginsberg to Allen Ginsberg

August 8, 1966

Dear Allen,

I trust your voice is getting better.

We'll drive in by car on Sunday, August 13, about 2:00 P.M. After some talk, we might prowl about the Village or go to a "happening" or find some offbeat movie or eat in a Chinese restaurant and/or go, if worthwhile, to the Village Gate. We'll play it by ear, so to speak. (In case something important comes up – for you, that is – we can postpone the visit, though I am getting lonesome for you and miss you.)

Blake's lines about the sunflower have also been with me a long time. There is a sadness lurking in the syllables of the poem that have always haunted me. The sunflower, symbolic of mankind, longs to escape the limits of this mortality for a region of immortal aspects. In the second stanza, does the "virgin shrouded in snow" imply a coldness or a barrenness? The end of the poem seems equivocal. What does the word "aspire," in next to the last line, mean? It means "long for," I take it; so that the youth and the virgin, as well as the sunflower, are still trapped on this side of the grave. Nonetheless, the poem has always worked a mysterious, nostalgic, and sad magic on me.

I am keeping busy, as ever, at my desk, writing slowly new poems and revising many other poems. At moments some days, I live less daily, finding myself setting a prismatic fringe about the moment; until some sudden insight, pouring light into me, makes me catch a glimpse where, as Wordsworth says, "All lay imbedded in a luminous light/and aspired with inward meaning."

Love to you from
Your father,
Louis

Louis Ginsberg to Hannah Litzky

August 16, 1966

[. . .]

I spent a day with Allen. We had long talks. We mentioned LeRoi Jones. Allen, while he thought Jones was going too far in his animosity, felt that was partly due to inroads of the White Establishment. I countered, if that is the whole burden of condonement, then we Jews should hate all Catholics for their Inquisition and all Christians for their injuries upon us for the so-called deicide, and we should hate all Germans for the six million murdered Jews. And where is Love, love, love? He finally yielded to my arguments.

We went to a group of Village poets cutting a record of their poetry. I was invited to read some of mine but I declined. Frankly I did not care to be included in meretricious and scatological passages.

At night we prowled amid the Village purlieus. We heard a combo which I disliked: they were too loud and too obscene. (Such things should be obscene but not heard.)

At an eatery we had a crowd, including Larry Rivers, the painter. I regaled them (aside from some puns) with my salad days when I lived in Newark and would, of an evening, take the tubes and hie myself into New York to give readings of poetry in converted stables in the Village with Maxwell Bodenheim, Clement Wood, A. M. Sullivan, Henry Harrison, etc.

People here in Paterson are beginning to ask for tickets to the joint reading of Allen and me on Nov. 23, so we ought to have a crowd.

Did you see the article about Allen in the *N. Y. Times Book Review*[1] yesterday?

By the way, what was the aftermath of the joint reading of me and Allen at the camp? (Do I sniff something untoward?)

[. . .]

Love from
Your brother,
Louis

Louis Ginsberg to Allen Ginsberg

August 29, 1966

Dear Allen,

How are you?

I am missing you. Hope you will come in soon.

I think Eugene and his family will be in Paterson Labor Day, Sept. 5, Monday. If you have nothing better to do, how about coming in, too, so we might have a family gathering?

Trident Press which looked with favor on my book of poems has merged with Simon and Schuster, and the President of the former Trident Press has frozen all decisions. His secretary tells me that, when he comes soon from Europe, he will get in touch with me. I am not sanguine: I hope for the best but almost surely expect the worst. I guess I'll send it again on its rounds.

Nonetheless, I am keeping busy, more than ever. My mind is fermenting with ideas, but, of course, ideas need the proper words, which we poets get by inspiration. The poet, I take it, consciously improves what unconsciously pours out from his subconscious. I guess it is a question of a controlled abandon. Controlled wildness. Koestler in his book, called *The Act of Creation,* says art is a marriage of the conscious and the unconscious. One matrix or frame of reference is crossed by another. Bronowski in his book called *Science and Human Values* declares: "The act of creativity lies in the discovery of hidden likenesses. The artist takes two facts or experiences which are separate; he finds in them a likeness which has not been seen before and creates a new unity." I like Lorca's notion: "Metaphor links two antagonist worlds by a equestrian leap of the imagination."

1. M. L. Rosenthal, "Poet and Public Figure," *New York Times Book Review,* August 14, 1966.

I am aware that you rely more on the outpouring of the subconscious without too much conscious interference. I daresay you make a minimum of so-called interference at the moment of your subconscious outpouring by having your mind instantly decide the competence or relevancy of the immediate utterance. Of course, late revision might improve the writing. Your telescoping, too, of images is fine, somewhat like Hart Crane, yet there is a danger in not quite getting the clues or connection so that the phrase seems obscure. The result is that the poem does not quite take the reader into his confidence but bars his way in. Be that as it may, there is no doubt a great deal in the spontaneous eruption or outpouring from the subconscious. I might say that I do more rearranging than you do.

Well, I am keeping busy these days.

Did I tell you I talked a half hour reading poetry at station WBAI-FM? They will let me know when the reading will be broadcast. My Detroit readings will take place in the Fall at the Wayne State University. The dates have not yet been fixed, but we hope, as the phrase is, "[to] firm them soon."

As I say, I am busy writing new poems and revisiting old ones. Sometimes I light firecrackers of the imagination and put them under clichés so see the latter break apart so I can make new combinations for felicity. Often in this way, I alarm syntax and fever phrases and get a luminous glow, so that, in the new aura of light, old familiar things are transfigured new and strange.

Will send you some newly published poems soon.

Love from
Your father,
Louis

P.S. Please pardon two-fingered, hit-or-miss typing of a raggle-taggle, tatterdemalion nature.

Louis Ginsberg to Allen Ginsberg

August 30, 1966

Dear Allen,

I have been haunted lately by the first sight of the first photo made of the earth from 240,000 miles near the moon. Though it was only a quarter earth, there it hung, limpid, serene, tranquil, rotating (one imagined) on its rounds, quiet, with no wisp of any suggestion of any turmoil on its surface. I thought what might an observer from, say, another planet wonder about the earth and whether it had intelligent beings and how far they had advanced. No one could detect any hint of turbulence on that tranquil, floating sphere.

Yet, down to earth, we do find humans in whom technical skill has outrun their ethical status, and the marvels of their inventions have not at all matched the quality of their souls. I guess the earth is now in the best condition for everything – except man.

I have perused your letter with much interest and care. It is a reasoned letter with an abundance of supporting statements and with an urban and urbane sense of a detachment that does you credit. I do not want to take anything away from the massive thrust of your splendid letter.

Nevertheless, according to my lights, I differ with you.

I wish to make these preliminary statements.

First, we see things, as a rule, not as they are but as we are. I am a liberal, with a vestige or residing of socialism of Eugene V. Debs type. You are more Left, no doubt influenced by the Naomi sentimental communism plus your own inbuilt rebellious attitude.

Second, as you intimate – but with a shift of emphasis – that one side is not all black and on the other side all white. As I phrase it, a three-quarters truth is more valuable than a half-truth.

Third, I still fail to see that the S. Vietnam struggle is entirely a civil war. While there may be some intricacies and partial involvement that may smack of civil war, and while Ky is by no means a democratic rule with no unblemished shield, yet, by and large, it was and is Communist aggression. For all your authorities, I can mass contra authorities: The people in S. Vietnam may not all be Marxists, but they have been aggrieved and trespassed upon by the Commies. What may have been an incipient civil war by dissidents against the government was soon engulfed by the Viet Cong and then by Hanoi with three cheers from China.

I will send you some pamphlets from whence I get my information. I am aware of the viewpoints of those you quote, but I will ransack my notes I have recently made of those who hold diverse views.

The main point I want to make is this as to why the other side does not negotiate. Johnson has said he will go anywhere and talk with anyone. My information reveals to me that the Administration is willing to include the

Vietcong at the table but *why only the Vietcong?* I am unalterably against negotiating *only with the Vietcong.* I would include them, with representatives of S. Vietnam (no matter what Ky says, he'll just have to knuckle down to the Administration position). I agree with R. Kennedy. Yet so far the other side – Hanoi, the Viet Cong, the Commies – have not at all responded!

Do you advise us to walk out without a face-saving device? I violently refute that. That way lies tragedy, for China and the Vietcong will take that as leeway to run amuck and rampant over small countries; and our name will be mud. That way lies world tragedy.

No, I don't remember your being especially impartial in the past. Later, you admitted discrepancies on the Commie side. I heard not a breath out of you when Stalin's name suffocated the people in an orgy of sycophancy. You ought to read *The God That Failed* to see the prefrontal lobotomy performed on a whole nation by Stalin. Yes, Stalin used the grave to correct mistakes. Well, later, when you had more experiences and traveled, then you saw flaws, but I had to keep fiercely fighting with you to make you admit them.

By the way, I don't at all blame Naomi. Her heart was in the right place. But she, with her noble, though sentimental wishes, had the best impulses misguided and traduced for the worst goals perpetrated by Russia.

There are, as you know, many intellectuals and professors who condemn your position, who feel that to negotiate only with the Vietcong is to let loose a wholesale war by the Commies. . . . Speaking about escalation, when the U.S. held off bombing for a while, was there a peep of a desire to talk from the Vietcong? No. A similar pause of our bombing would fortify the Vietcong in allowing them to bring greater masses of men down to the field of battle.

You talk about loosening control these days in Hungary. But we are talking about *those days* when the Soviets murdered the youth with their tanks. So there were, as you learned later, some semi-Fascist forces against the Commies. Does that excuse the Soviets from murdering or raping Hungary then?

About Bertrand Russell. I admire him as a genius and as a philosopher. He does some independent thinking, but being human, he can be wrong, too. For instance, what sticks in my throat about him was that, when the Soviets took out their missiles from Cuba, Russell praised the Soviets for their peaceful motives. But why did he not blame *them in the first place for bringing or stealing those missiles secretly into Cuba? That* he ignored and so, for me, he stained his impartiality, so-called.

I abhor war. I think we should not have gone into South Vietnam. I think the game isn't worth the candle. I think that the means is worse than the ends. Yet, after all is said, in the last analysis, I have searched my mind, and I cannot find any excuse or palliation for the aggression of the Vietcong, despite your array of authorities. I am gathering details to counterbalance your critics. To repeat, I am against negotiating *only with* the Vietcong; I would have them only as a part, with S. Vietnam, at the conference table.

Yours for the truth or as much of it as our fallible, personality-colored glasses can envision, to the best of our disability.

> With love,
> Your father,
> Louis

More anon.

Please pardon my hit-or-miss, two-fingered, raggle-taggle typing as I do it hurriedly, from the top of my mind.

Louis Ginsberg to Allen Ginsberg

September 27, 1966

Dear Allen,

I miss hearing from you.

How are you?

I received a call from Miss Belle Krass. She is the supervisor of the Cultural Committee of the Paterson YMHA. She told me the tidings that the house is well nigh sold out for our joint poetry reading on Oct. 23.

I'm coming in on Oct. 15, to hear you at the Town Hall. Can you get two complimentary tickets for me and Edith?

It seems, no doubt, that you have vast drawing powers. But, in addition, if I may say so, there is an added intriguing spice when both father and son – a poetic rarity – appear. If you see any opening, or a suggestion is made that both you and I appear, if you are so inclined, make such arrangements, say, in some neighboring city. What think you?

Some executive board members of the Paterson YMHA felt that, due to the parochial or small town atmosphere of Paterson, that I should try to persuade you to mitigate any "blue" or "raw" words. I said I would try. I wish you would.

When you get a chance from the pressure of your work, come in to see

Your father
Louis

Louis Ginsberg to Allen Ginsberg

December 8, 1966

Dear Allen,

As I wrote you yesterday, I am missing you and had planned to run in to see you in N.Y. but, since you will run into Plainview, I'll see you on Sunday.

Am keeping busy, now and then rubbing the Aladdin's lamp of poetry in hopes of summoning some clouds of wonder or some convocation of images to inspire me. Have written some new poems. Did you get the one I sent you, called "In Every Place"?

Am reading the papers and magazines aplenty and, as is my wont, drawing my own confusions, as good as the next man's. Some moments I feel that men accumulate more ignorance than they can assimilate and that people are a bundle of prejudices wrapped in misinformation and tied together with rubberbands of mistakes. And philosophy is solipsistic; it suggests unintelligible answers to insoluble problems amid conspiracies of misinformation and/or silence. Is life a mysterious arrangement of relentless logic for a futile purpose? I had these thoughts viewing a TV program of exploration of underseas where bizarre species of fish and eerie creatures all spawned and proliferated abundantly, only to eat each other or devour other species. This reminds me of my favorite topic: free will and determinism. I feel that there is more determinism than we realize. For instance, did we ourselves determine that we would be born human any more than a cobra or a python determined what it should be born or a maimed Negro what he should be born? I like what Nehru said about this subject: "Determinism is the cards we are dealt; free will is the way we play or use those cards."

Then, at other times, my mood is the opposite. I think of Shaw's statement in *Superman* that life is the effort of nature to multiply in forms that try to find a greater power of awareness of themselves. Could man be bits of nature vocal and thinking? As a poet, I feel that the joy of life is being used for a greater purpose than myself; that the brevity of life reveals its wonderful moments which urge us, in art, to transmute them so that they transcend mortality. That is one of the purposes of art: to perpetuate moments of deep awareness that in life are fleeting.

So it is that, these days when I awake, I am surprised to discover myself alive and to discover myself exploring the wonder of awareness and the astonishment of being a part of the impulse of all creation.

If only in our times of turmoil, the marvels of our products could match the quality of our lives! If only our efforts to reach the moon might be matched by our efforts to make peace and spread well-being over the world!

What put me in this mood? Well, I wrote a couple of poems and found my mind still glowing after being enkindled by incandescent phrases.

Despite the fact that my book of poems – now condensed and sharpened with the help of Norman Rosten – is still unpublished and still going on its rounds, I have infinite faith in it. Also, while there's life, there's hope.

Wish I could see you more often.

The years are flowing fast.

> Love from
> Your father,
> Louis

The bond between Allen and Louis Ginsberg, powerful to begin with, was strengthened even more in 1967, when they toured Europe together and gave significant joint poetry readings in Italy. For Louis, who had never traveled outside of the United States, the trip was especially meaningful. Allen was already scheduled to appear at a poetry festival in Spoleto, as well as at a function in England, so it seemed only natural that he meet and accompany his father and stepmother when they arrived in Europe.

Louis Ginsberg to Allen Ginsberg

March 25, 1967

Dear Allen,

Not seeing you much, I have to write to you.

Edith and I are planning to go to Europe about Aug 15 – Sept 7. (I have to start teaching shortly after Sept 7.)

1. Can you arrange lodgings for us – or give us addresses for same – in London, Paris, and Rome?

2. Will you be in London or Paris on these dates Aug 15–Sept 7? Maybe you can escort us??? How sweet it would be!

Please advise.

Your father,
Louis

Louis Ginsberg to Allen Ginsberg

Monday, June 26, 1967

Dear Allen,

It was a fine feeling I had to see you relaxed in our garden and at home. I trust any tangled knots in you were unraveled, and all crossed lines flow parallel and free. I would relish more interludes like yesterday.

I visited my travel agent. There is no direct flight to N.Y. from Venice, but there is one from Milan. Milan is three hours by train from Rome; while Venice is eight hours from Rome. So, I am having my travel agent confirm my departure to N.Y. *from Milan on the morning of Sept. 9.*

I look forward with much expectation to my first trip abroad. I'm sure it will be enhanced by your being with me. Maybe you and I will be able to exchange impressions, confidences and ideas so that we can journey deeper into each other.

Call me up before you leave.

Love from
Your father,
Louis

Louis Ginsberg to Allen Ginsberg

Friday, August 4, 1967

Dear Allen,

Received your card.

That is a good idea you mentioned: to address our emotions to the best of each side. The only trouble, as I see it, is that the worst of one side might erase the best of the other side. Can't blame you for wanting no part of escalation and want no part of either side, though I myself, while I want no part of escalation, yet, I have an historical umbilical chord to the ages-old heritage of the Jewish people from which I am sprung.

I like Tagore's words: "That which unites men is holy; that which divides men is unholy."

Here is a new poem I had in the current issue of the *University Review* (U. of Kansas City). How did you like that little piece of mine, called "Your Glance"?

Concerning the subject matter in the paragraph at the beginning about conflict in the world, these swim into my mind: "Writing is an attempt to settle one's conflict with the world. . . . Poets aim to find harmony amid an unharmonious world. . . ."

Says Emerson, "Literature is the effort of man to indemnify himself for his wrong condition."

"The world's imperfections are revenged by the poet."

Don't go to too many places without us. I'd like to see the Wordsworth country, and places of Keats and Shelley, my old and continuing poetic loves.

They say, some travelers do, that there is anti-American feeling in Paris. Maybe we could lop off a couple of days in Paris and add them to Rome and Venice? We'll see the lay of the land.

Browning wrote:

"Open
my heart and you will see
Engraved upon it 'Italy'"

All's well here, and Edith's excitement is mounting. We like flying so there will be no mounting apprehension! Stay well and wait for us on August 16.

Love from
Your father,
Louis

P.S. Pardon my two-fingered, rag-tag, higgledy-piggledy, hunt-and-miss typing!

Louis Ginsberg to Allen Ginsberg

Monday, September 12, 1967

Dear Allen,

We arrived safely after an eight and a half hour flight. At the Kennedy airport, Eugene and his whole family met us as did Harold and his family. We all had a small bite and soda and then Harold took us home.

We unwound and relaxed and are now back into the groove.

Dear Allen, I want to tell you that I was touched, as was Edith, by your devotion and love for us. You certainly made our European trip much more richer than it might have been. You were wonderful all around, and I love you more than ever.

Well, tomorrow I start Rutgers teaching again. Edith went back to work today.

I dispatched a letter to Stanley Eker in London and also my third book of poems, called *Morning in Spring*. Maybe he can do something for my book of poems.

How are your lodgings with Mrs. Pivano?[1] No doubt you are busy concentrating on your work. Tell Mrs. Pivano I regret we could not meet but hope to do so in the future.

When you get a chance, write to George Rapp of Rapp and Carroll, publishers. There is no hurry about that, as I want to hear first from Eker.

Monmouth College has invited both of us to give a joint poetry reading sometime in the Winter or next Spring. If you are interested, tell your agent to get in touch with them about dates, financial terms, etc. [. . .]

Otherwise, all is now quiet here. No doubt, many impressions and scenes have sunk deep into my subconscious and will in time, at least some of the impressions will swim up and be transmuted into reasonable facsimiles of poems.

When you get a chance, write me a letter and tell me how things are with you now. More anon.

> Love from
> Your father
> Louis

Allen Ginsberg to Louis and Edith Ginsberg

September 13, 1967

Dear Louis & Edith:

Still sightseeing – now Milan, Brera art museum & others, and vast Gothic cathedral the Duomo here to explore. Living in luxury in giant apartment at Pivano's – her husband designed the Olivetti and so is well off, she has secretaries, I have two room little suite-like section of apartment with my own keys, & invitations from Inge Feltrinelli to spend time in a giant Villa

---

1. Fernanda Pivano was Allen's Italian translator. Through Pivano and her husband, Allen was able to meet Ezra Pound.

out of town like the one we visited with Joel.[1] Meanwhile working, correcting translations [and] answering mail; leaving tonite for a few days in Florence and later will give small readings in bookshops in Naples and Turin. Don't know how long I'll be here. I'll stay a few weeks anyway.

Enclosed letter I got from George Rapp. I'll answer that I don't know your plans, that you may do something with Eker; and that I'll consult you, and that I think it's generally a good idea. We can transcribe my speech and use it for preface. Let me know what you decide with Eker, and you can also write Rapp if you wish, I'll tell him I'm forwarding you his letter – OK so all's going well.

How was your return? I hope you enjoyed yourself. I had a lovely time with you and be glad to travel with you anytime there's a chance. How did the pictures come out? All you need do is give them to photo place; get negatives and "contact prints," take home & examine & choose the ones you want enlarged to about "postcard size."

Enclosed another small tidbit of info on Bolivia from today's *London Times*.

Trying to straighten my affairs from longdistance; contracts etc. Peter sounds fine again, more or less back in shape & house in good order, so no worry there.

I'll write before I leave here. *Newsweek* had sketchy account of Rome arrest[2] I guess you saw. By eliminating background of 16 others arrested & history of arrests (probably oversimplification for mechanical space reasons) I appear in Image of an aging creep. What I'm pointing out is the inadequacy of modern media for actually reporting Event, and the consequent impossibility of public understanding of what's happening, and consequent vast errors of public mental judgment policy & action. One is "brainwashed" as Romney complains not thru any intention, merely that the abstraction necessary in mass media alters actual event, from tiny arrest to giant war.

OK – send me any Europe poems you write.

Love
Allen

[. . .]

---

1. Joel Gaidemak, Allen's cousin, lived in Italy, and he briefly hosted Allen and his parents while they were in the country.
2. On the evening of September 4, while Louis and Edith were still with him in Italy, Allen was arrested in Rome on the Spanish Steps, where he was attending a poetry reading. (Apparently, the police were alarmed by the congregation of the "hippie element" at the popular tourist site.) Allen was briefly detained but then released. Although there was never any real substance to the arrest, the incident was reported in the international media.

Louis Ginsberg to Allen Ginsberg

September 18 1967

Dear Allen,

Glad to hear from you.

Edith and I are still talking how splendid it was to travel with you and how you enriched our sight-seeing, what with your devotion and love to us.

Pleased with the letter from George Rapp. A week ago I sent the ms. of my third book to Eker. Let's see what he does with it. If he can't place it, I'll send it to Rapp or to you to send on to him. I would be delighted to have you use as an introduction your superb and moving instruction to me at our joint reading at the ICA.

I sent away to the ICA asking for the tape-recordings and offering payment for any charges. How will you get the words of your introduction? Will you get a tape, too, and how will you transcribe your words, in the fast moving talk?

(How about using your instruction among your prose pieces? It's a fine document that breaks new ground, I think.)

Meanwhile a copy of my mss. of my third book is also at an American publisher (Bobbs-Merrill Co of N.Y.). I hope for the best but expect the worst so it may be that my third book may come out in England.

(Incidentally, I have many, many poems which I debated putting into my third book. Some of these are equal to many in my third book, so I may begin gathering the best of them for a fourth volume.)

Under separate cover, will send you some mail for you that accumulated.

It has taken us a week of going to sleep early to free ourselves from the time lapse between two continents.

I took out the photos of numerous black and white ones. They came out well. Do you wish to see some? The colored ones are not ready yet.

Edith is already talking about traveling next summer. With her, who knows where we will find ourselves? She's eager to travel with you.

Love from Edith and
Your father,
Louis

Allen Ginsberg to Louis Ginsberg

{London}
October 17, 1967

Dear Lou —

Occupied here daily working on translations & making publishing arrangements etc. My *TV Baby* book[1] came out in London & will get you a copy when return possibly in 2 weeks. Rcd all yr. letters. Wrote to Eker encouraging him. I'll transcribe my ICA Intro soon's I get back. I suggest hold off till hear from Eker before sending mss. to Rapp. Enc. some gossip from *London Times* re Rapp & Carroll Publisher, present status shaky but hopeful maybe. Met Quasimodo & Montale etc here. Save ICA London tapes till I get back. Yes can include ICA intro in my prose book. Save photos till I return, I won't be here much longer.

[. . .]

I'm not sure my movements next summer — tentative plans for Japan-India but not sure & glad to see Mexico again if not geographically impossible, I'll know better in a few months. Happy New Year & happy birthday. Last line "Tight Rope Walkers" very clear & subtle.

Don't like Violence, & don't like SNICK [*sic*] intense hysteric anti-Semitism. However the assumption of total discount henceforth of Snick complaints about system & intensity of change-need, and also assumption of total acceptance of Israeli suppositions re Arab war will end in escalating antipathy & violence.

The main Moloch is violence in all forms: and the most massive center of planetary violence right now is centered in the heart of America—Pentagon CIA Military-Industrial complex, and every US citizen who participates economically in the military complex. The patient may die of cancer.

May be home soon — in haste.

Love
Allen

---

1. *T. V. Baby Poems* (London: Cape Goliard Press Ltd., 1967).

Louis Ginsberg to Allen Ginsberg

Saturday Oct. 21 {1967}

Dear Allen,

Received your letter of Oct. 17.

As I wrote you, Eker had nothing to report so I decided to send on a copy of my book to Rapp and Carroll. I now see the clipping that Rapp and Carroll are disintegrating. This is the second time a publishing firm that offered to publish my book has dissolved. Oh, well . . .

I'll hold the two tapes for your return so you can transcribe them.

Things are popping here with the anti-war demonstrations. There will be a massive one today in Washington. No doubt, the English papers abroad will tell you the results.

What have you been doing all this time?

Thanks for your good wishes on my birthday Oct. 1. I wake up each morning surprised to find myself alive but more than ever active and zestful.

Hope to see you soon.

Love from Edith and
Your father,
Louis

1968

In August 1968, Allen's nonprofit organization, Committee on Poetry, purchased a ninety-acre farm near Cherry Valley, an upstate New York town. The farm, intended as a retreat where Allen could work away from the pressures and interruptions of New York City, and where Peter could presumably avoid the drug and alcohol temptations of the big city, was very run-down and needed a lot of work.

Back in Paterson, Louis never ceased in his efforts to market his third book of poems, though he met with very little success. He was well aware of the small market for poetry books, in comparison to those of fiction or nonfiction, but he was becoming increasingly frustrated by his inability to find a publisher for Morning in Spring.

Louis Ginsberg to Allen Ginsberg

August 19, 1968

Dear Allen,

We miss you.

How are you there up at the farm? What improvements have been made?

Will you be at the farm Labor Day weekend; namely, Aug. 31, Sept. 1 and 2? If so, Edith and I will entertain the idea of motoring up there to see you, if there is room.

Did Eugene tell you he will be a participant in a radio program panel on "Space Law" on Station WEVD, on the dial 1330 AM, or 97.9 FM, Friday night, August 23, at 9:00 P.M.?

Robert Huff writes me that you and I are having poems facing each other in the next issue of his *Concerning Poetry*. Also, I am having two poems in *Poetry, Australia* and two poems in a scientific magazine called *Biology and Scientific Perspectives* issued out of Chicago under the auspices of the U. of Chicago.

How did you like the first installment of your Profile in the *New Yorker*,[1] dated Aug. 17? You came out well, a benevolent guru. The editors of that magazine phoned me, in connection with some corrections, that there will be an account of one of our joint readings, a bit about Edith, me, and our living room, not forgetting some of my puns which have infiltrated.

Write me, as I asked, whether you will be at the farm on Labor Day weekend.

All is well here.

Regards to all at the farm.

> Lots of love from Edith and
> Your father,
> Louis

P.S. I wrote for the second time to Rapp and Whiting, wondering whether the ten-month submission might hatch an acceptance? I am beginning to have doubts.

Louis Ginsberg to Allen Ginsberg

Monday, September 9, 1968

Dear Allen,

Glad to get your letter.

The postal from Untermeyer indicates that you, not I, will be in his revised *Modern American Poetry*. However, he did take a poem of mine for another one of his anthologies.

Enclosed find announcement of a course on N.Y. poets.

I have invited my close friend Gordon Bishop to come up with us the next weekend, unless you have strenuous objections. He deserves to come. (He has promised not to write anything about the farm.)

What new improvements have you made at the farm?

This Friday we start again our next year's teaching. Have now been on the Rutgers staff in the English Department for twenty-two years and still going strong and still finding it stimulating.

---

1. Jane Kramer, "Profiles, Paterfamilias" – 1.' *The New Yorker*, August 17, 1968. The second part of the lengthy profile appeared in the August 24 issue of *The New Yorker*. Both installments were combined and published in book form, as *Allen Ginsberg in America* (New York: Vintage Books, 1970).

Glad you are finding quiet and tranquillity to seep into your soul to enable you to tolerate with philosophic benignity the alarms and excursions and trepidations of the world, foreign and domestic.

If there are any foodstuffs you wish us to bring up, do write or phone.

Love, more than ever, from your father,
Louis

P.S. I but dimly remember the route to your farm. I think I get off at Albany, exit 24; then take Route 20; then route 6 to Cherry Valley. Is that right? Write.

Louis Ginsberg to Allen Ginsberg

Sunday, October 13, 1968

Dear Allen,

I am glad you are feeling better. I would like very much to see you.

Remarks you made recently have set off a train of thought in me. When I had heard that your fame had set high prices on your letters, somehow, on my part, I drew back from selling your letters to me. Somehow there lingered some sort of a taint of guilt in trying to batten on my beloved son's fame.

Yet, since your close friends are doing so, it occurs to me: why not do likewise? Especially so that, now in my seventy-third year, I have just a few years to go. I do not like to leave things to a whim of chance, but would like to tidy up my estate – just in case – and I would like to set things, financially and otherwise, in order.

I suggest, therefore, that when you come in here next time, let us, you and me, examine those packages and bundles in the bin where you have stored your things. Maybe there we can exhume many letters you wrote to me, letters, particularly, when we corresponded often in long, three-page letters on the meaning of life, on Communism, on world events, and poetry and so forth. Some more recent letters of yours to me I have on hand. Gathering all your letters to me, maybe, we can get them ready for a sale, as did your friends. Do you happen to have in your apartment any letters from you to me?

Think about the matter. I am planning to put things in order for future eventualities. There are other things I want to talk to you [about]. The days may seem long, but my years are growing short. I look forward to seeing you soon. Think on what I have written.

Love from Edith and your father,
Louis

Louis Ginsberg to Allen Ginsberg

Saturday night, November 16, 1968

Dear Allen,

Here is the letter from G. Rapp to you. I hope you pardon me for opening it to see what added information he might divulge.

I am pleased the prospects for my book look good. It may be fewer poems might prove advantageous.

Write to Mr. Rapp and tell him – as I shall – that we shall be glad to sign jointly the numbered copies.

Hint, too, that you hope (I do) that he might have printed simultaneously in London and America the edition.

Here is an article or review I wrote about Bennett Cerf's book of puns.

Ferlinghetti sent me a nice postal and a copy of your new book.[1] Congratulations! It looks rich with fine poems. I shall take an evening off to revel in it. The Wordsworthian transcendental poem[2] in your book is well worth the price of the book!

Love from Edith and
Your father,
Louis

On November 29, Allen was involved in a serious automobile accident, which left him with a broken hip and four cracked ribs. He had spent most of the fall in upstate New York, working on his farm and writing musical charts for William Blake's Songs of Innocence *and* Songs of Experience.

---

1. *Planet News* (San Francisco: City Lights Books, 1968).
2. See "Wales Visitation," AG, *CP*, pp. 480–482.

Allen Ginsberg to Louis and Edith Ginsberg

{Albany, New York}
December 7, 1968

Dear Louis & Edith –

All OK, pain mostly gone, pleasant wait in bed, read & write & eat and nap – sort of kindly vacation with occasional stabs or rib pain from leftover bronchial cough. Anyway, not smoking. How you doing Edith? Thanks for pretty card.

Love
Allen

Louis Ginsberg to Allen Ginsberg

Saturday night, January 25, 1969

Dear Allen,

How are you? How are you getting along on your crutches? Sometimes I become apprehensive and picture you stomping down the stairs and I worry lest a crutch slip on those narrow steps and you come sliding down. I hope you'll be careful.

Fate recently granted me a reprieve. I had been having long low grade headaches with drowsiness. My doctor took a few samples of my blood and felt suspicious that there might be a blockage of a kidney that might need an operation. Subsequently, my doctor took five X-rays which turned out negatives (hum). So, the doctor declared no operation was indicated but that one kidney was sluggish. As an antidote, he gave me pills (to increase circulation) and requested that I cut down on proteins. I am now feeling much better; and so, I say, Fate granted me a reprieve. Truth to tell, at my age of 73, anything can happen. I charged the doctor to keep me together, all in one piece for a while, as I have many poems to conjure up yet.

Had some new poems taken and will show them to you when they see the light of day.

My next reading is early in March when I make my annual flight to Detroit to talk on Humanities and Science and read my poems. Am taking Edith with [me], then, as usually, the night before, the two professors under whose aegis I read gather with their wives and families for dinner, and merriment plus witticisms abound about the table.

Our home here has been decorated and refurbished. All rooms have been painted or papered; my sun-room has an extension phone on my desk, and new shelves have been built along the windows. Our living room has been given special treatment: the air conditioner has been lowered; the radiator recessed; the fireplace broils painted white; the mantle-shelf colored a simulated antique motif; and a new russet carpeting is to be laid this coming week. It all looks clean and smug and cozy and warm.

I wish I could see you, as I miss you. When the weather relents, we'll trek up to your farm. Or maybe you'll be in N.Y. in mid-February so we may meet. It seems too long a time since I saw you.

Am still waiting for Godot. . . . If you hear anything from G. Rapp, let me know.

Did you have a chance to read my article called "My Son the Poet,"[1] which appeared in *Book Week* of the *Chicago Sun-Times*? I hope you like it. Let me hear your reaction to it.

Meanwhile, I am trying to eavesdrop on ideas and trying to get the right combination of words like the fortunate conjunction from words which never before met; so that they start mysteriously shimmering on a suffused aura of luminousness to change common things around me to something new and stranger.

I wish my love to you and hope I'll see you very soon.

Your father,
Louis

Louis Ginsberg: "My Son the Poet"

The first time I found out that Allen wrote poetry was when I paid a visit to him in his dormitory rooms while he was an upper-classman at Columbia University.

But before I note this, it occurs to me to mention an incident that happened while Allen was still in grammar school in Paterson, N.J. In the school yard during recess, a bully, taller than Allen, twitted him with an anti-Semitic remark and advanced to hit him. Allen stood there and let out a few sentences with a string of polysyllabic, highfaluting words. This stopped his would-be assailant in his tracks. He wondered what Allen meant, and in his wonderment the bully forgot his punitive intent and asked Allen what he had said. I believe that my son then suddenly felt the power of words. His facility later grew to felicity.

1. "My Son the Poet: 'The kids love him. . . . He is the voice of their secret dreams and desires,' " *Chicago Sun-Times Book World*, January 12, 1969.

To come back to my visit to his college rooms. While I was chatting with Allen and some boys, one said to me, "Mr. Ginsberg, do you know Allen is writing poetry? He has a poem in the college magazine."

Surprised, I said to Allen, "I didn't know you wrote poetry. Since when? Why didn't you tell me?"

He responded, somewhat diffidently, "I thought you didn't want me to write poetry."

Astonished, I fell back. Indeed, I took it as an affront. "I never told you that. How do you figure that out?"

"Well, one time when we were having some people over at our house, you said to them that you and your older son, Eugene, wrote poetry but that I was normal. So I interpreted it to mean that you wanted me to be normal and not write poetry."

"Allen, you misconstrued my remarks. I was only jesting. It is true, in a sense, that I don't want you to write poetry merely because Eugene and I wrote. If you write poetry I want you to do so only because you have an inner compulsion, because you feel you must write, and because you can't help but write poetry."

"Oh," declared Allen, "that's different. I do feel I must write." His face was wreathed in smiles.

"There is no joy," I continued, "like the joy of creative activity, the delight of unburdening one's self of what life precipitates in one, of making articulate what is inarticulate and imprisoned in most people, the exultation and exaltation of finding, at times, words happily mated, lucky words combining into vistas and visions."

And later, after I left, I wrote to Allen: "You, Eugene and I – we would live bad if we didn't write. And we'd write bad if we didn't live."

In the early years of my marriage, a shadow of sorrow fell on our family. My wife, Naomi, somehow developed a neurosis, which, as the years went on, thickened into a psychosis. She would spend two or three years in a sanitarium, then I'd take her out for half a year or a year. After that, ominous hints of her worsening condition made me take her back.

Once, during an interlude at home, she grew worse, and I planned to return her to the hospital. She divined this and declared one night she was going to kill herself, since she didn't want to be a burden to me and the boys.

At the party, all seemed to go well. A couple of times, when I hurried into the kitchen for something, she happened to be there. She winked at me and drew a finger across her throat. At dawn the next day, she slipped out of bed and slipped into the bathroom and locked the door. I had removed everything and had pushed my razor into a deep recess in the old fashioned medicine-chest. But then I heard her murmur, "I have it."

"Open the door," I cried, "or I'll smash in the glass panel of the door!"

She opened it and came out with blood oozing at both wrists. They were surface cuts, so I bandaged them and put her to bed. The boys stood there, shivering in their night clothes, panic in their eyes. What traumas, I thought, might sink into them and burrow into their psyches?

When, after a number of years, Naomi died from a stroke in a New York sanitarium, Allen was beside himself with grief, no matter how much he had foreseen the end. He was then on the West Coast, and he wrote his long elegy on the death of his mother, the poem called "Kaddish," the Hebrew word denoting prayer for the dead. In it he combined Biblical prayers and Walt Whitman–like lines. When I read the poem, I cringed in places, for it was too naked, too raw, too uninhibited. But there were many fine passages which rise to emotional, poetic utterance in his recapitulation of his mother's life and her death. Allen's writing of "Kaddish" gave him a vent for his grief, a safety-valve for his pent-up anguish so that the poem was a purgative and an exorcism of his grief-raged heart. His book helped him, as lines in "Macbeth" assert, to "cleanse the stuffed bosom of that perilous stuff which weighs upon the heart."

Allen is the most compassionate man I know. People will think this is a father's natural prejudice, but this is not so. He is interested mainly in the good, not in goods. He was born with a generous heart, and this kindliness, I conjecture, was accentuated by his heart-wrenching sympathy and love for his disabled, helpless mother which led to Allen's empathy and sympathy for all down-trodden, disabled, helpless creatures.

For instance, fate dredged up from the side of humanity a person called Hunkie [*sic*], a junkie. Early in Allen's life, when Allen was living in Yorkville, I came to visit him and noticed that a new overcoat I had bought him was missing. A typewriter was gone, too. "Where are they, Allen?" He confessed that Hunkie had stolen then them and pawned them to get money for a fix.

On my next visit, who was there, lying on the couch, but Hunkie? When he saw me, he sidled out.

"Allen, what's this?" I asked. "How can you let him in when he robbed you?"

Allen spread his hands apart and replied, "What else could he do? He was desperate."

But that was not the end. In and out of prison, Hunkie haunted him and came to batten on Allen. Later, Allen sublet an apartment of a literary friend who had an elegant library and fine records. It was not long before Allen noticed that books were missing. Who else was taking them out but Hunkie?

"He's helpless, he's struggling for survival," said Allen.

I remonstrated, criticizing Allen for his irresponsible attitude toward someone else's property.

"I'll pay back the amount, when my literary friend returns," he said.

To make a long story short, we bought books at a Fifth Avenue store to make up the loss. Allen's father paid the bill.

Later, when Allen became famous and got fat fees for his readings at colleges all over America, his generosity continued. Moderation in his kindness was no virtue to Allen. He organized a foundation called "Committee on Poetry, Incorporated." Eugene was the lawyer and Allen was the treasurer and the power behind the throne. He poured most of his money into that company. In 1967, Allen gave away $20,000. Who received money? His down-and-out friends, disabled unfortunates, poor poets almost going under, filmmakers, and, of course, Hunkie the junkie, cast out from jail and bobbing in the humantide.

"Allen," I admonished, "save some for your later years."

"They are desperate now," he replied. "I'll have it later."

In 1950, I married a second time and obtained a new lease on life. My second wife, Edith, was a divorcée with two children grown. She managed an office and could add and distract. Seriously, she was a very sensible, warmhearted, understanding woman whom my two boys took to. She created a warm household, just what they had needed for a long time.

Eugene was in New York where he established a law office and married a fine woman, who bore him five children. Allen lived with us. We assigned him a front upstairs bedroom for which he chose wall paper of an Oriental design, a hint of things to come. I offered to stake Allen and let him write unimpeded, but, after a year or so, he became restless and longed for the big city and its literary ferment.

He often came to visit us, bringing such friends as Carl Solomon, Gregory Corso, Jack Kerouac. Our house had a commodious garden with a huge cherry tree and borders of rose bushes and other flowers, and in it we often had cook-outs and plenty of room to chat and ruminate.

Here, too, Allen held long debates and arguments with me on all sorts of topics. Allen was way out in left field, an avant-gardist, a guru to the young leaders of the Beatniks. We argued about drugs. I held that no matter how he felt about marijuana, he should obey the law. "Too bad," I would say, "but the hippies want pot in every chicken." We also argued about the Vietnam War, politics, "the System," and what not. We fought furious battles about free verse and regular meter and rhyme and so on. I objected to his use of raw and obscene words, but I guess that was the generation. My nature and my circumstances shaped me, and his nature and circumstances made him. I suppose we see things not as they are, but as we are.

I felt that Allen relied too much on the surrealist outpouring of the subconscious, without conscious pruning, and that he was neglecting the age-old values inherent in poetry. My own nature inclined me to hold that in regular but flexible meter there is an elemental instinct for satisfaction in recurrent patterns with their variations, postponements and satisfactions. Robert Frost said: "Meter is moving easily in harness." Meter magnifies and heightens emotions. And rhyme, while not absolutely necessary, added pleasure through fresh expectations. It emphasizes and burnishes symmetry. It rings bells. It draws meanings neat and tight. It roves back, with rhythm, to the primitive interweaving of the senses in the tangled roots of elemental time, down to the threshold below the consciousness.

As time went on, Allen and I became more reconciled and saw more of each other's viewpoints. We began to feel, as I expressed it, that there are many mansions in the house of poetry. We began to practice poetic co-existence. Once, on a radio program with Allen, I mentioned that a writer claimed Allen was in rebellion against his father. "No," said Allen, "we are not antagonists but just different."

About three years ago the Poetry Society of America invited us to do a reading together. The announcements drew articles in the press, saying it was a confrontation: "In this corner the father, in that corner the son." We frowned on this. At the reading, we had an overflow crowd. Allen had his devotees, I had mine. Since then, we have read together at Los Angeles Harbor College, at Berkeley, Boston University, Paterson State College,

Rutgers Pharmacy College in Newark, Fairleigh Dickinson University, Brooklyn Academy of Music and at the London Institute of Contemporary Arts.

I usually come on first, neatly-dressed, the "Square" poet, and I intersperse my poems with puns and witticisms. Allen is picturesque and charismatic. He has a kindly owl-like face with long hair and ringlets and a wide beard which is his trade-mark. His orange shirt with beads and amulets disdain his shabby, creaseless trousers. He comes on with small, tinkling cymbals and chanting mantras and *Hare Krishnas.*

The high school and college kids love him. He is the audible voice, unabashed and uninhibited, of their secret hidden dreams and desires they themselves dare not voice. He is their guru, a prophet whose disarming manner and eyes, benevolent with love, capture them.

Often after our readings, we are asked questions of all sorts. I, who am older, seem optimistic. Allen, who is younger, seems pessimistic. He often goes to extremes and he reminds me of Henny-Penny, who, when a pebble fell on her head, cried that the sky is falling.

"What do you think of each other's poetry?" someone usually asks.

Allen says he likes much of my poetry and recites some. In fact, Allen has written an introduction to my projected third book of poems. Generally, I reply that, believing in poetic coexistence, I like much of his poetry and admire his courage. By and large, Allen's lines lash out, like Whitman's, with satiric flagellation of the hypocrisy and apathy and cruelty of the world. He has magnificent flashes of imagination as he pours out cascades of words. And the visionary side of his poetry is his search for exaltation in a mystical identification of compassion and his love for his fellow man.

If we bridge, in part, the generation gap, it is because we both have respect for the validity and integrity of each other's art and poetry.

Allen holds that, besides bridging the generation gap and despite our differences in manner and matter, we have in some of our poems a common denominator in our soaring from the material and physical to transcendent emotional and cosmic heights. In some of our poems, we both use the material world as a springboard into the spiritual.

Recently, Louis Untermeyer wrote to me: "You are good for Allen, and he is good for you."

Allen Ginsberg to Louis Ginsberg

RD 2 Cherry Valley
New York
January 31, 1969

Dear Lou:

Starting off tomorrow for Florida – I'll call you later tonite to get details on Clara – I have her address but no phone #.

Happy news your kidneys are in running order – It's lovely good luck you are still here for company and I feel sad I'm not more near your side – I hope what I'm doing is worth while – which is, precisely, setting up a refuge for people who need refuge – and the need for Balance here has kept me tied down (as well as the hip) more than I'd wanted or anticipated. I'd like to be able to leave this place running independently, or at least independent of my presence. It's getting along.

I got a lot of work done on music – have actually learned elementary notation and harmony & so have a new language & have written out some lovely tunes for Blake – which will last a long time & give pleasure & probably also make some $ to take care of farm.

I'll be in Miami a few days, first time in 16 years – (1953?) – Then short stops at Notre Dame and Ohio Wesleyan & Minneapolis and San Francisco & Denver & home to NY in 2 weeks so will see you then – I'll be in N.Y. Feb 17 – I will call soon as I get in.

I have Son the Poet which is very kind to me – what's amazing is the professional alertness of the prose style – style looks like you'd been writing for magazines in prose before, that's a whole new field open to you – as music is now to me.

OK – Love from
Your son
Allen

I'll probably have spoken to you before you get this. Love to Edith – We put in new floors insulated here too.

Louis Ginsberg to Allen Ginsberg

Friday, January 31, 1969

Dear Allen,

Here are two poems: one of yours and one of mine, both of which appear, facing each other, in the current issue of *Concerning Poetry*.

My poem, called "An Old Love," you glanced at one time and thought it was interesting. Indeed, it is one of those poems which now and then I allow to well up from my unconscious without too much scrutiny at first, and then I look at it curiously to discover what lurks there. As I recall it, when I wrote it, there hid, like some wavering shadow under the threshold of my consciousness, a thought of Naomi: it was as if I was trying to tell her, while she was in the sanitarium, with the wall of madness between her and me, that I wrote her a letter (which it seems that it did not reach her) in which I told her I still loved her, in spite of all the time that flowed by. It is one of those adumbrations that hide under the lines of the poem, and when you try to touch it, it slips away and eludes you. Still, there's the poem. What do you make of it?

All's quiet here. I start tonight on our second semester in Rutgers.

March 4 and 5, I fly with Edith to Detroit for a reading at Wayne State.

The Unitarian Church of New Brunswick asked me to come and talk to them on a Sunday, but their fee of $75 for two one-and-a-quarter hours sessions I thought too small, so I am declining it, unless they raise their ante.

Have you had an answer to your last note from Rapp? I have not heard from him yet.

> Love from Edith and
> Your father,
> Louis

---

1. See "An Old Love," LG, *CP*, p. 253.

Louis Ginsberg to Allen Ginsberg

Friday, May 30, 1969

Dear Allen,

How are you?

I miss you more lately.

Is this feeling a kind of omen? Meanwhile, my burial plot near the Newark-Elizabeth line waits very patiently while I am writing new poems to badger Death and bait oblivion. Maybe I'll rescue something of myself from the flow of Time.

I have been working on my book of poems, taking out what I think are weaker poems and putting in new and perhaps more modern poems. A number of times my book teetered on acceptance. I know it is better than some books of poems appearing, but I guess there must be a conjunction or confluence of interests or forces of people for its acceptance. Maybe by now I have enough exposure, thanks, in parts, to you, to have my book given consideration.

Am keeping all the windows of my senses wide open, ready to receive intimations of the marvelous or the light of magic or the invading light of a satori.

Had new poems accepted in a wide variety of magazines. When they are punished by publication, I shall send them to you to frown over.

By the way, I liked your statement in your *Playboy* interview[1] that "by the holy spirit I mean the recognition of a common self in all of us and our acceptance of the fact that we are all the same one." What is Holy? That which unites the souls of men. Romain Rolland declared, "One never knows where one begins and where one ends."

How is your farm? Have you made any moves to buy it for your own?

Our garden is now bursting with brilliant, even magniloquent, rose bushes, so prodigal and I may say even redundant are the uncounted loading the air with perfume, Keats would have relished the scene. Some roses, already too lush, are shedding their petals. Reminds me that nature is all bosom but no heart: she is eager to proliferate the species but is careless about the individual.

How do you like the pictures of the earthrise seen from near the moon? The earth looks innocent, blue-and-white, afloat in a black silence,

---

1. Paul Carroll, "The *Playboy* Interview: Allen Ginsberg," "*Playboy*, April 1969. Reprinted in AG, *Spontaneous Mind*, p.159.

voyaging along "in strange seas" of loneliness. Wonder whether any creatures in other planets wonder if there is any life in that roving globe of earth? A grandeur seems (to me) to halo the globe. I look forward to the excitement on July 20 when men from earth will step on the moon. What an historic epoch it will be! Maybe it will spur men on earth to look at the earth and say, "We are all in the same boat."

Some time in July, Edith and I will come up to your farm and stay, I think, till Monday morning. We two ought to get into closer communication with each other.

Love from Edith and
Your father,
Louis

Louis Ginsberg to Allen Ginsberg

June 19, 1969

Dear Allen,

How are you? What are you doing these days?

There is a wrangle going on between my desire to see you and my desire not to trespass on your time. So I shall let your inner compulsion suggest to you to come here to Paterson.

Lately I have been writing more than ever. In any case, in the Spring, I usually thaw and flow out more than at other times. Meanwhile, each morning I get up to explore the wonder of being still alive and trying, when I am in the mood, to translate that wonder or astonishment into lines or images of poetry.

Our garden is in full bloom, and I often ruminate in it, trying, as you may have heard me say, to ponder on imponderables, touch intangibles, and unscrew the inscrutable.

In my garden, I often think on the statement of various writers to the effect that man is the mind with which nature contemplates itself or the world looks at itself through man's eyes. Or, as Shaw said, "Life is the effort of nature to strive for a greater awareness of contemplating itself." And so I try. Cynics would say that life is the mysterious arrangement of merciless logic for a futile purpose.

Be that as it may, existentialists insist that, even though the world or the universe seems futile and absurd, the mind of man must wrench some design or pattern or reason, imposing order on chaos.

Strange, too, that breaths or sounds or collocations of words – the frailest things – have more power to last than temples that may crumble and empires that may fade and once haughty cities that vanish through Time.[1]

Louis Ginsberg to Allen Ginsberg

Friday, July 4, 1969

Dear Allen,

I enjoyed hearing your music to Blake. Some of it is really fetching.

When you are finished reviewing my book of poems, give one of ms. to Mr. Syare Ross and one to me. I am baffled as to why a publisher doesn't take it. I insist the ms. is good poetry.

I sent the article from *Book Week*, called "My Son the Poet," to Parkinson in Cal. Enclosed find his reply. Sometime we might go again to Berkeley. They seemed most receptive there of our joint reading.

Lately I did a few short surrealistic free verse pieces. Here is one which has been accepted by the revived *North American Review*.

RUMINATIONS

I bought stock in Time,
That rose,
Levitated by the sounds of the sunset.
If I stepped on my life,
I would step on bells.

I'll have to examine this sometimes, for I let my subconscious have its way without intrusion of the conscious.

Let me know when you will be back in civilization.

Love from
Your father,
Louis

1. The rest of the letter is missing.

Allen Ginsberg to Louis Ginsberg

RD 2 Cherry Valley
New York 13320
July 7, 1969

Dear Lou –

Enclosed Parkinson's letter in return.

"Ruminations" poem is strange & valuable – some kinda mystery there that's not logical but is real. The nearest I got to that style (including a single bell) is "Guru on Primrose Hill"[1] in *Planet News*. Your short poem's interesting reading.

Yes, you're definitely right, and now no need to even insist, your poems are really good, in the mss I have – (requiring a little selection), but the body of work is quite intense, and as perfect as many of the poems are it should have a publisher. I'm sorry I never intruded before but I didn't think I should (reverse nepotism) but the quality of the poems outweighs other thoughts, & the shame that you're not enjoying their publication shames me – I'll try & do what I can swiftly now.

Love –
Allen

Louis Ginsberg to Allen Ginsberg

Tuesday, August 26, 1969

Dear Allen,

I am delighted that you are delighted that I am delighted to have my new book of poems published by a good company like Wm Morrow and Co of N.Y.C.

I wrote them a letter and told them I accept their terms and would be pleased to sign a contract.

I told them you are finishing the Preface or Introduction to my book and would send it to them shortly. I also gave Mr. Landis your farm phone number (which, as you know, has been slightly changed).

1. See "Guru," AG, *CP*, p. 356.

Do send me the list of poems in the book so that I can begin to hunt in my scrap books for the places where the poems originally appeared.

When you are finished with the Xerox copy and the preface, send them on to me.

Naturally I am excited by the new book. Many people in the past, especially at my readings, have asked me for a copy of my book of poems; so, in due course, I shall have an up-to-date one.

If you can offer me some advice about promoting the book, about where to have advance copies for review sent, etc., I trust you will tell me, in due course.

Thanks for helping me weed out some poems.

Edith has an appointment with her doctor about some bladder trouble, so that I shall not know until Friday afternoon just when we shall motor up to your farm. I am in touch with Eugene so that it may be we shall synchronize our visit.

More anon.

Love from
Your father
Louis

P.S. Will call you up when I sign the contract. Till then, I am not saying anything to anybody.

L.

Louis Ginsberg to Allen Ginsberg

September 3, 1969

Dear Allen,

Eureka!

I have the contract from the Wm Morrow Co. I have scrutinized it [and] am satisfied with it. Will sign and send it off.

If there is an item (like fifty-percent of anthology reprints), well, as I haven't had a book of poems published for ages, I shall not demur. A man, long famished, [should] not quibble about food set before him.

Please send me the Xerox copy of my book. I wish to give it the final touches and send it to the publisher, together with the revised Table of Contents.

I'll bring up the signed contract when I visit you on the 13 of Sept.

If you have any suggestions toward the advancement of my book, I shall be grateful.

Everything looks propitious – and I am on Cloud 9.

Love from
Your father,
Louis

Allen Ginsberg: "Confrontation with Louis Ginsberg's Poems"[1]

I

Living a generation with lyrics wrought by my father, some stanzas settle in memory as perfected. "In this mode perfection is basic," W. C. Williams wrote, excusing himself for rejecting my own idealized iambic rhymes sent him for inspection. The genre itself seems imperfect on the XX Century page: a heavy leather Webster's International Dictionary published the same decade Louis Ginsberg (October 1, 1895–) was born defines *lyric* as "1. Of or pertaining to a lyre or harp. 2. Fitted to be sung to the lyre; hence, also, appropriate for a song; –"

Few lyres sounded aloud in Newark, New Jersey, in the 1920's, although in first editions of the then standard popular *Modern American Poetry* edited by Louis Untermeyer most of the poems anthologized still "rely greatly on the steady pace of iambics," including "A Quiet Street After Rain":

. . . While every front yard lawn is seen
Twinkling a myriad tongues of green.
Marvelous too, it is to see
A rose-bud dipped in deity!
Nearby a spider has begun
Upon a fence to thread the sun.

Continuing his attempts to perfect this form, L. G. received the anthologist's later praise: "You have the lyric touch. You know how to make words sing something as well as say something." Yet no literal music was intended. Originally these forms were fitted to music by Waller and

1. Published as "Introduction" to LG's *Morning in Spring*.

Campion, Blake sang his *Songs of Innocence & Experience* with his own voice unaccompanied; even Yeats wrote "with a chune in his head" we were told by Ezra Pound who consistently remembered the musical body of which these lyric forms were skeletons.

Though lyric words had parted company from music a century or centuries before, the standard Educational System anthologies are bulked with rhymed and metered stanza forms (including those of E. Dickinson) that look like the lyrics of short songs, that echo in the head with old tune fragments, that might be put to melody had students world enough and time, but which were written out of language symmetry rules adapted & patched together from differing ancient traditions and then labeled "traditional" in schoolbooks for a few decades in the early XX Century. English measures of stress drawn from Greek and Latin nomenclature originally definitive of pitch and quantity (vowel-length) of sound were applied to bold accent and weak; foursquare stanzas abstracted from song still chimed with parallel sounds at the end of parallel-cadenced lines prescribed as standard – such forms were read less and less aloud and more solely in the universe of the eye-page or silent mind and never sung from the lung. Since that mode of poetry lost track of music, its very rules confused the measures and weights of American speech, as W. C. Williams pointed out at the time. One collection of "representative American Poems for boys and girls" of 1923 "planned to meet the requirements of the College Entrance Board" with the following illustration of *Iambic Tetrameter*:

Thou too/sail on,/ O Ship/ of State,/

Nearly half a century later the student may have sufficiently wakened from a rhythmical hypnosis proposed above to notice that the only way to make affective spoken sense of *Thou*, *sail* and especially *O* is to pronounce them (contrary to schoolbook instructions) with expressive emphasis equal to the syllables *too* and *on* and *Ship*. *Iambic Trimeter* was illustrated in a manner that completely distorted the pronounceable sense of an exampled line:

Whose heart/-strings are/a lute./

In this case the stress indications for "strings are" literally reverses sensible emphasis and obliterates significance. Awareness of this fault of ear caused by rote degenerate lyric meter was Ezra Pound's contribution to U. S. prosody after the turn of the century.

Thus from Whitman's time thru Williams and Pound to Kerouac & Olson, Horace Traubel to Gregory Corso, early Eliot on to Ted Berrigan a new tradition of poets improvised prosodies echoing our actual speech our stutters our jazz our blue bop our body chant the tone leading of our vowels or whatever mystic zap-talk that came natural. "I'll kick yuh eye," W. C. Williams quoted from New Jersey town streets, as an example of musical phrasing which did not fit the metric system described in 1923 by the Secretary of the New England Association of Teachers of English as "particularly well adapted to the needs of English poetry . . . definite rules, which have been carefully observed by all great poets from Homer to Tennyson and Longfellow."

Ironically, a self-enclosed Academy rose to follow such "definite rules" (No playing tennis without nets! Frost rebuked prosodaic anarchists) and an intellectually frosty accentual prosody, non-physical or meta-physical and only remotely musical in nature, became the manner of versification professionalized at best from the later Eliot through John Crowe Ransom to the earlier Robert Lowell in the fourth and fifth decades of this century, and such stingy Rhythm was for a while the dominant mode of poetics in the giant Universities of cold-war megalopolis till the ampler-bodied and more naked breath'd tradition began to sound freely Prophetic a return to common sense in the robotic market places & electric media of apocalyptic planetary & pre-lunar-voyage times.

Ezra Pound's scholarly intuitions came true after the midcentury when a third generation of minstrel poets including Bob Dylan sang their poems aloud in contemplative rooms black alleyways or bardic halls thru microphones and a new consciousness that had broken thru the crust of old lyric forms like my father's evolved back to the same forms refreshed with new emotions and new subtleties of accent and vowel articulation.

II

Latent in the unsung written lyric form, songs are suggested, echoed or new-jived, whole melodies buried their voices resonant in the unconscious never sounded aloud – in a sort of timeless eternal Imaginary place where poets' minds dwell after the death of their bodies, and this is the subject of much of this mode of poetry. All poets from Shelley to Housman knew that melancholy immortality, their body impulses, sensations, consciousness & feelings embedded like flies in amber verse. I have resisted this mode as an anachronism in my own time – the anachronism of my own father writing the outworn verse of previous century voices, reechoing the jaded music in a dream-life of his own sidestreet under dying phantom elms of Paterson, New Jersey – at the very time that Paterson itself was (having been articulated to its very rock-strata foundations and aboriginal waterfall voice in W. C. Williams epic) degenerating into a XX Century Mafia-Police-Bureaucracy-Race-War-Nightmare-TV-Squawk suburb.

Yet if this nightmare world explodes it will all have been a dream with latencies, symbols, daydreams clairvoyant, & tiny perfect poems, archaic stanzas full of intuition and unconscious prophecy, faithful craft in outworn arts, triumphs of the meek and unmodish, forlorn ideals redeemed thru fatal changes, bankruptcy and prophecy confounded, mortality and immortality confounded – Beauty as Truth a last remaining tearful smile at dream's end.

Confronting my father's poems at the end of his life, I weep at his meekness and his reasons, at his wise entrance into his own mortality and his silent recognition of that pitiful Immensity he records of his own life's Time, his father's life time, & the same Mercy his art accords to my own person his son.

I won't quarrel with his forms here anymore: by faithful love he's made them his own, and by many years practice arrived at sufficient condensation of idea, freedom of fancy, phrase modernity, depth of death-vision, & clarity of particular contemporary attention to transform the old "lyric" form from an inverted fantasy to the deepest actualization of his peaceful mortal voice.

This last book of Poesy begins with a contemporary prophetic glimmer of the planetary catastrophe –

> When bombs on Barcelona burst,
> I was a thousand miles away –

that a third of a century ago established the permanent authoritarian bureaucratic police state so familiar to later generations in almost every country of the world. *Remembering Ruined Cities* follows with its house rubble déjà-vu superimposed on 416 East 34 Street, Paterson, New Jersey. The warning deepens *After the Blast*; next *Our Age*'s hallucination crowds downtown Paterson Central High School *Reporter's Class* with phantom-identity victims, till the poet himself is included with *Mr. Anonymous* among those *Lost in the Twentieth Century*.

The ancient recollection of cosmic-identity breaks through one *Morning in Spring* and *After the Rain*. Here the clearest, surest, oldest personal vision commonly recognizable to all human generations, squares and acidheads alike, is set forth as *Testament of Wonder*. These eternal generalizations are located perfectly in an *Autumn Leaf on a Pool* which, compared to Cleopatra's barge, displays in short magical verses an Emily Dickinson vision. *Night in Silver* sets forth artful lines plated with silent rhymes near to some pure tone imaginable while pictures flash on the mind:

> And with a shining crystal,
>   All shingled is the shed;
> Each icicle shows in it
>   A moon is tenanted.

Following thereon, *Morning in Ice* beacons from the abode of Shelleyan realization of Platonic personality where

> Trees are archangels thinking light.

This special gold radiance, seen through suburb-man's eyes as also through pastoral Wordsworth's in meadow buttercup, again manifests clearly around city houses:

> . . . I could see
> The street was like a long ravine of light.

Therefore *At the Zoo* the poet sees sacred monsters, & looking twice out through "Zoo" bars sees his own bestial person. A solitary humor among all this multiple identity frees the poet's imagination to exchange impressions with a caterpillar, comparing their visions and feet and doubts until

> The caterpillar crept away
>   In hurried ripples to a tree.

Time as the impression of *Something Timeless* recurs over and over in these three decades of poetry:

> The autos, the buses,
>   The traffic all,
> Like pageant, stream to
>   A festival.

That awareness clarifies all phenomenal perceptions even *Scents and Smells* to

The crisp fresh mint of violets tinct with chill;

and when specified to *My Love* the humor of world-identity ends sensationally when

In her thighs,
Africa sighs.

But the deepest tones are measured for death's woe and here at *Burial* in

The cemetery drugged with light

a single man's voice is heard slow word by word unalterable in eternity:

Through blur of years, I saw you go,
    From Time at last now moving free;

pronouncing farewell to *Olden Days*

We used to welcome Summers in
    With children by the shore,
But now how long the time has been
    We journey there no more.
For now our sons are tall and grown
    And Summers come and pass
So that I never leave alone
    Without you under grass.
The Summers move above your mound;
    The shore is full as then.
Long will you sleep beneath the ground
    Before I go again.

One by one all relations are resigned to oblivion: self, love, wife, mother,

And if sometimes spring up the tears
   That kennel loss of days we knew,
Be sure, my father, that the years
   Keep leading me more close to you.
In vain my striving to decode
   Some messages of hope and trust
Which truth has cached in that abode,
   That synagogue of silent dust.
For, with myself less busy now,
   I hear more clear your slender tones.
Mercy is flowing from your brow,
   Forgiveness streams up from your bones.

This agnostic compassion emotionally dense as any deity-faith completes a cycle of generations and is transmitted through myself in *Kaddish* as a litany in praise of Oblivion that buries mortal grief. A rational image of the mystery of life perpetuating life enclosed inside itself is presented as in a *Chinese Box* with its very last Question self-answered in terse rhymes terminating thought –

And what do the years
   Finally stow
In a box of wood,
   Narrow and low?

Is this the end? Yes, stoic, agnostic & melancholy as that XIX Century-styled closure must sound, *Conversation with My Skeleton* suspends further speculation:

"One short rhyme, when I am gone,
Time may break his teeth upon."
      . . .
Silent grinned my skeleton.

This Art is a last grim remnant of the transcendental flash that life was, the consciousness of consciousness vanishing: "Suddenly I remembered that I was dead." As in *Loneliness*, concealed in an anonymously formal sonnet, all human poets are

Lackeyed at last by fevers to the grave,
Where we sink cold, as is, above, the stone,
Unfriended, unaccompanied, alone.

It is the same absolute darkness & endless void that shades mortal appearance so tenderly spectral, that surrounds the commonplace *City Twilight* with conscious glory fading in god's shadowy eye:

And with a softness as of petals,
    Like fringe of lights above some boats,
As on a lake where darkness settles,
    So, lamp by lamp, the city floats.

Would that all sons' fathers were poets! for the poem and the world are the same. Place imagined by Consciousness, and the squared exact forms of these poems are tiny models of Hebrew-Buddhist Universes rhyming together in Imagination, as if Art were the one activity in the flux of Time wherein Place becomes completely self-conscious, *Terse.*

So I
Shall try

To hammer
My stammer

And beat
It neat

Exact,
Compact –

identical with itself Aeon to Aeon, climaxed Immortal. This Imaginary Place remarked earlier is precisely the subjective matter of this mode of lyric, an Evanescent Eternity as Weir'd as any invented by Poe (or mapped in the Zohar or unhexed after Avelokiteshvara's Prajna Paramita Sutra), to which this poet returns obsessively again and again in poem-trances even at "Morning in Spring":

> . . . until I knew
> I was the world I wandered through.

The same self of our odd universe recurs everywhere – observing a *Dragonfly*, upside-down in a *Lake in the Park*, glancing at a lion's "shaggy, uncle-bearded face" *At the Zoo*, or watching *At the Burial of My Mother*

> . . . the casket
> With one who gave me birth
> Take a curious leisure
> To sink to earth

–feeling a familiar little sensation named *Correspondences* by Baudelaire and recalled in the "page of Baudelaire" framed by *Snow at Midnight*.

Buried in anthologies unvocalized and lack-harp, hundred of lyrics in this mode by generations of poets whisper Eternal secrets of their Place. A frenzied feverish reader with third-eye open for a month may discover their reality & pathos – perhaps in a more leisure-populaced afterworld to our present apocalyptic Place such verses will be sounded aloud, Lizette Woodworth Reese herself syllable by syllable turned to electronic lyres. Living a generation with lyrics wrought in this mode by my father, some stanzas reflecting this Eternal Place settle in memory as perfected.

Louis Ginsberg to Allen Ginsberg

September 3, 1969

Dear Allen,

How are you?

Received a note from Mr. Landis of Morrow. He says everything is in fine shape. Your introduction, too, is fine, and he is happy indeed to have it. He further writes that I'll be able to have a final look at the poems when he sends me the galleys in about eight weeks.

You'll be interested to hear that the anti-war sentiment is mounting and that its waves are lapping into my Rutgers College evening classes. President Gross has asked us teachers to encourage our classes to participate in the Oct. 15 anti-war protests. Accordingly, I am planning to have my two classes air their views in class on Oct. 14. (I have no classes on Oct. 15.)

Love from
Your father,
Louis

1970

To Allen Ginsberg, American political and societal life at the turn of the new decade seemed to be reaching a flashpoint. December 11–12, 1969, he had testified as a witness for the defense at the Chicago Conspiracy Trial, in which eight leaders of the protest and countercultural movements were being tried for their participation in the events surrounding the 1968 Democratic National Convention in Chicago; the trial, one of the greatest farces in American judicial history, weighed on Allen's patience, causing him to again consider the lengths to which the government would go to silence its dissident voices.

The forthcoming months provided him with a hint of an answer, when he spoke with former attorney general Ramsey Clark, who filled him in on FBI director J. Edgar Hoover's smear campaign against Martin Luther King, Jr.; when he learned (again from Clark) of the ways narcotics agents had, for a quarter of a century, been dealing drugs, even as they tried to silence such dissident voices as those of Timothy Leary and John Sinclair by leveling bizarre drug charges against these men; when, on May 4, 1970, the National Guard in Ohio opened fire on antiwar protesters at Kent State University, killing four people. In Allen's view, America was a police state running amok.

Louis Ginsberg was likewise shocked by these and other events, but in his correspondence with Allen, he continued to defend the government, insisting that the sins committed by a few did not indicate a corruption of the system.

Louis Ginsberg to Allen Ginsberg

Tuesday, February 10, 1970

Dear Allen,

I thank you for those batches of circulars about various subjects and movements. I do not thank you at all, however, for the David McReynolds circular. It is a bundle of whitewashes, rationalizations, half-truths, three-quarters lies, etc.

The Panthers aim at violent overthrow of the government. I favor drastic reform. Violence breeds violence.

"The Panthers, at least officially, are not anti-Semitic," writes McReynolds. Wrong. Their leader, Eldridge Cleaver, has claimed in Algeria that he will train Panthers as guerrillas against Israel. In Paris he said – in a vicious and venomous lie – that the Jews are treating the Arabs like the Nazis. Ironically, the Arabs were with the Nazis against the Jews.

The Arabs could lose a hundred wars, but Israel could lose only one war – and then they are finished, kaput, driven into the sea, butchered and massacred by feudal Arabs. After the six million butchered by the Nazis, this is an abominable obscenity, namely, to want, as Eldridge does, and the Panthers declare – to wipe out Israel. Any Jew who shares with this view is a seeming renegade and seemingly treasonable (I am not talking about religion) but the fountainhead of that Jew's being and his historical heritage. So don't give me that slush, sludge, crap, shit, feces, excrement about New Left or three world orientation whitewash of the Panthers' anti-Semitism.

Wherever the Panthers are, there is intimidation and violence. In Newark, they blackmail poor Jewish storekeepers to fork over money for their Panthers' use.

Allen please don't send me any more crap whitewashing Panthers' anti-Semitism. *My rage will know no bounds!!!*

Yours,
Louis Ginsberg

P.S. In Arab lands, the Jews are harried, imprisoned and tortured. In Israel, Arabs are part of the country, are even in the Knesset. If an Arab guerrilla is wounded, he is treated the same as a Jew in a hospital. *Allen, no more Panther crap.*

L.G.

Allen Ginsberg to Louis Ginsberg

R.D. 2 Cherry Valley
New York 13320
February 15, 1970

Take it easy don't blow your top, I took it easy & didn't blow mine this last few weeks despite attacks of rage similar to yours in letter "My rage will know no bounds." I think probably the Panthers feel exactly the same emotions we do, and the Arabs feel that precise violent sense of outrage, and the Jews identifying with Israel feel that adrenaline brilliance pounding in the gorge & forehead.

I do imagine that it's as Burroughs suggests some sort of trust of giant insects from another galaxy operating thru manipulation of images to drive everybody out of their skulls in states of outrage so blind it will blow up the planet so the insects can take over. Or if the metaphor's too outlandish, its a trust of secret military bureaucrats (Israeli military vs. Egyptian military, Russian military vs. Pentagon) who have an interest in each other's mounting opposition – symbiosis like Narcotics Police & Mafia who have a mutual interest in keeping the junkies (100,000 in NY) persecuted as badly as Jews or Arabs or Blacks anywhere.

My direct experience of the Panthers hasn't been the same as your newspaper clips. I spent time smoking pot with Cleaver & Carmichael in Nashville while the *Nashville Banner* newspaper incited a riot to coincide with Carmichael's presence in Nashville & was with both of them the night of a violence which was blamed directly on them by U.P.I and *NY Times*. Panther means fight back when attacked. As I don't believe in this strategy I part ways with them there; and I think they've stuck to fighting back when attacked, and they have been attacked illegally & grievously, despite accountings of Reisel & others, in accountings by *Life* and ACLU & enormous mass of weekly reports I've read from dozens of cities in under-ground press for 2 years now, material which you haven't seen. Which I can send as I keep it all here in boxes, tho it will only fatigue the reader with such a welter of "institutionalized" violence that you realize the Panther cries are just what we hear, of unnumbered & unreported myriad illeg-alities, beatings, false arrests, insults, unconstitutional force & illegal court process so deep and vast from South where it's acknowledged to North where it's complained about, suffered thru, & bears scars on head from. Panthers in context are Irgun in context. The amazing thing is that Black Violence and Zionist Violence come head on like immovable force & unpushable object round the corner of the world, each with the same fear of extermination and violent sense of outrage. It is precisely the same anxiety that motivated Panthers-like military competence in Israel that motivates Dyan-like language and behavior & propaganda among the Panthers.

As I would not see myself as Black if I were black, I don't see myself as a Jew as I am a Jew & so don't identify with Nation of Jews anymore than I would of Nation of America or Russia. Down with all nations they are enemies of mankind! And nationalism is disease. If this be renegade treason etc remember that's precisely the rhetoric the Panthers apply to blacks who cooperate with white culture police.

You can't have Jewish integrity at the expense of Panther sympathy or Arab reality any more than you can have Arab integrity at price of Jewish extermination – Napalm & violence & bombing from Jewish or Arab hands has already escalated the problem beyond reasonable solution. I don't have a solution except not to take sides that involve bloodying anyone's ass or any kind of political violence. If however everyone insists on being violently right, then we will all have to suffer it through & die violently at various idiots' hands, Jewish idiots, Arab idiots, American idiots, Maoist idiots, liberal idiots, reactionary idiots. All the same violence and it's always proved wrong. By hindsight I wonder if WW II actually solved anything? How many more would've been killed unnaturally if Hitler had his madness enacted, than have already been killed as we've had our madness enacted? I dunno. Obviously no reality to that thought except as it's a thought entertainable among many nowadays.

I didn't read Dave McReynolds' circular. Generally his judgment is good. He was among the first to protest A Bomb drills, and in the 1960's was early organizer with Dellinger[1] and others of Anti-War movement. He then took a pacifist position on war buttressed with reasonable arguments against the Vietnam war which arguments are now considered universal – i.e. we have no right fighting their war, we shd hold elections as per Geneva Convention, it's wrong war wrong place etc. He also gave 10 years working against that war while others including myself had not yet had our consciences roused. He's not "communist." He may have different opinion re Panthers than you but his sincerity is unquestionable and it doesn't help reconciliation to refuse his essay any dignity. It's reconciliation or death for everyone, that includes you as well as Arabs and Panthers. So don't blow your top.

I'm meanwhile worried about Dellinger going to Jail, & the rest of the Conspirators,[2] because I suppose it's getting nearer I'm next unless I begin to shut up & give in and participate (i.e. pay taxes)[3] for the war. The thing that really amazes me is slow discovery of how much of my comfort & ability is the result of labor of others and suffering of other forms of life. I

---

1. Peace activist David Dellinger.
2. A reference to the Chicago Conspiracy Trial defendants (Abbie Hoffman, Jerry Rubin, David Dellinger, Tom Hayden, Bobby Seale, Rennie Davis, Lee Weiner, and John Froines).
3. Allen refused to pay the percentage of his income taxes allocated for the war effort.

don't think that we in US with all our ease are in a position to be very much outraged at disturbances being made by people living in subhuman or nonhuman circumstances. Be glad you're not black & living on River Street or behind the market by the Docks in Port-au-Prince & that I have a nice typewriter & comfy light to write you a letter with. Remember most people ain't got what to eat, and it's going to get worse.

Until we can recognize & solve Black problems we've created – like, in N.J. Mafia dominated police and politics that we've refused to acknowledge for over a decade tho blacks were outspoken about it – & that includes Paterson especially you know – we're not in position to lecture Panthers. I once asked Carmichael what he'd do if he were me – he said sensibly, "Pacify the white violence, calm the whites." Obviously that's one thing we *can* do, it makes no sense to lecture Panthers on their violent rebellion against the police until you can, at very *least,* say that the police and Mafia are not working together in NJ as well as Chicago, Cleveland, Detroit, etc.

Well OK, don't blow yr top, realize the actual problems drive people mad because they are maybe insoluble with present population pressure anyway. I blew my top with Eugene like you blew your top with me, rather than lay it back on you, & that's the net result of violence – passing it on down the line till it returns to the self. Well this is all obvious.

Regarding Reisel, Evans & Novak articles: They have reduced the number of probably killed by police to a Dozen or 10 depending on count; & blamed all violence on the Panthers. This is just doublethink. The number of publicized deaths may well be only a dozen. ACLU has more extensive analysis and details, even *Life* shows a different picture. I remember that the Panthers first began on West Coast after *years* of abuse of Blacks in Oakland, & I remember the context, Panther as "fight back when & only when attacked" from the beginning. You'd have to rewrite all the newspaper work SF 1960–65 to eliminate that context. Read Cleaver's book. OK

Allen

On top that, *White Panther* John Sinclair of Detroit, busted for 2 sticks of pot given to an agent who'd infiltrated his commune, & sentenced to 9 1/2–10 years by judge that thought Sinclair was a menace; then denied appeal bail & sent upstate northern Michigan prison away from direct contact with me or family or lawyers – I spent a week raising necessary $4500 for legal steps in Detroit for him & *still* he can't get out of jail on a charge which elsewhere is misdemeanor as with Samuel's son.[1] Physician cure thyself.

Louis Ginsberg to Allen Ginsberg

February 17, 1970

Dear Allen,

Your answer came to me. It breathes nobility. Your heart is in almost the right place. Yet you raise a cloud of complexities and then, above the battle, give a simplistic answer.

What you don't realize is that there is a hierarchy of guilt.

There are three-quarter truths, half-truths, one-eighth truths and so on.

One truth in this mundane world that you are blind to is this: The Jews in Israel are fighting for their lives; they are fighting for survival: they refuse to be butchered and wiped out by the Arabs.

That is why the Panthers, spreading anti-Semitism and aiding the Arabs, are, carried to a logical conclusion, doing or finishing Hitler's work: i.e., aiding the Arabs to wipe out Israel.

You listen to Cleaver's half-truth, but he did not reveal his arrant anti-Semitism. The fact that he is wronged does not give him the obligation or right to wrong the Jews or Israel which is fighting against its extinction. Cleaver who is violent against racism is himself rampantly racist.

No, I don't – nor do the Jews – have to be masochists to bow our heads before his venom.

If we carry his viewpoint to its logical conclusion, we have to be venomous to the age-old injustices perpetrated against not only the Jews but against all peoples by all peoples: the Crusades, the Inquisition, the Thirty Years' War, and endless destruction and evil of many people against many people.

To cancel out evil and say that all are equally guilty means that no one is guilty. You are wrong. As I claim, there is a hierarchy of guilt: something you fail, in your ardor for peace, to recognize.

It is easy to say, down with nations and up with universal mankind. In the

1. Efforts to free Sinclair eventually paid off when, on December 10, 1971, a "Free John Sinclair" benefit concert was held in Ann Arbor, Michigan. Among those appearing were Allen Ginsberg, John Lennon and Yoko Ono, Stevie Wonder, Bob Seger, Ed Sanders, and Phil Ochs. Fifty-four hours after the the concert, Sinclair was released from prison.

long run, I agree. But in the short run, there is no reason why one nation should try to wipe out another nation whose cohesiveness carries with it immemorial values of a heritage that enriched history and mankind.

I have read Cleaver's book. He was wronged. Does that mean he must wrong others? Those clippings show [he's] an anti-Semitic racist. He has only a part of a truth. I insist on my truth: I refuse to put my head on the block. I refuse to be a masochist or to agree that Israel should be obliged to be wiped out, a natural conclusion of the Panthers, led by Cleaver.

> More anon from
> Louis

Louis Ginsberg to Allen Ginsberg

April 7, 1970

Dear Allen,

How are you? Are you resting up at Ferlinghetti's?

Under separate cover, I am sending you, via first class mail, three copies of my new book of poems, *Morning in Spring*. One of the copies has a special inscription to you. The two other copies are autographed. Give one to Ferlinghetti. Maybe you might give one to Rexroth, though I had ordered a review copy sent to him.

Our party May 3 at the Alexander Hamilton Hotel seems to be growing apace. Nearly everyone is accepting our invitation; so that it seems to swell bigger than we thought. (Your photographer friend is coming with three assistants!)[1]

Reviewing the dates, we have as follows:

May 3, Edith's party at the hotel in Paterson.

May 5 the Louis Ginsberg–Allen Ginsberg joint poetry reading at the Paterson State College, at 8:30 P.M.

May 11 the Morrow–Gotham Book Mart Publication Day Party.

May 17 Hannah's party in Newark.

---

1. Acclaimed photographer Richard Avedon took a series of stunning family portraits at the book party.

Incidentally, the P.E.N. reading of you and me has been postponed to the afternoon of June 3. My publisher who wishes to attend, has been apprised of this date. I hope the date is not inconvenient for you. [. . .]

Drop me a long letter and tell me how you are.

Love from
Your father,
Louis

P.S. Regards to Ferlinghetti and Rexroth.

Allen Ginsberg to Louis Ginsberg

R.D. 2
Cherry Valley, New York 13326
May 5, 1970

Dear Louis:

Enclosed the P.E.N. card I said I'd send you. Also see on reverse my last turn onstage N.Y.C. for the season –

Visited Ramsey Clark, ex Atty Gen, who said J. E. Hoover had a microphone/bug tape of M L King (not photos) in "wild party" at motel which he played around Washington to undermine King's position, & which Hoover tried to publicize

– that the Junk problem could be solved by medical research for half the cost of one Polaris submarine

– that the history of narco agents peddling dope could be traced back a quarter century

– that he thought the Mafia was less influential than I estimated in General Dynamics, tho it was present

– that there was a heavy secret report the government was hiding, or not releasing so far, saying that LSD did *not* lead to chromosome damage.

Well that was interesting – OK – I'll go to Boston June 10, & then Buffalo 12–13 then back to farm.

Love
Allen

Louis Ginsberg to Allen Ginsberg

Monday, May 25, 1970

Dear Allen,

Thanks for your postal. I found my schedule. I shall meet you at times and places designated.

Book reviews are coming in. All are favorable. Did I tell you that the *Wall Street Journal* had a good word for my book? Am keeping clippings in a scrap book.

Received your letter. I deeply deplore the grievous injustice done Leary.[1] I agree with you that ineptness and stupidity in places in government are aggravating the bad situation. Yes, the system is corrupt BUT *only in part*. In other many parts, it is giving due process of law.

You ask what to do? Not violence. That brings counterviolence. "Trashing," burning of buildings by students, bludgeoning of professors result in mindless tyranny which tramples on the rights of others. That way lies madness, polarization and counterviolence (cf. rightist construction workers).

What to do again? The new movements of students, moderating influences, lawyers, etc NOW are infiltrating, crowding into congressmen's and senator's offices to warn them and press them to oppose the President and the Pentagon and to demand END WAR NOW. Congress is hearing this. All this is more effective; it is slower but more effective in working WITHIN THE SYSTEM OF DEMOCRACY. Don't burn the flag but wash it (Norman Thomas). Mindless idiots raise the Viet Cong flag and so admire totalitarian tyranny.

See you anon.

Love from
Your father,
Louis

1. Timothy Leary faced lengthy prison sentences and staggering fines as the result of several minor drug busts. Federal officials and narcotics agents favored the use of draconian punishment for minor drug offenses as a means of silencing political dissidents – an abuse of power that did not go unnoticed by Allen and many others.

Allen Ginsberg to Louis Ginsberg

RD 2
Cherry Valley, New York
May 27, 1970

Dear Lou:

Enclosed note from Y. & yr reviews.

Regarding Leary & system being corrupt "BUT only in part. In other many parts, it is giving due process of law." It seems to me you are depending on nonspecific generalizations that do not take account of your basic inexperience with police corruption because you have led a *sheltered* middle class life the last 50 years, and not stuck your neck out, and in fact supported the system particularly in matters of narcotics policy and Indochina War policy until only recently. If you took an activist role in reform I think your experience of the almost universal corruption of police state in US would be more nearly that of the younger generation. However regarding specific police corruption, the series in *NY Times* end of last month, which I read thru carefully today, paints a picture of irreversible and total corruption of law enforcement. My own previous studies in area of narcotics lead to following facts;

1) by 1925 Lindner Decision Supreme Court, all junkies had right to go to Doctors (like present small scale Methadone experiment, or English system)

2) systematic evasion of this constitutional decision, systematic lobbying and propaganda created a whole practice of denial of constitutional right of medical treatment to junkies for the last 45 years. This was accompanied by universal corruption in Narco bureaus, with Fed State & Local fuzz themselves peddling heroin and cocaine.

3) 70 percent of NY crime is attributed to junkies caught between Fuzz and Mafia squeeze; over 60 percent court cases; 40% males and 70% females locally incarcerated are junkies; there are now estimated 100,000 to 200,000 junkies in NY as result of police corruption; and

4) THEREFORE THE MAIN STATISTICAL BULK OF COURT, PO- LICE & CRIME & PRISONERS IN NY (and other large cities, situation same) IS DIRECT CONSEQUENCE OF POLICE CORRUPTION. In other words quite simply, New York would be safer without police. This same applies to Paterson where the exact same statistics now apply.

Leary's incarceration is byproduct of this corruption. When I asked you what to do, my question was really, how can we stop violence being done to us by the government? I know you are not perhaps the right person to ask inasmuch as, to the extent that you even knew it existed, you have been a firm if not vehement supporter of that violence, and for that reason now that the war and police state conditions seem questionable to you I think you might have some clearer idea of how to halt it. The problem is, that there is now built up in US such vast police state locally that even with intelligent mayors like Lindsay, the police in NY are all together out of civic control and are an army unto themselves, and a completely corrupt army. And I think that now both Congress and judiciary are helpless before secret police and military, even if there were an attempt to curb the power of both. I don't think you realize how serious the situation has become, there does not seem to be any way back; and I regret to see that you tend to siphon your outrage off on "mindless idiot" violent protesters; you must realize that the theory of trashing leading to polarization leading to police state is an excuse for liberals to vent their anger on a smaller scapegoat group than themselves; and that police-military state did not develop because of these tarsiers but preexisted before the trashing began; that the tarsiers are trashing because they claim the police state ALREADY exists; and that if one is going to assign blame for police state, it would be more appropriate to question the vast majority of middle class who have supported the military violence in Vietnam which began over 15 years ago. Speaking of trashing I am sorry you burned my letters from India.

It is the "unacknowledged & unreported crimes" that doom America – the idea that "our motives were pure but we just made a mistake etc." It was evil from the beginning, it involved CIA secret police brainwashing in USA and training of police state Diem in Michigan State U., it involved Nationalist China opium fields in Burma, it involved Tungsten lobbies, it involved the fact that we are racist in our consciousness, and that we consume 60% of world's raw material production with only 6 or less % population.

What it boils down to is that unless we reduce our standard of consumption to 1/10 the present, probably, we will continue to be at war with "under-developed" nations as we habitually call them, for control of their resources. As long as we exploit nations we create communism; communism is the mirror image of capitalism, and in the end they are about the same.

Meanwhile Leary is in Jail, I've written Justice Douglas asking for explanation, since his decision was actually unconstitutional.

I think total pacifist unilateral disarmament is the only way out here, in Israel etc everywhere; Leary's practicing that, he's the only one I know except Dellinger. The difficulty of your position is that you like to select who you'll be violent to, one year the Vietnamese, one year the Weathermen. It would be a lot more emotionally satisfying to me to see you get violent against someone bigger than you like the CIA or the police or the Capitalist system as well as the OGFU or the communist system; nonetheless I don't suppose that would solve the problem of pacifying the scene, so that's dead end too.

Well I don't know where this will all end, I just don't see any way out. I think Mafia, CIA, Military, Police etc have now too powerful a physical hold on US technology for any basic change to be effected by the pacifist democratic means I and others practice. It's like a cancer metastasis in the body politic. You know the budget statistics?

Total Fed Tax Receipts 1969	$147,875,000,000
"Defense" Budget	81,240,000,000
Veterans Benefits	7,640,000,000
Interest on debts due to wars past present future	15,791,000,000
total 1969 expenditure war past present future or 70% of Federal Budget	104,601,000,000

The main business of Govt is now that of WARS; just as with local police *the main business is war against the citizenry.* See statistics p. 1.

OK – Love
Allen

Just spoke with Ramsey Clark on phone who agreed w/me about Junk problem.

Louis Ginsberg to Allen Ginsberg

June 5, 1970

Dear Allen,

I certainly enjoyed our readings – and tiffs – in our recent radio readings, including the one at the P.E.N. Club.

I am very reluctant to trespass on your time when you are so taxed by the pile of letters descending on you. Yet your admonitions on the ending of my poem, "To A College Girl on the Barricades,"[1] what with my own ambivalent attitude, compels me to rethink what I meant at the end of the

---

1. See "To a College Girl on the Barricades." LG, *CP*, p. 282.

poem and to solicit your own thinking on the ending of my poem. I like this poem of mine, but, as I say, I am heckled by my ending.

First, background. If the girl is raging against the rigidity of the college or the college's assistance in this unjust war, in either case her violence in abetting destruction of the college property constitutes a counter-measure. If it be argued, as well it might, that the government is using violence in S. Vietnam, should she follow that bad example of government violence by meeting it with her own violence? Two evils or two wrongs do not make a right. Second, if she is destroying property or smashing windows of innocent storekeepers, why should she vent her rage on them?

Second, often the mindless violence is a sign of political dementia to think that these pathological characters, especially the Weathermen, can overturn a powerful government.

Again, the violence of the fanatics who mistake themselves for saints, roils up the know-nothings, the incipient Fascists, and the vigilante groups; so that in their blind countermeasure, they vote for [George] Wallace and [Ronald] Reagan and even use counter-measure force. I am with the construction workers who resent the carrying of the N. Vietnam Communist flag, but I am against the use of force by the construction workers. I say, with Norman Thomas, "Don't burn the flag; wash it." I fail to see the logic of the stormtroopers, alias students, who, wanting a more democratic society, bray blindly for a totalitarian suppressive regime.

So, I am against violence being used by students in order to cure the violence of the government. They may get short-term advance but long-term retrogression and suppression. Said Nietzsche, "Those who set out to kill monsters should take care not to turn themselves into monsters."

Broad, accelerating, widespread non-violent protests and dissent toppled Johnson and will topple Nixon in due course.

Now as to the poem, in the last two lines, do I mean that the girl has been carried away into violence by her outrage against the actions of the college? Strange is it indeed that her violence should breed counter-violence. Is her outrage against the war carrying her away into violence? Here I can understand her rage, but still I must say it is counter-productive and follows a bad example of the violence of the government. In any case, I shake my head and feel sad at such a delectable nymph's being carried away into violence.

How about having the last three lines read:

"I know your feelings against the war,
Yet it is strange to see you so carried away

By more than the paddy wagon!"

If you can suggest another ending, let me hear from you.

Love from
Your father,
Louis

P.S. I cut out some redundant lines about her use of "billingsgate" (which is the use of vile language uttered by fishmongers at Billingsgate, a place in London where wives sell fish).

Louis Ginsberg to Allen Ginsberg

Thursday, September {?} 1970

Dear Allen,

Enclosed find an article about you and Corso in the current *Village Voice*.

I enjoyed my stay at your farm. Despite our wrangling about the Panthers, I shall think there is much to be said on both sides.

This morning I had a phone call from a student in Syracuse University. They want both of us to read. I gave the student the Edmiston-Rothschild Management's address. Let them take it from there.

Thanks you for sending me all those brochures breathing peace. I shall peruse them soon. I must say, though, with my own time running out slowly and with so many poems germinating in me and seeking release, it is difficult to spread oneself in so many worthwhile projects and movements.

[. . .]

My new college term begins this month on the 15 of September. It will be my 24 year, I believe. I received a small raise in salary.

I notice that, in our forthcoming college term, the dates of Oct. 26 to Nov. 4 will be a recess, a sort of moratorium, to allow the students to practice the Princeton plan; that is, for the students to go out in the field to work for a new congress against the war.

Give my regards to the folks at your farm.

Keep well and stay calm.

Love from
Your father,
Louis

1971

Allen Ginsberg to Louis and Edith Ginsberg

Over Michigan
2.30 PM Monday
April 12, 1971

Dear Louis & Edith –

Passed the week at Kent State school & drove to Cleveland (after overnight stay at Kenyon plenty talk with Gary Snyder & learned some new yoga postures & hand symbol mudras from him, & taught him new mantra & gossiped) then 2 days in Cleveland, read at Case Western Reserve & reminded them their entire administration was involved in Biological Warfare/Institute Defense Analysis –

Plane in sunshiny misty day passing across Lake Michigan now – huge flat blue waters fringed with puffy cloudbanks –

Read in High School this morning in Cleveland – third time now, after Washington – had also read at Kent H.S. (gave them classroom assignment to invent a May Day ritual to end War. "Pillow fight all over campus" the best answer).

Going to Wisconsin state now – stay there then Milwaukee a couple days.

Then to Wyoming. Voice holding out OK tho a little strained on top notes for singing.

Easier traveling with Gordon[1] who in Folk/Rock jargon is the "roadie" or road manager, making phonecalls registering at hotels arranging airtickets & carrying Harmonium case – so I get time to write notes like this – goofy trip, awful luxury – can't last too long (the Airplane Age, I mean, not me) –

Love to you Lou & Edith – Yr son,
–Allen

---

1. Gordon Ball, manager of Allen's Cherry Valley farm. Ball recorded many of Allen's lectures on this reading and lecture tour, and edited them into *Allen Verbatim*.

Louis Ginsberg to Allen Ginsberg

April 19, 1971

Dear Allen,

Received your letters. Glad you are O.K.

I miss you. I miss, also, with a feeling of nostalgia, our past summer vacations with you to Europe and to Berkeley. We seem to move closer into each other on those vacations together. Edith, too, misses them. Maybe next summer, we three can commune and intermingle our spirits. (I feel I have not too many years to go, though I am now feeling fine.) (Still, as you've heard me repeat,

"Always at my back I hear
Time's winged chariot hurrying near.")

Things are running smoothly here. I am still teaching and gladly doing so. Edith is still at work in her office and likes it. I guess she'd rather work than stay at home where she gets restless.

Did I tell you I received the second royalty report from William Morrow. My book is still selling, especially the paper-bound book. It has not been reviewed by *Poetry* or the *N. Y. Times Book Review*, but I am hoping they will do so.

I am getting a few invitations to read on my own "write." Some pan out, some peter out. One I have finalized, if I may use that awkward word, is a reading at a convention, the N.J. Teachers of English, on Sept 24, '71.

Let me know of your plans after you reach San Francisco. (There is a P. S. of America, Celeste Heights, friend of mine whom I have alerted that you will read where she teaches at Davis, the U. of Cal.)

Regards to Larry Ferlinghetti.

How is my paper-bound book faring in his City Lights Bookshop?

Eugene was here in Paterson with his brood recently during the Passover. We had a fine meal. Have you had matzo balls recently? We ate them to our hearts' content. [. . .]

Keep writing me letters for I want to hear more details of what you are thinking, doing, and reading.

I read a great deal and, as you've heard me repeat, draw my own confusions. I keep my composure, in a turbulent world, by composing.

At my desk I putter a great deal, hoping to find an accidental inevitability of felicity. In imagination, I hear remarks from my desk. My sheet of paper says "Try to [. . .] in fewer phrases"; my loitering pen-knife tells me, "Whistle neatly"; my burning lens of magnifying glass urges me "To try to focus my meaning more sharply." My stapler tells me "To try to write or staple the moment to the momentous." Who knows: if I am lucky, I'll save something from impermanence.

This Wed. I'm going into N.Y. to meet my publisher, James Landis, of Wm Morrow Co.

Well, I really meant to say, most of all, that I miss you very much. Keep writing to me. Regards to Gordon Ball. (I like him. He is a courteous gentleman with gentility. Tell him to remind you to write to me.)

Love from Edith and
Your father,
Louis

Allen Ginsberg to Louis Ginsberg

City Lights[1]
1562 Grant St. S.F., California
May 3, 1971

Dear Louis –

Sitting on a rug on wooden floor by fire-pit with hot water kettle hung from 15 foot ceiling, surrounded by 4 wooden pillars upholding Maidu-Indian style log rafters in Gary Snyder's new house in Sierra mountains of California – been here since before May Day – will stay a week.

Pressure of business unfinished so great that I've canceled Australian trip & will stay here in California & edit writings & edit recordings & make 2'nd Blake album[2] while Miles is still in USA – otherwise opportunity passes & can't be reconstructed since he alone has the key to all the tapes he indexed. So I'll stay here thru the fall.

Going in to post office now so I'll send this note – no electric here either, beautiful Japanese style temple/household that Snyder build with crew of Zen/woodsmen friends.

1. Although Allen used the City Lights address in heading this letter, he actually wrote the letter in Nevada City, California.
2. Allen's second album of Blake songs, never released as intended – parts were released on his *Holy Soul Jelly Roll* boxed set – was produced by Barry Miles, an old friend and future biographer.

I'll be up in that room in City Lights –
When you leave for Israel?

Love Son Allen

Louis Ginsberg to Allen Ginsberg

May 5, 1971

Dear Allen,

Glad to hear from you in your letter of May 3.

I presume, as you write, that your heavy load of work will keep you from flying off to Australia. Wish you didn't have so much work so that you might be with us to enhance our trip to Israel and Greece!

We leave on June 15 on an overnight flight to Israel. Will spend a few days in Tel Aviv and then tour various places, visiting Jerusalem where I want to see the Wailing Wall, aching with ancient memories of Jewish nation. (I get less religious and more Jewish with time.) After spending eleven days in Israel, we fly to Athens to spend two days there; then by boat (where we sleep each night), we visit a number of islands like Delos, Mykonos, etc. We'll be in Istanbul for a day.

I have written to our distant relatives in Tel Aviv, whom you saw; also to some friends there: I have also written to Alan Ansen in Athens but have not yet heard from him. We return from our foreign sojourn on July 6.

Let's try the next summer around to be together, because that's the time we explore the best adventures.

We have three more weeks of college classes and then joy will be unconfined and I'll gorge on expanded leisures.

Have had new poems accepted. Here's one just published in the *Christian Science Monitor.*

Besides working at new poems, I am gathering other poems, published and unpublished, and putting them together for a new book. I revised some old poems that have refused to hatch oblivion in my drawers but still glisten with feeling or pulse with life.

I keep percolating myself, while I wait to be surprised or ambushed by the delight of two dissimilarities joining in a partnership of similarity beneath their skins to accost me with joy of felicity.

Of course, I am reading the papers and see old reputations bleaching on the rocks of errors, while the History is bleeding from many wounds. Still, I am an incorrigible optimist, and Time surprises us with unexpected loopholes . . .

Stay sober till we meet – which I hope will be soon.

Regards to Snyder and Ferlinghetti.

Love from Edith and
Your father,
Louis

Louis Ginsberg to Allen Ginsberg

May 24, 1971

Dear Allen,

Received your postcard from Bixby Canyon. I revived memories of delightful and happy times we had there with the idyllic scenery seeping its romantic influences into us.

I trust your sitting and meditating there gives you vibrations from cosmic forces so that these vibrations sink deep down into the secret, subterranean passageways of your being, so that they counteract and soothe the eruptive and bad reverberations of the turbulent world that beats upon and molests your composure![1]

As for me – as I have no doubt written you – I try to put a halo around the commonplace or a nimbus around the status quo. By that I mean, not so much to hide the reality but to reveal what is behind the reality. That is, I try to contemplate myself perceiving the focusing forces that urge me to discover the network of relationships or network of correspondences that converge on the pinpoint of my consciousness here in the sunlit sun-room of my home. As I wrote in my book of poems, "Time looks through the poet into the timeless."

Be that as it may, coming down to brass tacks, we are leaving, as you know, on the evening of June 15 for an overnight flight to Israel. In Tel Aviv, the Vekselmans have written me they will pick me up where we will be lodged in a hotel. A few days later, in Jerusalem, I am to give a poetry reading, arranged by a friend of mine who works for an Israel official.

1. See "Bixby Canyon Ocean Path Word Breeze," AG, *CP*, pp. 559–567.

A little later, I shall send you our itinerary, if you so desire one. After about ten days touring Israel, we get on a steamer to visit several Greek islands, some of them, no doubt, where burning Sappho loved and sang. I am hoping the claret air of Greece which Henry Miller praised will also let me inhale its euphorical influences.

Meanwhile, I read the current papers and feel like a lost footnote trying to keep from being swept into the deep chasm-like Credibility Gap.

Maybe, while I am away from America — which I love — I'll get a better perspective of my nation now struggling for a soul. Meanwhile, using one of my own phrases, I am mainlining myself with dreams and hopes and optimism.

I see the "Radical Left is split by a Cleaver."

I trust we shall get together soon before Time leaks out of me.

Love from me and Edith.

Regards to Miles and Ann and Gordon.

Louis

Louis Ginsberg to Allen Ginsberg

Wednesday, August 18, 1971

Dear Allen,

I was wondering why I haven't heard from you for so long a time.

I received your long letter with the messages and enclosures. I glanced at them and will soon read them carefully. They poured out on me baleful tidings and omens and depressing evils. Will address myself to them soon.

I note you are going to India for a week. It seems a horrible tidal wave of evil is sweeping over Bangladesh and India's frontiers.[1] Russia's lining up with India and China with Pakistan. Hope fervently there's no devastating confrontation.

Read in the papers about the Living Theatre in Brazil.[2] While Brazil is brutal, I question the prudence of the members of the Living Theatre to venture into wilds of Fascism where human wolves do not know the

---

1. Flooding and famine had combined to decimate India (and Bangladesh in particular), killing countless people and leaving an estimated 7 million homeless refugees in camps.
2. The Living Theatre, a troupe of actors long known for the controversial political and social nature of their performances, were being detained in Brazil, supposedly for marijuana possession. Allen suspected that the CIA-trained authorities in Brazil were trying to silence the group – suspicions that grew even stronger when he heard tales of the group members being beaten and tortured.

thought of freedom. The U.S.A. needs their ministrations into civilizing knownothings here. This does not, of course, excuse the C.I.A. of contributing to the evils.

What beast, according to Yeats, is now shuffling or slouching to foal horror on horror . . . to give birth to a dark age of helpless refugees? Seems the chancelleries are sounding boards or echo chambers of euphemisms masking lies and cosmetic phrases hiding atrocities.

Still, Tricky Dicky has done something to bring a bit of sunlight appearing at the end of the tunnel: I think it is a good thing – to give the devil his due – of trying to establish relations with China.

I note those fine and majestic lists of literary works of yours! More power to you!

That was a good figure of speech about the so-called comfort in the lounge of a burning ship. Hope, somehow, the fires will be put out. Well, I can't say that you are not doing your part. More power again to you!

Summer here is slowly ebbing away. I have written some new poems, some about the war in S.V. and others about my trip abroad.

I am trying to edit and tighten my ms. of my projected fourth book of poems: taking some out and adding some new ones.

Hope, when you get back, we can do some joint poetry readings, if you are in the mood. But do as you please. I am loath to pressure you.

I received a phone call from the Hackensack YMHA, telling me your agent is agreeing that you and I will read there on Oct. 26. Do you know about it?

Call me up before you jump off to India. How are you going?

What's new about the farm and what is its status?

> Love from Edith and
> Your father,
> Louis

Louis Ginsberg to Allen Ginsberg

n.d. {ca. December 1971}

Dear Allen,

This surging poem[1] is fine! Has excellent rhythm which is emphasized by the telling rhyme.

1. See "September on Jessore Road," AG, *CP*, pp. 571–575.

I have two suggestions. As I heard you read it, the poem is too long and taxes one's patience. I'd omit at least two pages, including the 3 stanzas on p. 4, as these mar the general unity of the poem.

Best wishes and love from your father,
Louis

P.S. Come in soon, when you are free from pressures.

L.

1972

Allen Ginsberg to Louis Ginsberg

{San Francisco, California}
January 7, 1972

Dear Lou –

Finished reading poem[1] several times – it's an advance ideologically beyond roots, that is to say, a further idea – but it is a lot happier & the statement does depend on a lot of generalizations & unattached radiances – Is there any way to even out the verse, condense it &, if possible, introduce more evidence of the senses from some specific visionary experience in yr writing room over last 20 years?

Better talk in detail when we meet.

Why not work on, work up, this poem as a solid statement of high mind?

Love,
Allen

Louis Ginsberg to Allen Ginsberg

Tuesday, January 11, 1972

Dear Allen,

Glad to hear from you.

Thanks for sending me your suggestions about my long poem called, "When the Walls of My Room Flew Away." I shall mull over the poem to gather more evidence of the senses from some visionary experience which I know I had a number of times.

1. See "When the Walls of My Room Fell Away," LG, *CP*, pp. 323–326.

I am sending you a short poem called, "A Woman Acted Queerly in a Bus."[1] Of course, sending you a poem is like sending coals to the proverbial Newcastle. But – aside from the fact that X. J. Kennedy took it for her new poetry magazine, called *Counter Measures,* and commented, among other things, that "it was nearly a wonderful poem" (be that as it may) – I thought you might be interested in the poem. The lines' inception rose in me some time ago – many years and griefs ago – when once or twice or more, I was riding with Naomi on a bus, and she made twitches and strange motions. Her actions were sadly amusing to the passengers who soon thought better of it.

When you get a chance and have an inner compulsion to visit the old homestead, don't check that impulse but come in.

With love,
Your father,
Louis

Louis Ginsberg to Allen Ginsberg

February 10, 1972

Dear Allen,

Did you see the article on Yevtuchenko in *Time,* Feb. 14?

The magazine reports that when Eugene McCarthy saw Yev's lines about the Statue of Liberty & "the death of freedom" (in U.S.), McCarthy said to the translators, "Are you going to be associated with this crap?"

Why does Yev. bridle at questions about Russian Jews when Russia keeps up churning anti-American vituperation against *everything* in America? Nothing at all good in America. And how about putting dissident writers in Russian insane asylums?

I'd like to meet you in a debate on this subject.

Also, on LeRoi Jones' inflammatory and incendiary and poisonous rhetoric.

Did you hear that now Huey Newton declares that we (the Blacks) should drop the gun and work in the system?

Did you, Allen, hear anything good about America? Do tell me.

Louis

---

1. See "A Woman Acted Queerly in a Bus," LG, *CP,* p. 295.

Allen Ginsberg to Louis Ginsberg

{San Francisco, California}
February 15, 1972

Dear Louis –

Getting ready for one or two musicals here, & then will leave for Hawaii, Fiji & Australia on 27 Feb.

Tomorrow will go upstate to spend couple days on the land owned in common with Gary Snyder and also one Richard Baker who is the teacher at the Zen Center here in S.F. Meditative Forest Community. I may buy some more land this year – for my own use not COP Inc.

Received Shenker's *Times* piece[1] – nice photos – I don't know whether yr. terminology about my writing being "unselective, undiscriminating . . . unstructured" is accurate language if you examine accurately the use of those words. You use as per dictionary. As I publish only a fraction of what I scribble the first two words you use are not used with discrimination. As for structure I thought we had long ago agreed that rhyme & stanza do not monopolize concept of structure. "Ungrammatical." That's almost O.K. sometimes as I model syntax on mind flow, but if I were really insistent and asked you for examples of ungrammatical speech you would likely have difficulty finding more than a couple of actual examples of actual ungrammatically used words. Check it out? You occasionally tend to use words somnambulistically. You do tend to fall into stereotypes when you talk about post Whitmanic verse forms. Remember the Bible didn't rhyme and had other structure, like vowel assonance. Re repetition, litany & double-clause sentences balanced etc like you say, "watch out for hardening of your platitudes."

Larry[2] is on phone making Australian reservations, he'll take his son Lorenzo 9 years old to see world down under –

Anyway, rest of Shenker article very lovely and characteristic – yes I saw Jerry Tallmer's *Post Kaddish* review[3] & yes it sure did occur to me that you must been exasperated & tired out by the whole scene w/Naomi. In a way the play *Kaddish* sentimentalizes it further unnecessarily.

---

1. Israel Shenker, "The Life and Times of Ginsberg the Elder," *New York Times*, February 13, 1972.
2. Lawrence Ferlinghetti.
3. Jerry Tallmer, "Lament for Naomi," *New York Post*, February 11, 1972.

OK – I'll write in a couple of days. Feeling OK, arranging music and business –

Love
Allen

Louis Ginsberg to Allen Ginsberg

February 17, 1972

Dear Allen,

Received your February 15 letter.

Yes, in the interests of truth and in all honesty, I *apologize* for the words "unstructured" in affiliation to your verse. It is, indeed, structured. That word must have caught itself, entangled on the flow of my garrulousness, in my mensentopause. I trust you'll pardon my mensentopause.

About the word "unselective," I reserve judgment in order to meditate on it. I feel that you think anything you pour out of your unconscious or subconsciousness, is, *ipso facto*, self-sufficient as being spontaneously authentic.

Also, often you are ungrammatical. However, these last two peccadilloes are nits compared to the outpouring of an avalanche of Whitmanlike lines which are incomparably Ginsbergian in flagellating the hypocrisy and apathy of the public.

I have always thought that your epithet "anachronist" regarding my poetry was wide of the mark. I aim at an equilibrium, in my flexible traditional verse, but the regularity of the meter and the naturalness of the speaking voice, as T. S. Eliot said, "The life of poetry is the recognition and evasion of regularity."

Yes, I shall scrutinize the "hardening of my latitudes and the constriction of my platitudes and the arteriosclerosis of my views."

Hope your tour of the Australian venture comes through. Do keep writing me letters, as I miss you.

Love & Kisses from
Your father,
Louis

P. S. Regards to Ferlinghetti.

Louis Ginsberg to Allen Ginsberg

February 20, 1972

Dear Allen,

After my enduring many years of grief and horror at seeing my wife disappearing helplessly into insanity, how can you use such an unfeeling, frivolous, and wretched term as that I was merely "exasperated?"

Love,
Your father,
Louis

Allen Ginsberg to Louis Ginsberg

{San Francisco, California}
February 20, 1972

Dear Lou –

Working w/musicians – enclosed interview w/Yevtuchenko may answer some of your questions about him – he'll probably get in trouble for indiscretion of the interviewer in printing comments that were meant probably to be off the record –

I'll phone you before I leave on 28th for Australia.

I didn't mean to come down too hard on your nice *Times* interview. Re selectivity I publish only a little of what I write – the selectivity comes that way – skim off the peak perfect moments of spontaneous composition – after years of practice you get to develop the improvisational facility – now I'm experimenting with improvising blues onstage – as advised by Tibetan yoga teachers – odd new turn.

Love
Allen

We read (Ferl, Duncan, Whalen, Kay Boyle, & others) at Farmworker's Union benefit & Yevtuchenko telegrammed following poem –

"I bless you
Farmworkers w/American land

The end of all bastards
Would your sufferings end.
I bless you
Allen Ginsberg, Omissar of American lit
Each poet
Is a farm worker
If even a little bit."

                                    –E. Y.

He's over-heroic & over starry but means well & plays a different public role
– dangerous.

Allen Ginsberg to Louis Ginsberg

                                    Adelaide, Australia
                                    March 16, 1972

Dear Louis:

Spending time with aboriginal song men whose epic connects with Eternal
Dream Time – we all sang together in concert halls –

Very busy – 1 or 2 readings a day – Day after tomorrow with
Voznesensky in Melbourne & Sydney, & then to Central Australia Ayers
Rock a holy rock mountain with ancient Petroglyphs in the center of
Australia – then north to Aruhein Land – Then to San Francisco at end of
month.

Met A. D. Hope the national poet, a Blake fan.

Sitting in Moderne Hotel Australia looking over Adelaide late afternoon
parks and towers in golden sunlight thinking of you – Love as ever –

Improvising a lot of Blues poetry on the harmonium during readings
now –

Ferlinghetti & son Lorenzo off 2 days on big river house boat. Love,

                                    Your Son,
                                    Allen

Allen Ginsberg to Louis and Edith Ginsberg

On top of Ayers Rock, Australia
March 24, 1972

Dear Louis and Edith –

Flew into central Australian Aborigine sacred rock pictured here, climb up to meditate, & thought of you so sending love right here from the top, my face covered with delicate little flies buzzing –

I learned a few aboriginal songs. Readings here well received, saw lots of Voznesensky & read with him. . . . Next up to Aruhein Land north, different Abo. Tribes & arts. I'll stay till month's end & head back to San Fran.

Allen Ginsberg to Louis and Edith Ginsberg

Madison, Wisconsin
April 19, 1972

Dear Louis and Edith –

Lovely trip so far – giving reading tonite in Madison – Marched with several thousand students a few hours ago to State Capitol & got on the megaphone & sang Vietnam War 10 year Blues, rhymed improvised bardic – Well, have you phoned & written your legislators insisting on end of War? Only if you do that will war end, otherwise it drags on. Parents should take the responsibility, not leave it up to college kids. On to Notre Dame! Love Allen

Allen Ginsberg to Louis and Edith Ginsberg

{Denver, Colorado}
May 24, 1972

Dear Lou & Edith –

Been living here at Hilton in luxury cheap room till end of this week, every day going down singing Vespers hour with teenage peace vigil geniuses on State Capitol steps – reading Kerouac's unpublished giant Denver mss. of quarter century ago[1] & walking nostalgic streets here, Neal & Jack both ghosts –

I'll go up to Montana for a few weeks, never been there – seems easier to detach myself & float loose wandering like homeless Buddhist than stay sunk in phonecalls & correspondence in N.Y.C. – also in these crucial weeks of planet war & bombing I want to see mid American emotions & landscape –

Sorry I didn't get back for birthday party, but poesy called me here & bid me stay & mourn & watch the Rockies – I'll be back sometime in June I guess. [. . .]

I'll give a reading the 30th at Montana State Univ. & then read again up north further in Missoula – maybe hitchhike back, on the road, I bought a new pack & an old down sleeping bag & poncho waterproof so am ready for almost any voyaging – lovely U.S. Western nostalgia of open road – that's what bemused me, reading all Kerouac's youthful lyric prose. All well here – See you soon.

Love
Allen

In July, Allen traveled to Florida, where he attended the Republican National Convention and the Democratic National Convention. The main issue, as always, was the Vietnam War, but by 1972, the counterculture was all but dead, and the conventions, for the most part, were uneventful.

Allen Ginsberg to Louis and Edith Ginsberg

{*Miami, Florida*}
July 12, 1972

Dear Louis & Edith –

I pass by here [Famous Lincoln Road Mall, Miami Beach] every day – Arthur has his office in the building at right in this photo – been inside the Convention Hall – Amazing collection of Middle Class liberal folk and

---

1. *Visions of Cody.* This Kerouac novel was published later in the year, with an introduction written by Ginsberg. This introduction, slightly expanded and altered, was published, along with some of Neal Cassady's correspondence, as *The Visions of the Great Rememberer* (Amherst, Massachusetts: Mulch Press, 1974).

freaks – sort of a revolution inside – Gawd knows what'll come of it – Hope it evokes peace – Clara was fine – Love Allen

Louis Ginsberg to Allen Ginsberg

July 21, 1972

Dear Allen,

I trust you are finding things favorable and benign up at your farm.

Sometimes thoughts swim up in my mind from our conversations. I find, then, that statements which you make in your zealous espousal of peace are inflammatory and wrong and extreme.

For instance you equate the "Good Germans" of the Nazi period with the "Good Americans" during the Vietnam struggle.

I am constrained in rising anger to refute your incendiary falsity.

The "Good Germans" did not – or could not – as Americans and a good portion of Americans did – [succeed] in toppling one president, Johnson, in opposition to the war.

The "Good Nazis" did not turn inside out a political party over a convention in which 80% had not been delegates before. Never was Hitler, etc. in danger of being ousted by the angered Germans, as was the case in the recent Democratic Convention. There is an ever rising tide of anger against the war.

Moreover, in the press, atrocities are revealed and broadcast to the detriment of the leaders of the government. This did not happen to the leaders of the German Nazi Party.

To continue, the exposure of the Pentagon Papers, the Berrigan affair, the crumbling of the credibility of American officials – all these make it a lie – if unconscionable (as in your case) – to equate the supine "good" Germans with an ever increasingly angry people of America. How different all this abyss between Germany (Nazis) and America.

Why are you so given to extreme and inflammatory statements?

P.S. One day you have given up hope for America. In another day, you see rescue of such hope when a major political party is turned inside out to provide an option or opening for a reversed and better day. Only in America. "Wash the flag – not burn it."

P.S.S. [*sic*] I read the papers and draw my own confusions – which are as good (or as bad) as the next man – or the so-called experts.

As ever,
Your father,
Louis

Allen Ginsberg to Louis Ginsberg

{Cherry Valley, New York}
September 24, 1972

Dear Lou:

Here's the Kansas letter, Ok yes let's meet students. Also yr. clipping from Evans & Novak "Hanoi Embraces Arab Terrorists." I think all nations involved have used terror on greater or lesser scale; you are especially sensitive to terror against the Jews. Reverse the picture, imagine an anti-Israeli column in Hanoi – "Israel Embraces American Terrorists" (which Golda Meir did). "A Pox on Hanoi" and not "A Pox on U.S., Israel, Arabs, & Americans" is partial and ignores too much of the total interrelationships. Are Americans better than Arabs? Are Jews better than Indochinese? Are Arabs better than Jews? Are Indochinese better than Americans? Are Jews better than Arabs? Are Americans better than Indochinese? Are Indochinese better than Arabs? Have the Indochinese suffered more than the Americans? Have the Jews suffered more than the Arabs? Have the Arabs suffered more than the Indochinese? Etc.etc. Is Arab terror not terror? Is U.S. terror not terror? Is Evans & Novak less terrifying than N. Viet Army Newspaper? We're all in a hell of terror.

Love,
Allen

Allen Ginsberg to Louis Ginsberg

Cherry Valley, New York
September 26 {1972}

Dear Louis:

[. . .]

I don't understand the Israel-Arab situation and I don't feel partisan. I think both sides are following deathly suicidal policies – anxiety reactions which increase lethal pressure rather than decrease – and both sides are sleepwalking into catastrophe – So I feel there is little I have to say except *AH* which is irrelevant to the conceptual fury – like Lion's mouth – I imagine as the *official* position-feeling of the Israel community. Unofficially probably people feel there a lot of bohemian variant mellowness & strangeness on Arab and Israeli sides both.

In other words I guess no reason for me to run away from the situation, a trip/reading with you to Israel. So anything you arrange & think appropriate, O.K. I'm not going to be provocative there, the situation is too scary and tragic, but I'm not a Zionist. My own suggestion wd be to let back in all the Palestinian Arabs & make it a non-Jewish state, secular state. Roughly that's the nearest I can see to a resolution of the conflict. I'm not sure this opinion is practical, and I'm not sure this opinion is emotionally safe to express in Israel. Nor would I be insistent on formulating it. Nor will the question necessarily arise. Nor do I feel sure this is an answer. But as I can't *hide* my doubt over the validity of the *official* Israeli military/political/moral position re Arab refugees, Vietnam, the tactics of counter-violence, alliance with U.S. military etc. you should not be disappointed or emotionally overexcited if I articulate my consciousness frankly. I've already been in *more* difficult/ emotional pressure situations in Cuba and Prague where my recalcitrant eccentric complaining got me thrown out of the countries by morally outraged governments. I don't guess we'd get into any such trouble in Israel; but I want to feel free to retain any kind of clarity & independence of opinion I can and not get into a situation where, finally, I feel I have to submit to mass or bureaucratic opinion in order not to "offend" or in order to protect my traveling companions from high blood pressure anger attacks.

In other words yes alright let's go to Israel but without me being locked into some kind of silent submissive heavy-hearted acquiescence to Golda Meir –?!

Really I don't know what to say. See, I don't feel sure of my own opinions but I can't form them in advance & guarantee that they'll be agreeable.

And it may turn out that my judgment is too heavy & we get there and all that's at issue is fun and music & poetry and not some hideous Arab-Israel willful mental death struggle. And it might do some good if we went. Why shd. I be too cowardly to face it?

What wd. you like for Birthday? I'll be in N.Y. before this weekend, & call – How is Canada reading arrangement?

Love
Allen

Louis Ginsberg to Allen Ginsberg

September 27, 1972

Dear Allen,

I received your lucitration. It is true we are all *more or less* guilty, but your lack of perspective and your black-or-white indignation and your wishful blinking of gradations and hierarchies of guilt – all *blur* your judgment.

Take Israel. When the U.N. partitioned Palestine, the Arabs descended on Israel to wipe it out. The Israeli advised no Palestinians to flee, but the Arab countries panicked the Palestinians to flee, telling them they'd come back later. Remember, in all this, that the Jews lived in Palestine from time immemorial and had rights, too. Don't forget this.

After the wars – which the Arabs aimed to *wipe out* Israel (don't forget it) – those Palestinians who remained, they now live in peace, have rights, obtain sanction jobs, have equal treatment, and even have members in the Knesset.

Israel offered to take back a portion of the hate-filled Palestinians and pay indemnity for the lands taken. But the Arab insist that *all 1 1/2 million* Arabs be taken back. This enormous number would swamp Israel 2 1/2 million and engulf it and wipe it out. Should Israel choose suicide? The Arabs want to wipe out Israel which now depends on its survival upon itself. After the Holocaust of 6,000,000 Jews in Germany and the widespread anti-Semitism, especially, in Russia, Israel, as a survival remnant, depends on its life on its own efforts, in spite of bluntly idealistic Jews like you.

Israel condemns terrorism. The Jewish Defense League, with its American leader, has been eschewed and condemned by all Israeli leaders.

While I am not unaware of the guilty position in all peoples, history has dealt harshly with Jews; and my inheritance of its immemorial culture makes me sympathetic with Israel's struggle for survival.

I bitterly regret your own so-called, above-the-battle, astropheric idealism, which blinds you to the rights of Israel as a viable nation.

Louis Ginsberg

Louis Ginsberg to Allen Ginsberg

November 10, 1972

Dear Allen,

I enjoyed your stay here at the house, but it was marred by your arguments, which were either unencumbered by logic or were of a specious hair-splitting variety.

You read this enclosed clipping, but failed to realize or respond to the fact that the Jews have a humanitarian view while the feudal Arabs maul their imprisoned Jews.

Your ignorance of the Jewish situation distresses me and seems to widen a gap between us.

How about your reaching for Jewish Israel bonds instead of hungering after alien gods?[1]

Louis

---

1. A direct reference to Allen's Buddhist faith. Earlier in the year, at the Dharmadhata meditation center in Boulder, Colorado, Allen had taken formal Buddhist vows. His teacher Chögyam Trungpa Rinpoche, bestowed upon Allen the title "Lion of Dharma."

Louis Ginsberg to Allen Ginsberg

February 12, 1973

Dear Allen,

Congratulations on your being elected to membership in the National Institute of Arts & Letters!

I am delighted that my son has been bestowed this high honor. I am very proud of you.

Come home soon so that I may embrace you and kiss you in happy delight at your new laurels!

Your father, with love,
Louis

Allen Ginsberg to Louis Ginsberg

c/o City Lights
156 Grant Ave SF
May 5, 1973

Dear Louis –

Been in L.A. almost a week – reading once in Pomona College, and then two evenings downtown in an auditorium sharing stage with Baba Ram Dass (formerly Richard Alpert)[1] – we raised $5000 in two nights for Tim Leary's lawyers – so this part of trip was success – and I stopped cigarette puffing & smoking living upstairs a vegetarian "mucuous-less" diet yoga food shop

---

1. Richard Alpert (Ram Dass) worked with Leary at Harvard.

eating avocado papaya melons & beansprouts & nuts for several days – had been puffing nicotine a month again, but came off easy.

Los Angeles sure has grey cloud of smoke overhanging the sky to the mountains behind the huge flat city – giant freeways wind over hills & thru cities and it takes an hour to go visit friends over these huge bands of concrete in space-ship like cars.

I'll be up at City Lights as of tomorrow May 6 Monday – I'll write from there.

Love
Allen

Watergate gushing truths – It's like a woolen sweater – unravel one thread and the whole cloth finally comes apart – If the thread keeps unraveling the whole fabric of "mass hallucination" public imagery will fall – and what *should* be seen is that all of Vietnam – all the "Brainwash" imagery that Romney complained about in 1968–was also a giant Watergate-type conspiracy. That's basically what the Pentagon Papers proved. But the illegality of the war has yet to be publicized – as present Cambodian Bombing is awful Nixon gratuitous horror show, no good reason, all subterfuge & commerce, as the French say.

I'm OK – my leg comfortable in cast adorned with red hearts scrawled in felt tip color.[1]

– Love Allen

When do you move?

Allen Ginsberg to Louis and Edith Ginsberg

City Lights
{San Francisco, California}
9 A.M. May 22, 1973

Dear Lou & Edith –

Been out here 2 weeks, saw McClures who, painting their house dark azure blue, say hello to you – I am staying at Ferlinghetti's office – Larry

1. On January 21, while at his Cherry Valley farm, Allen slipped on a patch of ice and broke his right leg.

and I drove up to the Sierra Mountains and visited Tim Leary in Folsom Prison – thin & pale & alert – and then to Gary Snyder's temple-like house in the Ponderosa pine woods – Next summer I'll take some money and build a cabin up here with local workmen – I'll be here another week & then → Chicago → Vancouver → Cherry Valley June 4 to go to hospital. Leg feels fine.

Love
Allen

Allen Ginsberg to Louis Ginsberg

{San Francisco, California}
May 31, 1973

Dear Louis –

Back from visiting Gary Snyder in Sierra Mountains, and with him & Ferlinghetti doing a reading in honor of Rexroth down at Santa Barbara – Tonite a benefit for Leary, then plane June 1 to Chicago, and June 2 to Vancouver, and home to Cherry Valley June 4, hospital and see you in NYC a week after that. Leg OK, very comfortable.

Love
Allen

Allen Ginsberg to Louis and Edith Ginsberg

{Amsterdam}
June 23, 1973

Dear Louis & Edith –

The poetry festival here went happily – the director A. Van der Staay asked about you, and said he'd invited you and me next year. Well OK let's see. You should get a letter in the next months. Are you OK!? Happy Summer Solstice. I'll go to Amsterdam for a few days, then London – Love Allen

Louis Ginsberg to Allen Ginsberg

June 29, 1973

Dear Allen:

We received your postcard and we are glad you are having a good time.

It would be an adventure for us three to go to Amsterdam next summer.

I don't want to press you but we have a good offer for you and me to read poetry at the William Patterson State College. They are anxious to have us come in the fall. Would it be too much for you to suggest or to agree to read sometime in October or November? When do you expect to come back?

I am feeling better and hope to see you soon. How are you doing on your crutches? When do you expect to discard them?

As you know we will be in our new quarters on July 16th at 490 Park Ave.

Love and take care of yourself
Edith and Louis.
Louis

Allen Ginsberg to Louis and Edith Ginsberg

c/o Burroughs
Flat 18, 80 {} St. St. James
London SW1
n.d. {ca. early July 1973}

Dear Louis & Edith –

Got your June 29 letter – I see Louis signed his name with close-near same control as before, so I hope his hand is steadying again.

Prices here same as U.S. inflated – the only stable currency is Swiss Franc & German Mark at the moment. Hotel was expensive, first night – 5 pounds or 12 dollars for tiny fleabag room no bathroom. Meals in average restaurants are 2 pounds (cheap) – already 5 dollars. Burroughs is thinking of moving to Southern Ireland or Costa Rica somewhere cheaper – his income is shrunk from books, and his rent & food cost too much. He's selling his archives to Swiss library & putting his money in Swiss Francs. So that's an economic report.

I saw a CIA fellow here who'd just been to Washington who said Nixon'd tried to take over CIA and FBI for his own use, so they didn't cooperate (like they *already had* Ellsberg's psychiatrist's files) but let the White House secret police (plumbers) blunder into a giant self-made trap.

My leg is healing. I began putting some weight on it this last week in London. In a day or so I'll go to a doctor and get Xrayed & diagnosed to see if I can switch to a cane. If so I'll be in better shape to travel. I have all sorts of invitations to Switzerland & Italy & northern England (Scotland) but have been hanging around London, did the International Poetry conference readings with Auden and MacDiaruided and others, and did some TV and radio. You were lucky to be here in '67 – there was lots of money & lots of spirit & fine clothes – the economic depression has hit and there's less obvious spirit, poetry readings are duller and more formal, clothes are less showy, there's less of a center & less spirit – people more mature but no community poetic vivacity. I'll be giving a poetry reading at a 500 seat theater here – proceeds to charity an actor's fund – and see what can be done to enliven the scene. [. . .]

I'm having a good time – people still like me & respect my poetry – but I shudder to think what hassles a younger unknown person would have to go thru to find food & lodging.

I expect I'll stay on till early or mid August, and then come home & spend a week with you in Paterson & then go visit farm & hang around New York for a month. In mid-September I plan to go to Wyoming on a meditation study retreat for 3 months. I'll take two weeks off of that for a fast reading tour to raise money to keep farm going and build a house (shack – about $5000) in California on the land there near Gary Snyder – Phil Whalen & I will both be able to use it, in future. But I don't think Patterson College reading be convenient then as I'll be flying around too fast on that 2 week Fall trip. I'd rather do it anytime after December 15 – early January or February Louis – my schedule will be – in Meditation retreat Sept 15–Dec 15 except for

Oct 15–25 }
    On the road, mostly Midwest, reading
Nov 8–18 }

That'll be the first time I hit heavy yoga practice, sitting immobile 10–12 hours a day 10 days at a time, mixed with teaching & technique discussion. I don't know too many poets except Gary Snyder & Phil & Diane di Prima who have that experience – it'll be useful.

Summer weather here, I lost my one shirt, and walk around on crutches in Bib-overalls and T-shirt with Bomb statistics under bright blue sky. Last night had party in my honor at *Turret* bookshop in a little alley in Kensington Church walk – a hundred people or so, nearly everyone I knew well, I stayed up till AM babbling to Harry Fainlight & other poets.

This afternoon the first day I've stayed home to answer letters and get my papers straight.

Send me report on your hand & foot condition Louis. Love as ever – see you in about a month.

Love
Allen

Louis Ginsberg to Allen Ginsberg

490 Park Avenue
Paterson, New Jersey
July 21, 1973

Dear Allen,

How are you?

How is your leg?

I made an agreement – at the suggestion of your dates – for our joint poetry reading at the William Patterson College on Feb. 20, '74. Our fee is $1000. I hope this is O.K. (Do you have to let your agent know about the date?)

We moved at last after much packing and profusion of cartons, and miscellaneous impedimenta. I took Thoreau's admonition to heart, "Simplify" – and cast off many things that, to get out of sight, we buried in the cellar and bin. We have four attractive rooms. In my study, a commodious one, we have a couch, called a high-rise, for your sleeping in with us.

I am in fair condition with hopes that my partially numb right hand will get better.

Write what you are doing and how you feel.

Regards to Mr. Burroughs.

Love from Edith and
Your father,
Louis

Allen Ginsberg to Louis Ginsberg

{Teton Village, Wyoming}
September 17, 1973

Dear Lou:

Began sitting this morn 6:30 AM with food & tea breaks – will sit daily till 9 PM for next two weeks, uninterrupted silent no-thought – a rest and pleasure. Hope you're as tranquil as a lotus on a golf-pond. Any news, write me here for the next month. I won't move. No newspapers unless I make special effort so won't know the latest massacres till later. I'll be out on way to Baltimore Oct 15th. You'll get schedule by then from Rothschild.

OK – I'll write if I have a Vision – Love Allen

Allen Ginsberg to Louis and Edith Ginsberg

{Teton Village, Wyoming}
September 21, 1973

Dear Lou & Edith –

Been sitting meditation 6:30 AM–9 PM with food breaks – Interesting subjective experience of pain in legs & boredom dissolving into a sort of transcendence of identification with body & opening up of awareness of breath itself as a sort of free spirit bigger than the body self as usually played. This goes on another 2 weeks maybe then some technical studies. Great trip. Lovely scenery! – Love Allen

Louis Ginsberg to Allen Ginsberg

n.d. {ca. fall 1973}

Dear Allen,

Glad to get your letter and your postcards.

Pleased you are doing well in your meditation and clearing your mind – or what takes its place – of trivia and impediments in order to see – or think you see – the larger circle. Let *seems* be *is*.

I am hanging on, despite my ailments, or, rather, trying to ignore them.

I haven't written much but hope to warm up soon. I wonder what sentences, as Kafka wrote, "are waiting for me and impatient to coil about my pen-point." Had a poem, "Twilight" (symbolic), published in the magazine section of the *Chicago Tribune*. Another poem, called "Midnight Streets," will appear next month in the *Midwest Quarterly*.

My birthday passed quietly with friends and relatives calling up or sending me cards. Well, I'll try to hang on till 80, etc.

I am working slowly on my fourth book of poems, *Our Times*, and hope to get it in shape by the end of the year. Maybe, somewhere or other, a publisher is waiting for it?!?

Stay sober till we meet.

Love from
Your father,
Louis

Allen Ginsberg to Louis Ginsberg

{Teton Village, Wyoming}
October 14, 1973

Dear Louis:

[. . .]

"It's a question of winning this war – or another Auschwitz." If all interpretation of phenomena – this situation – is narrowed down to this one interpretation – which is an image of past – then you enforce that interpretation on the situation, and no other. So either the war is won or it's Auschwitz. I hope your interpretation is not correct. I should pray that it's not. You leave Israel no space this way – no space to transcend or alter a fixed interpretation. It's a case of double bind, both sides absolutely decided on a fixed closed interpretation of the same situation, each side with a mirror-image horrific interpretation, victory or death. There should be room left for withdrawal & compromise & reinterpretation of phenomena on both sides. Space is what's needed: "A new world is only a new mind." Mental space is needed, everywhere. In a way, even Auschwitz is not as bad as a close down of all imagination, a shrinkage of all mental space, & a clinging to a duality of total power or total fear. It is perhaps too late to behave otherwise, but both sides have been enacting a self-fulfilling prophecy.

There is no God. Everything is permitted.

Meditation I'm doing here isn't exactly transcendental. We just sit 10 hours a day doing nothing but breathing, "like pigs." Mental images, fantasies, recollections flash by, over & over, till the mind wears out its dreamings – the same films repeat in mind's eye day after day till they fade somewhat and become more transparent – "I am Allen Ginsberg the poet . . . what am I doing here . . . Victory or Auschwitz etc . . ." and after all varieties of imagination of that are played out for the 50th time these mechanical images begin losing potency & another present sentience occasionally flashes [by] – what it feels like to be in a body without thoughts – Something like the immediate presence of mind space the instant after I broke my leg – a more realistic appraisal of situation than habitual repeated visual-verbal thought formations recycling thru consciousness – kind of an uncanny sense of the realness of the mindless Aspen trees losing their leaves. So it's not exactly un-locatable Transcendental Meditation – it's more exploration of larger mental space – Still haven't come anywhere clear yet except flashes – and a good inventory of my mental furniture to date. It's very boring "like an operation without anesthetics" says the Tibetan teacher – in the sense of painful just to sit there & do nothing, watching my favorite sex fantasies & political angers repeat over & over till they begin to look like the empty stereotypes they are. There's 60 people in the room sitting & I've screwed everyone already 60 times & gone on to you & Edith & Naomi & Grandma & repeated that till the old movie fades & gone on thru Auschwitz-Israel several dozen times till I see it's a thought-formation rather than a present reality. But without consciousness of fantasies we get trapped in them & *act them out,* as if they were the only reality.

This is the general direction of the last few weeks experience – nothing definite except a sense of interesting relief to be more familiar with habitual pattern of "entertainments" created by my own mind trying to create a self which ultimately is – not there at all – first an empty indifferent sympathetic sentience – like the Aspen trees losing leaves. Mountain tops all around covered with light first winter snow, I get up at 6 AM, full moon over the peak top 4,000 feet above my motel balcony.

OK – See you next week – I'll call when I get to Cherry Valley Oct 20 –

Love
Allen

Allen Ginsberg to Louis and Edith Ginsberg

{Teton Village, Wyoming}
December 1, 1973

Dear Louis & Edith –

I'll be leaving here (Teton Village) on Dec 6 – stop over a day in Salt Lake to give reading – and arrive back in N.Y. on December 7 evening – so I'll be in Paterson on the 9th probably – I have reading in Connecticut the 10th & then free again. Money coming in from readings will afford the loan you asked for & repayment to Gene of money he put out. I have no regular bank account & can't cash the enclosed English check – Edith, can you give it in for payment in Paterson? Enclosed.

This last week here is mostly sitting 10 hours a day crosslegged – I watch snowy mountainside with fixed eyes unfocused, sitting inside my body immobile, observing thoughts rise and fall & repeat themselves. Effort of attention here is to cut or limit space-travel daydreaming by attention to breath leaving nostrils – & so re-focus attention on present space & present empty mind filled with space. Nothing else to report except I'm reading *Denver Post,* White House soap opera. I see Vesco was linked to dope traffic! Gee!

O.K. love to you – Not seen the comet yet, have you? I get up at 6:30 AM but it hasn't showed above Gros Ventre Mountain range on S. E. horizon yet. Sky blue & mountains crystal clear & snowytopped now.

Love, Allen
Again

Louis Ginsberg to Allen Ginsberg

December 22, 1973

Dear Allen,

I see that Aba Elan said, at the Geneva conference, that Israel would offer compensation to displaced Palestinians (or to Palestinians who fled, though some who remained were well treated and a few rose to the Kenneset).

How about compensation, Aba Elan added, to those thousands of Jews driven out by the Arabs without any compensation for their homes and possessions???

As for Jerusalem, when, in a previous war or partition, the Arabs took possession from East or Old Jerusalem, no Jews were admitted there. All slept well in other countries. No protests.

No right of possession by force? True, but how about Russia usurping possession of Poland, Czechoslovakia, Romania, East Germany? What arrant, brazen hypocrites!

As for Rev. Dan Berrigan, he is decompartmented – he is riddled by Christian anti-Semitism. He charges Israel of not abolishing poverty. What nation has done that?

What crimes against humanity has Israel engaged in, according to Berrigan? It has treated Arabs well & attempted to integrate them into the body politic.

He accuses Israel of savagery. What damned nonsense! Israel is fighting for its existence and refused to accept national suicide pleasantly.

Israel does not want Arab territories. It wants to trade them for national security and [the] right to exist.

Sometimes, Allen, in your astral heights, you are perilously close to taking the position of a renegade Jew.

I'd like to debate this question on the lecture platform where restraints would keep us both safe from hysterical outbursts.

More anon.

Yours for Israel with an honorable, safe, peace!
Louis Ginsberg

Allen Ginsberg to Louis Ginsberg

December 28, 1973

Dear Lou:

The whole Palestinian/Israeli problem is so complex, like a family quarrel, that I don't find anybody's accusations helpful. Probably Berrigan makes it too black & white but the astringency of his challenge makes for good discussion if anybody wants to discuss it, which I'm not sure is common.

Everybody expert tells me different stories, actually, so I have no fixed mind, except on a few facts I know from direct contact there. There is as much racism among Israelis as among Arabs whom some pro-Israelis see as a "mob." There is the absolutely real problem of displaced Palestinian Arabs and that's a major or the major place of thought.

I haven't read Berrigan's complete statement and don't think it's so bad as everybody makes out – because of the real criticism of American – "Imperialist" – style of politics & life that probably Golda Meir & Dyan & the high rise hotels in Israel represent. There probably *is* a difference between Meir and the original socialist Zion.

I think the worst thing on both sides is the attempt to browbeat everybody into agreement "Victory or Death" that seems sick.

I don't know YSA personally no? Read their actual statements so all this rhetoric "I accuse you" is meaningless, some kind of red flag to rouse anger and contention.

Any move taken in anger or anxiety causes spread of anger and anxiety.

The harshness of tone of Berrigan may be more objectionable than what he's said as far as ideas.

To lump all "Arabs" together apparently is as mistaken as lumping all Israelis together. There are a lot of Israelis who think Golda Meir's style is "imperial" i.e. get what you can by force, for your side, & screw the other side. American Jewish opinion may not be the same as native-born Palestinian Jewish opinion. It is not black & white. No amount of love physical or emotional can simplify the scene.

I have absolutely no idea what the solution to the problem is. Yours was "Victory or Buchenwald" and that's no solution that's a remote slogan.

Resolution of the conflict seems to be hung on the Palestinian refugee problem. No matter who is playing that up, the people are real & will not vanish for anyone else's convenience.

The attack on "radical self-haters" is based on the flat statement that "genocide is the real aim of the Arab 'revolution'." I think that that statement is probably inaccurate, and is an inflammatory escalation of the actual Arab position and fantasy. Such statements are based on extremist propaganda (the mirror image would be an Israeli politician threatening to A-bomb Cairo) by Arabs but are not the actual Arab position. This use of the "Genocide" threat in the editorial confuses matters because it is not a practical realistic appraisal of other side's motives and grievances. It is used as a flat statement to inflame your reactions. It is much more damaging than Berrigan's speech to any real understanding.

Re Palestineans: Some "fled," some were "displaced," and some were driven out by force. This is a fact that cannot be gotten around or *bought off with money*. At least I guess so, judging from other fights. Actually I don't really know, and I doubt that you do, or Aba Elan. Maybe somebody actually on the land might know, and I doubt they're being consulted.

I couldn't agree more that all governments Russia in E. Europe and U.S. in So America Philippines Greece Indochina etc are hypocrites. In fact the entire U.S.A. (Turtle Island as the Indians knew it) being taken by force – and raped by ourselves ever since – is still suffering the bad effects of that seizure & it may yet poison the whole world w/mercuric smog.

I doubt that Berrigan is an anti-Semite and I think it's dangerously paranoid for Jews to make that their first reaction. In the first place it's a tangle of language – the Arabs are Semites. So you'd have to accuse him of being anti-Jewish. And he's probably not anti-Jewish when you put it that way, you know.

There's too much to argue about and too little real information, at least on my part – I'm hoping you don't assume you for your part are completely informed on living actuality there: Israel "has treated Arabs well & attempted to integrate them into the body politics" – a statement like that which I see as not complete or accurate, but a sort of well meaning gloss over a real tragedy and a real conflict which is not even perceived by you as a conflict – could lead to endless ignorant contention between us.

I don't believe the situation of "debate" with one side making points against another, as if one side could "win," "truth" is a useful attitude here. Exchange of real information would be more useful. I don't think either of us have any real idea what's going on and all rhetorical language like "theological anti-Semitism" – "Victory or Buchenwald" – "I accuse you" – "Radical self haters" contributes to the confusion. I suppose Berrigan's generalizations also might have.

The really difficult thing is, the U.S. has about been taken over now by the military – and this Israeli crisis with 2.2 billion war aid to Israel & the psychological strengthening of Jackson, Kissinger & the hawks, plunges the U.S. deeper into irreversible military control economically psychologically & politically – and so sets barriers to any kind of reversal of U.S. imperial policy all over world, and barriers to reversal of ecological self-destruction & economic burn-out. Watergate might have been beginning of roll-back of military dominance in U.S. but that has not happened, and I feel that military hawk folk in U.S. like Jackson are being strengthened – and the whole fearful role of the military – by their firm pro-Israeli stand – rallying Jewish liberals (who might otherwise be anti-military) as well as middle-road people – all confused by scary modern world – to take on apathetic attitude toward Pentagon CIA etc. I mean, "if they weren't strong who would save Israel so maybe I should shut up & let someone else run the world . . . even if it's Jackson & the Pentagon" – And that attitude *will* end the planet.

Thus the whole problem of official Israeli O.K. of Vietnam war – and working relationship of Israeli military & U.S. military – is still a great hangover and interdependency. This is a whole aspect of world context to remember. It is just "She had to say it." But just as she uses U.S. military, U.S. military uses her & Israel hawks to increase control on philosophy & economics here, right now, these past weeks – All Congress afraid to attack Defense Dept & automatically granting huge defense budget intimidated by military's crucial role in beefing up Israel. One thing hangs on another in a weird way. I think it is oversimplifying to say "Israel has no other way to deal with Palestine problem than get U.S. arms & take on the whole Arab world & Russia too." I think that somewhere in here is a primary mistake of choice & road that leads Berrigan to use his accusative word "Imperial" on Israel – in this huge context.

So there's a real dilemma here – not a matter just of psychological warping on my part if you want to see it as that – there's a vast unsolved political problem – that has its roots perhaps in the first attempt to use any force at all in the wartime settlement of Jews in Israel – and that leads back to Germany. So the chain of aggression is unbroken. These problems won't be solved by passing on aggression & pain to others, whether inadvertently or consciously. The Germans didn't see the Jews as humans – not with same eyes as themselves – and Jews at least in U.S. don't see the Palestinian Arabs as human – not with the same eyes – but as a mob as you called it – or a vague mass of people that *should* be satisfied & happy with Jewish influx into their territory, but somehow *aren't,* maybe because they're not educated or they're of a weird religion or have primitive habits etc. That seems to be the basic problem of distortion of perception of others. To the extent that this split vision continues on all sides a resolution is hopeless, and hope to find a permanent security by armed force even 2.2 billion worth is a will o' the wisp.

I don't think most of the Jewish/Israeli argument or rhetoric or language that I've seen takes into account the real basic problem. In fact most of the public discourse does *not* even go as far into flexibility of imagination as the *actual* political settlement at Geneva will be. I mean positions & concessions that were inadmissible a year ago – and which would have brought up "accusations" of "self hatred" or "treason" etc –

may well be the practical compromises found at Geneva. So there's an element in the situation of a sort of patriotic overstatement, and like all political patriotism, accompanied by a little emotion flagwaving emotional blackmail so to speak – "Don't you love me?!" "How dare you say things like that to me?!!" "I'm your mother! What do you mean I'm selfish! You're crazy!" etc. If you get what I mean. They lay that kind of emotional blackmail on you in Russia, too, if you disagree with their heroic policies. So you or I just have to look carefully and not accept statements – and positions based on statements – like "Genocide is the real aim of the Arab" or "Victory or Buchenwald."

OK – I haven't been very precise historically. I don't know enough about the actual history –

Love
Allen

I understand Jean Genet has written an essay or made a speech criticizing Palestinian Arabs for male chauvinist hypocrisy.

I enclose your clippings as they're related to my reply, OK?

P.S. Regarding oil: It would be wise for the U.S. to develop solar, wind, & other decentralized electric sources. The whole fight over preserving oil resources is something characteristic of oil-industry capitalist monopoly & industrial-military alliance on a mentally & economically static plane of fixation. The entire "crisis" is out of ecological context anyway. Cost of Alaska pipeline would be enuf to R&D to create solar or ocean current power forms. If there's a crisis, the reaction to ask for more oil is neurotic as a junky looking for a fix. That's part of whole context.

Hope you can read this. I wrote it fast off the top of my head.

Louis Ginsberg to Allen Ginsberg

January 9, 1974

Dear Allen,

So you are no more against the war against Hitler? What caused Hitler? Many things. The Versailles Treaty? Partly.

But before I go into that, do you know that Commies, during the rise of Hitler, said, "Let's make things worse so the people will turn against the Nazis and for us!"

Thus, the Commies joined with the Hitler rowdies and louts to beat up Socialists and liberals. And thus they (the Commies) connived with the Nazis. (You blame me, a liberal, with guilt by association; by the same token I blame you, with your taint of communism in the debacle in Hitler days.)

Well, then, the Nazis, creating chaos with the Commies, turned against them too.

But suppose, for the sake of argument, I take your logic. Then, what caused the Versailles Treaty? (Does history make man, or man make history? Both. A megalomaniac turns evil times to his advantage.) Then, with your logic, what caused the causes and, prior to that, what caused the causes that causes the causes and that begat that and prior to that, what begat – and so on infinitum. Or as Emerson said, "By a chain of countless rings, the nearest to the farthest brings."

So, at last, we reach the Garden of Eden, and there they ate of the forbidden apple. On the other hand, God said, "Increase and multiply." So who is to blame? And why the equivocation of God? What caused that?

In other words, your opposition view to the war against Hitler (who aimed to kill all his so-called enemies – Jews, Commies, gypsies, etc.) is based, I think, on false logic.

More anon.

Louis Ginsberg

P.S. And how are you going to undo ages of history?

Allen Ginsberg to Louis Ginsberg

RD2
Cherry Vally {New York}
January 28, 1974

Dear Louis –

All this about Hitler is a nonsensical argument, you realize, & let's not prolong it. I mean, & said on phone, or meant to say – as follows:

I am not Allen Ginsberg of 1942, it is now 30 years later, I'm 3 times the age I was then & my whole experience of the universe has changed.

The abstract animosity I felt toward Hitler as a newspaper symbol then is not the same as my understanding of today. My approach would be different.

As you remember, for instance, U.S. intelligence report concluded Hitler liked to have Eva Braun shit on him. For some reason it never occurred to the U.S. Government to conduct psychedelic "warfare" making wide & funny use of this fact in giant world headlines. It may not have changed the course of history, or it might have. In any case the same imagination that created international Hitler conditions somehow found no use later for image-use of his coprophiliac masochism.

The world has to be re-thought from the bottom. Israel's unimaginative death-disposal of Eichmann a decade ago prefigured an unimaginative view of the Arabs or any "enemy" today.

I am not a pacifist (this in relation to war, Hitler or non Hitler wars) but do realize the imagination is only rarely used in problem solving on political level (except by maniacs like Hitler!).

There was something "square" about the outside world's reaction to Hitler – encouragement of the capitalism that fostered him, indifference to fascism & to Jewish extermination, late fury of self interest, restitution of Krupp empire & Cold War later, & adoption of Hitlerian methods in South America covertly & Indochina overtly. The "war against Hitler" solved nothing except local problem temporarily in a world where all problems *are* as you noted interconnected. Part of the problem is authoritarianism & (Communist) militarism, police state. Part is capitalism which is a sort of economic authoritarianism.

That's what I meant when I sd. on phone I am reconsidering "Hitler" as an image, and especially my own emotional relationship. I remember at the age of 14–15 I talked for war & by age 16–17–18 grabbed a 4F as not to fight in the war I talked. I was nuts in every direction as an adolescent. I suppose the whole world was, is. I don't see reason to retain my 1940–1943 worldview as a permanent understanding of the universe. There is a tendency to take the WWII as a fixed jelled fact over & done with, one's opinion need never review it. But mind changes all the time. No reason not to. No need to fix thought-forms forever. Even Hitler can be turned upside down. Nothing to be afraid of or get mad or startled at. The imagination is supreme, "a new world is only a new mind," as W.C.W. said. I'm not disputing facts about Buchenwald. I *am* reevaluating Soviet English & U.S. hypocrisy in the final debacle, was Stalin as "bad" as Hitler or not? Is U.S. "American Century" and all that catastrophe of last decade any better than "Good German" thousand years image? Is Rusk better then Eichmann? Is Westmoreland more virtuous than Bormann? Is Nixon holier than Rudolf Hess? Is the average American "better" than the average German? These are all open questions. There's no fixed reality you can put on ice & say stop thinking – OK –

Love
Allen

I think I'll Publish a piece on Berrigan controversy for *Liberation* mag.

Allen Ginsberg to Louis Ginsberg

{*Cherry Valley, New York*}
February 16, 1974

Dear Lou –

Saw the *Times* piece, enclosed. I'm sure Arab armies are barbaric and the story true, I guess. Barbarism of that kind is now universal, as you know, including U.S. barbarism especially noteworthy in S.E. Asia, it present where it is refined mechanized & made scientific as in Saigon where there are 200,000 political prisoners habitually undergoing electronic torture according to Kennedy subcommittee on refugees.

As a matter of fact I think it likely that under conditions of increasing mechanization everyone on earth every race is barbaric and of course there are stories of Israeli barbarism & torture of prisoners for information, which I believe are also true, as far as I can ascertain.

I don't however think the enclosed clipping will prove an argument that the Israelis under pressure were or will be less barbaric than any other race – there is nothing about the Jewish race that makes it superior to other races in these matters, or inferior, as other races occasionally claim. Basically I am anti-racist & anti-nationalist in every direction where I can be coherent –

The main problem is how to avoid nationalism without sacrificing the joy of particularism, localism, "nationalism" and provincial folklore – oddly it is State Nationalism (as in Cuba, Russia, & U.S.A. etc) which suppresses folkloric ways & minority cultures. So how to balance healthy particularism, or Nationalism (earth-folk-ways) against armed egoistic nationalism that seems to be insoluble problem.

JAWEH & ALLAH BATTLE![1]

is the title of a new poem I'm finishing typing. It's only by abandonment of nationalistic allegiances that people can end the war which is generally manipulated by States above the folk. There are pacifist groups still in Israel and the Arab countries that cling to some notion of brotherhood rather than unsoluble conflict. It is an idealistic position but under present hysterical circumstances I see no other road – all other roads of armed conflict lead to mass murder as in the clipping you send. As I myself would not physically fight for either side if I could help it, so I can't advise others who have chosen to support fights or fight themselves. I wouldn't advise others to do what I wouldn't do – which as I said was a flaw in my own pro-war position 1938–9–42 age 12–16. See you in a few days.

Love, son
Allen

Allen and Louis Ginsberg's debate over the crisis in the Middle East reached a new level after Allen's essay "Thoughts and Recurrent Musings on Israeli Arguments" appeared in the March 11, 1974, issue of Liberation. *A furious Louis Ginsberg responded with a letter to the magazine's editor.*

1. See "Jaweh and Allah Battle," AG, *CP*, pp. 614–616.

Louis Ginsberg to the Editors of *Liberation*

March 16, 1974

The Editors
LIBERATION
New York, NY

Gentlemen:

I read, with great unhappiness, the article by my son, Allen, re: Berrigan and Israel in your February 1974 issue.

I am enclosing an answer to his article, called "A Letter to My Son, Allen Ginsberg."

I hope you will like to print this letter in your forthcoming issue.

I shall thank you for your courtesy in the matter.

Sincerely yours
Louis Ginsberg

Louis Ginsberg to Allen Ginsberg

{March 16, 1974}

Dear Allen:

I read, with commingled disappointment and distress, your article on the Arab-Israeli Conflict in the February, 1974 issue of *Liberation*.

You falsely accuse Israel of "military and nationalistic chauvinism."

What would you? Would you have the Israeli waving aloft prayer-shawls and Bibles to meet the oncharging cannon and tanks that charged forth to annihilate the country of Israel?

When, in 1949, the U.N. sanctioned the country of Israel, its Arab enemies, surrounding, bayed about its imprecation and fell upon Israel to wipe it out.

Israel was forced by abominable events to set up a state for survivors who crawled away from Hitler's unspeakable butchery of Jews and others. When the smoke of Jewish bodies burning in Nazi crematoriums rose in question-marks to Heaven, hardly a nation heeded. So, as I say, the Jews were forced to flee to their own hospitable nation.

Israel is the legitimate expression of the historic separation of the Jewish people for the national liberation.

Who helped Israel defend herself from being destroyed or wiped out? All nations sat on their hands. Only America aided Israel with arms. Did you want Israel to accept graciously the Arab invitations to suicide? Thus, as I main, it was "Victory or Buchenwald."

Allen, you (and your New Left cronies) are ready to help liberate all oppressed groups – except your own.

Your single example of mistreatment of an Arab is in violent contradiction of the general benevolent treatment of Arabs in Israel. The Arabs who chose to stay in Israel (after being urged by Arab nations to flee and then return after Arab victory) – these Arabs are well treated. Their lives are enhanced by better housing, sanitation, jobs and education.

Contrast this with the brutalization of such Jews as lived in Arab countries. These Jews were harried out cruelly, expelled with only the clothes on their backs (that is, if they were not imprisoned).

Israel, contrary to what you aver, does not wish to humiliate anyone. As Golda Meir said, "We victors are suing for peace, while the vanquished are threatening war to wipe us out."

It pains me that you, a Jew, bend so far back while you think you are standing straight.

Another thing: I suggest that, instead of panting after strange gods, you should search more for the long roots of your very being – roots that reach down to immemorial ancient times and are fed by the rich heritage of the illustrious history of the Jewish race with Justice for all – a history that harvests a resonant and luminous glory.

Allen, your lofty and aloof disdain has been bruised by the facts.

Your unrealistic, above-the-clouds viewpoint has been ransacked by events.

With love,
Your father,
Louis Ginsberg

Allen Ginsberg to Louis and Edith Ginsberg

St. Louis Airport
April 22, 1974

Dear Louis & Edith –

Here reverse page is the speech I wrote for Peter to deliver – I knew he would be able to make it heard clearly in the polite atmosphere of N Book Assn.[1] and be able to answer Press questions in line with our common opinions & information as on his war-statistics T-shirt, which he made & wore to the ceremony (mentioned is this week's *Time*) – also he was participant in the Beat "prophetics" mentioned – Also knew he'd be funny & enjoy it with Ed Sanders – & Denise & Anne Waldman who went –

Flying around, writing a few new poems too, enjoying reading & singing & getting some publishing business done like this speech, & a letter to Internal Revenue denying them war taxes April 15 (I withheld the 1/3 of taxes = 100 billion military to 300 billion budget) – a lot is simple & clear – right action right speech right labor right energy right mindfulness right meditation right clarity & peace –

Love to you
Allen

Allen spent most of the summer and early fall in the Sierra Nevada range, working with Gary Snyder, Peter Orlovsky, and a group of local laborers on a cabin, which Allen hoped would serve as a West Coast retreat similar to his farm in Cherry Valley. Snyder had already built a cabin nearby, in a beautifully rustic area about twenty miles from Nevada City, California, and Allen looked forward to having a place nearby. The physical labor, Allen quickly discovered, was more than he had bargained for, but he found that he enjoyed it.

---

1. Allen had recently won the National Book Award for poetry for *The Fall of America*. Since Allen was out of town at the time of the awards ceremony, Peter Orlovsky delivered his acceptance speech, in which Allen used the occasion to launch an attack on United States foreign policy, from the Vietnam War to U.S. involvement in the recent overthrow of the Allende government in Chile. The speech was eventually published as a small booklet, *"The Fall of America" Wins a Prize,* and was later reprinted in *Deliberate Prose* (pp. 19–20).

Allen Ginsberg to Louis Ginsberg

{Nevada City, California}
June 1, 1974

Dear Louis:

This town is bigger than Cherry Valley, but I am 20 miles away in woods. Snyder has a beautiful tile roofed Jap style farm style house here, & in another part of the woods is a complete tiny Zen temple with sitting hall. I'm building 3 room hermitage. Been holing & axing stumps & clearing the site all week. Leaving now for Sacramento airport to pick up Peter. Good healthy outdoor life working all summer. I'll get rid of half my potbelly I hope – Love Allen

Louis Ginsberg to Allen Ginsberg

June 13, 1974

Dear Allen,

Enclosed find the letter to you re Berrigan, which appears in the current – May–June 74 – *Liberation.*

Did you get the *Zenger's* recording of our dialogue in San Fran. hotel room?[1] To my surprise and delight, on Father's Day, June 16, *The N.Y. Times* in its *op.ed.* page in the editorial section, reprinted a big excerpt! Did you hear about it? Would you like me to send you a copy of this?

How are you doing in your woodland clearing building your Zen Meditative center?

We are all OK.

Mail me letters about what you are doing.

Love,
Your father,
Louis

1. Stephen M. H. Braitman, " 'Slice of Reality Life' Interview with Allen & Louis Ginsberg," Zenger's, May 22, 1974; reprinted as "Violets Are Blue: On Father's Day, the Ginsbergs 2," *New York Times,* June 16, 1974.

Allen Ginsberg to Louis Ginsberg

{Nevada City, California}
June 18, 1974

Dear Louis –

No I didn't see the *N. Y. Times* so if you have a spare copy please send it to me here – I hope they edited it neatly.

Glad *Liberation* published your letter, but I think it is more rhetorical than factual, point by point, particularly "general benevolent treatment of Arabs by Israel," yr phrase. That wasn't my experience a decade ago there, and isn't anything like the version you hear from Palestinian Arabs, even as reported in the *Times*.

Work here's gotten to stage of foundation of cabin dug & ready for concrete, rocks are drilled for peg-holes on which to rest pillars made of pine which we felled and stripped a hundred yards away.

I am camping out in a beautiful circle of ponderosa pine, sleep at night under stars. I don't have writing paper or envelopes at moment – It's hard to do paperwork which is why I depend on postcards.

Peter labors all day long digging & skinning trees and has astonished everyone here with his endurance and solidity – there is a frontier-like cult of work here but the local woodsman carpenter Buddhist hippies never saw anyone so fanatically working as Orlovsky. I don't think the place would get done if he weren't around to open the earth & move rocks.

Most of the money for building was already set aside when I came up here but probably I'll need more $ so I'll sell some papers to Columbia this summer – some of Kerouac's letters probably.

I sent you back the *Zenger's* interview? I don't have a copy so keep it safe, which I know you do.

Meanwhile I'm learning about axes, draw knives, hammers & nails, drills and wheelbarrows – There's no electricity so everything on spot must be done by hand. Fortunately Gary Snyder helped cut a truck path thru the brush and so we can deliver lumber, rocks, cement & plumbing, Planning nice outhouse and outdoor summer kitchen.

And Summer solstice, several nites ago, we all put on a play by McClure in the starlight on the meadow between Gary's house and the site I'm working on —

Love
Allen

Best to Edith.

Louis Ginsberg to Allen Ginsberg

June 27, 1974

Dear Allen,

Enclosed find the excerpt, which appeared in the *N.Y. Times* op. ed. page 21 of June 16, '74.

I had sent a Xerox copy of this to Ferlinghetti, asking him to forward it to you. I sent him also some poems of mine for possible use in his forthcoming *City Lights Journal.*

I'll send you an article on our poetry reading when I get Xerox copies soon — it's from an underground paper, called *The Phoenix.*

San Fran. certainly gave us plenty of notice, producing about seven stories. I'm saving them all in my folder.

All's quiet here. I'm reading much but liking less. Had a couple of new poems published in minor places.

I feel well except that, as before, I can't walk much. No improvement there. I'm taking, with the approval of my doctor, vitamin E and C pills to see if they will help.

Edith sends her love. She is busy scurrying around with friends on odds and ends.

Peter certainly must be a great helper with his physical prowess. Give him and Gary Snyder my regards.

Write soon.

Shall I send you paper and envelopes?

Love from
Your father,
Louis

Allen Ginsberg to Louis Ginsberg

{*Nevada City, California*}
July 10, 1974

Dear Louis

Hard work for me potbellied city-lax,
pushing wheelbarrows empty up hill, shoveling red dirt
into a sieve, shaking out fine Mexican-red dust,
lifting iron spoons full w/clay into flat-bed jeep,
mixing gravel from old gold mines with measures of grey concrete
with red clay dust, to color kitchen floor, then
watering hardened concrete with hose so it won't crack
And logs, draw knives strip bark, chisels smooth out branch holes,
tumbling round posts over each over a bed of two pine laid parallel,
helping dig foot deep holes for porch stone foundation
All work done in a month — then unseasonable rain —
days under apartment-high ponderosa's dripping water
onto lean-to roofed with black and white plastic rolls,
sleepingbags muddy wet at dawn, squirrels scampering away from
   our apples,
deer at Gary Snyder's pond-edge in garden —
Unexpected rain ending sweaty labor, a few days
sheltered indoors, reading Zen koans or Lu Yu's
eleventh century laughter about his drunken white hair —
Now sun's out, Wednesday sky's blue,
Cool wind in pines dries housetops and grass fields —
Trial to re-stack wet lumber to dry in sunlight,
Load the truck with second hand windows to take to Marysville
to dip in vats of chemical paint remover, and on to Frisco
to Poetry reading this Friday w/McClure & Snyder,
Benefit small Island attacked by Yamaha Industries Tourism —
Small sample of Great natural world eaten by human cancer —
I read your friend Bluefarb's letter but could not make head or
   tail of it —
Yes he reasons well, but poems my stepmother likes he thinks are
   off track,
he doesn't believe in Jahweh but he wants me to believe,
He doesn't practice religion but wants me to practice what he

rejected –
He doesn't respect my learning but wants me to respect his
    bookishness –
He takes things personally and denounces my vanity –
It's too confusing to argue when neither of us know what we're
    discussing
and meanwhile pseudo-peace in mid-east makes all previous
    reasons vain –
assertions of sovereignty yesteryear today are bargained away today –
Meanwhile lumber must be piled properly or it'll warp
And what I'm learning is not history or Kabbalah
but bruises on my hands and knees, splinters from rough cut
    wood
and how difficult it is to master the "primitive"
the old story, how I lost track of shelter and food, given them in
    cities,
and how hard and beautiful both seem when worked for by hand.
I'll write in a few days when returned from the white-hilled city –
Meanwhile we have each other's love while still alive –

> Son,
> Allen

Louis Ginsberg to Allen Ginsberg

July 15, 1974

Dear Allen,

Received your letter of July 10.

It was interesting as a lavish and exuberant outpouring of concrete details – a rich flood as from a big cornucopia of details, pouring out in unrestrained specific details of your physical labors: "the red clay dust, chisels, deep holes for porch stones," etc. It all reads like a litany or prose poem of concrete edge – appealing, touch-sensation artifacts. My muscles got tired from those labors almost Herculean. Nothing like youth!

When will you finish this miniature temple?

[. . .]

I am lying fallow poetically. Wrote a few poems recently.

Am reading the *N.Y. Times* as usual. Glad Ehrlichman was found guilty. (What an arrogant, self-serving, unctuous, bloated toad he is.)

I ponder imponderables & try to touch intangibles, etc. etc.

I posture my mind on majestic passages of memorable lines. I like this one: "The greatest mystery is not that we are thrown up, by chance, between a profusion of matter and of stars, but, that, in that prison we should be able to get out of ourselves images sufficiently powerful to deny our insignificance." Malraux

I miss you and look forward to your letters.

Love from
Your father,
Louis

P.S. *Scatological Dept*

Nixon once sacked Cox, the lawyer, now an auto sticker reads as follows "Nixon is a Cox-sacker!"

L.

Allen Ginsberg to Louis Ginsberg

{Nevada City, California}
July 22, 1974

Dear Louis:

Floor down now about complete – next step frame of cottage including log beams we cut skimmed & chiseled cleaner.

I shouldn't have been so condescending "your friend Bluefarb" as he's my friend too so forgive me that rhetoric, a flaw.

Glad Allen Jr's [*sic*] got a girl & car license. I'll go to Boulder, CO July 28–Aug 11 to teach in Buddhist Academy – Poetics.

Today Sunday sat down with all the mail. I'm losing weight & getting a few minor new muscles & am browner. Love Allen

Louis Ginsberg to Allen Ginsberg

August 12, 1974

Dear Allen,

Was glad to hear your voice from Boulder, Col. and to hear you were O.K.

These days are traumatic for the nation. Tricky Dicky, caught in the toils of his own machinations, proved to be victim of his own inner depredations. *Character is destiny!*

A great sigh of relief went over the nation – and me. It proved that, in our democracy, defective as it is, the Constitution is alive and well. I felt glad to be an American.

Also there is a difference between the "good" Germans and "good Americans." In Nazi Germany, perhaps the Nazis, at gunpoint, cowed the Germans so that they could not overthrow Hitler. But here in America, twice they overthrew a president, once when the anti-war protests forced Johnson to resign, and now, when the judicial process, plus the hostility of the Americans to Tricky Dicky's illegalities, forced him from office.

I do think there is hope for America.

As I told you, a crew, under the auspices of the Board of Education, took videotapes of an interview with me and will show it in the public schools as an example of Patersonians in successful careers. They want to do one with you when you come home.

I am enclosing a letter from my epistolary friend who still wants us to come to Marquette, Michigan, in the fall. The terms he agreed on are $1000.00 plus $500 for expenses. He says he is in touch with your agent.

Thoughts to posture one's mood on:

Schools aren't what they used to be and never were.

"The purpose of life is perpetual astonishment."

"Life is the force in nature that strives to attain a greater power of contemplating itself." Shaw.

"Man's intelligence is the universe of becoming aware of itself." Asimov

"It is a wonder that those who are against the establishment don't insist on reinventing the wheel, which came out of a bolurgeois society." Sol Alinsky

----

Well, Allen, I'm still hanging on! Oct 1, in two months or less, I'll be 79. Intend to make 80. Meanwhile, when I get up in the morning, I try to explore the surprise and wonder of finding myself enjoying the astonishment of being alive; so that, in poems, I celebrate the amazement of life.

Write me long letters because I miss you very much.

> Love from
> Your father,
> Louis

Allen Ginsberg to Louis Ginsberg

> *Allen Ginsberg*
> *Allegheny Star Route, Box 963*
> *Nevada City, California 95950*
> *August 13, 1974*

Dear Louis –

Enclosed *Phoenix* clipping. Back in Sierras roof being put on today by carpenters & Peter & Denise – I'll spend day answering mail.

Chögyam Trungpa asked me to help found an arts school community in Boulder as adjunct to meditation center[1] – he was interested in the Buddhist meditators also becoming poets. So I'll probably spend more time in Boulder & around Rocky Mountains in far future, running a poetry school from a distance & in residence a few months of the year. There were 2000 students at last session of this "Naropa Institute," I just left to come back here & finish cottage. Work should be done within a month – as far as the solid body of the house – after that, beds & shelves & details have to be carpented up. . . . Finished *First Book of Blues* & gave that to Anne Waldman to publish.[2]

All fine here.

> Love
> Allen

1. The Jack Kerouac School of Disembodied Poetics, at Naropa Institute in Boulder, Colorado.
2. *First Blues*. (New York: Full Court Press, 1975).

Received advance copy of *Allen Verbatim,*[1] Gordon Ball's editing of my mouth-spouting 1971. They'll send you one.

Allen Ginsberg to Louis Ginsberg

{Nevada City, California}
September 8, 1974

Dear Lou –

Sorry long 2 week silence I've not been able to get to desk writing, getting more involved with building side porch out of oak poles, and notching & sawing & creosoting wood lintels, and cutting tarpaper and insulation to block chinks in the frieze between log rafters under the roof. House now has roof asphalt shingles and siding on outside, next put in inside sugar pine walls and windows, doors, a stairway, shelves & closets –

It's so beautiful that I hope you'll be able to come out here next spring and stay awhile – house is on nice level ground in the woods near a flat meadow so you won't have trouble getting around – surrounded by blue oak trees, tall ponderosa pine like a thinner Muir woods, and manganita red-branched brush, with mossy rocks all around like in the Forest of Arden – and in front of the cottage there's a large platform of bedrock which has a dozen mortar holes for grinding acorns & grass seeds – the spot was domesticated hundreds of years ago, so it's an auspicious site.

I'll be working here till Oct 1 and then 2 weeks in San Francisco and on way home around Oct 15. I have a Dharma Festival reading date in S.F. Oct 7 – so can't go to Marquette with you then, but could meet you on the way back & see you home around Oct 15 – I'll write a note to Rothschild about that. Enclosed your copy of Livingston's letter.

I liked the poem about leaky lifeboat you sent – swift & to the point. I'm sending it on to Gregory Corso since the inspiration was his. The poem has no excess & says what you think fast.

I don't think Nixon's passing & pardon will make much difference to essential problems & guilts in America, as I said in the National Book Award speech half year ago – Ford & Laird were always chief hawks on the war, in fact 10 years ago it'd been unthinkable that those nuts & creeps allied w/military-industry would be in Complete Control. Johnson & Nixon

1. *Allen Verbatim,* ed. Gordon Ball (New York: McGraw-Hill, 1974).

passed but the Military-industrial-Police network is *more* powerful & secure than ever. Rockefeller was always bad, with his family & himself, an awful exploitative capitalist Ludlow-massacre Attica-massacre record. One great political-economic-technical question is Energy and how to get off the petrochemical addiction which is burning down the world's veins – Rockefeller as Governor destroyed mass transit, hiked up the subway fare, build giant highway system. He has mental & physical addiction to gasoline & thus is a terrible choice.

Ford has been a mass murderer also re Vietnam. Nixon was got on petty burglary, not on the war crime much vaster scale, secret illegal bombing of Cambodia. The press, public & politicos refused to face the deeper problem & facts. So I don't think much has been gained at all, Johnson & Nixon gone – I prayed for Johnson remember. It's the states themselves & the people that are guilty not just Nixon, because they elected him knowingly, and accept Ford knowingly. There's been no reversal of basic energy and military destructiveness, and the war in Vietnam continues as big as ever as far as killing and U.S. funding of the killing. I'm sorry you still "feel glad to be an American," in addition, because such nationalistic vanities are not essential to local rooted well being – as you remember from earlier Socialist days, *Nationalism* is a curse & generally an excuse for businessmen & real estaters to kill Indians, wage wars on forests, & "civilize" the world for their own selfish centralization of power. Large nations as Solzhenitsyn pointed out are a curse & one had better identify with one's own nature, one's own locality, one's own *watershed* – the source of one's own delights.

I like provincialism, localism, folklore, individuality, as did the founders of the "nation" and think that the American Century has been a piece of egotism and violence equal to any in world's history. The egotism is the worst. International energy monopolies fronted by Ford & Rockefeller now run America and Nixon's obvious disgrace hasn't changed that manifest egotism of leaders & people in America at all. The problem in U.S. finally is really the people, their bourgeois hypocrisy – living fatly off nature while destroying it everywhere for their fat – and calling that "normal" & "Progress." Nature's revenge will be slow and awe-ful.

Very interesting group of young woodsmen & women here all hard working. Carpenters living off the land improving it, selective timber cutting, building ponds & gardens enriching the locale, and all of them know personally exactly where their water comes from & where & how their shit is disposed, not like mechanized middle class which is enslaved to robot dreams, ignorant of its own waste. See, the idea that 7,000,000 people in N.Y. knowingly or unknowingly dispose of their shit into the ocean is enough to undo the foundations of the entire nation. It's a piece of arrogance & stupidity you could find in science fiction, about a bunch of slobs who tore down their own planet and died —

Love,
Allen

I'll send photo of house when I make one soon.

Louis Ginsberg to Allen Ginsberg

September 12, 1974

Dear Allen,

I was relieved to get your letter and to know you are well.

Your idyllic description of your dwelling is interesting and has marvelous therapeutic value. The elemental forces of nature, seeping into your system, must have a salutary effect on your psyche.

(Still, I don't think that you are any more superior or benefitted by knowing where your excrement goes, if I do not. That is a specious argument of yours.)

I agree that the industrial military complex is a danger but what shall we do with the growing armaments of the Soviets? I know your head is up in the clouds of pushing for an ideal peace assented to by the Commies, but I never trusted nor trust the Commies, say what you will. Peaceful co-existence and slow, mutual agreement might in time bring a peaceful convergence.

The judicial process is faulty, but it is the best we have. I am proud to be an American, though I perceive its faults. The worst form of government is a democracy — *with the exception of all the others.*

[. . .]

When will you come to these parts?

Love from your Father,
Who is hanging on,
Louis

Allen Ginsberg to Louis Ginsberg

{Nevada City, California}
September 30, 1974

Dear Lou –

This will reach you late but happy birthday anyway, and enclosed some traditional birthday geet for present, as I haven't been out of woods shopping for 2 weeks – also a photo – I'll try to call you Oct first if I can get a ride out to the highway –

Packing up to leave for S.F. the morning of Oct 3 Wednesday & be at City Lights for about 10 days before leaving for east – may do some readings on the way, haven't heard definitely yet –

House inside & outside siding now on, & windows & doors being hung right now, woodstove cleaned for installation & closets & sink put in after I leave during the next week – Expert carpenter friend of Snyder be staying in it all winter making it wind & rain proof in cracks in exchange for the rent – so all's well & I'm in healthy shape – you too?

Love
Allen

Maybe we come out here next summer visit.

Louis Ginsberg to Allen Ginsberg

October 5, 1974

Dear Allen,

Glad to get your letter dated Sept 30.

Thanks for your generous birthday check. I banked the major part of it till I ponder what to get.

Those photos were fine. You certainly engaged in salutary labors. Edith pounced on the pictures to exhibit to her friends. (Incidentally, Edith is your most loving, loyal and fierce devotee, who will not brook any criticism of you.)

Eugene gave me a birthday party with Harold's family and with cake and candles and all fanfare, as did our friend Ruth Lipset.

Once upon a time, the precipitous height or promontory of 80 seemed out of reach; now, at 79, I am gradually near the top of the rarefied plateau, which I think I soon clamber upon, and from which I'll, no doubt, look with benign demeanor on the landscape below, viewing it with a philosophic mien and, I hope, a quiet and satisfactory tranquility, believing that I did what I wanted to do the most with what innate, modest talents I had. (I am happy and fortunate, I think in having two such fine sons who enhance my old age.)

I am feeling O.K. except, as you saw in San Fran., my legs with arthritis make it hard for me to walk much.

Enclosed find an article re Bernstein's forthcoming project, in which you are mentioned.

I am also enclosing small clippings of puns. Show these latest spasms of my punning to Ferlinghetti and his secretary, if you will.

Meanwhile, now and then, I keep my aesthetic antennae alert for vibrations of inspiration. I guess we search for beauty to exalt our lives. From the perishable, I try to snatch the imperishable, and to snare the vibrations of the momentous behind the vibrations of the moment.

It's like kindling a spark from the strange and unfathomable mystery of life to illuminate the mystery of the self. So, I think – or at least, I hope (as I wrote in one of my poems in my third book) – to leave some bright remnant of myself behind.

Come soon.

> Love from Edith and
> Your father,
> Louis

Allen continued his active involvement in the poetics school at Naropa Institute, and he was now spending most of his summers on campus. The visiting faculty during the summer of 1975 was especially impressive, with Allen and codirector Anne Waldman being joined by William S. Burroughs, Gregory Corso, Diane di Prima, Ed Sanders, Ted Berrigan, John Ashbery, Peter Orlovsky, and Philip Whalen. The campus had the feel of a Beat Generation reunion.

A few months later, Allen heard from another old friend. Bob Dylan was organizing a group of wandering musicians – the Rolling Thunder Revue – which would be traveling from state to state, playing unannounced concerts in the minstrel tradition, and Dylan wondered if Allen might be interested in joining the troupe.

Louis Ginsberg to Allen Ginsberg

August 9, 1975

Dear Allen,

How are you these days, "the most August time of the year?"

How is your health?

Are you being besieged by an avalanche of trivia?

I received the three books you sent. I am deep in *Meditation in Action* by Chögyam Trungpa. I'll try to transfer the heart of his message to the deeps [*sic*] of my heart and blend the two there. Give him my regards when you next see him.

The Paterson Library has invited us – father and two sons – to give a poetry reading. Mr. Leo Lichleberg spoke of renting a school auditorium. The date may be pinned down, if you will, when you come home at the end of August.

I asked Dr. Sam Berg about the Levys, who spoke with me on the phone. I am enclosing his answer. Return it soon.

I am working on a blank verse poem about our trip from Boulder to Santa Fe. Some felicities are wandering into the poem.

We miss you. Hope your health is improving.

Now and then I try to conjure wonders heretoformed by the dancing letters of the alphabet. Felicitous combinations kindle sentences to luminescence to make light to be shed on objects about me, luminous and numinous.

Regards to Trungpa, Anne Waldman and her boyfriend, Peter and Denise and Gregory (if he is behaving).

I look forward to seeing you soon.

Write when you are in the mood.

Love and kisses from Edith and
Your father,
Louis

Allen Ginsberg to Louis Ginsberg

P.O.B. 382
Stuyvesant Station
{New York City}
October 27, 1975

Dear Lou –

I received money from sale of Kerouac letters so here's the $500 I borrowed from you a couple months ago. Seems to be definite that I'll be leaving Monday with Bob Dylan and troupe of musicians & singers – I don't know what my role will be – wander around stage in Merlin costume or velvet Uncle Sam hat or sit on side on meditation cushion, I'll see. I'll bring yr poem along & analyze it –

Love
Allen

"Thanks for the Loan" – see you in short time and I'll write & call.

Allen Ginsberg to Louis Ginsberg

{Newport, Rhode Island}
November 4, 1975

Dear Louis –

Beautiful day with Dylan in Lowell Mass, beginning early afternoon visiting Kerouac's grave plot & reading the stone "He honored the world"[1] – We stood in the November sun brown leaves flying in wind & read poems from *Mexico City Blues,* then we sat down, Dylan played my harmonium, Peter beside him, & we traded lines improvising a song to Kerouac underground beneath grass & stone. Then Dylan played Blues chords on his guitar, while I improvised a ten stanza song about Jack looking down with empty eyes from clouds – Dylan stopped guitar to stuff a brown leaf in his breast pocket while I continued solo voice, & he picked up his guitar to pluck it on the beat perfect to the end of my stanza – little celestial inspired ditty on Kerouac's grave – all recorded for movie then shot many other scenes in Catholic statue grotto Jack wrote about, near an orphanage – Dylan conversing w/statue of Christ –[2]

Staying here a few days, then to Stockbridge –

Dylan wants to do some scene related to Sacco & Vanzetti when we get to Boston – Thoreau near Walden – A Bicentennial picture – we shot some scenes on Mayflower replica, & at Pilgrim Plymouth Rock.

Stay well, hang on, more work to do to come –

Love
Allen

Louis Ginsberg to Allen Ginsberg

November 7, 1975

Dear Allen,

Glad to get your letter.

It was interesting, to say the least, to hear of your adventures with the

---

1. The headstone actually reads. "He honored life."
2. Some of the best of these scenes were presented in *Renaldo and Clara,* the lengthy film documentary of the Rolling Thunder Revue tour.

Bob Dylan troupe. That was an interesting scenario at the grave of Kerouac. Will the movie be shown?

All is quiet here. I am busy at my desk, reading, writing and trying to lasso the elusive and unfound, the unimponderable.

Am working on my fourth book of poems, *Our Times,* and hope to send it on to seek its fortunes soon.

(If you know of a publisher who is [looking] for a book of lyric poems, saturated with philosophic implications, let me know.

Write me a letter soon.

Regards to Peter, Denise, and also Bob Dylan.

Love from Edith and
Your father,
Louis

Allen Ginsberg to Louis and Edith Ginsberg

York Harbor, Maine
November 10, 1975

Dear Louis & Edith —

Traveling w/theatrical-musical troupe seems to be the nature of what I'm doing — just like in old 1930's movies, with people crying, menstruating, drinking, meditating, singing till 7 AM & sleeping all day before getting on the bus. Still looking for my "big chance" to do an act onstage. Meanwhile busy conceiving scenes & shooting improvised charades w/ Dylan & Joan Baez — Peter hauling luggage, Denise preparing dressing rooms — the concerts are beautiful — Love Allen

Allen Ginsberg to Louis Ginsberg

{In air}
November 18, 1975

Dear Lou —

On way to Utah somewhere over midwest, farms squared below under clouds — Sudden departure from the Rolling Thunder company for side trip to read poetry – one problem with this tour is that musicians are so preoccupied with their rock style I haven't had a chance to perform before audiences except in the movie we're improvising – In Massachusetts I read part of "Kaddish" in a resort motel before a convention of Maj jong playing grandmothers – odd, half-real half messy-ear'd ladies – cameras rolling & Dylan & Peter O. listening –

What is amazing about the theater is the enunciation of vowels & syllables in rhythmic progression by Dylan who seems to me to be epitomizing all the Americana poetics from Poe thru Vachel Lindsay thru the poetry-jazz experimenters of a decade ago – He's able to stand up & chant/recite/sing intricately regularly rhymed irregular-lined narrative poems to continuous downbeat & instrumental background, making a combination of music & poetry, with emphasis on the words, that maybe hasn't been performed as *theater* since the Greeks. His very mouth seems to keep rhythmic tune, as well as his stomping feet. Real poetic genius transcending anything I've seen invented for utterance – tho maybe I've heard better words from Kerouac, but the combination of Terpsichore, Clio (narrative poems), Thalia, Erato, & Calliope among Muses is rare – Dance, history, theater, poetics & music. So the tour has been a poetic vision – I hope before the run is out you get a chance to see the show – maybe we'll get it to some theater in N.Y., there's talk.

Meanwhile cloud cover below hides the landscape, & my mind is in the sky anyway – perhaps am too detached from earth this month – See you soon. [. . .]

Love
Allen

Allen's full-time involvement with the Rolling Thunder Revue came to an end in December 1975, when his father became ill and was diagnosed with cancer. Louis had grown very weak, and Allen felt a strong urge to spend as much time with him as his crowded schedule would allow. Nevertheless, in late January, he left for Europe, where he had business to attend to in Brussels and Paris. Allen had always loved Europe, but with his father's illness weighing heavily on his mind, the old, familiar places seemed gloomy. "Paris is a mirage, poetry is a mirage, I am a mirage," he wrote in his journal on February 1, the same day that he wrote a more cheerful letter to his father. To Louis, he mentioned that he had stayed up all night and watched the sun rise, with all its romantic implications; in his journal, he was much more blunt: "Dawn is white and empty."

Allen Ginsberg to Louis and Edith Ginsberg

{Brussels}
January 28, 1976

Dear Louis & Edith:

Flew all nite & landed 9AM Brussels – staying at Mayfair Hotel, antiseptic modern. I don't have much to do here except use up free chits for taxis and restaurants given by the *Pocket Theater* that invited me – they put on *Kaddish* in 1969. Going to museums to see Breughel paintings I saw with Peter [and] Gregory in 1957. I'll spend a week in Paris with Gregory & Jocelyn, and correct proofs at my publishers, new and old translations need work. Nothing is new but old Europe. Sitting in Common Market building to write this card. See you in a couple weeks – Love Allen

Allen Ginsberg to Louis and Edith Ginsberg

{Paris}
February 1, 1976

Dear Louis & Edith:

Paris still mirage, snowy streets grey skies & I'm here so short a time with nostalgia for your company & Peter's which I had here long ago – prices high in restaurants – $15 meal – Gregory & Jocelyn own a 2 room w/ kitchenette apartment 9th floor w/balcony & elevator in ritzy building on Right Bank. George Whitman of Seine bookshop sends his love as do Gregory & Jocelyn. Stayed up all nite & watched dawn on the Seine. There's the Deux Magots Café on postcard, passed these last nite, a male gigolo offered services – same tolerant Paris. Be home to go to Washington this Thursday – Love Allen

Although his health continued to decline, Louis Ginsberg hung on. He now needed assistance in bathing and getting dressed, and Peter Orlovsky helped Allen with such tasks. Allen wanted to be with Louis in his final days, but there was no way of knowing when those days might be, so Allen divided his time between his father's home in Paterson and his work and obligations elsewhere. In late March, he flew to Colorado to teach a brief course on Charles Reznikoff, one of his favorite Russian poets. In May, after returning home for a visit, he rejoined the Rolling Thunder Revue for several performances. He stayed in constant contact with Louis, either by telephone or through a series of postcards that he mailed while he was on the road.

Allen Ginsberg to Louis and Edith Ginsberg

[Boulder, Colorado]
Sunday Noon
April 4, 1976

Dear Louis & Edith –

I'm staying in this hotel 1890's style near Anne Waldman & Michael Brownstein, making curricula plans & writing up grant application papers for next year. Anne & Mike send you their love & hellos. I am teaching Reznikoff to poetry class – I get more and more moved by his simplicity – The short life-stories he tells are just like Abe & Anna, Abe and Arthur, & your laundry horse stories, in detail. I must read you a dozen pages when I get back, I think you'll like it – It's a simple form *you* could use now – just to tell simple anecdotes covering a whole life-span – one-half page biography tales of Sam Freiman, like.

I am busy on phone with lawyers and PEN club still trying to get Leary out, & been talking to him on phone.

Chompa Chompa Lama returned here with one of his old teachers & is giving lectures next week on the feminine principle and all sorts of ideas about the arising of consciousness out of the "womb" of empty space. If he manages to describe how the universe began, I'll let you know.

Peter wrote, said he'd phoned you. If you need any strong arm call him, while I'm away.

W.S. Burroughs III, Bill's *son,* also a writer, will teach his father's prose-poetry in my class tomorrow.

There are no jobs for little Alan here – work is *hard* to find everyone says – I'll be willing to support him here, with help, this summer, if necessary for the trip.

O.K. Love to you

Allen

Allen Ginsberg to Louis Ginsberg

Estes Park, Colorado
May 21, 1976

Dear Louis:

Busy Days – Dylan asked me to phone Gov Brown's office & give him congratulations on winning in Maryland. . . . Politics raising its head – Rain over Rockies, so I've been indoors all day making Buddhist guest-lists for the concert near Boulder – Dylan asked me (drunk) to recite during Intermission – & I've been practicing with musician for my next recording date June first – Love as ever Allen

Hang on!

Allen Ginsberg to Louis and Edith Ginsberg

{Denver, Colorado}
May 23, 1976 {next stop Salt Lake}

Dear Louis & Edith:

Spent all day in misty rain in giant sports stadium, grass wet & muddy; 27,000 youths & maids came out to concert, which built energy & passion in the music till everyone was dancing & cheering. At intermission Dylan casually said to me over his shoulder, why don't you go out & read some poetry during intermission? So I went out with a microphone before the curtain & read an 8 line poem "On Neal Cassady's Ashes" (we were outside of Denver Colo.). That's the biggest audience I ever had. I'll be home soon – Allen

With the arrival of the summer sessions at Naropa, Allen found himself back in Colorado, teaching poetics classes. He had instructed Louis to call him if he needed him. When he left for Boulder, he kissed his father good-bye for the last time.

Allen Ginsberg to Louis and Edith Ginsberg

{Boulder, Colorado}
June 14, 1976

Dear Louis & Edith –

Here's the New Jersey Bell $38 check, sorry I'm so late, I forgot, too much paperwork to keep track.

It's Sunday, I'm taking it easy looking at the mountains from my balcony, seeing students, reading mail.

I miss you and wish you were here or I was there – I'll be back for a week [July] 10 unless you call for me sooner.

[. . .]

The students this year are smarter, better read more "serious."

Dana, the girl who liked you so much, got married yesterday here, and I went in my tuxedo to her wedding party for an hour last nite. She said to send you her kisses Louis.

I'll phone & write in the next instant –

Love
Allen

POSTSCRIPT

Louis Ginsberg died in the early-morning hours of July 8, 1976. Allen was still in Boulder, teaching his customary summer session at Naropa, when he received the news. He immediately boarded a flight to New York, and while in transit, as his plane crossed over Lake Michigan, he composed a slow blues piece to commemorate his father's passing. "Father Death Blues" became his most moving piece of music, as well as the centerpiece of a sequence of poems he had been writing over the recent months.

Don't Grow Old

I

Old Poet, Poetry's final subject glimmers months ahead

Tender mornings, Paterson roofs snowcovered

Vast

Sky over City Hall tower, Eastside Park's grass terraces & tennis courts
beside Passaic River

Parts of ourselves gone, sister Rose's apartments, brown corridor'd high
schools —

Too tired to go out for a walk, too tired to end the War

Too tired to save body

too tired to be heroic

The real close at hand as the stomach

liver pancreas rib

Coughing up gastric saliva

Marriages vanished in a cough

Hard to get up from the easy chair

Hands white   feet speckled   a blue toe   stomach big   breasts hanging
thin

hair white on the chest

too tired to take off shoes and black sox

Paterson, January 12, 1976

II
He'll see no more Times Square
honkytonk movie marquees, bus stations at midnight
Nor the orange sun ball
rising thru treetops east toward New York's skyline
His velvet armchair facing the window will be empty
He won't see the moon over house roofs
or sky over Paterson's streets.

New York, February 26, 1976

III
Wasted arms, feeble knees
    80 years old, hair thin and white
        cheek bonier than I'd remembered –

head bowed on his neck, eyes opened
    now and then, he listened –
  I read my father Wordsworth's *Intimations of Immortality*
"*. . . trailing clouds of glory do we come*
    from God, who is our home . . ."
        "That's beautiful," he said, "but it's not true."

"When I was a boy, we had a house
    on Boyd Street, Newark – the backyard
        was a big empty lot full of bushes and tall grass,
    I always wondered what was behind those trees.
When I grew older, I walked around the block,
    and found out what was back there –
        it was a glue factory."

May 18, 1976

IV
Will that happen to me?
Of course, it'll happen to thee.

Will my arms wither away?
Yes yr arm hair will turn gray.

Will my knees grow weak & collapse?
Your knees will need crutches perhaps.

Will my chest get thin?
Your breasts will be hanging skin.

Where will go – my teeth?
You'll keep the ones beneath.

What'll happen to my bones?
They'll get mixed up with stones.

June 1976

V
Father Death Blues
Hey Father Death, I'm flying home
Hey poor man, you're all alone
Hey old daddy, I know where I'm going

Father Death, Don't cry anymore
Mama's there, underneath the floor
Brother Death, please mind the store

Old Aunty Death Don't hide your bones
Old Uncle Death, I hear your groans
O Sister Death how sweet your moans

O Children Deaths go breathe your breath
Sobbing breasts'll ease your Deaths
Pain is gone, tears take the rest

Genius Death your art is done
Lover Death your body's gone
Father Death I'm coming home

Guru Death your words are true
Teacher Death I do thank you
For inspiring me to sing this Blues

Buddha Death, I wake with you
Dharma Death, your mind is new
Sangha Death, we'll work it through

Suffering is what was born
Ignorance made me forlorn
Tearful truths I cannot scorn

Father Breath once more farewell
Birth you gave was no thing ill
My heart is still, as time will tell.

July 8, 1976 (Over Lake Michigan)

VI

Near the Scrap Yard my Father'll be Buried
Near Newark Airport my father'll be
Under a Winston Cigarette sign buried
On Exit 14 Turnpike NJ South
Through the tollgate Service Road 1 my father buried
Past Merchants Refrigerating concrete on the cattailed marshes
past the Budweiser Anheuser-Busch brick brewery
in B'Nai Israel Cemetery behind a green painted iron fence
where there used to be a paint factory and farms
where Pennick makes chemicals now
under the Penn Central power Station
transformers & wires, at the borderline
between Elizabeth and Newark, next to Aunt Rose
Gaidemack, near Uncle Harry Meltzer
one grave over from Abe's wife Anna my father'll be buried.

July 9, 1976

VII

What's to be done about Death?
Nothing, nothing
Stop going to school No. 6 Paterson, N.J., in 1937?
Freeze time tonight, with a headache, at quarter to 2 A.M.?
Not go to Father's funeral tomorrow morn?
Not go back to Naropa   teach Buddhist poetics all summer?
Not be buried in the cemetery near Newark Airport some day?

Paterson, July 11, 1976

Allen's devotion to his father continued long after Louis Ginsberg's death. With Michael Fournier at the Northern Lights Press, he saw Louis's Collected Poems *into print. It was a beautiful book, containing all three of Louis Ginsberg's previously published volumes of poetry, as well as the unpublished* Our Times *and a large selection of previously uncollected poems. Eugene Brooks wrote the book's introduction, while Allen reprinted his essay on his father's poems, originally published in* Morning in Spring. *The "family business" went on.*

Allen wrote other published and unpublished poems about his father, including a second "Don't Grow Old" poem, which was included in his Plutonian Ode *collection of poems.*

"Don't Grow Old"
I
Twenty-eight years before on the living room couch he'd stared at
    me, I'd said
"I want to see a psychiatrist – I have sexual difficulties –
    homosexuality."
I'd come home from troubled years as a student. This was the
    weekend I would talk with him.
A look startled his face, "You mean you like to take men's penises
    in your Mouth?"
Equally startled, "No, no," I lied, "that isn't what it means."

Now he lay naked in the bath, hot water draining beneath his
    shanks.
Strong shouldered Peter, once an ambulance attendant, raised him
    up
In the tiled room. We toweled him dry, arms under his, bathrobe
    over his shoulder –
he tottered thru the door to his carpeted bedroom
sat on the soft mattress edge, exhausted, and coughed up watery
    phlegm.
We lifted his swollen feet talcum'd white, put them thru pajama
    legs,
Tied the chord round his waist, and held the nightshirt sleeve
    open for his hand, slow.
Mouth drawn in, his false teeth in a dish, he turned his head
    round
Looking up at Peter to smile ruefully, "Don't ever grow old."

II

At my urging, my eldest nephew came

To keep his grandfather company, maybe sleep overnight in the apartment.

He had no job, and was homeless anyway.

All afternoon he read the papers and looked at old movies.

Later dusk, television silent, we sat on a soft-pillowed couch,

Louis sat in his easy-chair that swiveled and could lean back –

"So what kind of job are you looking for?"

"Dishwashing, but someone told me it makes your hands' skin scaly red."

"And what about office boy?" His grandson finished high school with marks too poor for college.

"It's unhealthy inside airconditioned buildings under fluorescent light."

The dying man looked at him, nodding at the specimen.

He began his advice. "You might be a taxidriver, but what if a car crashed into you? They say you can get mugged too.

Or you could get a job as a sailor, but the ship could sink, you could get drowned.

Maybe you should try a career in the grocery business, but a box of bananas Could slip from the shelf,

you could hurt your head. Or if you were a waiter, you could slip and fall down with a loaded tray, & have to pay for the broken glasses.

Maybe you should be a carpenter, but your thumb might get hit by a hammer.

Or a lifeguard – but the undertow at Belmar beach is dangerous, and you could catch a cold.

Or a doctor, but sometimes you could cut your hand with a scalpel that had germs, you could get sick & die."

Later, in bed after twilight, glasses off, he said to his wife

"Why doesn't he comb his hair? It falls all over his eyes, how can he see?

Tell him to go home soon, I'm too tired."

Amherst, October 5, 1978

III
Resigned
A year before visiting a handsome poet and my Tibetan guru,
    Guests after supper on the mountainside
we admired the lights of Boulder spread glittering below
        through a giant glass window –
After coffee, my father bantered wearily
"Is life worth living? Depends on the liver –"
The Lama smiled to his secretary –
It was an old pun I'd heard in childhood.
Then he fell silent, looking at the floor
    and sighed, head bent heavy
        talking to no one –
           "What can you do . . . ?"

                        Buffalo, October 5, 1978

*In 1995, Allen published a limited-edition poster/poem of "Visiting Father &
Friends," a dream poem not unlike his "White Shroud" dream poem, which dealt
with the resolution of his relationship with his mother.*

Visiting Father & Friends
I climbed the hillside to the lady's house
There was Gregory, dressed as a velvet ape,
japing and laughing, elegant handed, tumbling
somersaults and consulting with the hostess
girls and wives familiar, feeding him like a baby,
He looked healthy, remarkable energy, up all night
talking jewelry, winding his watches, hair over his eyes,
jumping from one apartment to another.

Neal Cassady rosy faced indifferent and affectionate
entertaining himself in company far from China
back in the USA old 1950's-1980s still kicking
his way through the city, up Riverside Drive without a car
He hugged me & turned attention to the night ladies
appearing disappearing in the bar, in apartments
and the street, his continued jacknapes is wasting time &

everyone else's but mysterious, maybe up to something
Good – keep us all from committing more crimes,
political wars, or peace protests angrier than wars"
cannonball noises. He needed peace to sleep.

Then my father appeared, lone forlorn & healthy
still living by himself in an apartment a block up
the hill from Peter's ancient habitual pad, I hadn't
noticed where Louis lived these days, somehow obliterated
his home condition from my mind, took it for granted
tho never'd been curious enough to visit – but as I'd no place
to go tonight, & wonder'd why I'd not visited him recently,

I asked him could I spend the night & bed down
with him, his place had bedroom and bath
a giant Jewish residence apartment on Riverside Drive
refugees inhabited, driven away from Europe by Hitler
where my father lived, now – I entered, showed me his couch
& told me to get comfortable, I slept the night, but woke
when he shifted his sleeping pad closer to mine I got up
– he'd slept badly on a green inch-thick dusty
foam rubber plastic mattress I'd thrown out years ago,
poor cold mat upon the concrete cellar warehouse floor –
so that was it! He'd given his bed for my comfort!

No no I said, take back your bed, sleep comfortable
Weary you deserve it, amazing you still get around,
I'm sorry I hadn't visited you before, just didn't know
where you lived, here you are a block upstreet
from Peter, hospitable to me Neal & Gregory &
girlfriends of the night, old sweet Bohemian heart
don't sleep in the floor like that I'll take your place
on the mat & pass the night ok.

                              I went upstairs, happy to see
he had a place to lay his head for good, and woke in China.
Peter alive, thought drinking a problem, Neal was dead
more years than my father Louis no longer
smiling alive, no wonder I'd not visited this place

he'd retired to a decade ago, How good to see him home, and take
his fatherly hospitality for granted among the living
and dead. Now to wash my face, dress in my suit
on time for teaching classroom poetry at 8 am Beijing,
far round the world away from Louis' grave in Jersey.

November 16, 1984
6:52 A.M.
Baoding, P.R.C.

On April 5, 1997, following a brief illness, Allen Ginsberg died of cancer – the same
illness that had claimed his father two decades earlier. Some of his cremated remains
were buried in Louis Ginsberg's grave.

INDEX

NOTE: AG's works appear directly under title;
works by others under author's name

A NOTE ON THE TYPE

The text of this book is set in Linotype Garamond Three which is based on seventeenth-century copies of Claude Garamond's types, cut by Jean Jannon. This version was designed for American Type Founders in 1917, by Morris Fuller Benton and Thomas Maitland Cleland and adapted for mechanical composition by Linotype in 1936.